ASSASSINATION

the Royal Family's 1,000 year curse

David Maislish

First published in Great Britain by Pen Press

ISBN13: 978-1-78003-148-4

Cover design by Jacqueline Abromeit

Author photograph by Gerald Fass

Assassination – the Royal Family's 1,000 year curse

Power, glory, wealth; yes, they all came with the crown. But for English and British monarchs there was something else – somebody: a rival, an enemy or a madman would try to kill every single one of them.

As we travel through 1,000 years of history, learning how each monarch won the crown (and a third of them had no right to inherit the crown from his or her predecessor), it will become apparent that there were one or more attempts to kill every person who became king or queen; and many of the attempts succeeded.

Poison, arrows, daggers, swords, pistols, rifles and bombs ensured that over a quarter, perhaps as many as half, of all English/British monarchs were murdered. It was not just the ones we all know about, such as Edward II (the red-hot poker) and Edward V (one of the princes in the Tower), but also many others, with relentless research revealing that the 1,000 year curse has meant that no king or queen escaped at least one attempted killing.

Even in the twentieth century, we will find twelve attempts to kill the monarch – and one of them succeeded.

Here is the history of England and Britain without the things that sent us to sleep in school; instead interweaved with a series of murder and attempted murder stories.

Was there really a 1,000 year curse? Can it be true? Read on and decide for yourself. The evidence is here.

Acknowledgements

My thanks to Claire Spinks, who edited the first complete manuscript; to Catriona Watson at Pen Press, who dealt tirelessly with typesetting and the numerous amendments; and to my daughter Lucy, who corrected the original text chapter by chapter and also selected the illustrations.

DMM
September 2012

Author's note
With very few exceptions, I have limited the images to what I consider to be the most realistic available image of each monarch and of each assassin or assassination or attempt.

By the same author
White Slave, 978-1-90475-498-8: the true story of Captain James Riley; shipwrecked with his crew in 1812 off the coast of Morocco, enslaved and struggling for freedom.

Also available as an eBook.

Contents

Family Trees

Illustrations

Cover image – Burglar – © INSADCO Photography / Alamy

p1 Meeting of Edmund Ironside and King Canute – © Timewatch Images / Alamy

p7 King Hardicanute – © Mary Evans Picture Library / Alamy

p11 Edward the Confessor, from the opening scene of the Bayeux Tapestry – this image is in the public domain – source: Wikipedia

p17 Harold II of England– this image is in the public domain – source: Wikipedia

p21 Harold Godwinson falls, from the Bayeux Tapestry – this image is in the public domain – source: Wikipedia

p23 France, Calvados, Falaise, equestrian statue of William the Conqueror – © Hemis / Alamy

p30 Duke of Normandy – © Epics / 2011 Getty Images

p31 Statue of King William II from Lichfield Cathedral – © Stephen Dorey / Alamy

p34 The Rufus Stone Memorial, New Forest – © Greg Balfour Evans / Alamy

p36 Henry I of England – this image is in the public domain – source: Wikipedia

p42 River lamprey Lampetra fluviatilis – © Natural Visions / Alamy

p43 Statue of King Stephen from Lichfield Cathedral – © Colin Underhill / Alamy

p48 Henry II's tomb – © Interfoto / Alamy

p49 The Angevin Empire – this image is in the public domain – source: Wikipedia

p55 Richard the Lionheart statue – © Carole Anne Ferris / Alamy

p61 King John's tomb – © The Art Gallery Collection / Alamy

p67 Henry III's tomb – © Time & Life Pictures / Getty Images

p74 Edward I – © Getty Images

p76 Edward I and his would be assassin – © Gustave Dore / Getty Images

p263 James II – this image is in the public domain – source: Wikipedia

p272 "King Billy" (William III and Mary II) – © Getty Images

p285 Queen Anne – this image is in the public domain – source: Wikipedia

p296 George I – ©World History Archive / Alamy

p299 (top) Rugelach – source unknown, believed to be in the public domain, please contact the publisher if you believe copyright has been infringed

p299 (middle) Rogalik – this image is in the public domain – source: Wikipedia

p299 (bottom) Croissant – © imagebroker / Alamy

p307 George II – this image is in the public domain – source: Wikipedia

p311 George II Battle of Dettingen – © SOTK2011 / Alamy

p317 George III – © PRISMA ARCHIVO / Alamy

p323 Margaret Nicholson – © Getty Images

p327 Attempt on the life of George III – © Getty Images

p331 Despard on Scaffold – © Mary Evans Picture Library / Alamy

p335 George IV as Regent – © The Art Gallery Collection / Alamy

p348 William IV – this image is in the public domain – source: Wikipedia

p359 Queen Victoria – © Getty Images

p365 Oxford's assassination attempt – © World History Archive / Alamy

p369 Queen Victoria: attempted assassination – © Pictorial Press Ltd / Alamy

p370 Pate's assault on Queen Victoria – © The Print Collector / Alamy

p379 McClean shooting at Queen Victoria – © World History Archive / Alamy

p389 King Edward VII – © Lebrecht Music and Arts Photo Library / Alamy

p402 Sipido's attack on King Edward VII – © Look and Learn Ltd

p403 Sipido aged 13 – source unknown, believed to be in the public domain, please contact the publisher if you believe copyright has been infringed

p406 Maud Gonne Munsey 1903 – © Mary Evans Picture Library / Alamy

p411 Four Kings; George V, Edward VIII, George VI and Edward VII – taken by Queen Alexandra – this image is in the public domain – source: Wikipedia

BRITISH ISLES BATTLEFIELDS MENTIONED IN THE TEXT

Culloden
Killiecrankie
Dunkeld
Stirling Bridge
Bannockburn
Prestonpans
Pinkie
Flodden
Dunbar
Towton
Marston Moor
Stamford Bridge
Wakefield
Boyne
Lincoln
Grantham
Winceby
Bosworth Field
Stoke Field
St Albans
Shrewsbury
Lowestoft
Mortimers Cross
Barnet
Worcester
Ashingdon
Evesham
London Bridge
Tewkesbury
Sandwich
Winchelsea
Lewes
Sedgemoor   Edgehill   Northampton   Hastings
Edgecote Moor   Naseby

CANUTE
the first King of England

30 November 1016 – 12 November 1035

It was the year 1014, and the Battle of London Bridge was raging. On one side the Anglo-Saxons led by King Ethelred, and on the other side the invading Danes led by King Canute.

The Anglo-Saxon leaders made for the middle of the bridge, eager to engage the Danes. Fighting alongside King Ethelred were two of his sons, Edmund and Edward. Young Prince Edward raced ahead. Spotting Canute, Edward urged his horse onward, wielding his sword to left and right, determined to plough through the mayhem and to attack the Danish king. In the din of the screams of the fighting and dying, Edward came right up alongside Canute. Edward wasted no time; grasping his heavy sword with both hands, he raised it high above his head, about to strike before Canute could defend himself.

Jarl (Earl) Thorkell the Tall was riding on the other side of

1

Canute, and he saw that his leader was in peril. But Thorkell was in no position to stop Edward – Canute was in the way. Suddenly, with amazing quick-thinking, Thorkell took hold of Canute's arm and pulled him off his horse, throwing Canute to the ground. So, Edward's blade sliced the thin air and cut right through Canute's empty saddle, sinking deep into his horse's back, the animal's blood spraying in all directions. The resourceful Jarl Thorkell had saved the man who would become the first king of all England from the attempt to kill him.

Ethelred was being aided by his ally, King Olaf of Norway. Olaf realised that with the Danes forcing the Anglo-Saxons backwards and taking almost all the bridge, it was time for drastic measures. Fortunately, Olaf had a plan. He ordered some of his men to manoeuvre their boats beneath the bridge and then tie ropes to the supporting posts. That done, they rowed off, pulling the posts away until the bridge collapsed, killing many of the Danes and giving Ethelred victory. It was the origin of the rhyme, 'London Bridge is falling down'.

We could have started with Hengist and Horsa, the Jute brothers from Jutland (Denmark) who conquered Kent in the fifth century, or with Cerdic King of Wessex (the West-Saxons) in south-west England who had landed in the sixth century with warriors from his Gewisse tribe from Saxony (south of Jutland), or with Cerdic's descendant Alfred the Great. However, these men and others were kings of a region; none of them was king of the whole country.

In fact, even by the ninth century England was not a kingdom; it was made up of seven separate kingdoms, each with its own king. So there was no 'King of England'. Then, in 866, the Danes landed and set about the conquest of all the regional kingdoms. The heroic resistance of Alfred, a man who struggled against illness (thought to have been Crohn's Disease) throughout his life, resulted in the country being divided between the Danelaw (the part occupied by the Danes) and the territory controlled by the Anglo-Saxons. Of all the Anglo-Saxon leaders, Alfred alone kept his crown, but it was only the crown of Wessex.

Next there were invasions from Scandinavia by the Norsemen, who established a kingdom in the north. After they had been expelled, the Vikings arrived, followed by a new wave of Danes. King Sweyn of Denmark marched his army south, slaughtering all opposition. By 1014, Sweyn had conquered most of the country, and he had forced Alfred's descendant, King Ethelred, leader of the Anglo-Saxons, to flee to Normandy. There, Ethelred joined his second wife, Emma, who had already taken their children, Edward and Alfred, across the Channel to the court of her brother, Duke Richard II of Normandy.

All seemed lost, and then just five weeks later there was good news – King Sweyn had died. Ethelred saw his chance, and he returned to England. However, there was no let up by the Danes as Sweyn's son, Canute (or 'Cnut'), took over. Despite defeat at the Battle of London Bridge, Canute won victory after victory.

Ethelred was known as Ethelred the Unready, *un-raed* meaning 'no counsel', suggesting that he was ill-advised or did not take advice. Badly advised or not, Ethelred maintained the Anglo-Saxon resistance; and when he died, he was succeeded by Edmund Ironside, the older of Ethelred's two surviving sons by his first wife.

Edmund went on the attack, winning several minor battles. Then, in 1016, he was heavily defeated by Canute at the Battle of Ashingdon in Essex. Although it looked like the end for the Anglo-Saxons, it was not. They had fought so effectively, nowhere more so than at the Battle of London Bridge where Edmund's half-brother Edward nearly killed Canute, that the Danes agreed to the division of the country. Rule of the land to the south of the River Thames was given to Edmund, with Canute taking the rest of England. The two kings also agreed that if one of them died, then the other would take his territory.

If ever there was an invitation to murder, that was it. Six weeks later, on 30th November 1016, Edmund was killed (said to have been stabbed by someone crouching in the pit below as Edmund went to the toilet). That left Canute, an exceptionally tall and strong man, as king of both territories. This was the moment when Canute became the very first King of all England.

Canute's year of birth is not known for certain. The earliest of several suggested dates is 981, and that possible year of birth for the man who would become King of England was the start of a thousand-year curse for all English monarchs. None of them would escape the curse; someone would murder, or at least attempt to murder, every single one of them.

As king, Canute knew that his first task was to eliminate all the Anglo-Saxon claimants to the crown. With Ethelred dead, those claimants started with his children. From Ethelred's first marriage, his son Edmund Ironside had already been murdered. Edmund left two sons, Edward and Edmund. They had to be dealt with, so Canute seized them and sent them to the court of his half-brother, King Olof of Sweden.

Exile seemed a reasonable solution from everyone's point of view, at least everyone except Canute. Little did the princes know that the soldiers taking them to Sweden were carrying a letter from Canute to Olof asking him to kill both boys. Fortunately for the princes, King Olof was unwilling to put them to death. Instead he sent them to Kiev where his daughter was the queen; but she did not want them, so she sent the princes on to Hungary where her son-in-law was the king, and there the two boys lived at court. That allowed the 28 x great-granddaughter of the older boy, Edward, to sit on the throne today.

Next, Canute dealt with Eadwig, brother of Edmund Ironside and the last surviving son of Ethelred's first marriage. Eadwig had tried to raise resistance to Canute's rule, so Canute had him murdered.

The other threats to Canute's crown were Ethelred's sons from his second marriage, Edward and Alfred. Canute could not get to them as they were safe in Normandy with their mother, Emma.

Undaunted, Canute shrewdly strengthened his position by marrying Emma of Normandy, the widow of King Ethelred[1]. Yet despite invitations to come to their new stepfather's court in England, the two princes wisely remained across the Channel.

With all his rivals out of the country, Canute divided England into four regions, appointing governors for three of the regions and ruling Wessex himself. He then returned to Denmark (Canute was by now King of Denmark, Norway and part of Sweden), leaving Wessex under the control of a fierce warrior named Earl Godwine, a descendant of King Aethelred (Alfred the Great's brother and predecessor as king). Godwine had deserted his fellow Anglo-Saxons and joined Canute's side on the death of Edmund Ironside. Improving his position further, the ambitious Godwine married Gytha whose brother, Ulf, was married to Canute's sister, Estrith. Godwine became in effect the Viceroy of England during Canute's absence, his only rival for power being Leofric of Mercia (the Midlands), whose wife, Godgifu ('the gift of God'), is better remembered by the Latinised version of her name, Lady Godiva.

Several years later, Canute returned to England. Although his crown was secure, Canute was well aware that he had not dealt with Edmund Ironside's sons who were safe in Hungary, nor had he dealt with Ethelred's two surviving sons who were safe in Normandy.

However, none of the four princes raised a challenge, and having ruled England for nearly 20 years, King Canute died in 1035. The first King of England, and also the first in the unbroken list of monarchs to have been the victim of an attempted killing. Thanks to Jarl Thorkell, the attempt failed.

****

---

1 A widow was allowed to marry one year after her husband's death; not earlier, as that would put the parentage of a child in doubt.

KINGS OF ALL OR PART OF ENGLAND BEFORE HAROLD

The Anglo-Saxons

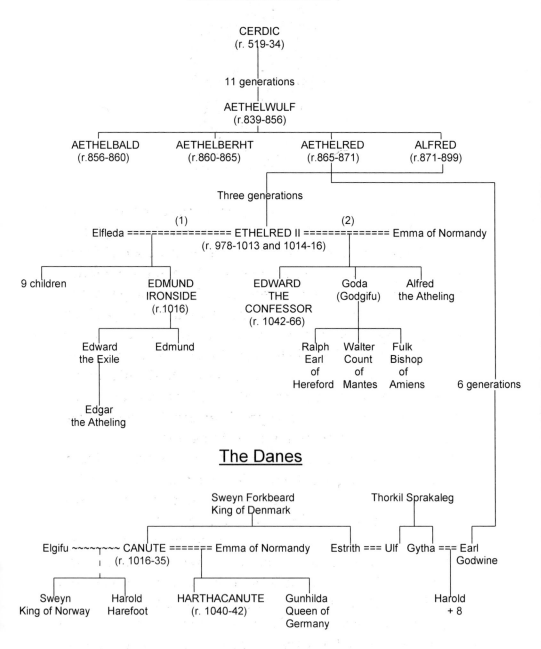

CERDIC
(r. 519-34)

11 generations

AETHELWULF
(r.839-856)

AETHELBALD (r.856-860) — AETHELBERHT (r.860-865) — AETHELRED (r.865-871) — ALFRED (r.871-899)

Three generations

(1)
Elfleda ================ ETHELRED II =============== Emma of Normandy (2)
(r. 978-1013 and 1014-16)

9 children — EDMUND IRONSIDE (r.1016) — EDWARD THE CONFESSOR (r. 1042-66) — Goda (Godgifu) — Alfred the Atheling

Edward the Exile — Edmund

Ralph Earl of Hereford — Walter Count of Mantes — Fulk Bishop of Amiens — 6 generations

Edgar the Atheling

The Danes

Sweyn Forkbeard King of Denmark

Thorkil Sprakaleg

Elgifu ~~~~ᴛ~~~ CANUTE ======= Emma of Normandy (r. 1016-35)

Estrith === Ulf   Gytha === Earl Godwine

Sweyn King of Norway — Harold Harefoot

HARTHACANUTE (r. 1040-42) — Gunhilda Queen of Germany

Harold + 8

HARTHACANUTE

12 November 1035 – 8 June 1042

By the time he died, Canute had given his oldest son, Sweyn, the rule of Norway. Canute's two younger sons, the illegitimate Harold Harefoot and the legitimate Harthacanute son of Emma of Normandy, were left to fight over England and Denmark.

There could be no real dispute as far as England was concerned; the Anglo-Saxon Church would never willingly accept the right of a bastard to inherit the crown. So Harthacanute was acknowledged as king. However, he had no time for England as his priority was to secure the Danish crown and defend it from the challenge of King Magnus of Norway, who had already ousted Sweyn. That left the illegitimate Harold Harefoot to assume the rule of England.

In no time at all, Harold decided that if he was acting as the king, then he ought to be the king. He is sometimes called Harold I, but Harold Harefoot was never crowned; he was merely regent for his half-brother, not king at all.

Harold Harefoot was not the only one to see an opportunity. When they learned that Harthacanute was in Denmark, the two princes in Normandy became over-confident. Recklessly, in 1036 Ethelred's sons, Edward and Alfred, each decided that it was time to return to England. Apparently they did so in response to a letter from their mother, Emma, urging them

7

to join her in Winchester. They had been tricked, the letter was a forgery. Harold Harefoot was luring the two princes to England in order to kill them.

Edward came first. He landed near Southampton with a party of Norman soldiers. Meeting no opposition, they started to ride inland. They must have enjoyed their gentle progress through the English countryside, until suddenly armed horsemen came at them from all sides. Edward's landing had been discovered; it was an ambush. A violent conflict saw Edward and his forces fighting for their lives. Edward was the target, and he came under sustained attack. But he had learned to fight in England and had learned horsemanship in Normandy. Skilfully controlling his horse as he lashed out at his assailants, Edward beat off all the efforts of Harold Harefoot's men to kill him. Now the balance of the conflict changed, and it was the Danes who were fighting for survival. The few who had not been killed rode off at speed.

It was time for Edward to reconsider the situation. He realised that the Danes were not just escaping, they were going to seek reinforcements. Edward's reduced numbers would have no chance. He knew what he had to do. Edward quickly returned to Normandy.

A few months later, Alfred decided to make his move. He landed near Dover. Aware of how close his brother had come to disaster, Alfred brought 600 Norman horsemen – more than enough to deal with any adversaries. He had reckoned without Earl Godwine. On Canute's death, Godwine had pledged his support to Harthacanute. Then the new king was occupied in Denmark fighting Magnus, and Godwine realised that he had gambled on the wrong brother. Godwine was desperate to find a way to ingratiate himself with Harold Harefoot. Alfred provided the opportunity. Godwine hastened southwards with a substantial force, but the cunning Godwine had no intention of taking on Alfred's forces in open battle. The story is told in the Anglo-Saxon Cronicle:

"As Alfred and his men approached the town of Guildford

in Surrey, thirty miles south-west of London, they were met by the powerful Earl Godwine of Wessex, who professed loyalty to the young prince and procured lodgings for him and his men in the town. The next morning, Godwine said to Alfred: "I will safely and securely conduct you to London, where the great men of the kingdom are awaiting your coming, that they may raise you to the throne." … Then the Earl led the Prince and his men over the hill of Guildown… Showing the Prince the magnificent panorama from the hill both to the north and to the south, he said: "Look around on the right hand and on the left, and behold what a realm will be subject to your dominion." Alfred then gave thanks to God and promised that if he should ever be crowned king, he would institute such laws as would be pleasing and acceptable to God and men. At that moment, however, he was seized and bound, together with all his men. Nine-tenths of them were then murdered. And since the remaining tenth was still so numerous, they, too, were decimated[2]. Alfred was tied to a horse and then conveyed by boat to the monastery of Ely. As the boat reached land, his eyes were put out. For a while he was looked after by the monks, who were fond of him, but soon after he died…"

Why did Godwine not kill Alfred straight away? Possibly he wished to take power by having the only Anglo-Saxon claimant to the throne in England in a feeble condition and under his control. If so, his plan failed; he would have to think again.

Across the North Sea, Harthacanute signed a peace treaty with Magnus under which each kept his kingdom and promised that if he died childless, the other would be his successor. Now Harthacanute could sail for England. He expected his half-brother to resist, but a civil war was avoided when Harold Harefoot conveniently died. Harthacanute returned as undisputed king.

---

2 In the 1920s, the remains of several hundred Norman soldiers were found to the west of Guildford. They were bound and had been executed. The grave was dated to c.1040.

Once in England, Harthacanute's thoughts turned to the succession. He was unmarried and therefore had no legitimate children. So he invited Prince Edward, his half-brother (Emma was the mother of both), to return from Normandy and join the court as the appointed heir. Edward did so, but heirs can be impatient.

A few months later, on 8th June 1042, King Harthacanute was the guest of honour at the wedding feast in Lambeth near London given by Lord Osgod Clapa on the marriage of his daughter Gytha to Tofig Pruda ('Tofig the Proud'). The King was in good spirits, drinking with the bride and groom and mixing with the guests. It was all very joyous. Barely noticed, an attendant walked over to Harthacanute and refilled his goblet. Continuing his conversation, Harthacanute took another swig. Suddenly, the King's eyes opened wide into a stare, he suffered a violent convulsion, staggered forward and fell face-down to the ground. It was some time before Harthacanute regained consciousness. He was carried away, unable to speak, dying a few hours later. Perhaps it was a stroke, but more likely it was poison. Who was the culprit: Edward or Godwine? We will never know. The only clue is that, possibly for other reasons – possibly not, once he was king, Edward sent Osgod Clapa into exile. Did he know too much?

So, the first three kings of England all became victims of the curse. Canute survived an attempt to kill him, Harthacanute was murdered and the third (Edward, whose reign follows) survived an attempt to kill him. As we shall see, the survival ratio would deteriorate for future monarchs.

****

EDWARD THE CONFESSOR

8 June 1042 – 5 January 1066

With Harthacanute dead, in 1042 an Anglo-Saxon from the line of the kings of Wessex took the throne as *'Eadwerd Englalandes cyncg'*. Descendant of Alfred the Great, son of King Ethelred and of Emma of Normandy, Edward was the first 'English' King of England. He was a tall handsome man, dignified and strong-minded, but like so many English kings he had a terrible temper.

Emma must have been a remarkable woman. She was the wife of two kings (Ethelred and Canute) and the mother of two kings (Harthacanute and Edward). Remarkable or not, after his coronation Edward seized all his mother's lands and possessions as punishment for favouring her other son, Harthacanute; or perhaps the letter inviting Edward and Alfred to return to England was not a forgery after all. Anyway, another person was much more of a problem. Edward was very wary of Earl Godwine of Wessex, the most powerful man in the kingdom, whose support Edward needed if he wanted

THE GODWINES

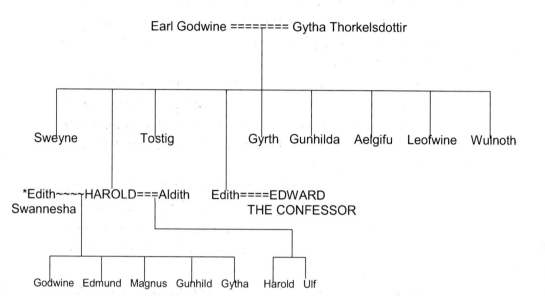

Earl Godwine ========= Gytha Thorkelsdottir

Sweyne   Tostig   Gyrth Gunhilda Aelgifu Leofwine Wulnoth

*Edith~~~~HAROLD===Aldith   Edith====EDWARD
Swannesha   THE CONFESSOR

Godwine Edmund Magnus Gunhild Gytha   Harold Ulf

* Although not a Christian marriage,
  the children were treated as legitimate

12

to keep the crown. He received that support, but it came at a price. It included creating the Earl's eldest son, Sweyne, an earl, and marrying Earl Godwine's daughter, thereby ensuring that one day Godwine's grandson would rule England – or so Earl Godwine thought.

Before long, Earl Godwine saw his new plan destroyed. To everyone's amazement, once married, King Edward took a vow of chastity. Edward said that it was a religious decision, but just as likely it was the best way to avoid producing a Godwine heir to the throne.

Earl Godwine was not deterred. He demanded the grant of earldoms to four other sons: Harold, Tostig, Gyrth and Leofwine. Then the Godwines started to exercise their power, refusing to obey Edward's commands and inciting rebellion across the country.

When he was returning home after visiting Edward, Count Eustace of Boulogne stopped for the night in Dover. Eustace sent out some soldiers to seek lodgings, unaware that Earl Godwine had given instructions to the townsfolk not to be of any assistance. Encountering hostility, one of the soldiers killed a citizen; then a citizen stabbed the soldier, and a violent affray developed. Men and women were slaughtered, and children were trampled underfoot as the soldiers rode off leaving seven of their number dead.

Furious at the insult to his brother-in-law Eustace, King Edward ordered Earl Godwine to lay waste to the town. He refused, and the matter turned into a trial of strength between the Anglo-Saxon Godwines and Edward's Norman favourites.

Within days, the two armies faced each other. However, Godwine hesitated and allowed negotiations to commence. The Norman Archbishop of Canterbury, Robert of Jumieges, announced that the Godwines were plotting to kill the King, and he appealed for assistance. Support soon arrived, and now that he was heavily outnumbered, Godwine was forced to accept Edward's terms. Edward banished the Godwines from England, and he sent his own wife, Queen Edith (Earl Godwine's daughter), to a nunnery.

Had it really been an attempt to kill Edward? All that can be said today is that if Godwine had attacked before Edward's reinforcements arrived, Edward's death would have been the likely result.

Across the Channel, the Godwines raised an army, and in 1052 they invaded England. King Edward was forced to reinstate all the Godwines to their former positions. But within a few months, Earl Godwine was dead; he had choked whilst dining with the King. Godwine lay speechless for three days, and then he died. A stroke is the accepted diagnosis, but murder was a reasonable suspicion. As if a motive were needed, Edward had invited Godwine to dinner in order to challenge him about the blinding and murder of King Edward's brother, Alfred, all those years ago.

Regrettably for Edward, the elimination of Earl Godwine did not solve anything. Godwine's second son, Harold, took his father's place as Earl of Wessex and as the most powerful and troublesome man in the kingdom, the first son, Sweyne, having died whilst returning from a pilgrimage to Jerusalem.

There was another problem, and Edward had created it. With his declared chastity, he would never have children, so questions began to be asked about the succession. Who would be the next king? The main contender, still living in Hungary, was Edward the Exile, the son of King Edward's half-brother, Edmund Ironside, Edmund's other son having died. Edward recalled Edward the Exile, and in 1057 he landed in England with his wife and children. This solution failed when the Exile died two days after his arrival in London. Again, murder was a strong possibility, and Harold (who may have escorted the Exile on the last leg of his journey) was a prime suspect, perhaps the only suspect.

Having failed to deal with the succession, Edward was confronted with a more pressing matter. In 1065, there was a rebellion in Northumberland against the repressive rule of Harold's brother, Tostig, who had doubled taxation. King

Edward summoned his forces, intent on marching to Tostig's aid, but the nobles, led by Harold, refused to obey the summons. The northern rebellion became ever more violent, and Tostig had to flee to Norway. Across the sea, the exiled Tostig would plot his revenge, having accused his brother, Harold, not just of failing to come to his aid, but of having incited the rebellion in the first place.

Edward, now elderly and frail, was the real loser. The nobles' direct challenge to Edward's authority shook him to the core. The distraught King fell ill, perhaps suffering a stroke. He lapsed into a coma, awakening at intervals, often delirious and talking nonsense. It would only get worse.

When Edward died in early 1066, he of course died childless. This left the Exile's son, Edgar the Atheling (Anglo-Saxon for a noble or, as in this case, the heir to the throne), as the leading claimant by inheritance. He was only 12 years old; how could he rule the country? Someone else had to be found.

Edward's nephews Ralph of Hereford and Walter of Mantes, the sons of Edward's sister Godgifu, had once been possible heirs. However, Ralph had died in 1057, a broken man following a catastrophic defeat by the Welsh that left him known as 'Ralph the Timid', and Walter had died in 1064 while in the custody of Duke William of Normandy. The Duke's eyes must already have been on the English crown.

In any case, heredity was not yet the sole basis for succeeding to a throne. It was usually obtained either by a deal, appointment by the former king, or by sheer power. As far as power was concerned, Harold had no rivals in England. In an effort to bolster his claim, Harold announced that on his deathbed, King Edward had nominated him as his successor, the ambiguous words said to have been: "I commend this woman [meaning Queen Edith, Harold's sister] and all the kingdom to your protection".

Other reports say that the dying king merely pointed at Harold. Its significance is a matter of conjecture. Whatever happened as Edward died, it is clear that the next day the

Witenagemot (from Anglo-Saxon *gemot* – 'meeting', and *witena* – 'of wise men'), a council of senior clerics and nobles, confirmed Harold as king. He wasted no time, and within 24 hours he had been crowned in Westminster Abbey.

Built on the site of a monastery, Westminster Abbey was Edward's great legacy. It was named the west–minster to distinguish it from St Paul's, which was the east–minster; a minster being a church or cathedral attached to a monastery.

Although Edward lived long enough to see the abbey completed, it was little more than that. Westminster Abbey had a busy first few days: on 28th December 1065 it was dedicated in Edward's absence because of illness, on the morning of 6th January it hosted Edward's funeral, and on the afternoon of 6th January it staged Harold's coronation.

Edward was remembered as 'Edward the Confessor', that is a saint who had led a holy life. Worshipped by his successors, he became the patron saint of kings, difficult marriages and separated spouses. For a long time he was also the patron saint of England. During the fourteenth century he was replaced in that role by Saint George, yet Saint Edward the Confessor remains to this day the patron saint of the Royal Family.

In retrospect, Edward's escape from murder at the hands of Harold Harefoot's men before becoming king and by Earl Godwine's men after becoming king enabled him to establish England as a country freed from the Danes.

But worryingly, the marriages of Emma of Normandy to Ethelred and then to Canute, both no doubt designed by the Normans to ensure a dynasty of Norman kings of England, had produced two kings of England (Harthacanute and Edward) who died childless. The Normans would have to try a less subtle method, and yet again it would involve the killing of a king.

****

HAROLD

5 January 1066 – 14 October 1066

Now that he was king, Harold was faced with two threats: King Harald III of Norway (known as Harald Hardraada) and Duke William of Normandy.

It all started with Harold's brother Tostig, who was still living in exile. When he heard that Harold had taken the crown, Tostig, eager for revenge, wasted no time in encouraging Harald Hardraada to invade England. They set sail, with Harald Hardraada demanding the throne of England under the treaty between his predecessor Magnus and Harthacanute. The claim was that Magnus became entitled to the English crown when Harthacanute died childless, and Harald Hardraada was the inheritor of his nephew and predecessor Magnus's rights.

Harold immediately rode north to deal with the mightiest warlord in Europe (Hardraada meaning 'a hard ruler'), who had landed with an army of 15,000 men carried across the sea in 300 ships. In a brilliant victory, Harold defeated the invaders at Stamford Bridge near York on 25th September 1066, killing Tostig, Hardraada and the majority of his army. It needed only 30 ships to carry the survivors back to Norway.

William was next. Born in 1028, Duke William of Normandy was the illegitimate son of Duke Robert of Normandy and Herleve, the daughter of a tanner (a maker of leather). As a result, William grew up in Normandy as 'William the Bastard'. However, he was Duke Robert's only son, so despite his illegitimacy William succeeded his father as Duke of Normandy as decreed in his father's will.

Again, Edward the Confessor's mother, Emma of Normandy, provided the link. She was the daughter of Duke Richard I of Normandy, William's great-grandfather. It made William the second cousin once removed of Edward the Confessor – and that was one of William's claims to the English throne. Sensibly, he did not overplay that hand, because relying on heredity would be admitting that Edgar the Atheling, the son of the Exile, should be king. Edgar was, after all, the grandson of Edward's half-brother, Edmund Ironside.

William's main claim to the throne was that Edward had promised him the succession in gratitude for the years of sanctuary in Normandy. This is rather doubtful as William was only 14 years old when Edward left Normandy, and Edward must have known that William's illegitimacy would be an issue for the Anglo-Saxon Church.

Nobody in England was listening; Harold had already been crowned. William was incensed. He complained bitterly to the Pope that Harold had sworn to acknowledge him as Edward's heir. William said that this had happened in 1064, when Harold had been sent to Normandy, supposedly to confirm Edward's promise of the succession. Harold's ship was blown off course, and he landed in Ponthieu where he was seized and held for ransom. William secured Harold's release, and in return Harold is said to have sworn on oath that he would accept William as the next king of England. As with William's other contentions, this Norman justification for the invasion sounds rather contrived. Probably William felt that if someone with no right at all was going to be king, it might as well be him.

Harold's response was to say that Edward had nominated him as the next king, it had been confirmed by the Witenagemot, and that was an end to the matter. William was not impressed. He knew very well that the Godwines had been Edward's main opponents for years, responsible for the murder of Edward's brother Alfred, and continually fomenting revolts. Harold was hardly the man Edward would promise the throne to on his deathbed; at least, not willingly. Yet, in Harold's favour, he was of the royal house of Wessex, he was Edward's brother-in-law, and although probably no one knew it he was Edward's eighth cousin three times removed (see page 6). More to the point, there had been no adult Anglo-Saxon alternative.

Critically, King Henry I of France had died, leaving as his successor the eight-year-old King Philip. With France having an infant king and being governed by co-regents, one of whom was William's father-in-law, the French threat to Normandy was much diminished, so William felt safe in leaving Normandy with his forces to seize the English crown. Having waited for the Pope's approval, that is exactly what William did.

Three days after the Battle of Stamford Bridge, William's army landed in Sussex and took up position near Hastings. By now Harold was back in London, celebrating his victory over Harold Hardraada. When he was given the news of William's landing, Harold wasted no time. He was eager for battle. Harold set about raising a new army, and then he marched south to confront the invader.

The two armies were each about 7,000 men strong. Harold's forces were nearly all on foot as although senior Anglo-Saxons rode to battle, they generally dismounted to fight. They were armed with swords, axes and javelins. Standing ten ranks deep on firm ground on the summit of Senlac Hill, their flanks were protected by marshland on either side. The Normans were a combination of mounted knights, infantry and archers. William commanded from the centre with his Norman knights. They were supported by Flemish and French to the right and Bretons to the left.

First, William's archers let fly, but to little effect. Then, William told his infantry to advance. As the invaders moved forward, the Anglo-Saxons hurled their javelins at William's left flank. The Bretons' advance was halted with scores of them killed, and the survivors turned and ran away downhill. Seeing the opportunity for easy killing, many of the Anglo-Saxons broke from their line and chased the Bretons as they fled.

William countered by directing some of his knights to attack the Anglo-Saxons who had run ahead and become detached from their main army. The Norman knights now trapped and slaughtered all the pursuing Anglo-Saxons.

With the momentum in his favour, William sent a contingent of knights forward. They reached Harold's men, but the Anglo-Saxon line held fast, and the Normans fell back in disarray. Again, many Anglo-Saxons raced after the retreating knights, and when those pursuers were separated from their main force, William attacked with the rest of his knights. Just as before, the pursuing Anglo-Saxons, all on foot, were encircled and killed.

Naturally the Normans later claimed that both retreats had been tactical moves, intended to draw the Anglo-Saxons forward so that the cavalry could destroy them. Perhaps.

Despite the reverses, Harold was not finished. He commanded his men to return to the original defensive formation. However, having suffered heavy losses, the line was much shorter. As a result, there was firm land between the flanks and the marshland. Protection of the sides had gone, and William had seen it.

His confidence soaring, William ordered his infantry and cavalry to charge. The Anglo-Saxon line still held, but William's knights could now attack the flanks of Harold's army from the firm ground on either side, and they did so to deadly effect. Yet, although Harold's position had deteriorated, the issue was still in doubt as the Anglo-Saxons protected themselves with their large shields, desperate to hold out until nightfall.

The battle had lasted a very long time, over nine hours. In half an hour it would be dark, and then both armies would have to withdraw. They would only be able to resume fighting at dawn.

At this crucial stage, it was vital for the Normans to use all their available resources in a massive effort to gain victory, as Harold could expect to receive reinforcements by morning. The Normans had one resource that had been largely unemployed – their archers standing to the rear, hardly letting fly at all for fear of hitting their own men. William rode back and shouted at his archers, ordering them to shoot high into the air so that their arrows and bolts would fly over the Norman attackers and come down on the enemy. This was a strategy he probably adopted not in the expectation of causing many deaths, but rather to force the Anglo-Saxons to raise their shields above their heads to protect themselves from the falling arrows, so weakening the wall of shields the Norman infantry and horsemen were struggling to breach.

The archers took hold of their crossbows and aimed high. Within seconds, a shower of arrows and bolts rained down on the Anglo-Saxons.

One arrow changed the course of English history. Puzzled at the strange sound overhead, Harold instinctively looked to the sky, and at that moment, as he gazed upwards, an arrow hurtling to the ground struck him in the eye.

The death of Harold

21

Now the Normans broke through the disintegrating wall of shields. Already mortally wounded, Harold was hacked down beneath his standard of the golden dragon of Wessex, his two surviving brothers having already fallen. After a final stand by Harold's housecarls, the remaining Anglo-Saxons, beaten and leaderless, fled. A number of Norman knights pursued them, but as they rode through a gully known as the Malfosse in the near-dark, they were ambushed and many Normans were killed before the Anglo-Saxons ran off. Then Duke William arrived and met up with the surviving fifty Norman knights. As Count Eustace of Boulogne was explaining what had happened, suddenly an Anglo-Saxon lying on the ground feigning death leapt to his feet intent on killing William. First he struck Eustace between the shoulder blades so forcefully that blood spurted from Eustace's nose and mouth; then, turning to William, the Anglo-Saxon raised his sword – but he was killed before he could strike.

It was over, and somewhere there was a Norman who did not even know that he had killed the King of England.

Yet it was not the end of the Godwines, because far from the battlefield some of them lived on. Two of Harold's sons and his daughter, Gytha, managed to escape. They fled to the court of King Sweyn Estridsson of Denmark. King Sweyn was the son of Ulf and Estrith (Canute's sister), who were the children's great-uncle and great-aunt. Gytha later married Grand Prince Vladimir Monomakh of Kievan Rus, a state (covering much of present-day western Russia) that had been established by Norse settlers. In time, the Godwine blood would flow through the five sons of Gytha and Vladimir into several European royal families, and as we shall see, through the marriages of Edward II and Edward III, back to the English Royal Family.

The last Anglo-Saxon King of England had perished; nevertheless his descendants would wear the crown.

****

WILLIAM I

25 December 1066 – 9 September 1087

William marched into London with his conquering army. He was crowned King of England in Westminster Abbey on Christmas Day 1066 by Ealdred the Archbishop of York. The Anglo-Saxon church was in no position to object to the crowning of a bastard. Of course, William was not claiming the crown by inheritance, he was claiming it by conquest. Perhaps illegitimacy was not such a problem after all. Anyway, rather than take responsibility, Ealdred asked the assembled crowd if it was their wish that William should be crowned king. Very wisely, no one objected.

The Conqueror and his compatriots were not really French. They were actually descendants of Viking marauders. In 911, after the Vikings had attacked Paris, French King Charles the Simple allowed a group of Vikings under the leadership of Rollo to settle in northern France on condition that they would protect the coast from future Viking invaders. The settlers were called the Northmen (in Old French: *Normanz*), and their land was known as Normandy, which later included the Channel Islands (today in French: *Les Isles*

FAMILY OF WILLIAM THE CONQUEROR

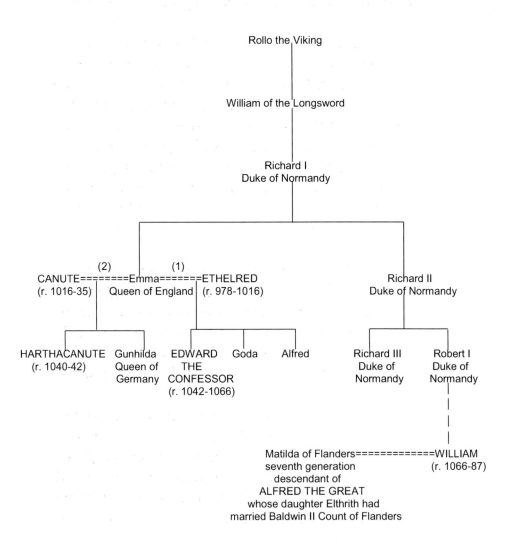

Rollo the Viking

William of the Longsword

Richard I
Duke of Normandy

```
          (2)                    (1)
CANUTE========Emma=======ETHELRED              Richard II
(r. 1016-35)  Queen of England  (r. 978-1016)  Duke of Normandy


HARTHACANUTE  Gunhilda   EDWARD    Goda    Alfred    Richard III  Robert I
(r. 1040-42)  Queen of   THE                         Duke of      Duke of
              Germany    CONFESSOR                    Normandy     Normandy
                         (r. 1042-1066)


                          Matilda of Flanders=============WILLIAM
                          seventh generation             (r. 1066-87)
                          descendant of
                          ALFRED THE GREAT
                          whose daughter Elthrith had
                          married Baldwin II Count of Flanders
```

Anglo-Normandes). Rollo's grandson Richard became the first Duke of Normandy, and Duke Richard's great-grandson was William.

Having succeeded to the dukedom of Normandy at the age of seven, William was lucky to survive to adulthood. Many senior Normans thought that they had a better right to rule than a bastard. One of them decided to do something about it. In the depth of the night in the castle-keep at Vaudreuil, a man crept into the room where William, still a young child, was fast asleep. Drawing his dagger, the man reached out, stabbed the sleeping child repeatedly and then ran off. However, the assailant had made a mistake; in the dark he had murdered the boy lying next to William. After that, William was more heavily guarded.

Once crowned King of England, William spent most of his reign fighting to retain his kingdom against the English, the Welsh, the Scots and the Danes, and he did so with great success. William was a tall, fierce-looking man with exceptionally strong arms. The Anglo-Saxon Chronicle describes him as "very stern and violent". By the standards of those times, that meant a lot.

William and his wife, Queen Matilda (granddaughter of King Robert II of France and seventh generation descendant of Alfred the Great), had ten children. There were six daughters: Adeliza, Cecilia, Agatha, Constance, Matilda and Adela; and four sons: Robert, Richard, William and Henry. With so many children, at least one of them was bound to cause trouble. So it was with the first son.

The problem was that with their overwhelming success in battle, the Norman leadership was not being killed at the customary rate for those times, and their sons were becoming restless. It must have seemed as though they would never inherit their fathers' titles.

Brave and ambitious Robert may have been, but he did not have the reputation of being clever. When he was 25 years old, he decided that it was time for him to become Duke of

Normandy. His father had England, that was enough. Robert confronted his father and demanded the dukedom. William was not interested; he refused. That demand did not endear Robert to his father, nor to William and Henry, his surviving brothers; the second son, Richard, having been killed by a stag while hunting in the New Forest.

Predictably, the hostility turned to violence. One evening after dinner there was a ferocious brawl between Robert and his supporters on one side, and his two brothers and their supporters on the other side. Apparently it started when his brothers, probably the worse for drink, dumped stinking liquid on Robert's head from the gallery. King William stopped the fight, but he refused to punish the pourers of the liquid. Shouting abuse and threats, Robert stormed out, bent on revenge.

Robert went to Normandy, and with money provided by his mother, he recruited his own army. He attacked Rouen, where his forces were beaten back. Then, Robert went to his father's enemy, the King of France, and asked for help. King Philip, always jealous of Norman power, sent Robert a contingent of soldiers.

William was not a man to rest idly, waiting to be attacked. If Robert wanted a fight, he could have it. Having sailed to Normandy, William led his army in battle against Robert, defeating him at Rémalard. Robert withdrew to the east of Normandy, and barricaded himself and his men in the Castle of Gerberoi.

Charging after his son, William besieged Gerberoi Castle. Three weeks went by, and Robert knew that by waiting any longer, his position would only deteriorate. So Robert and his men rode out of the castle to attack, catching William completely by surprise.

With William's army being considerably larger than Robert's, surprise would not be enough. Robert realised that his best chance of victory would be to kill his father. After William's death, his army would have nothing to fight for and even better, Robert would be their new ruler. It seemed to be the perfect solution.

Riding in full armour, Robert made for the centre of the fighting where he found William, and he engaged his father in combat. By now William was nearly 50 years old; Robert gained the upper hand, and he pressed his advantage. Then, with a savage slash at William's side, Robert injured his father, causing a wound to William's arm from which he would never fully recover.

Robert continued the assault, going for the kill. However, William had his senior knights near him, and one of them saw that his king was in danger. That knight, whose name was Toki, attacked Robert, driving him away from his injured father. Now more of William's men came to his aid and helped him from the field of battle, but not before Toki had been killed.

William's forces withdrew. Next, King Philip of France changed sides. With that development, despite victory Robert's position was no longer promising. It was time to talk.

The Norman nobles wanted some sort of agreement, as many of them had impatient sons fighting alongside Robert. Yet negotiation would not be easy with Robert having tried to kill his father, the King of England. Despite his reputation of not being clever, Robert dealt with the issue by explaining that he had not realised that the armoured man he was fighting was William, and that as soon as he had recognised his father's voice he had immediately withdrawn. Toki was not there to contradict him.

Accepting the excuse, William tried compromise. He offered Robert the dukedom of Normandy, but only on William's death. Although it was not what he wanted, Robert accepted that it was the best deal available, so he agreed to the bargain and returned to court.

All was quiet for some time. Then, in 1083, Queen Matilda died in the convent to which she had been sent by William, angry at her for supporting Robert. It provoked the grieving

Robert to rebel once more, and he made for France where he was welcomed by King Philip. From now on, Robert would be the centre of all opposition to William in Normandy and the surrounding territories.

One of those territories was the Vexin, which had always been a source of dispute between Normandy and France, each holding part of that region. There were constant disturbances on the border, and matters worsened with raids into Norman Vexin by French troops.

William decided to deal with the French. In 1087, he led his army into France, murdering and laying waste as they proceeded. He took the town of Mantes, which was set on fire, possibly by the fleeing citizens, and it was then sacked by the Normans in the most brutal manner.

The fighting was over, and William decided to ride through the deserted town to survey the fate of the inhabitants. Whilst relishing the murder and destruction, William rode too close to the burning buildings. Suddenly, flames shot out from a doorway and William's horse reared in fright. Now an elderly fat man and holding on with his damaged arm, William was unable to keep control. He was thrown to the ground as the horse turned sharply, and William suffered a serious internal injury, perhaps caused by the pommel of his saddle thrusting into William's abdomen as he fell.

Gravely wounded and in pain, the ailing king was taken to Rouen. William realised that the end was near, and he knew that he had matters to deal with; in particular, the succession. There were no kind words for Robert, William said that he was unfit to rule. Robert had taken up arms against him, had tried to kill him and had wounded him – a wound that had later led to his fatal injury. Even now, Robert was at the court of William's greatest enemy.

William made it clear that he did not wish to divide the inheritance. With his second son having died, he announced that everything should go to his third son, also named William.

The Archbishop of Rouen interrupted William to remind him that he had sworn on oath that Robert would succeed to the dukedom of Normandy. Breaking an oath taken on the Bible was a risk too far when he was about to meet his Maker. So William reluctantly confirmed that Robert would become Duke of Normandy. England was another matter; it had come to William by conquest not inheritance, and in William's view it was therefore at his disposal and not subject to any hereditary rights. The Conqueror gave the English succession to his third son, William, handing him the crown and sceptre. Then, King William told his son to leave for England so that he could claim the throne on his father's death before Robert could react.

A few days later, William the Conqueror died. He was buried in Caen. Unfortunately, the injury suffered in Mantes had caused William's abdomen to swell. At the funeral, the bloated corpse would not fit into the stone coffin. As they struggled to squeeze William in, his stomach burst open and the putrid contents sprayed over the mourners. Everyone ran away to escape the foul stench. During the French Wars of Religion the corpse was dug up and the bones were scattered on the streets. Some were later returned to the tomb, but the same thing happened during the French Revolution. All that remains of William in his tomb is his left thigh bone.

What of Robert? Denied the crown of England, which he considered to be his birthright, he determined to obtain it in battle, in many ways copying his father. But he failed. Robert ended up imprisoned in Cardiff Castle, where he remained until his death 28 years later. Not unreasonable for causing the death of his father. However, the attempted murderer of William when he was a child escaped without punishment.

****

CHILDREN OF WILLIAM THE CONQUEROR

WILLIAM THE CONQUEROR
(r. 1066-87)

Robert Duke of Normandy — Richard d. 1075 — Adeliza — Cecilia — WILLIAM II (r. 1087-1100) — Agatha — Constance — Matilda — Adela — HENRY (r. 1100-35)

The tomb of Duke Robert

WILLIAM II

9 September 1087 – 2 August 1100

King William II, known as William Rufus because of his red hair, was the third son of William the Conqueror. He succeeded his father as King of England in 1087.

William Rufus is said to have been a repulsive character. The Anglo-Saxon Chronicle pronounced him "hateful to almost all his people and odious to God".

With William taking the crown ahead of his older brother, several Norman nobles who supported Robert rebelled. William easily defeated the rebels, exiling the survivors to Normandy. However, Robert was still a threat, so William invaded Normandy and crushed Robert's forces in battle. The two brothers then made a truce that put much of Normandy under William's control. One of the terms of the truce was yet again that if either of them should die childless, the other would be his successor.

William triumphed once more when the Scots invaded England; he drove them back over the border. Then, having fallen out with the Church, William was involved in further fighting in England, Scotland, Wales and France. But despite delivering victories, William was despised by his people for his savagery and high taxation. Among the very large number of people who hated William II was his younger brother, Henry.

In August 1100, William Rufus was hunting in the New Forest near the south coast with Henry and six other lords. At a certain moment, William found himself alone to one side of a clearing. Suddenly, a single arrow flew across the clearing and struck William in the heart. He died instantly.

On being told of his brother's death, Henry rode with two lords to Winchester, where he seized the royal treasury. Early the next morning, William's body (which had been left where he had fallen) was thrown on to a cart by some peasants, taken to Winchester and buried. Two days later, Henry was crowned king in Westminster Abbey.

The timing was everything. Henry was hungry for the crown. He knew that William, a homosexual, unmarried and without children, had agreed that if he died childless, his older brother, Robert Duke of Normandy, would succeed to the throne. Robert had gone to the Holy Land on crusade, but he was now on his way back, having won a reputation as a hero and having obtained a wife and a substantial dowry in Italy on his way home – a dowry that would enable him to raise an army. Once Robert had returned, Henry's chance might be gone.

Henry had a novel claim to the throne. He could not demand it as brother of William II, that suggested that his older brother Robert should be crowned. Instead, he relied on a custom that existed at times during the Roman Empire of being born 'in the purple'. Under that system, the succession did not go to the oldest son of the late emperor, rather it went to the oldest of the sons who had been born after their father had been crowned, because only those sons had been born to an emperor. Robert and William were born whilst their father was merely Duke of Normandy, Henry was born in England after William the Conqueror had been crowned king. On that basis, William

Rufus had been a usurper and Robert had no claim at all.

Of course, with two brothers dead and leaving no children, and another brother travelling somewhere in Europe, Henry was the only claimant immediately available to be crowned.

So, although the death of William Rufus was said to have been a tragic accident, if anyone had an interest in arranging it at that time, it was Henry. It need hardly be said that murder was already within the range of Henry's accomplishments, to which can be added his subsequent reputation of being the cruellest of all the Norman kings.

With regard to the 'accident', the facts make it almost impossible to see anything in this other than murder.

The man who shot the arrow was Sir Walter Tyrrell, Lord of Poix in Normandy. He is said to have claimed that William had been hiding behind some cover, and had stood up and shot an arrow at a passing deer, wounding it. Then another deer had run past, and Tyrrell, who was standing on the other side of the clearing, had shot at that second deer, had unfortunately missed it completely (despite his renown as an expert shot), and even more unfortunately William was still standing up and by an amazing piece of bad luck the arrow glanced off an oak tree and struck him in the heart. Regrettably, William was unaware of the danger, as at that very moment he was shielding his eyes from the sun. For a final piece of misfortune, despite being struck in the chest, William fell forward to the ground, forcing the arrow through his body, thereby ensuring his death.

One account claims that when Tyrrell was asked how he did not see the King, he replied that he had mistaken the King's red beard for a squirrel. Whether he said this or not, the fact remains that all the excuses made to suggest that this was an accident were just too ridiculous. In all probability the King was murdered, although the story of an accident was accepted at the time. Perhaps accusing the new king of being part of a conspiracy to murder the last king would not have been a good idea.

The Rufus Stone in the New Forest

Tyrrell later denied that it was his arrow that struck the King. That denial is not assisted by the fact that Tyrrell instantly made for the coast, where a boat was waiting to take him to Normandy. He never returned to England.

More circumstantial evidence points at Henry. Apart from Henry needing to stake his claim before Robert returned from crusade, William was refusing to allow Henry to marry Edith, the daughter of the King of Scotland and the niece of Edgar the Atheling. That was a union that would hugely increase Henry's acceptability as king.

Murder was not a predicament in itself, but there was a pitfall; if Henry killed the King, it might endanger his chances of the succession as far as the Church was concerned. He had to get someone else to do it.

The Clares were great friends of Henry; the family was descended from Geoffrey Count of Eu, the son of Duke Richard I of Normandy. Gilbert de Clare and Roger of Clare were two of the lords at the hunt. After William's death, when Henry rushed to Winchester, it was the Clare brothers who travelled with him. At Winchester, they were met by William Giffard, who was the Lord Chancellor and the uncle of Gilbert and Roger, and he helped them to seize the royal treasury. Then Giffard, Gilbert and Roger rode with Henry to London, where he claimed and obtained the crown.

Were they rewarded? The day after the murder, William Giffard was installed as Bishop of Winchester; Gilbert de Clare was already Earl of Hertfordshire, he would soon become Lord of Cardigan; Roger inherited his father's Norman lands and was appointed one of Henry's most senior military commanders; their brother Robert of Clare was appointed Steward to the King and was granted the title of Lord of Little Dunmow; another of the Clare brothers was a priest, he was given the abbacy of Ely.

But why would the Clares select Tyrrell? They had to choose someone whose presence would not be suspicious – Tyrrell (whose grandfather had fought alongside William the Conqueror at Hastings) was an unsurprising invitee to the hunt. They needed someone who was a good shot – Tyrrell was an expert marksman. They needed someone who would not be available for questioning or trial after the killing – Tyrrell lived in Normandy, and was clearly willing to leave England for good. Most of all, they needed someone who was close to the other conspirators and whom they could trust – Tyrrell was married to Alice, sister of Gilbert de Clare and Roger of Clare.

Walter Tyrrell, having returned to Normandy, brazenly selected the stag's head for the motif on his shield. Then, funded by whatever reward he may have received for the cold-blooded murder of the King, he went on crusade and died in the Holy Land.

****

HENRY I

3 August 1100 – 1 December 1135

Henry seized the throne in 1100 on the death of his brother, William II. It was at a time when the oldest son of the Conqueror, Duke Robert, was travelling in Europe, coming home from crusade.

Having missed out again, Robert decided on invasion. He landed with his army near Portsmouth; but Henry bought him off, and Robert returned to Normandy. It was not long before the two brothers were once more at war. On the fortieth anniversary of his father's landing in England, Henry conquered Normandy. The victory was well received by the English, and many saw it as a reversal of the humiliation of Hastings.

Despite defeat, Robert was still a threat, so Henry had him locked up, first in Devizes Castle and then in Cardiff Castle. He remained there for the rest of his life.

Henry had solidified his position by marrying Edith, daughter of the King of Scotland and niece of Edgar the Atheling. That marriage, together with the fact that Henry had been born in England, helped to establish him as an English king in the eyes of many of the Anglo-Saxons. Even better,

HENRY I and MATILDA

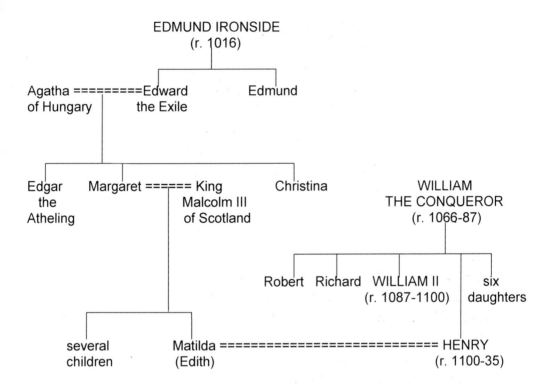

EDMUND IRONSIDE
(r. 1016)

Agatha =========Edward   Edmund
of Hungary   the Exile

Edgar   Margaret ====== King   Christina   WILLIAM
the   Malcolm III   THE CONQUEROR
Atheling   of Scotland   (r. 1066-87)

Robert   Richard WILLIAM II   six
                  (r. 1087-1100) daughters

several   Matilda ============================ HENRY
children   (Edith)   (r. 1100-35)

Henry's children would be the great-great-grandchildren of King Edmund Ironside. However, the marriage itself was a rather loose arrangement, as Henry is believed to have fathered more than 20 illegitimate children.

Being the youngest son, Henry had been destined to become a bishop, so he received a far better education than any of his brothers. That enabled him to introduce many judicial and financial reforms. Nevertheless, to his subjects Henry's reputation was that of a ruthless and cruel man. The greatest illustration of his cruelty is provided by the tale of Eustace de Pacy and Ralph Harnec, two feuding nobles who had exchanged children as hostages for good behaviour. Eustace decided to continue with the feud, so he blinded Harnec's son. Harnec complained to Henry. Having considered the matter, Henry announced that Harnec was now entitled to blind Eustace's two daughters – this, despite the fact that those two girls were Henry's own grandchildren, Eustace having married Henry's illegitimate daughter, Juliane. After the two children had been blinded, the furious Juliane demanded to see her father. Henry agreed, he had no difficulty in justifying his decision, it seemed perfectly reasonable.

Juliane stormed into the hall in the Castle of Breteuil, carrying a crossbow. She lifted it, aimed at Henry and let fly; but with Juliane struggling to hold the heavy weapon steady, the arrow missed. Immediately seized and imprisoned, Juliane climbed out of a window, jumped into the moat and escaped. In later years, Juliane and Henry agreed to put it all behind them, and they were reconciled.

In 1119, Louis VI of France invaded Normandy, determined to seize it for William the son of the imprisoned Duke Robert (that son being called 'the Clito' – the Latin equivalent of Atheling). He met Henry at the Battle of Bremule. Victory was Henry's; but even as the French were retreating, one of the Clito's supporters, a Norman knight named William Crispin, spotted Henry who had dismounted. Crispin ran at Henry, raised his sword and aimed a blow at the King's head. But the sword hit the collar of Henry's hauberk (chainmail shirt) and drew no blood. Before Crispin could attack again, Roger of Clare struck him down and took him prisoner.

Having dealt with the French, Henry suppressed troublesome nobles in England and then came to an arrangement with the Church. He had now done everything possible to secure his position as king. His remaining concern was to ensure the succession for one of his children.

Henry had two children with Edith, or Queen Matilda as she came to be known: Matilda and William. There may have been two more children: Euphemia and Richard, both of whom died at an early age. The crown seemed to be destined for William. It was not to be.

In November 1120, the court was returning to London from Normandy. As King Henry was preparing to board ship, the captain of a new vessel named the White Ship begged Henry to cross the Channel with him, the captain claiming that his father had carried William the Conqueror to England in 1066. Henry was not interested, he wanted to travel on his own ship; but he said that his son, William, would travel on the White Ship. By the time the White Ship started its voyage, it was dark and everyone on board was totally drunk. Shortly after leaving Barfleur, the White Ship struck a submerged rock and was holed below the water-line. The story is that William escaped in a small boat, later returning to the sinking vessel to rescue one of his illegitimate half-sisters, the Countess of Perche. Unfortunately, so many other people jumped into the small boat that it sank, and everyone in it drowned, including William.

Apparently, King Henry's nephew, Stephen, had been on the White Ship, but had disembarked just before it set sail as he was suffering from diarrhoea. Lucky man; Stephen would take advantage of his 'luck'.

William's death left Matilda as Henry's heir, and there would be no sons to take priority unless the King remarried, for Queen Matilda had died in 1116. Princess Matilda was a haughty, argumentative woman, but there was a greater problem. At the age of twelve, Matilda had been married off to the 32-year-old Holy Roman Emperor King Henry V, and she had spent most of her life in Germany, having been sent there to prepare for her marriage when she was only nine. If she became Queen of England, the Holy Roman Emperor would become king, and England would in effect become part of Germany. That was unacceptable.

Desperate for an alternative to Matilda, there was a movement among some of the barons to promote William the Clito to be the next king. To counter this, Henry began to advance the candidacy of another nephew, Stephen, the son of Adela, Henry's favourite sister. Then, in a frantic effort to provide a new male heir, Henry married Adela of Louvain. It was in vain; despite Henry's impressive record, there would be no children.

The situation became less complicated in 1125, when the Holy Roman Emperor died leaving no children. His widow Matilda returned to England, where she was grudgingly accepted as Henry's heir by the barons. She was then, at the age of 26, forced to marry the 14-year-old Geoffrey, son of the Count of Anjou. That only created a new problem because the Norman barons did not want to be ruled by Angevins, their traditional enemies. But they lost their alternative heir in 1128, when the Clito died of wounds received in battle.

Next, Matilda quarrelled with her husband and went to live in Normandy. So Henry recalled her to England, where she succeeded in making enemies of just about everyone. Aware of the difficulties with Matilda, Henry continued to assist his nephew Stephen in obtaining land and wealth to compensate for any shortcomings in his entitlement to claim the throne by heredity.

Then, in 1129, Geoffrey of Anjou succeeded to the title of count, and he demanded the return of his wife. Henry was only too pleased to see Matilda leave, as was the entire court. Matters developed two years later, when Matilda gave birth to a son, Henry Plantagenet. The succession was now assured, although the barons still hated Matilda and objected to her Angevin husband.

Almost an irrelevance, in 1134 Henry's oldest brother, Robert, died in Cardiff Castle. As Robert left no surviving legitimate children, it did at least mean that Henry was truly entitled to the crown and Matilda was entitled to succeed him.

However, nothing ever went smoothly where Matilda was concerned. She again fell out with her husband, and she went to live in Rouen, her father's principal town in Normandy. King Henry rushed there to see his grandson. Yet Henry's pleasures would be few, as most of his time was spent arguing with his unpleasant daughter. The aged king seemed to have been badly affected by Matilda's constant aggression.

It was not only Matilda who caused trouble, so did her husband. The Count of Anjou called for the delivery of several castles he claimed Henry had promised to him. Henry refused, so the Count destroyed one of the castles. True to form, Henry retaliated ruthlessly. Matilda was horrified by her father's excessive cruelty, and she returned to her husband.

Henry was now 68 years old, in poor health and increasingly upset by his daughter's conduct. At least food remained a pleasure. One evening at dinner, the agitated king sat alone awaiting his meal. A servant brought in a large dish piled high with lampreys. These fish were a notable delicacy of the time, and were known to be a favourite food of the King. However, Henry had been specifically forbidden from eating lampreys by his physician, and that prohibition was well known at court and no doubt just as well known in the King's kitchen.

By the time the meal had been presented, Henry had already consumed sufficient alcohol to relax his judgment, and he ate all the lampreys. Who was responsible for serving the lampreys to Henry? Did he insist on them himself? Did someone instruct the kitchen to serve the King what was known to be a dangerous food for everyone and particularly for him? Or was it simply a mistake?

A lamprey

Lampreys are jawless fish that look like eels, and can be anything from five inches to three feet long. They have a scaleless skin covered in mucus. Shaped like a tube, the fish has a round mouth containing rows of dagger-like teeth, and it also has a tongue on which there are three teeth. Some species of lampreys are parasitic. They attach themselves to other fish with their sucking mouth, and then they use the toothed tongue to scrape away the flesh of their host, drinking its blood.

Not surprisingly, eating lampreys can lead to food poisoning. Henry awoke the following morning with a fever, accompanied by acute indigestion. He died several days later.

Was it the lampreys, or was it Henry's fragile state following Matilda's verbal assaults that really caused his death? No one can tell. We do not even know if he really died of food poisoning or whether he had a heart attack. If the latter, then Matilda's conduct may have been the cause of Henry's death.

Matilda or the lampreys? Perhaps one daughter succeeded where the other daughter's arrow had failed.

****

STEPHEN

22 December 1135 – 25 October 1154

When King Henry died, the selection of his successor was not quite as simple as he had hoped.

Henry left one surviving child, Matilda, whom he had named as his heir. However, Matilda and her second husband, the Count of Anjou, were not wanted by the Norman barons. Worse for Matilda, she was immobilised by pregnancy and could not travel to England. Obviously Henry's numerous illegitimate children, of whom only Earl Robert of Gloucester was a power in the country, could not be considered. So apart from Matilda, the only realistic contenders for the throne were Henry's nephews, the sons of his sister, Adela. She had married the Count of Blois and they had eleven children, but by 1135 only four of her sons were still alive. The oldest, William Count of Sully, said to have been mentally deficient, remained in his wife's lands in Sully. Henry, the youngest, was Bishop of Winchester. That left Theobald and Stephen.

The barons wasted no time; they declared their support for

the older of the two, Theobald. Crucially, when Henry died, Theobald was in Blois in central France, Stephen was in Boulogne on the Channel coast. Stephen rushed to England, and with the backing of his brother, the Bishop of Winchester, Stephen claimed the throne. In addition, someone was found who was happy to swear that on his deathbed Henry had appointed Stephen as his heir. Fortunately for Stephen it was believable, as everyone knew that he had been King Henry's favourite since the death of Prince William. Once again, the first man on the spot had the advantage; Stephen was crowned king, and on receiving financial compensation, Theobald agreed to remain in Blois.

STEPHEN and MATILDA

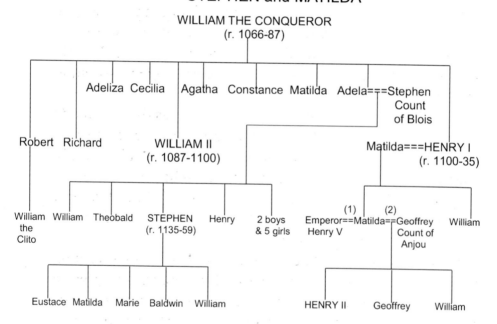

Stephen was a powerful character, and at first he was popular. His weakness was the fact that he was not a great military commander, nor was he blessed with good judgment. With Matilda fuming in Anjou, trouble was inevitable.

Early in the reign, the Scots invaded. Peace was only obtained by ceding the northern cities of Doncaster and Carlisle and most of the northern counties of Cumberland and

Westmorland. Stephen had shown weakness, now others took advantage. Several barons rebelled; they were overcome, but Stephen allowed them to go free to cause more trouble. Then, one after another, many of the barons declared their support for Matilda. Stephen did not react, but eventually Matilda did. In 1139 she landed in Sussex with an army commanded by her half-brother, Earl Robert of Gloucester.

Rebellions turned into civil war, with castles won and lost on both sides, and the country dissolved into anarchy.

In late 1140, there was a serious development when Earl Ranulf of Chester seized Lincoln's royal castle and declared for Matilda. Stephen had to react. He marched his army north and besieged the castle. However, Stephen had been too slow; shortly before he arrived, Ranulf had slipped away to seek help from his wife's father – Earl Robert of Gloucester. Surprising Stephen, Earl Robert appeared outside Lincoln with Matilda's army. There was no choice; Stephen set out to meet the challenge.

Earl Robert's army advanced and swept aside the guards posted by Stephen. Yet Stephen had the advantage as he held the higher ground. Then, over-eager for battle, Stephen rashly abandoned his strong position and marched down to the plain below the city. Earl Robert could not believe his luck. Even before Stephen's army had formed its line, Earl Robert's knights had begun their charge.

Stephen wanted to attack, not defend. He ordered his men forward, but when they saw that Earl Robert had the greater numbers, Stephen's mounted barons deserted and fled. Then the wings of Stephen's army were routed. All that remained was the centre, and that was soon surrounded. Here stood Stephen with his knights and soldiers as the enemy approached on horse and by foot. The royalist square was assaulted from all sides. Earl Robert's men moved in, certain of victory.

This was the great opportunity to kill Stephen, end the civil war and elevate Matilda to queen. Although his judgment was poor, Stephen's courage was not in doubt.

Now he showed it, resisting bravely as those around him were felled. Stephen fought like a lion at bay, lashing out with his sword time and again until the blade broke. Then he attacked with his hand-axe, laying unmercifully into those who would kill him until the shaft of his axe shattered. Exhausted, defenceless and encircled, he was unable to fight and unable to flee.

At the very moment when Earl Robert's men were moving in for the kill, a foot-soldier decided that he would be the one to slay the King. Taking careful aim, the soldier hurled a large stone at Stephen. It struck him on the head, spinning Stephen round and knocking him unconscious. All fighting stopped, with the King lying motionless on the ground, blood flowing down his face, apparently dead. The battle was over, and Earl Robert's men prepared to carry Stephen's body away so that it could be shown to the populace as proof of his death.

Suddenly, Stephen stirred; he opened his eyes and slowly he regained consciousness. The stone had not killed him, it had saved his life. With the fighting over, it was now too late to kill the King.

Stephen was taken to Bristol near Earl Robert's south-western stronghold of Gloucester. Locked up and fettered in chains, Stephen's future looked bleak as Matilda made her way to London. The majority of churchmen and barons quickly swore allegiance to Matilda. They had forgotten about her arrogance. Within days, and before any coronation, she cancelled grants of land and titles and then she increased taxation. Now people started to cause trouble in the streets. The mood of the Londoners became so hostile that Matilda was forced to leave the city.

As a result, those still supporting Stephen saw an increase in their numbers, and the civil war started once more. Not long after the renewal of hostilities, Stephen's wife saw to it that the scales were balanced. While Earl Robert was besieging Stephen's brother, Henry, an army raised by the Queen (also named Matilda) besieged the besiegers, and Earl Robert was captured. So the two Matildas (first cousins) exchanged King

Stephen for Earl Robert.

Stephen immediately took the offensive, and the civil war became increasingly brutal, until in late 1147, Earl Robert died of a fever. With the loss of her military commander, Matilda despaired, and she left for Anjou, never to return to England.

King Stephen now felt secure, and he set his mind to ensuring the succession for his first son, Eustace. Unfortunately, there was a new problem. Stephen had fallen out with the Church, and the bishops refused to accept Eustace as heir to the throne.

Although the death of Matilda's half-brother had improved Stephen's position, the death of her husband would have quite the opposite effect. When Geoffrey of Anjou died in 1151, Matilda's son Henry Plantagenet became Count of Anjou, and he found himself with a powerful army. Two years later he landed in England, and warfare recommenced. However, barons on both sides had lost their enthusiasm; they wanted an agreement rather than a battle. All of them feared death or ruin if they backed the wrong side. At almost the same time, young Eustace died. Stephen had had enough. He was now old and weary, and he had no interest in procuring the succession for his sole surviving son, William (the second son, Baldwin, having died in infancy).

So the civil war ended with a deal: Stephen would remain king until his death, then his son William would inherit all his father's private estates; but Matilda's son, Henry Plantagenet, would succeed to the throne.

A few months later, in October 1154, Stephen died. It was a sudden illness, said to have been a bowel disorder. Very convenient timing for Henry Plantagenet.

The attempted killer of the King at Lincoln is unknown. That stone-thrower was also the man who unintentionally saved the King's life, so condemning England to another 13 years of civil war. But maybe someone had more success with poison.

****

HENRY II

25 October 1154 – 6 July 1189

On the death of King Stephen, Henry Plantagenet succeeded to the throne under the agreement that had settled the civil war. However, Stephen's only surviving son, William, was not content to abandon his right to inherit his father's crown. He engaged Flemish mercenaries to assassinate Henry when he was visiting Canterbury. The assassins travelled to Canterbury and lay in wait. But Henry had learned of the plot, and he fled to Normandy where he remained until the danger had passed. The plot was abandoned. Four years later William died, and as neither William nor his brothers left any children, the threat from the Blois family ended.

Henry's father, Count Geoffrey of Anjou, used to wear a sprig of bloom on his helmet. The plant was called the Broom Flower or *planta genista* (*planta genet* in French), and from that came first his nickname and then years afterwards the family surname and the name of the Plantagenet dynasty.

King Henry II ruled a vast territory. From his father he inherited Anjou, Touraine and Maine; from his mother he inherited Normandy; and from his grandfather Henry I (via Stephen and Matilda) he inherited England. Before his accession, Henry II had married Eleanor of Aquitaine, the former wife of the King of France (the marriage annulled on the grounds of consanguinity, but in truth because after 14 years of marriage she had not produced a son), and she brought Henry the lands of Aquitaine, Poitou, Gascony and Auvergne. Later, Henry inherited Brittany from his brother. As a result, Henry ruled England and the western half of present-day France.

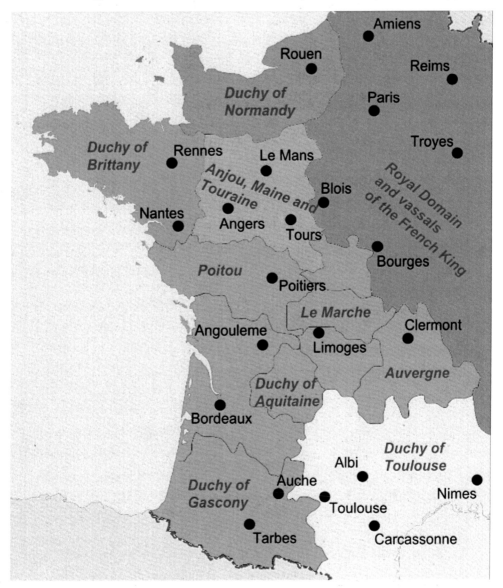

The Angevin continental territories

England's growing status was enhanced when Nicholas Breakspear was elected the first and only English pope,

Adrian IV, who is said to have authorised Henry to conquer Ireland.

Short but strong, Henry had tremendous energy and intelligence as well as an impressive knowledge of languages and the law. He also had a fearsome temper. His problems came from those closest to him, and one by one they reduced him from greatness to a weak old man.

Early in the reign, Henry appointed his friend and Chancellor, Thomas Becket, as Archbishop of Canterbury; Becket having been ordained a priest one day earlier. Becket immediately discarded the friendship and opposed Henry's efforts to increase royal control over the English Church. The main clash came about when Becket refused to allow a lay court to try a priest who had been accused of rape and murder. Leniency of church courts towards priests they had convicted was commonplace; the church courts could not pass a sentence of blood, and they were unwilling to incur the expense of imprisonment. So penance was usually as far as it went.

Matters came to a head when Becket complained to the Pope (no longer Adrian IV, who had died, supposedly by choking on a fly in his glass of wine) and started excommunicating Henry's supporters, threatening to do the same to Henry. The King's temper exploded and his rash words led to four of his knights riding to Canterbury where they murdered Becket. The whole of Europe was outraged. Becket was declared a martyr; he would later become a saint. King Henry was forced to do penance and required to walk barefoot to Canterbury, to be scourged by 80 monks who beat him as he walked past them wearing sackcloth and ashes.

Henry also fell out with his wife, partly because of their conflicting strong personalities, but also on Henry's side because of his lack of interest in a woman who was twelve years his senior, and on Eleanor's side because of her husband's large number of illegitimate children. Queen Eleanor was particularly incensed at having in the palace the son of a prostitute, a boy named Geoffrey who would later become the Archbishop of York.

The royal couple had eight children: William who died young and four more boys: Henry, Richard, Geoffrey and John. There were also three girls: Maud, Eleanor and Joan. The sons would continually cause trouble.

Henry favoured his youngest child, John, and was always concerned to see to his future. When Henry was negotiating a marriage for John, he decided to give him three castles in Anjou. The oldest son, also called Henry, had already been crowned King of England so as to ensure a smooth succession on his father's death, and he was therefore known as the Young King, although he was in reality a prince. The Young King was impatient for power, and he demanded that his father give him England, Anjou or Normandy to rule. He also objected to John being given any castles.

When Henry rejected all of the Young King's demands, the Young King made for the court of King Louis VII of France, and his equally rebellious brothers Richard and Geoffrey followed him. Queen Eleanor argued that she had the right of gift of the territories she had brought to the marriage, and she decided to join her three sons. But she was caught before she could leave England and was imprisoned by her husband.

In time, Henry made peace with the three princes. Then a dispute over a castle caused the Young King and his ally Geoffrey to fall out with Richard. The Young King went on the attack and ravaged Richard's territory of Aquitaine. Richard called on his father for support, and Henry set out with troops, heading for Limoges. On approaching the town, they were ambushed, and arrows rained down on Henry and his men. One arrow penetrated Henry's armour, but the armour was strong, of the highest quality. Although the arrow drew blood, the wound was minor; a man with lesser armour would have been killed.

Having joined up with Richard, father and son set out to confront the Young King in the hope of forcing a settlement. As they neared his castle they were spotted, and archers on the battlements took aim and let fly their arrows at Henry and his knights. One arrow sped through the air bound for Henry. Just as

CHILDREN OF HENRY II

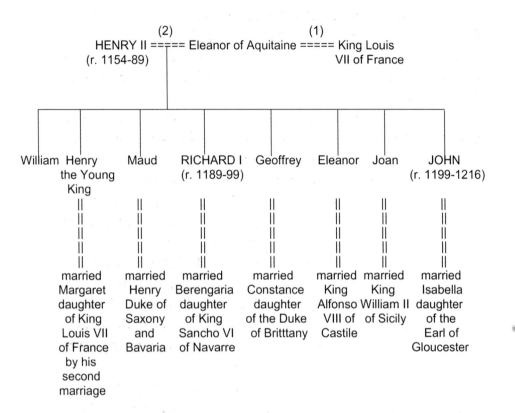

```
              (2)                              (1)
        HENRY II ====== Eleanor of Aquitaine ===== King Louis
        (r. 1154-89)                               VII of France
```

William	Henry the Young King	Maud	RICHARD I (r. 1189-99)	Geoffrey	Eleanor	Joan	JOHN (r. 1199-1216)
	married Margaret daughter of King Louis VII of France by his second marriage	married Henry Duke of Saxony and Bavaria	married Berengaria daughter of King Sancho VI of Navarre	married Constance daughter of the Duke of Britttany	married King Alfonso VIII of Castile	married King William II of Sicily	married Isabella daughter of the Earl of Gloucester

the arrow neared its target, Henry's horse reared, raising its head high, and it was struck a fearful blow. If the horse had not lifted its head at that very moment, the arrow would have pierced the King's breast. Another lucky escape for an English monarch.

The negotiations came to nothing. Then the Young King fell mortally ill. He died of dysentery in 1183, his only child having died in infancy.

Now King Henry had to reassess the succession. He decided to give Anjou, Maine and Normandy to the oldest surviving son, Richard; Geoffrey already ruled Brittany having married the duchess; Aquitaine was to go to the favourite son, John. The problem was that Richard had been installed as Duke of Aquitaine when he was 14 years old, and he refused to surrender it to John as part of the arrangement.

There was only one way to deal with Richard. Geoffrey and John were sent to Aquitaine with an army to force him to submit. They failed as Richard repelled the attack. Then, in 1186, Geoffrey took part in a tournament in Paris. In the 'mock' fighting, Geoffrey was knocked off his horse and trampled to death. Only Richard and John were left.

Seeing an opportunity for mischief, King Philip of France, who was keen to acquire Plantagenet lands, advised Richard that Aquitaine was only the start and that Henry was planning to disinherit Richard completely, leaving everything to John. As a result, Richard confronted his father and demanded formal recognition as heir to all his father's lands. Henry refused to do anything of the sort.

With the dispute unresolved, the ageing king fell ill whilst at Le Mans (the principal city of Maine). Taking advantage of his father's infirmity, Richard attacked with the support of King Philip. Henry had the southern part of the town set alight in an effort to halt Richard's advance. Then, as the fire raged, the wind changed direction and Henry was forced to flee, accompanied by 70 knights. The French gave chase, eager to seize the opportunity to kill Henry, but they were slowed down whilst crossing a stream whose waters were high. That enabled Henry to make good his escape, and he reached a hilltop from where he watched his birthplace burn to the ground. It was a total disaster.

The victors summoned the exhausted Henry to discuss terms. He had to accept whatever was demanded; principally recognition of Richard as his heir, and an amnesty for those who had rebelled. Henry was therefore able to require one thing in return. He obviously needed the names of all the treasonable subjects who had fought against him and who were to receive the amnesty.

Henry retired to Chinon. The next day a horseman arrived and delivered the list of names into Henry's hands, no one believing that this was anything more than an administrative requirement to enable the appropriate document to be prepared for Henry's signature. They were mistaken; Henry wanted to know who was on the list. He untied the parchment, unrolled it and set his gaze at the top of the column of names.

To Henry's complete surprise and bitter distress, the first name was that of his favourite child, John. This was the very son he had been fighting for and whom he dearly wanted to be his successor. John could not have done more to kill his father if he had thrust a dagger into his heart. Henry flew into an uncontrollable rage, suffered a violent fit and collapsed on the floor.

After telling the illegitimate Geoffrey (the prostitute's child) that he was the only true son and all the others were bastards, Henry fell into semi-consciousness, intermittently gathering his remaining strength to abuse Richard and John.

Hounded to the point of death by the son who had attacked and harassed him, and mortally wounded by the son dearest to him, Henry lost the will to live. He died a day later of a cerebral haemorrhage – killed for sure if 'killed' means that someone caused his death. A miserable end after having survived the earlier attempts to kill him, saved first by his armour and then by his horse.

****

54

RICHARD I

6 July 1189 – 6 April 1199

When Richard succeeded his father, he finally achieved his ambition to rule all his mother's and his father's territories. However, he had absolutely no interest in England. In fact, he could speak very little English, and throughout his reign he would treat the country as little more than a source of manpower and revenue, preferring to live in his duchy of Aquitaine.

Richard was a tall man, and like most of the men in his family, he was red-haired with a wild temper, fearless and violent. No English monarch has such a romantic reputation, renowned through the ages for gallantry and virtue. Yet although he was called the Lionheart[3], Richard's considerable military prowess was largely employed in the slaughter of unarmed innocents.

After the death of his father, Richard travelled to London to be crowned, having released his mother from imprisonment. The coronation left London smouldering. First, the circling of a bat around Richard's head during the ceremony was seen as an evil omen. Then mass murder took over. William the Conqueror had brought to England a number of Jewish

---

3 An epithet he gained not on crusade, but by putting down the Aquitanian barons who had previously fought for him.

merchants and their families to help stimulate the economy, and he and his successors always considered it their duty to protect them. During Richard's coronation, several Jews who had come with gifts for the new monarch were beaten to death. With no effort being made to stop them, the mob poured on to the streets and set fire to the homes of all the Jews in London, and then killed most of them as they fled. After that, the Jews in other towns were murdered; every man, woman and child in Lynn, Norwich, Stamford and York.[4]

Having left the Jews to their fate, Richard's attention turned to their homeland. Once crowned, he started preparations to enlist an army to go on the Third Crusade with his ally, King Philip II of France. Their mission was to re-take Jerusalem from Saladin[5]. Richard set out in the summer of 1190, and he made his way to Messina in Sicily where he was to meet up with Philip.

Richard disliked King Tancred of Sicily because of the way he had treated the widow of the former king; and that widow was Richard's sister Joan. Tancred was holding Joan prisoner and would not hand over her dowry to which she was entitled under her husband's will, and to which the new king (who was not his predecessor's legal heir) had no right. When the citizens of Messina refused to allow Richard's soldiers into the town or provide them with supplies, fighting broke out. Richard took the opportunity to devastate the entire city. Tancred speedily released Joan, and he later agreed to give her 20,000 ounces of gold and to send a similar amount to Richard.

With one problem solved, another arrived. When he was twelve years old, Richard had been betrothed to Alys, the sister of King Philip II, the man who had helped Richard to

---

4 In 2004, the remains of 11 children and 6 adults were found at the bottom of a medieval well in Norwich. Examination results dated the remains to the twelfth century and suggested that the victims had been thrown into the well; and DNA testing showed that the individuals were related to one another and that they were Jews.

5 Also an epithet: Salah ad-Din – Righteousness of the faith. His real name was Yusuf.

be appointed heir to the English throne. Now Richard refused to go through with the marriage. A few days later, Richard's mother, aware of the rumour that Alys had been the mistress of her husband, Richard's father, landed in Sicily with a more acceptable bride, Berengaria of Navarre. The irate Philip promptly left for the Holy Land with his forces.

Richard decided to follow him. During the voyage, three of Richard's ships, including the one carrying Joan and Berengaria, were caught in a storm, and they ran ashore near Limassol on the coast of Cyprus. The survivors were taken prisoner by King Isaac Comnenus, who also seized Joan's gold. Not one to take such an insult quietly, Richard sailed back and conquered Cyprus, slaughtering a large number of the inhabitants.

While still in Cyprus, Richard married Berengaria. There would be no children as he was not particularly interested in relationships with women, perhaps more interested in men; that being confirmed when he later did penance for sodomy.

Having dealt with Cyprus, Richard set sail for Acre in the Holy Land, where he joined the forces of Philip and of Duke Leopold V of Austria in besieging the town. After a month, Acre was taken. The victory turned sour with a row about the division of spoils, and Richard had his soldiers tear down Leopold's standard from the town walls and throw it in a ditch, Richard telling Leopold that such honours were only for kings. Now Richard had fallen out with Philip and Leopold. Both of them had had enough, and they returned to Europe.[6]

The terms of the surrender of Acre included a payment by Saladin and the release of Christian prisoners in return for the lives of the citizens. Saladin paid the required amount and handed over Christian prisoners. Richard was not satisfied, claiming that Saladin had not handed over all the Christian prisoners. He ordered the massacre of the 2,700 captives he

---

6 There is a story that the French crusaders took home with them vines from the Jerusalem Hills together with some of the wine produced there. Coming from near the gates of Jerusalem, the wine was called *Porte de Dieu* – Gate of God, or in Hebrew: *sha'har-adonay*.

had taken, together with their wives and children. Richard looked on from a balcony as each of them was beheaded and disembowelled.

With no one left to kill in Acre, Richard marched to Arsuf, where he won a notable victory. Then he discovered that the route inland was blocked by Saladin's forces. Realising that it was unlikely that he could take Jerusalem, Richard agreed a three-year truce.

After 16 months of crusading, it was time for Richard to return to England, all the more urgently because of information he had received about mischief by his brother John, who was trying to depose Richard's Justiciar (chief minister). On his return voyage, Richard's ship was detached from the fleet during a storm and forced to seek shelter in Corfu. Fearing that he might be taken prisoner, Richard and four companions dressed as Templar Knights and took passage on a pirate ship bound for the north Adriatic. In another storm the pirate ship was driven ashore to the east of Venice. Unwilling to risk another sea voyage, Richard decided to travel overland in disguise. Within days he was recognised when he aroused suspicion by spending money too lavishly at an inn near Vienna, in the lands of the same Duke Leopold whom Richard had publicly insulted in Acre.

Richard was seized by Leopold's soldiers. On learning of Richard's capture, Holy Roman Emperor Henry VI ordered Leopold to hand over his captive, promising Leopold part of the ransom. Then Richard's brother John and King Philip of France offered money to the Emperor if he would keep Richard in prison. The offer was rejected. Instead, after a year and a half of fairly comfortable confinement, Richard was freed on swearing an oath of vassaldom and paying a ransom of 150,000 silver marks, which had been collected by dowager Queen Eleanor, partly by pawning the crown jewels. It was a massive payment, impoverishing the English treasury and the heavily-taxed English, especially after similar depletions had been caused by the need to finance Richard's crusade.

A term of Richard's release demanded by Duke Leopold was the release of Leopold's second cousin Isaac Comnenus, who had been locked up in silver chains as Richard had promised not to put him in irons.

Anyhow, Richard was now free. He reached England in March 1194, when he was once more crowned. The reason for the second crowning was that Richard feared that his oath of vassaldom to the Emperor implied subservience, so he might have forfeited his status of king. Being crowned again gave him a fresh start.

Within two months, Richard had left for France in an effort to recover castles lost by his brother John during Richard's absence. This brought Richard's total time spent in England during his reign to six months. It was more than Queen Berengaria, who did not set foot in England while she was queen. Richard reclaimed the lost castles, and for five years he continued the war against Philip, generally with success.

In what seemed to be a trivial diversion, in early 1199 a peasant discovered a hoard of Roman treasure whilst ploughing a field near Chalus in the Limousin. The peasant dutifully took the treasure to his lord, Achard of Chalus. News of the find soon reached Richard's ears. Richard was the overlord of Achard, and he considered that just as the peasant was required to surrender the treasure to Achard, so Achard was required to surrender the treasure to him. Achard refused. It was not a clever move.

As was to be expected, Richard rode out with a large force and besieged Chalus Castle. There were some minor skirmishes, and the time for an assault was approaching. Realising that his situation was hopeless, Achard offered to surrender if he and his men were allowed to leave with their arms. A deal was of no interest to Richard. He swore that he would take Chalus by storm and hang any survivors.

That evening, Richard decided to ride around the castle so that he could select the best point of attack. He set out, but dark as it was, it was not dark enough to prevent Richard from being spotted from the castle walls. An archer, Bertrand de Gourdon, took careful aim with his crossbow and let fly with a bolt. Richard was hit in the left shoulder. Defying the searing pain, Richard made light of the wound, and he rode back to his camp where he gave the order to attack. The assault on Chalus began as an attempt was made to extract the bolt from Richard's shoulder; but the shaft of the projectile broke whilst it was being pulled out, leaving the iron bolt deep in Richard's flesh.

Chalus Castle with its twenty or so defenders soon fell, and the survivors were taken prisoner. All but the archer were hanged.

A 'surgeon' was summoned. He dug into Richard's shoulder with primitive instruments, removing the bolt, but leaving a gaping hole in its place. Within hours, gangrene had set in. It was obvious that death was approaching. Eleven days after receiving the wound, Richard died.

The archer had been brought to Richard shortly before his death. According to legend, Richard ordered that the man should be set free with a reward of 100 shillings. As usual with the Lionheart, the facts are less endearing than the legend. One version is that the archer was sent to Richard's sister, Joan, who had him flayed and then torn apart by wild horses; another that one of Richard's senior knights had the archer whipped and then hanged; another that he was skinned alive and then hanged. This may not have been at Richard's direction, although it would have been true to character.

Either way it was a brutal execution, even for a man who had killed the King.

****

JOHN

6 April 1199 – 19 October 1216

The youngest of the eight legitimate children of Henry II, throughout his youth there was no reason to believe that John would ever become king. So, although he was his father's favourite, little was done to provide him with wealth or land. He therefore became known as John Lackland.

Yet he would become king; and even before that he was, with Richard's Justiciar, the joint-ruler of England while his brother was on crusade. Richard must have had an inkling of what might happen if John was left to his own devices, because before departing for the Holy Land, Richard had ordered John to leave England for three years. Their mother, Queen Eleanor, talked Richard into revoking the decree.

He should not have given in. Throughout Richard's absence on crusade, and then during Richard's imprisonment, John was scheming with Philip of France, stirring up rebellion in England while Philip seized Richard's lands on the Continent.

Once Richard was back in England, although he stripped John of most of his possessions, Richard forgave his brother; and John fought loyally alongside Richard in the quest to regain the continental lands. So much so, that the childless Richard nominated John as his heir. That nomination was followed in

England and Normandy on Richard's death, despite Arthur, the son of John's deceased older brother Geoffrey, having a better right to the crown according to the rules of heredity. However, John's claim was rejected in Anjou, Maine and Touraine, where the 12-year-old Arthur was recognised as ruler. So John paid King Philip a large bribe, and he helped John to oust Arthur.

Having arranged for his marriage to Isabel of Gloucester to be annulled by the Pope on the grounds that John and Isabel were half second cousins, John married the 12-year-old Isabella of Angoulême. His new bride brought John vast estates, but her fiancé, Hugh of Lusignan, was not happy to have lost Isabella, and he complained to King Philip. For some time Philip ignored the complaints of the Lusignans, but after they received further mistreatment from John, Philip took their side and seized two of John's castles in Normandy.

Naturally, John went on the attack, and at first he was successful. He captured his nephew, Arthur, who was imprisoned and then murdered, possibly by John's own hand. Then the fighting went badly, and John returned to England having lost nearly all his continental lands, most significantly Normandy.

John spent years preparing to recover his inheritance. His first need was money, and that meant higher taxes. It led to resentment and the threat of rebellion, which John struggled to restrain. Next, John fell out with the Pope over the choice of the new Archbishop of Canterbury. The Pope rejected the nominees of the King and of the monks, and instead put forward Stephen Langton. John refused to accept the Pope's nomination. As a result, the Pope excommunicated John and placed England under an interdict prohibiting all church services other than baptisms and confessions of the dying. John did not care, because now he could confiscate church estates and accumulate more money.

It was not quite that easy. Excommunication had consequences; one was that it released John's subjects from their oaths of allegiance, and that encouraged the barons to rebel. Eventually, John made peace with the Pope, and on making promises and payments, the interdict was lifted and the excommunication was rescinded. However, the rumblings of rebellion had started, and they would not be halted.

Ignoring the problems at home, John went to war against France in an effort to regain the lost territories. John won several victories; then, at the Battle of Bouvines an English/German/ Flemish army was decisively beaten, so ending John's hopes of recovering Normandy. In October 1214, John returned to England, and he returned to an unsettled country, with many of the barons on the brink of warfare. They resented having to bear the cost of John's peace with the Pope, they were furious at having had to pay for the unsuccessful war with Philip, and now John wanted to increase taxes.

Both sides gathered their forces, and the barons presented John with a list of demands, which he immediately rejected. John retaliated by seizing the estates of the rebel barons. Civil war was now inevitable. The rebels took Bedford, about 50 miles north of London, and then they marched south. When they reached London, the gates were opened to them, and they settled there and held the city.

In an attempt at compromise, or perhaps it was merely to buy time, John agreed to a meeting at Runnymede, a meadow on the south bank of the River Thames not far from London. After some negotiation, the terms of a charter (later called Magna Carta) were agreed. This document curtailed royal power and set out in detail the rights of all subjects, including their entitlement to trial by jury.

Happy with their success, most of the barons returned to their castles. They had celebrated too soon, because once they had left, John decided that he did not need to keep promises to rebels. He appealed to the Pope to annul the charter.

The Pope agreed, and he ordered the excommunication of many of the rebel barons, placing an interdict on their lands. However, Archbishop Langton refused to enforce the Pope's decree, and the Pope suspended from office the very man whose appointment he had worked so hard to secure. Ignoring Langton, the bishops applied the Pope's orders, the charter was annulled and the civil war began once again.

Winning significant victories, John subdued the north and east of England, the principal territories of the rebel barons. Their last stronghold was London, and John prepared to attack. In desperation, the barons invited Louis, son of King Philip of France, to take the crown of England. Now John had to deal with the expected invasion. Unfortunately, John's fleet was destroyed in a storm, and Louis was able to land in the south-east at Thanet and then move on to London.

John retreated northwards, but when he reached Kings Lynn he was laid low with dysentery. In a reduced state, John set out for Lincolnshire in October 1216, travelling around the bay known as the Wash by way of Wisbech, while his baggage train took the more direct but hazardous route across the four-mile-wide estuary where the Wellstream River flowed into the Wash. It certainly was hazardous. Those in the baggage train who were not swallowed by quicksand were swept away by the incoming tide. All John's treasure and all England's crown jewels were lost; not a single man in the baggage train survived.

Having taken the safer route, John struggled on and arrived at Swineshead Abbey to the west of Boston. Here his condition deteriorated. It was blamed on a meal of peaches and fresh cider. The next morning John set out with his entourage. He got as far as Newark, where he died a few days later.

There is an alternative version of John's death. It tells of how the Pope wanted to end the conflict between England and France. He believed that there was no way to accomplish this while John lived, for although John and the Pope were now reconciled, John had always caused trouble. So the Pope instructed a monk to travel to England and poison John.

Having crossed the Channel, the monk caught up with John's party as they reached Swineshead Abbey. Once there, the monk produced a letter from the Pope, and was invited to enter. He offered his services in the preparation and serving of the King's meal. Now he was ready to strike.

Alone in the wine cellar, the monk carefully poured some of the poison into a carafe of wine. He carried the carafe into the dining room and offered the wine to the King. John instructed the monk to drink some first. The monk drank a little, believing that a small amount would not be lethal. He did not realise that the poison was lethal even in small quantities, although slow-acting. As a result, the monk was initially unaffected, so John took a glass and drank his fill. John's life lingered on as his condition deteriorated on the journey to Newark, where he died. Still in Swineshead Abbey, the poisoner monk, the murderer of the King, also died.

The poisoning story was rumoured at the time and was revived in the sixteenth century, when it was taken up by Shakespeare in *The Life and Death of King John*. The story may have been inspired by Tudor anti-papalism. On the other hand, for an English king to die of 'natural causes' was rare, and peaches and cider were unlikely killers.

In all probability another King of England was murdered.

****

CHILDREN OF KING JOHN

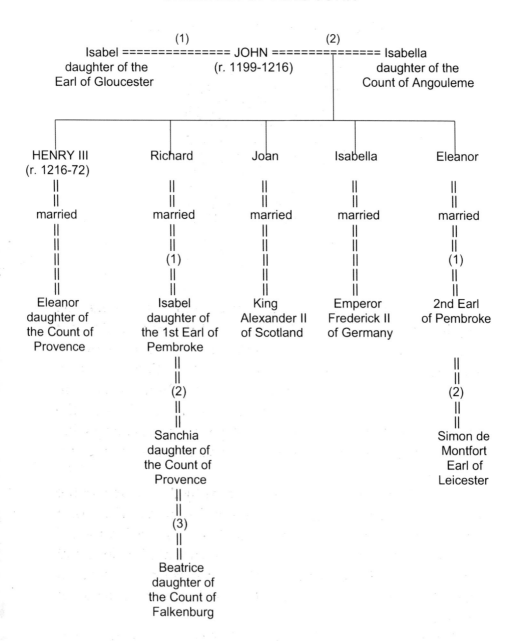

HENRY III

19 October 1216 – 16 November 1272

King John had married a girl aged twelve, so he had no legitimate children for seven years after the wedding. It meant that when John died, his first son was only nine years old. Henry succeeded his father in the weakest position of any new English monarch. Not only was he a young child, but London and most of the south-east were in the hands of Louis, the Dauphin[7], and the north of the country was controlled by rebel barons. On top of this, the crown jewels and the royal treasury had been lost.

Yet all these problems were overcome by the wisdom of the men who governed England during Henry's minority. For a start, the death of John took away much of the rebels' cause and support. Victories for Henry's forces on land at Lincoln and at sea off Sandwich led to a deal. All the rebels were granted an amnesty, and a bribe ensured that the Dauphin returned to France.

Finally, in 1227, at the age of nineteen, Henry took over from the men who had safeguarded the kingdom for him.

---

7 The heir to the French throne, meaning 'a dolphin' – the creature on the heir's flag.

When Henry signed a reduced version of Magna Carta, there appeared to be nothing to prevent an untroubled reign.

Then Henry appointed Peter des Roches, the Poitevin Bishop of Winchester, as his principal adviser. Wasting no time, des Roches granted positions and privileges to dozens of his kinsmen who had made their way to England. The barons were furious at this foreign invasion, and they forced Henry to replace des Roches and to send his countrymen back to Poitou. For several years Henry avoided further trouble; but it was weakness rather than wisdom that sustained him, and the barons grew ever more powerful.

In 1236, Henry married Eleanor of Provence, the younger sister of the Queen of France. Now came the first attempt on Henry's life. The unsubstantiated story is that in 1238, in the dead of night, an assassin managed to get into Woodstock Palace. He crept along the corridors, moving from room to room until he reached Henry's quarters. Drawing his dagger, the assassin advanced to the side of Henry's bed. To his disappointment, Henry was not there. In what was a rare occurrence for a king in those days, Henry was spending the night in his wife's bedroom. The would-be murderer escaped, as did Henry.

Following in the footsteps of des Roches, Queen Eleanor saw to it that many of her family and countrymen came to England to populate the court and move on to positions of power. They were joined by the King's half-brothers, because Henry's mother, who was only 28 years old when King John died, had married Hugh X of Lusignan, the son of Hugh IX of Lusignan from whom she had been stolen by John so many years earlier. Catching up on lost time, she bore Hugh nine children; and they all wanted positions at their half-brother's court.

Not surprisingly, the barons were even more enraged. The situation was aggravated by high taxation imposed by Henry to pay for an unsuccessful attempt to regain continental lands, for a crusade that never took place, and for a failed adventure to gain the crown of Sicily for his second son, Edmund.

In 1258, the threat of rebellion and a shortage of money forced Henry to sign the Provisions of Oxford under which he agreed to the formation of a Council, with half of the members to be selected by the King and half to be selected by the barons. Henry swore that he would follow the advice of this Council. He also agreed to the meeting three times a year of a parliament made up of magnates, bishops and the King's legal advisers.

Like his father after Runnymede, Henry did not keep his word. He continued to rule autocratically. However, there was one person who was not content to sit and look on as Henry ignored his obligations. A young man named Simon de Montfort had arrived from France in 1230 to make a claim to the earldom of Leicester. As the younger son of the nephew of the fourth earl, his case was doubtful to say the least, yet by force of personality and determination he succeeded to the title. In 1238, he married Henry's widowed sister, Eleanor. Now Simon had influence at court as the King's brother-in-law and in the Council as one of its most powerful members. Simon's authority increased as many of the barons and much of the populace gave him their support in the quest to restrict foreign influence at court and to force Henry to keep the promises he had made in the Provisions of Oxford.

Henry agreed to resolve the dispute by arbitration. The arbitrator, King Louis IX of France, was horrified at the proposition that royal power should be restricted, and he ordered the annulment of the Provisions. It was asking for trouble. Open warfare broke out in 1264, with Simon leading the rebels as the champion of Parliament and enemy of the foreigners. Extraordinary, because Simon had clearly been a fortune-hunting foreigner himself.

The rebels' main strongholds were Northampton, Leicester, Nottingham and London. Within days, Henry had taken three of those cities. Only London remained, and it was the key to power.

Rather than making for the capital, where victory would have ended the war, Henry marched around the city to the royalist stronghold of Rochester, intent on relieving it from a besieging force. Even after routing the besiegers of Rochester, Henry might have marched to London. Instead he decided to capture Tonbridge, and then he proceeded to secure the towns on the south-east coast. That done, he turned inland and made for Lewes in Sussex, having left behind substantial forces to hold the coastal towns.

Simon set out with his army, and they made camp four miles from Lewes. Although he knew that Simon's army was approaching, Henry posted a party of only four men on the ridge overlooking the town to keep a look-out. Three of those men returned to the town to eat and drink, and the remaining soldier fell asleep. That allowed Simon to position his army, totally unseen and unhindered, less than two miles from the King's forces.

In the morning, with knights to the front and infantry behind, Simon's men advanced. Despite being taken by surprise, the royal army managed to form its line just in time. The rebel army was divided into three divisions abreast, with a fourth commanded by Simon himself to the rear. Henry's army was also divided into three divisions abreast, but without a fourth division behind. The men who might have formed such a reserve had been left to garrison the coastal towns.

The engagement took place across all three divisions, with Simon's left (made up of Londoners) meeting the King's right, commanded by Henry's son, Prince Edward, first. The rebels' assault was unsuccessful as Prince Edward and his men rebuffed the attack, forcing their opponents to flee in disorder. If Edward had then used his troops to reinforce the centre and left of his father's army, there is little doubt that Simon's army would have been defeated.

Instead, Edward's emotions took over. He wanted revenge on the Londoners for insulting his mother when they had pelted her with rotten vegetables and eggs as she sailed down the Thames. Edward led his men (the elite of Henry's army) in pursuit of the fleeing remnants of the rebel division, chasing them from the battlefield, killing as many as possible until there were no more to kill. When it was over, he found himself over three miles from Lewes and out of sight of the battle. On the way back, Edward stumbled upon Simon's baggage train. Never one to miss an opportunity for easy killing, Edward and his forces attacked the baggage train, not stopping the slaughter until they had mistakenly killed the royalist prisoners being held by Simon.

Meanwhile, the real battle had been continuing. After vicious hand-to-hand fighting, the rebel right division broke the royalist line, and then Simon advanced with his reserves to support the centre. They quickly began to overpower the royalists. Undaunted, Henry and those around him fought on in the hope that Prince Edward's forces might shortly return.

Here came the opportunity to end the battle and the war. Simon's knights rode forward, each seeking his own target. One of them made for the King, the knight's lance pointing at Henry's chest. At the critical moment something happened. Perhaps the attacker's horse stumbled, perhaps the King managed to turn away. As the lance was thrust forward with murderous intent, it narrowly missed Henry, instead sinking deep into the body of his horse. Henry fell to the ground; but the moment had passed, the opportunity lost. The attempted killing of the King had failed. Soldiers rushed to Henry's side, and they dragged the heavily-armoured monarch to a nearby priory.

Victory was completed, with Henry's soldiers and knights retreating into marshland around the River Ouse, half-covered by water now that it was full tide. Many of them drowned as the mud sucked them and their horses down.

At last, with the battle all but over, Prince Edward arrived with his men. Seeing the disaster before them, the majority turned and fled, leaving Edward to take refuge in a friary. The following day, surrender terms were agreed, with the royal army laying down their arms and the King and Prince Edward taken prisoner. No physical harm was done to either of them, because Simon and his supporters were monarchists; it was just that they wished to limit the monarch's powers as agreed at Oxford.

With the King under rebel control, the country was governed by the Earl of Leicester (that is, Simon de Montfort), the Earl of Gloucester (Gilbert de Clare) and the Bishop of Chichester (much of the clergy having supported the rebels in their moral crusade).

They summoned a parliament in 1265 that was made up of 23 barons, two knights from each county and two citizens and burgesses from each of the major towns and boroughs. With part non-nobility non-clergy membership for the first time, this was the origin of the House of Commons.

As always, one man became the absolute ruler. Simon began to govern as a dictator. With the King now a figurehead and a dictator in power, the mood of the barons and the populace changed. Gloucester withdrew to his estates. Then, one day when he was out riding, Prince Edward escaped from confinement. He rushed to join Gloucester and the others opposed to Simon's rule.

Ten weeks later, at the brutal Battle of Evesham, the two sides met once more. King Henry was at the battle, still in the custody of Simon and his knights as they fought in a circle around him. As Simon and his colleagues were slaughtered in the effort to kill all the Montfortian leaders, one of Prince Edward's knights, not realising whom he was attacking, struck Henry across the face with a sword, knocking the King to the ground. By pure chance, Henry was not killed. Looking up, the desperate Henry, bleeding severely from the face, screamed out, referring to his birthplace, "I am Henry of Winchester, your king! I am Henry your king!". The attacker held back, and Henry was rescued and removed from danger as the battle came to an end.

Surrender by traitors did not lead to a negotiated peace. Most Montfortians not already killed were butchered after the battle. Simon was dead, so when the fighting ended, his corpse was decapitated, his private parts cut off, his body dismembered and his trunk thrown to the dogs as an example to would-be traitors. It was also a lesson to others not to show clemency to a defeated king.

Henry reigned for another five years. Nevertheless, the principle of regular parliaments containing barons, knights and citizens was maintained.

However, there was a matter of greater importance for Henry: the reconstruction of Westminster Abbey. That building is the main consequence of the failure of the attempts to kill the King at Lewes and Evesham.

CHILDREN OF HENRY III

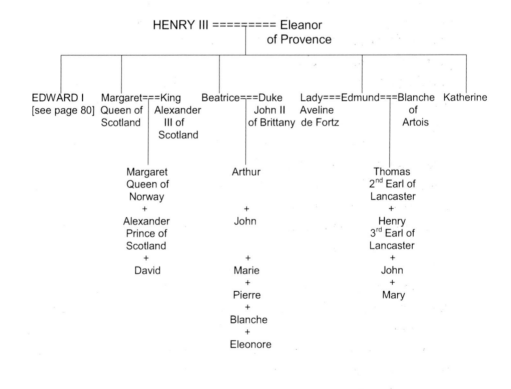

HENRY III ========= **Eleanor of Provence**

| EDWARD I [see page 80] | Margaret===King Queen of Scotland / Alexander III of Scotland | Beatrice===Duke John II of Brittany | Lady Aveline de Fortz ===Edmund=== Blanche of Artois | Katherine |

Margaret
Queen of
Norway
+
Alexander
Prince of
Scotland
+
David

Arthur
+
John
+
Marie
+
Pierre
+
Blanche
+
Eleonore

Thomas
2nd Earl of
Lancaster
+
Henry
3rd Earl of
Lancaster
+
John
+
Mary

****

EDWARD I

16 November 1272 – 7 July 1307

After the victory of the royal army at Evesham, followed by the killing of the surviving Montfortian soldiers, peace reigned in England.

With Edward's record of slaughtering fleeing Londoners at Lewes and surrendering Montfortians at Evesham, it is no surprise that the papal legate invited Edward to take part in the Eighth Crusade. Edward set sail in 1270, taking 1,000 knights with him. He also took his wife, Eleanor of Castile. Edward and Eleanor had married in 1254, when he was fifteen and she was thirteen. She would bear him fifteen children.

By the time they arrived in Tunis, where King Louis IX of France had been trying to establish a Christian kingdom, Louis had died and the Eighth Crusade was over. So Edward journeyed on to the Holy Land to take part in what would be the Ninth Crusade. Shortly after landing, Edward's knights joined the other crusading forces in attacking the town of Qaqun. Edward was denied the opportunity of further killing when, despite his objections, a truce was agreed.

The crusaders then moved on to relieve Acre from a siege led by the Sultan of Egypt. Next, Edward took Nazareth, after which he had all its inhabitants (Muslims, Jews and even some Christians) massacred. As the armies prepared for further slaughter, one of the emirs sent a representative to discuss terms with Edward. When the negotiator arrived, he was quickly ushered into Edward's room.

It was a trick, this man was a member of the secret order of Nazaris. They were a sect of the Ismailis, themselves a split-off from the Shiite Muslims. Their creed required them to kill those whom they regarded as their enemies.

The founder of the order, Hasan bin Sabah, taught his followers that anyone who did not believe as he did was a legitimate target for murder. He lived in what is now Iran, and he demanded total obedience, recruiting impressionable young men, and indoctrinating them until they became fanatics. They were then schooled in deception so that they could infiltrate the lands of their enemies and live there quietly without revealing their true purpose. Trained to kill, they operated not by open warfare, but by murdering the leaders of their enemies, usually with a dagger and preferably in public. That meant that the murderer was invariably apprehended and executed. It was actually the desired result, as Hasan bin Sabah had promised the killer that he would be a martyr and would go to Paradise to be rewarded with 72 virgins.

People believed that these young men must have been drugged with hashish to carry out such missions. For that reason they became known as 'Hashishim', which in time was corrupted to 'Assassin' – a word later adopted in many languages for the killers of prominent people.

Suddenly the Assassin drew a large dagger from within his robe and leapt forward. Edward was unprepared for the attack; nevertheless he managed to turn to the side, and he was stabbed in the arm. However, Edward was a formidable adversary, so tall that his nickname was 'Longshanks'. The injured Edward kicked out at his assailant and then picked up a stool with which he hit his would-be murderer, knocking him to the floor. Now Edward leapt on top of the man, and they grappled fiercely until Edward managed to wrench the dagger from the Assassin's hand, although not before Edward had been slashed across the forehead.

Having heard the noise of the scuffling, armed men came running to Edward's aid, and the Assassin was killed. Edward's wounds were not of themselves life-threatening, but the dagger had been dipped in poison. After several days the wounds turned a dark colour, and there were fears that the poisoning would be fatal. Eleanor realised the danger and – so the doubtful story goes – she sucked out the poison. Then the skills of the court physician ensured Edward's recovery. Now it was time to return to England.

Edward and the Assassin

On the journey home, news arrived that King Henry III had died and that as the first son Edward had been proclaimed king, heredity now being the accepted test. As the fourth king named Edward, he was initially called Edward IV following

Edward the Elder, Edward the Martyr and Edward the Confessor. Some time later it was decided that the numbering of English monarchs should start afresh after the Norman Conquest (supporting the dynasty's claim that they founded the English nation), so Edward became known as King Edward, then Edward I when his son was crowned Edward II.

Edward replenished his treasury by selling confiscated estates back to the barons who had sided with de Montfort. Suitably enriched, Edward's first target was the Welsh. The self-appointed Prince of Wales, Llewellyn ap Gruffydd, refused to pay homage to Edward, so in 1277 Edward marched his army into Wales and defeated Llewellyn and his forces with great bloodshed. Five years later, Llewellyn and his brother, Dafydd, led a rebellion against English rule. Edward took his army back to Wales, and after some early reverses he crushed the Welsh, Llewellyn being killed and decapitated. Dafydd escaped, but he was eventually handed over, tortured and executed. Edward then built a series of castles across Wales to ensure the continued subjection of the Welsh and the incorporation of Wales into England.

Now it was time for the Scots. When King Alexander III of Scotland died in 1286 by 'falling off a cliff at night', his successor was his granddaughter, Margaret of Norway (Alexander's daughter had married the King of Norway). Edward insisted that Margaret marry his heir, Edward Prince of Wales, so that the crown of Scotland would be obtained by the Plantagenets. The plan failed when the seven-year-old Margaret died at sea while travelling from Norway to Scotland. Then the Scottish lords asked Edward to decide which of the several contenders for the crown should be their king. He selected John Balliol, who was a 3 x great-grandson of King David I of whom Alexander III was a 2 x great-grandson. Balliol went on to rule Scotland as Edward's puppet.

With the Welsh and the Scots suppressed, Edward turned on the Jews. They had served a useful purpose by raising money for the crown and for the citizens, mainly through their foreign contacts. As such, they were treated as chattels of the King and were entitled to his protection. However, Edward was now able to borrow money from the Lombards and Florentines, so he banned the Jews from moneylending and most other trades, and ordered them to wear a yellow badge. It was not enough, so he had 600 Jews imprisoned in the Tower and held for ransom. On payment of the ransom, 300 of the Jews were hanged and many more were dragged from their homes and killed.

The murder of the Jews enabled whatever they had left of value to be seized by the Crown, as Jews belonged to the King and consequently so did their assets when they died. Now that they were destitute, the Jews were no longer a source of tax revenue. In 1290 by the Edict of Expulsion, Edward confiscated their remaining property and expelled the surviving Jews from England. Many were thrown overboard by sailors on the voyage to France. The Edict also provided that no Jews could return to England, and any who were found were to be decapitated.

Borrowing from Lombards and Florentines would bring problems. When it was time to repay, as Christians they could not be murdered so easily. Also, they had a country to return to, so taxation of moneylenders had to be limited.

It was also in 1290 that Queen Eleanor died. Three years later, Edward decided to marry Blanche, the half-sister of King Philip IV of France. Philip agreed, provided Gascony was handed over. As Edward waited for his bride, Blanche was dispatched to marry the son of King Albert I of Habsburg, the founder of the dynasty. Philip told Edward that it was no problem, he could have Blanche's sister, Marguerite, instead. But Marguerite was only 11 years old, and the 55-year-old Edward angrily rejected the proposal. So Philip seized Gascony, and Edward declared war.

With the war against France going badly, Edward again turned to the Scots. He humiliated Balliol by summoning him to Westminster, and the Scottish barons rebelled. Then Balliol renounced his fealty to Edward and made a treaty with the French. That was something Edward could not allow. In 1296 he marched into Scotland with his army, stopping en route to sack Berwick, killing all 11,000 inhabitants and razing the town to the ground. After defeat at Dunbar, Balliol was forced to abdicate and was imprisoned in the Tower until he was released into the custody of the Pope. Having lost their king, the Scottish barons surrendered.

That surrender did not end the spirit of resistance; a Scottish army led by William Wallace won a significant victory over the English at Stirling Bridge, and he followed up with a guerrilla campaign. In the end, Wallace was defeated at Falkirk. The Scots handed him over, and Edward had Wallace hanged, drawn and quartered.

War with France continued for another five years, after which a truce was agreed. One town was transferred to the English, and the 60-year-old Edward married Marguerite, who was now a more acceptable 16 years old. She went on to bear him three children.

However, the Scots would not be subdued for long, and in 1306 they crowned Robert the Bruce as their king. Bruce was a 4 x great-grandson of King David I, and was of similar origin to Edward, being a descendant of Robert de Brus, a Norman knight who had fought at Hastings. Edward marched north to do battle, but he died in 1307 before reaching Scotland.

Said to have been one of the greatest of the Plantagenet kings, the failure of the Assassin to murder him enabled Edward and his forces to slaughter thousands of Christians, Muslims, Jews, pagans, Welsh, Scots, French and Arabs either in battle, after battle, or with no battle at all, having already slaughtered thousands of his own countrymen.

****

CHILDREN OF EDWARD I

Eleanor ========= EDWARD I ========= Margaret
daughter of   (Marguerite)
King Ferdinand III   daughter of
of Castile and Leon   King Philip III
                                            of France

daughter	died 1255 – stillborn	Thomas Earl of Norfolk
Katherine	died 1264 – aged 3 months	
Joan	died 1265 – aged 8 months	Edmund Earl of Kent
John	died 1271 – aged 5 years	
Henry	died 1274 – aged 6 years	Eleanor
Eleanor	died 1298 – aged 29 years	
Juliana	died 1271 – aged 4 months	
Joan	died 1307 – aged 35 years	
Alphonso	died 1284 – aged 10 years	
Margaret	survived Edward I	
Berengaria	died 1278 – aged 2 years	
daughter	died 1278 – at birth	
Mary	survived Edward I	
Elizabeth	survived Edward I	
EDWARD	survived Edward I	

EDWARD II

Edward I had fifteen children with his first wife, Eleanor of Castile, and three children with his second wife, Marguerite. Yet when Edward died, only three daughters and one son (the fifteenth child) of his first marriage were still alive, and the crown would be inherited by that fifteenth child: Edward Prince of Wales – the new title for the heir.

King Edward II took over a powerful country, albeit in debt and with trouble in Scotland. However, his greatest problem came from the companion selected for him by his father. The companion was Piers Gaveston, the son of a Gascon knight who had ridden with Edward I in battle. Prince Edward showered Gaveston with gifts, giving greater confidence to a man who had no respect for his seniors and was hated by all of them. In time, Edward I became aware of the situation, and when young Edward asked his father to grant Gaveston the title of Count of Ponthieu, the enraged king banished Gaveston from England.

Predictably, Edward II's first step as king was to recall Gaveston. Edward then created him Earl of Cornwall, a title usually reserved for members of the Royal Family, bringing with it substantial estates and wealth. Next, having arranged for his niece to marry Gaveston, the new king left for France to celebrate his own marriage to Isabella, the daughter of King Philip IV. And it was Isabella who, being the 7 x great-granddaughter of Gytha, daughter of King Harold, introduced more Anglo-Saxon blood to the English royal family.[8]

At the coronation Gaveston, dressed in a purple outfit embroidered with pearls, carried the crown, and after the ceremony Edward gave Gaveston the best of Queen Isabella's jewels and wedding presents. So it went on, and with the increased authority and wealth going to his head, Gaveston started to behave almost as a second king, showing total contempt for the barons and treating them as his servants. They would not put up with that for long, and soon they demanded his removal. Facing opposition from the entire nobility, Edward had to give in. He sent Gaveston to Ireland as Lieutenant, at the same time giving him more properties in England and in Aquitaine.

Over time, the solidarity of the barons waned, and with the support of some of them Edward was able to recall Gaveston. He immediately reverted to his old ways, publicly insulting the barons at every opportunity. Once more, the barons demanded that Gaveston be exiled. This time they wanted to ensure that their victory was permanent, so they also insisted on widespread reforms, including the necessity for their consent to the appointment of all high officials and control of finance. Edward resisted, but Gaveston's increasingly outrageous behaviour led to the barons making it clear that if he was not exiled, the alternative was civil war. Gaveston went – within weeks he was back; and in 1312 the barons declared war on their king.

Edward and Gaveston hurried north, stopping in Newcastle. Then, on learning of the approach of the barons' army, they

---

8 Of course, some had already been introduced by William the Conqueror's wife Matilda (a descendant of Alfred the Great) and by Henry I's wife Edith (a great-granddaughter of Edmund Ironside).

escaped in a boat. Callously leaving the Queen and the royal household behind, they made their way to Scarborough Castle. Edward then headed for York to raise troops.

The barons' leader was the Lord High Steward, Edward's cousin, the Earl of Lancaster. He stationed his forces between York and Scarborough so as to prevent Edward and Gaveston from being re-united, while the barons' main army besieged Scarborough Castle. Gaveston had no stomach for a fight, and he surrendered. He was thrown into a dungeon at Warwick Castle and later beheaded. Having demonstrated their power and dealt with their main target, the barons agreed to withdraw their forces.

Now the King began to deal with his duties. A few months later the first of his four children was born. That was the only good news. To avoid unnecessary bloodshed, the English commander of the besieged Stirling Castle agreed to surrender it to the Scots if an English army did not arrive by Midsummer's Day, so Edward had to march north. He arrived just in time to save the castle, but was then heavily defeated by Robert the Bruce at Bannockburn. The humiliated Edward returned to England, where he had to face the Earl of Lancaster. Not having been at Bannockburn, Lancaster's position was greatly strengthened, and he was able to secure the appointment of his nominees to all the principal offices of state in place of the King's men.

While Lancaster consolidated his position, Edward spent his time indulging in his lifelong priorities: profligacy and pleasure. Inevitably, a new version of Gaveston appeared. Hugh Despenser became the King's close companion and adviser in much the same way as Gaveston, although at first he was more diplomatic. Naturally, Queen Isabella became his implacable enemy. Yet although she was now a much stronger woman than the young queen who had to stand and watch her husband and Gaveston, she held her fire.

Elsewhere, others began to cause trouble, and disorder broke out across the country. There were revolts in Wales, in

Ireland, in Bristol and elsewhere, accompanied by raids into the north of England by the Scots, feuding between the Welsh and the English, between Edward and Lancaster, and between Lancaster and other barons. Lancaster was the loser. After being taken prisoner, he was beheaded in Edward's presence.

With his main antagonist dead, Edward had yet another chance to establish his authority. Instead he let Hugh Despenser and his father, also named Hugh Despenser, rule the country. They were descendants of William the Conqueror's steward, *despenser* being French for 'steward'.

In 1322, Queen Isabella's brother was crowned King Charles IV of France. Minor warfare started between England and France, and in an attempt to arrange peace, the Pope suggested that Isabella should travel to France to negotiate with her brother. Surprisingly, Edward agreed. By this time, the Despensers had ensured that Isabella's estates had been sequestered, her allowance had been reduced and young Despenser's wife had been appointed to watch over the Queen and examine her correspondence. She was after all French and not to be trusted while a state of war existed with France. If so, why trust her to negotiate? Probably Edward and the Despensers were glad to see her out of the way, and even happier to avoid having to deal with Charles themselves.

Off Isabella went, reaching Paris in 1325. Before long she had negotiated a truce and the return of Gascony and Ponthieu to Edward. With the two territories restored, Edward was required to go to France in order to pay homage, acknowledging that he held the territories under the sovereignty of the King of France. However, the Despensers feared for their lives if Edward should leave the country. They were also afraid of going to France with him, where their host would be Isabella's brother. As an alternative, in what they probably considered was a brilliant move, the Despensers proposed that the Crown Prince, 12-year-old Prince Edward, should be granted the titles to the two territories and then he would be the one to pay homage. The King foolishly agreed, and young Prince

Edward travelled to France. Now Isabella had the heir under her control.

Charles immediately confiscated the two territories. That was only one piece of bad news for Edward. In addition he was told that Prince Edward would remain with Isabella, and that Isabella was now openly living with Roger Mortimer Baron Wigmore. A former supporter of Lancaster, Mortimer had escaped from the Tower when his supporters broke through the wall of his cell on the feast day of the Tower's patron saint, St Peter-al-Vincula (St Peter in chains), all the garrison being totally drunk at the celebratory banquet. Even worse for Edward than the loss of his wife and son, Isabella and Mortimer were planning to invade England.

It would not be so simple for Isabella. King Charles could not countenance his sister's adultery, and he expelled her from France. Ever resourceful, Isabella and Mortimer found refuge at the court of the Count of Hainault, Holland and Zeeland, whose wife was Isabella's cousin. For her next step, Isabella negotiated the marriage of Prince Edward to the Count's daughter, Philippa. Being a descendant of Gytha the daughter of King Harold, Philippa introduced more Anglo-Saxon blood to the royal line.

More importantly, the Count paid over a dowry, and that enabled Isabella to assemble an army. On 23rd September 1326, Isabella and Mortimer landed on the coast of Suffolk with 700 soldiers. They were joined by many of the barons with their troops. Hatred of the Despensers had made the raising of an army by the King impossible, and Isabella was greeted in town after town, eventually being welcomed into London. Edward and the Despensers fled to the West Country. It brought no safety, and the older Despenser was captured and executed. As Isabella's troops marched west, King Edward and young Hugh Despenser tried to get to the Despensers' island of Lundy in the Bristol Channel where the steep cliffs made an attack impossible. They failed, as the wind was against them, and their ship was blown back to the mainland. Within days

EARL GODWINE'S TRIUMPH

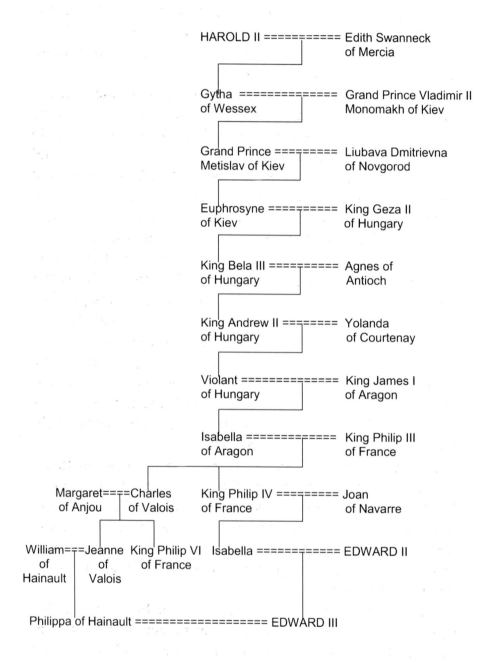

HAROLD II ============ Edith Swanneck of Mercia

Gytha =============== Grand Prince Vladimir II of Wessex — Monomakh of Kiev

Grand Prince ========= Liubava Dmitrievna Metislav of Kiev — of Novgorod

Euphrosyne ========== King Geza II of Kiev — of Hungary

King Bela III ========== Agnes of of Hungary — Antioch

King Andrew II ======== Yolanda of Hungary — of Courtenay

Violant ============== King James I of Hungary — of Aragon

Isabella ============= King Philip III of Aragon — of France

Margaret====Charles   King Philip IV ========= Joan of Anjou   of Valois   of France — of Navarre

William==Jeanne King Philip VI Isabella ============ EDWARD II of   of   of France Hainault Valois

Philippa of Hainault ================== EDWARD III

86

they had been betrayed, and they were seized and taken to Kenilworth Castle.

Young Despenser[9] was tried, convicted and brutally executed, the charge of sodomy lowering Edward's reputation even further. However, the She-Wolf of France, as the English called Isabella, had not finished.

Mortimer summoned the great lords, and they agreed that the King should be deposed; Parliament soon followed. Edward was informed of the decision and was asked to abdicate in favour of his son. He refused. Then he was told that if he refused again, not only would he be deposed, but his son and his family would be deposed as well. The thought of Mortimer as king was too much for Edward; he abdicated, and on 1st February 1327, Edward III was crowned king.

Edward II was placed in the custody of the Earl of Lancaster, the brother of the executed Earl. Despite their history, Lancaster treated Edward reasonably well. Then Edward was put into the hands of less friendly gaolers: Thomas Lord Berkeley and his brother-in-law, Sir John Maltravers. Berkeley's father had been imprisoned by Edward and had died in gaol, his estates having been given to Hugh Despenser. Isabella had restored to Berkeley his inheritance, and he had married Mortimer's daughter. With Edward in Berkeley Castle, there was no doubt where the new gaolers' sympathies lay.

At first the imprisoned Edward seemed to be no threat at all, but within a short time the popularity of Isabella and Mortimer plummeted. For a start, the deaths of the Despensers diminished much of the hatred of the former king. In addition, Isabella and Mortimer were recognised as adulterers, and now Mortimer was acquiring power and behaving as arrogantly as young Hugh Despenser.

With a growing mood of sympathy for Edward II in the country, a group of men led by Thomas Dunhead broke into Berkeley Castle, released Edward and fled with him to Corfe in Dorset. Edward was swiftly recaptured and returned to his

---

9 His descendants include US President Bush.

prison. Soon after this, a plot to rescue Edward, instigated by a Welsh knight, was betrayed to Mortimer. Clearly imprisonment and deposition were not enough. Mortimer sent a man named William Ogle to Berkeley Castle with a letter for Maltravers and Sir Thomas Gurney, the two men who, under Berkeley, shared the duty of Edward's safekeeping. Berkeley was to be kept out of the way while Maltravers, Gurney and Ogle dealt with matters.

They are said to have selected a death for Edward that would satisfy the need for revenge by causing abominable pain, that would be appropriate for his sins, and that would not be detected as murder should the public ever view Edward's body.

In the depths of Berkeley Castle a poker was placed in the open fire, remaining there until it was red hot. Edward was brought in, stripped of his clothes and forced to lie face down on a table in the middle of the room. Two men held him down as two others took hold of Edward's legs. His legs were pulled apart and a hollowed straight cow horn with the point removed was thrust into Edward's anus. Next, a heavily gloved man took hold of the poker and thrust it through the cow horn and up the anal passage of the former king. It was said that his screams could be heard beyond the castle walls.[10]

As planned, those viewing the body saw no blemishes or wounds, but Edward's face was said to have been horribly contorted with the anguish of intolerable pain.

What of the murderers? Berkeley, Ogle, Gurney and Maltravers were arrested three years later. Berkeley claimed ignorance of the plot, and was acquitted. Ogle and Gurney were convicted of murder, Maltravers of being an accessory. They all fled to avoid their punishment. Gurney was killed during his attempted escape. Nothing more was heard of Ogle. As for Maltravers, after living for 14 years on the Continent, his sentence of outlawry was remitted and his estates were restored to him.

10 Some believe the story to be untrue and that he was strangled or suffocated.

Those who instructed them to murder an English king escaped – but not for long.

CHILDREN OF EDWARD II

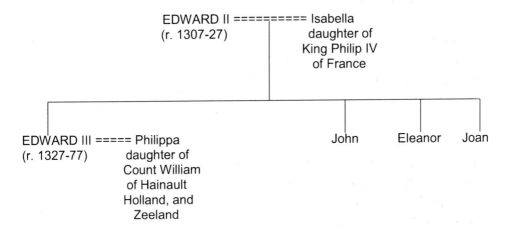

EDWARD II =========== Isabella
(r. 1307-27)   daughter of
                       King Philip IV
                       of France

EDWARD III ===== Philippa   John   Eleanor   Joan
(r. 1327-77)   daughter of
                  Count William
                  of Hainault
                  Holland, and
                  Zeeland

****

EDWARD III

1 February 1327 – 21 June 1377

When Edward II was murdered, his first son had already been crowned King Edward III. Despite being only 14 years old, he had in some ways been party to the deposition and murder of his father, although he was a very junior figure in the conspiracy. Edward III's reign began with him still in a subordinate position. All power remained in the hands of his mother and Roger Mortimer who was now Earl of March (the English-Welsh borderland).

With the English crown settled, it was the French crown that was next in question. When King John I of France died aged five days in 1316, his heir was his half-sister Joan. To avoid having a four-year-old queen whose legitimacy was in great doubt following her mother's conviction and imprisonment for adultery, the French declared that the Salic Law applied to the succession. In fact the Salic Law was no part of the law of France; it was the law of the Salian Franks.

The Franks were a group of Germanic tribes, the post-Roman conquerors of the land that became known as France (even now called *Frankreich* in German). One of those tribes lived in Salland (now north-east Holland), and they were therefore called the Salian Franks. Four of their kings became Holy Roman Emperors, but the dynasty ended in the twelfth century on the death without issue of King Henry V, the husband of Matilda (daughter of King Henry I of England). After that, the laws of the Salian Franks, the Salic Law, ceased to have effect.

Nevertheless, as it suited their purpose, the French adopted it. But they did not adopt all the Salic Law, they only took the part they needed: the provision stating that a woman could not inherit property. Next the French were able to say that as women could not inherit property, it followed that they could not inherit the crown. That allowed John's uncle, Philip, to become king as Philip V. When Philip's successor, his brother King Charles IV, died in 1328, he left a daughter. Of course she was now barred from the succession by the Salic Law. Next in line was Charles's sister Isabella, and she was also barred by the Salic Law. After Isabella came her son, and that was King Edward III of England. It was disastrous for the French; yet they still had hope, because when Charles died, the Queen was pregnant. So they waited – but it was a girl. Now Edward was unarguably the heir. In desperation, the French adopted a stricter interpretation of the Salic Law: that women could not inherit the throne and men could not inherit the throne through a woman. It meant that Charles's cousin, Philip of Valois, could be crowned.

The counter-argument put forward on behalf of Edward was scarcely less inventive. He appealed to the Pope asserting that as Jesus claimed the throne of David through his mother, Mary, Edward could claim the throne of France through his mother, Isabella. It did not work.

Realising that the matter could only be advanced through war against her own family and countrymen, Isabella did not pursue Edward's claim. She merely told the French that her son, the son of a king, could never do homage for his continental territories to Philip of Valois, the son of a count. Nevertheless, Edward did so after Philip VI was crowned, but only subject to

Edward's claim that he was the one who should really be the king of France.

In truth, Isabella and Mortimer were more concerned with their own position. That position was supposedly endangered by a plot to restore Edward II to the throne. The plot had been inspired by a rumour that Edward II was still alive, the rumour having been started by Mortimer so as to evade an accusation of murder. Mortimer immediately ordered the execution of one of the leading conspirators, Edward Earl of Kent, Edward II's half-brother.

As always, the barons turned against the holders of power when their own were being executed. The opposition championed the young and powerless Edward III, while Mortimer behaved as if he were the king. There were fears that Mortimer intended to have Edward killed so as to take the throne himself. Having procured the deaths of Edward II and the Earl of Kent, it is likely that Mortimer had plans, or at least a desire, to kill Edward III. However, before Mortimer could act, Edward struck. The young King and several supporters gained access to Nottingham Castle. They stormed into Mortimer's room and arrested him. He was tried and hanged. Edward took power, sending his mother, Isabella, to live at Castle Rising in Norfolk where she miscarried Mortimer's child.

The murderers of Edward II had now been dealt with. Yet it was not the end of the Mortimers; Roger had twelve children with his wife, and the descendants of his first son, Edmund, would in time have a crucial role in the monarchy – one of them would be the next King Edward.

As time went by, Edward III succeeded in unifying the country, taking no revenge on those who had supported Mortimer. Edward even restored to Mortimer's son his father's confiscated lands and the title of Earl of March. Now Edward could deal with his neighbours. He suppressed the Scots and liberated the north of England. Next he turned to deal with Scotland's ally, the traditional enemy: France.

The French moved straight away and invaded Gascony.

This was the beginning of a war that would last for decades, although not continuously. It would therefore be known as The Hundred Years' War. At first the two enemies were involved in minor skirmishes, making alliances and raising funds.

Then, in 1340, a French and Genoese naval force gathered at the mouth of the Zwyn River near the town of Sluys on what is now the Netherlands-Belgium border. It was clear that they were preparing for an invasion of England.

Edward assembled a fleet of 200 ships, loaded them with soldiers, and took command, sailing south to attack. The ships were cogs, small vessels each carrying thirty to forty men. In land battles Edward had fought with men-at–arms (armoured swordsmen), with a company of archers to each side. So he sailed his navy in groups of three vessels, one with men-at-arms and one with a company of archers to each side. The only true naval tactic was to ram enemy ships. Otherwise the battle would be fought by sailing near a French vessel so that archers could let fly at those on board, after which the cog would draw up alongside, enabling the men-at-arms to jump into the vessel and attack with their swords.

The fleet sailed towards Sluys on Midsummer's Day, inviting the French to sail forward, the sun in their eyes. Barbanera, the Genoese Admiral, saw a trap, and he advised French Admirals Quieret and Behuchet to go to sea and spread their forces. They ignored the advice and stayed on the defensive within the harbour, lashing their ships together.

Unopposed, the English advanced to attack the immobile target. All the enemy vessels were showered with arrows, rammed and boarded. Hand-to-hand fighting took place on virtually every French ship. According to one account, with a French defeat looking certain, Behuchet headed for Edward. Behuchet believed that if he killed the English king, it would turn the battle. He clambered from ship to ship, making his way towards the King, who had already boarded the line of French vessels. Finding Edward, Behuchet raised his sword and ran at him. He took a mighty swing, but in the bustle of the fighting

Behuchet was jostled, and he struck Edward a heavy blow on the thigh. Despite the protection of armour, Edward suffered a painful wound; but the attempt to kill him had failed. He was helped away to be tended by his physician. By nightfall, the French fleet had been totally destroyed, although the Genoese in their galleys were able to row away in the dark.

More than 16,000 of the French perished, most of them having drowned. Behuchet was taken alive. Invariably, a captured enemy leader would be held for ransom; apart from being a source of money, it set a precedent for when the tables were turned. On this occasion an angry Edward ordered his men to hang Behuchet, and this gives substance to the story that he had tried to kill Edward and had wounded him.

With victory, the threat of invasion disappeared. However, the Italian bankers failed to produce sufficient funds to enable Edward to progress the war on land, and a truce was agreed. Then, the principal Italian bankers went bankrupt as Edward demanded more loans, but failed to pay the interest due on existing debt. From now on, taxation, plunder and ransom would have to sustain any fighting.

Financed by increased taxation, the war started again as Edward, assisted by the Crown Prince, attacked town after town in France, executing thousands of their citizens if they had resisted, but few, if any, when they surrendered immediately. In 1346, King Philip's army was engaged, and the heavily outnumbered Edward won a massive victory at Crécy. The French losses were 4,000 knights plus a greater number of lower ranks. English losses, hard to believe, were said to be only 40. The King of France escaped. All he could now do was to encourage his ally, King David II of Scotland, to invade the north of England. He did, but King David was defeated and taken prisoner, to be held for eleven years until he was ransomed.

Most of the benefits of victory ended in 1349 with the arrival of bubonic plague. The disease was called the Black Death because of the dark bruising caused by haemorrhages under the skin. It spread from central Asia via rats and fleas on board ships, killing between one-third and one-half of the population of England (a population of about four million) in attacks in 1349, 1361 and 1369. It had the same effect throughout Europe.

However, plague did not stop war, and in 1350 off Winchelsea, Edward's navy engaged the galleys of Castile, which had been raiding English shipping. Edward sailed in a cog named 'The Thomas', and in another cog sailed Edward the Crown Prince, by now called the Black Prince because of his black armour. He was accompanied by his 10-year-old brother John, called John of Gaunt as he had been born in Ghent.

One of the enemy vessels made for Edward's ship, determined to secure victory by killing the King. This vessel was armed with catapults, and once within range, iron bars and large stones rained down on Edward's cog. Many on board were killed, others injured, as the Thomas was dismasted and its hull was crushed. The Thomas started to sink, but before it went down, leaving the King and the others on board to drown, grappling hooks were attached to one of the Castilian galleys. Then the Thomas was pulled alongside, and the King and his men jumped on to the galley, killing those on board and taking it over. Victory came swiftly, with the majority of the Castilian vessels seized or sunk. Another attempt to kill an English king had failed.

Still the war with France rumbled on, the Black Prince winning a great victory at Poitiers in 1356, and capturing the new King John II of France. He was taken to England to be held for ransom.

At last, in 1360 terms of peace were agreed giving Edward everything he really wanted; full sovereignty over Gascony, Poitou, Aquitaine, Ponthieu, Calais and other areas in northern France, and agreement by the French to pay a huge ransom for their king. In return, Edward abandoned his claim to the French crown. King John was allowed to return home before full payment of the ransom on leaving his three sons as hostages.

One of them ran off to France. Perhaps concerned that the lives of the other two sons were at risk, King John voluntarily returned to captivity in England where, still a prisoner, he died in 1364.

With the plague over, England prospered. The reduced population meant a lower demand for food and a smaller supply of labour, so food prices fell and wages rose. Economic recovery only reactivated the desire for war, and the fighting resumed, although by now Edward had passed leadership of the army to his sons.

The rank of 'duke' had been held only by the King or his sons as dukes of French territories. Edward decided to create duchies in England and to bestow the title on members of his family. The King's third surviving son, John of Gaunt, married the wealthy daughter of the first Duke of Lancaster (the grandson of Edward I's brother). When the Duke died, the King granted this title to John. Lionel, John's older brother, became Duke of Clarence (of Clare (*Clarentia*) in Ireland), while his younger brother Edmund became Duke of York, and the youngest, Thomas, became Duke of Gloucester.

As time went by, Edward became increasingly feeble, and with the Black Prince incapacitated by dysentery, England's fortunes declined. When Edward approached death, little more than Calais was left of the French possessions, and the Black Prince and Lionel Duke of Clarence having died, John of Gaunt was the effective ruler of England. John was now immensely wealthy, having inherited his father-in-law's lands. When his wife died, leaving three children who survived infancy (Philippa, Elizabeth and Henry), John married Constance of Castile.

The King's wife also died, after which he was besotted with his grasping mistress, Alice Perrers, lavishing jewels and property on her. A former lady-in-waiting to the Queen, she had been Edward's mistress since she was fifteen. Edward died in 1377. It was said to have been a stroke, but gonorrhoea was suspected. Could it be that Alice Perrers, or her charms, caused his death?

It was the death of a king who had become weak in his later years, but Edward's military successes had seen English power increase through much of his reign. So much so that until his decline, killing him was his enemies' only hope for victory – and both attempts failed.

CHILDREN OF EDWARD III

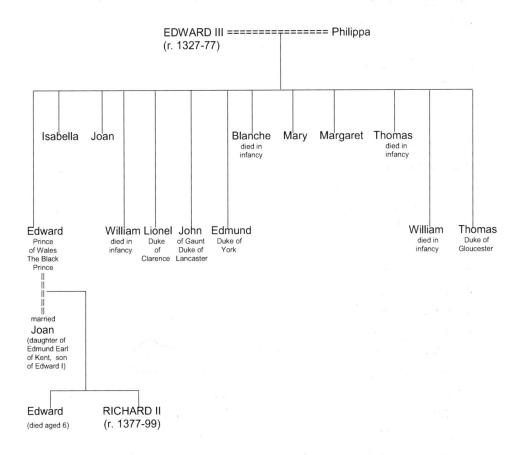

****

RICHARD II

21 June 1377 – 30 September 1399

By the time the ageing Edward III died, his wife had borne him thirteen children. There had been eight sons, three of whom died in infancy. Edward the Black Prince, heir to the throne, died three years before his father. The Black Prince had two sons: Edward who died in childhood, and Richard who inherited his grandfather's crown as Richard II.

Yet the families of Edward III's four other sons would in time play a more important part in England's history. They were Lionel Duke of Clarence (who had already died), John of Gaunt Duke of Lancaster, Edmund Duke of York and Thomas Duke of Gloucester.

With a ten-year-old king and no official regent or regency council, Richard's uncle, John of Gaunt, continued to be the most powerful man in the kingdom.

It was a time of discontent because of the continuing war with France, heavy taxation to pay for it, no plunder or ransom, and rising prices. The nobility and the merchant class were not the only ones who were restless; for the first time an emboldened peasantry showed its power in the Peasants' Revolt. They were

THE FOUR DUKES (SONS OF EDWARD III) AND THEIR HOUSES
ON THE ACCESSION OF RICHARD II

1377

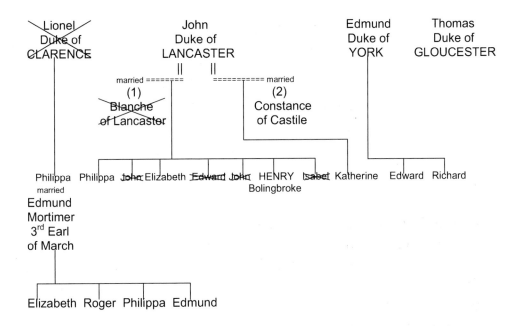

Lionel
Duke of
CLARENCE

John
Duke of
LANCASTER
‖   ‖
married ======   ========== married
(1)   (2)
Blanche   Constance
of Lancaster   of Castile

Edmund
Duke of
YORK

Thomas
Duke of
GLOUCESTER

Philippa   Philippa John Elizabeth Edward John HENRY Isabel Katherine   Edward Richard
married   Bolingbroke
Edmund
Mortimer
3rd Earl
of March

Elizabeth Roger Philippa Edmund

inflamed by the speeches of a priest, John Ball, but their leaders were Wat Tyler and Jack Straw.

In mid-1381, the mob made its way to London, and they burned down John of Gaunt's palace, the Savoy (the finest mansion in England, formerly owned by the Count of Savoy). Gaunt was unharmed as he was safe far to the north. Foreigners were the next target as the homes of the wealthiest merchants, the Flemings, then the homes of the moneylenders, the Lombards, were set ablaze. At least 150 Flemings were killed, most of them decapitated as they were dragged from sanctuary. Dozens of Lombards suffered a similar fate.

After the killing and looting eased, the peasants demanded that the Chancellor, who was the Archbishop of Canterbury, should give them an account of the tax revenue raised in the last five years and details of how it had been spent. Of course they did not get a satisfactory response, in fact no response at all. So they beheaded the Archbishop and the Treasurer.

Now the 14-year-old King came into his own. Richard bravely rode out to meet the mob at Mile End, an area of open land to the east of London. He addressed the peasants with confidence, agreeing to all their demands, promising an end to serfdom, to limit the price of land rental and to abandon rules capping wages. "I will never go back on my word" pledged Richard as the cheering peasants prepared to return to the countryside, not realising that going back on his word was something that Richard would do whenever it was to his advantage.

Ball, Tyler and Straw were not satisfied, and they remained in London with many of their supporters. A further meeting was arranged at Smithfield (formerly Smoothfield), just outside the city walls. Apparently Tyler, with several thousand men behind him, adopted an impertinent attitude, taking the King by the hand and calling him 'brother'. With some difficulty, Richard remained calm, and he confirmed all the promises he had made at Mile End. Having failed to intimidate Richard, Tyler stepped right up to him and demanded a drink. Now

Richard lost his Plantagenet temper and ordered Tyler's arrest. The Lord Mayor struck Tyler to the ground, and a squire ran him through with a sword.

With outstanding quick-thinking, Richard told the restless mob that their leader was dead, and as he was their king he was now their captain and they should follow him. They walked into the trap, and Richard led them into the countryside where they were surrounded by troops. He then allowed the peasants to return to their villages, although the unrest continued for some time, only ending with the executions of Ball and Straw.

Richard's next move was to revoke all the concessions he had made at Mile End. Ominously, Richard had discovered that giving his word and then breaking it, combined with severe punishment of opponents, was the way to secure his throne.

The following year, with both of them aged fifteen, Richard married Anne of Bohemia, daughter of the Holy Roman Emperor. There was little political advantage, but a foreign queen was always preferred; taking an English queen would give her family increased power and would cause dissent within the nobility.

Having dealt with the rebellion, Richard's kingship was unopposed, although he was still bound to take into consideration the views of the barons and Parliament. He created an inner council of his favourites, and they were showered with titles and properties. Inevitably, Richard went too far, falling out with the barons and Parliament over his wanton extravagance and demands for higher taxes. Forced to compromise, he agreed to hand over considerable power to a Commission of Government. Later to be known as 'the Lords Appellant', the members of the Commission targeted Richard's favourites, and they published an appeal (or charge) of treason against five of Richard's inner council. The Appellants' leader was Richard's uncle, the Duke of Gloucester; another member was the Duke of Lancaster's son, Henry Bolingbroke. Gaunt was not available to make peace as he was abroad, engaged in what proved to be an unsuccessful attempt to obtain the crown of Castile as his second wife's inheritance.

Realising that the differences could only be resolved by battle, Richard's Chancellor raised an army, but he was defeated by the Appellants' forces. That allowed Appellant troops to march into London, where they were welcomed by the citizens. Next, the Appellants seized the Tower and the King. Then several of those close to the King were executed, and control of the household was taken from him.

Order was restored when John of Gaunt returned to England. In what seemed to be a minor matter, after John of Gaunt's second wife died of plague he married his long-time mistress, Katherine Swynford (the daughter of a Flemish herald[11]), who was his daughters' governess and whose sister was married to Chaucer. By the time of the wedding, Katherine had already borne Gaunt four illegitimate children, who were later legitimised by Parliament.

With Gaunt's support, Richard made peace with Parliament, agreeing to pardon the Appellants and all those who had supported them apart from 50 men whose names were on a secret list to be kept and seen only by Richard. Next, Richard announced the recovery of all his powers, accompanied by a promise of peace with France – to the people that meant no increased taxation to pay for war. As a result, all was quiet, but then Richard fell out with London when he fined the citizens for refusing to provide him with extra funds. Richard lost another supporter when his wife died of plague in 1394. There had been no children; her only legacy was having introduced the practice of women riding side-saddle.

Uncharacteristically, Richard's promise of peace was kept as he secured a truce with France, underlined by his marriage to Isabelle, the six-year-old daughter of Charles VI.

It was time for revenge. In 1397, former Appellants and their supporters were exiled or executed. Richard even had the

---

11 An officer who announced proclamations and carried messages between those of high rank.

leading Appellant, his uncle the Duke of Gloucester, murdered while in the custody of Thomas Mowbray (himself a former Appellant) – Mowbray was rewarded by being created Duke of Norfolk. Now the Houses of the sons of Edward III were effectively, apart from Richard, only Clarence, Lancaster and York.

However, some of the former Appellants remained free. In particular Henry Bolingbroke, son of John of Gaunt, was not touched. He had the benefit of being the son of the King's principal supporter.

With Richard having such a young wife, a child was far off, so the succession became an issue. The House of Clarence was next in line, Lionel having been the second son of Edward III after the Black Prince (ignoring William who died in infancy). Lionel Duke of Clarence had long since died. His heir was his daughter Philippa, and she had married Edmund Mortimer 3rd Earl of March. He was the grandson of the Mortimer who had been responsible for the deposition and murder of Edward II. Philippa and Edmund's first son was Roger, and after his father's death he became the 4th Earl of March. He was the designated heir to Richard, being the grandson of the Duke of Clarence; and Philippa having died in 1382, he was the rightful heir until Queen Isabelle had a child.

The Houses of the next of Edward III's sons, Lancaster and York were waiting in the wings. In 1398, Roger 4th Earl of March was killed in battle fighting against a rebellious clan in Ireland. He left as his first son Edmund, who became the 5th Earl of March; he was the new heir to the throne. The late Earl also left another son (Roger) and two daughters (Anne and Eleanor).

Then came an altercation whose effects changed the course of English history. Henry Bolingbroke informed the King that Thomas Mowbray Duke of Norfolk had told him that the two of them were on the secret list of fifty, that they were in imminent danger, and that they should act before they were seized. Naturally, Mowbray denied having made the treasonable remarks.

THE THREE ROYAL HOUSES
AFTER THE DEATH OF THE DUKE OF GLOUCESTER AND OF THE THIRD AND FOURTH EARLS OF MARCH

1398

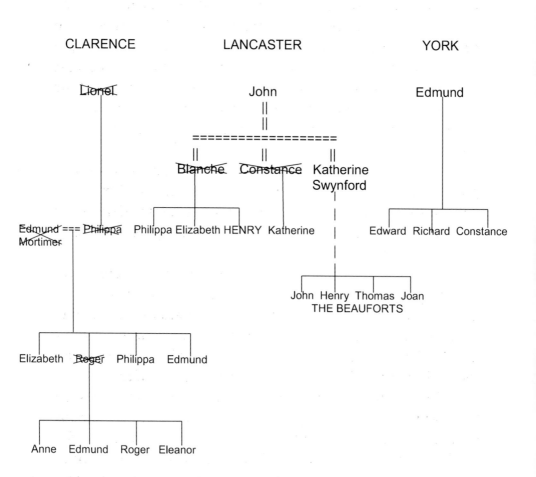

The row was investigated by the King, by Parliament and by a commission. In the end it was ruled that the truth of the matter should be decided by combat. That way, Richard would secure the death of one of the last Appellants. Unfortunately, there were complications. If Henry Bolingbroke won, his power and popularity would be vastly increased; if Henry was killed, Richard would lose the vital support of Henry's father, John of Gaunt. At the last moment, Richard intervened and ordered that Bolingbroke was to be exiled for ten years and that Mowbray was to be exiled for life. Mowbray died a year later. Henry was not so obliging. He took up residence at the French court, having secured Richard's promise that despite exile he would still receive his Lancastrian inheritance when his father, John of Gaunt, died.

With all his enemies executed or in exile, Richard's absolute power went to his head. Taxes were increased, those who annoyed Richard had to pay for a pardon, his personal spending soared, he sat on a giant throne, and all in his presence had to look to the ground.

In February 1399, John of Gaunt Duke of Lancaster died. Claiming that Henry Bolingbroke's name was one of the fifty on the secret list, Richard extended Henry's exile to life, and, breaking his word yet again, Richard seized Henry's Lancastrian inheritance. Then, with an air of over-confidence, Richard set off with his army to take control of Ireland.

If Richard thought that Henry Bolingbroke would accept the position and remain quietly in France, he was very much mistaken. Henry assembled a small force and made for England. The whole of the North raced to support him. Nobles were opposed to the confiscation of property, townspeople feared more taxes to pay for Richard's court and favourites, and peasants with memories of Wat Tyler had good reason to hate the King. All of them backed Henry's avowed claim: his inheritance, no more than that – he was no traitor.

Richard hurried back from Ireland and landed in Wales, ready to be joined by his supporters. But there were few.

Most significantly, the Duke of York, faced with choosing between two of his nephews, sided with Henry. He was no doubt still bitter at the murder of his brother, the Duke of Gloucester.

The two armies moved towards the north-west, where Richard took his position in Conway Castle in north Wales, protected by its impregnable fortifications. Henry sent ambassadors to negotiate with him. True to form, the King had already told the members of his Council that he would have to accept Henry's demands, but that as he was agreeing under duress, he had no intention of keeping to the bargain.

This time, knowing that Richard's word was worthless, Henry would be equally, in fact even more, duplicitous. Richard agreed to restore Henry's inheritance and to abandon control of Parliament. Next, Richard was to travel to Flint to meet Henry and seal the bargain, having received a promise made on oath of safe conduct. So Richard left Conway Castle; but halfway to Flint, Richard was ambushed, and he was taken to London as Henry's prisoner. The waiting Londoners pelted Richard with rubbish as he rode into the city. It was particularly painful for a man who was almost obsessed with refinement; a man credited with the invention, or at least the introduction, of the pocket handkerchief.

Encouraged by the widespread support, Henry changed his ambition. It was no longer his inheritance, now Henry wanted the crown. But how could he gain it with a semblance of legality? No king really wanted to win the throne by force, as that justified someone taking the throne from him by force. So Henry established a committee to look into the issue. The committee decided that a king could be deposed if he was guilty of great crimes, and obligingly announced that Richard was guilty of just such crimes. However, they could not find it in themselves to declare that Henry was next in line. The House of Clarence was senior to Lancaster.

There was no alternative, it would have to be by force. In September 1399, while still in the Tower, Richard was compelled to abdicate, and Henry simply took the throne as Henry IV, everyone ignoring the fact that the heir of Clarence, the eight-year-old Edmund 5th Earl of March, was next in line. Henry dismissed Edmund's prior right by saying that Edmund claimed through his grandmother Philippa, the daughter of the Duke of Clarence, so it was not a direct male line such as his own; even though the Salic Law did not apply to the English crown. The result was a perverse balancing of the scales, as the descendant of the Roger Mortimer who sought the throne of Edward II when he had no right to it, was deprived of the throne to which he had every right. Here was the origin of the Wars of the Roses. Henry was the red rose of the House of Lancaster and Edmund was the House of Clarence – the white rose of the House of York was yet to enter the fray.

Richard was moved from the Tower to Leeds Castle in Kent, then to Pickering, and finally to Henry's castle at Pontefract in Yorkshire, commanded by Henry's step-brother, Sir Thomas Swynford.

An effort was now made to reverse Richard's deposition, as supporters of the former king stormed Windsor Castle intent on murdering the new king. However, Henry had learned of the plot, and had left for the safety of London, a city still anti-Richard. It took little time for Henry to capture and execute the rebels. Now he knew that he could not allow Richard to remain alive.

Killing an ex-king would not bring the same disapproval as killing a reigning king, but it was still hazardous. It would have to be done in an unobtrusive manner. Just as Edward II's body had to be shown, so would Richard's. One evening, when Richard had retired for the night, the door of his room was locked shut. He would never see it open again, not for food, not for drink, nothing. The cries of the ex-king went unheeded, the banging of his fists on the inside of his door was ignored; demands, pleas, prayers – it made no difference. In February 1400, Richard collapsed, fell unconscious and died. Starved to death, leaving his second wife a widow at the age of ten.

The curse had struck again; another English king murdered. It must have been on the orders of Henry IV. What else could he have done? Accepted a promise of good behaviour from Richard? Hardly. Who locked the door? Very likely Sir Thomas Swynford. His reward was to be appointed the Governor of Calais. It was a prestigious position, but more importantly it would keep him permanently out of England.

****

HENRY IV

30 September 1399 – 20 March 1413

Henry Bolingbroke became Henry IV in 1399 on taking the throne for the House of Lancaster from his cousin, Richard II. Bolingbroke was not Henry's family name, rather it was the name of the castle in Lincolnshire where he was born. He had been born on Maundy Thursday (the Thursday before Easter, commemorating Christ's last supper), and at the age of fifteen he started the practice of giving alms to the poor every year on his birthday. Later it became the tradition for the sovereign to do the same every Maundy Thursday, even though not that sovereign's birthday.

Once crowned, Henry dealt with his father John of Gaunt's children by Katherine Swynford, barring the possibility of the Beauforts ever inheriting the throne by inserting a prohibition to that effect in their Declaration of Legitimacy. Henry had young children and no brothers, so his three half-brothers were a threat. With the passage of years, things would not turn out quite as he had planned.

At the age of fourteen, Henry had married Mary de Bohun, daughter of the wealthy Earl of Hereford and Essex, and she bore Henry four boys and two girls. However, Mary died at the age of twenty-four while giving birth to their second daughter. So Mary did not live long enough to become queen.

THE THREE ROYAL HOUSES
ON THE ACCESSION OF HENRY IV
(excluding many of those who would play no part in providing later monarchs)

1399

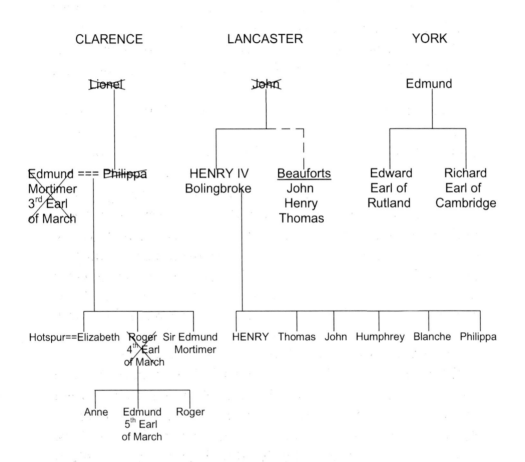

CLARENCE   LANCASTER   YORK

Lionel   John   Edmund

Edmund === Philippa   HENRY IV   Beauforts   Edward   Richard
Mortimer   Bolingbroke   John   Earl of   Earl of
3rd Earl   Henry   Rutland   Cambridge
of March   Thomas

Hotspur==Elizabeth   Roger   Sir Edmund   HENRY   Thomas   John   Humphrey   Blanche   Philippa
       4th Earl   Mortimer
       of March

Anne   Edmund   Roger
       5th Earl
       of March

King Henry IV, or Henry the Usurper as he came to be known, had already suffered one brush with death by the time he was crowned. That was following the incident when he accused Thomas Mowbray of treason.

Henry and Mowbray had been ordered to resolve their dispute in trial by battle; in effect, a duel. A fight to the death between two English dukes was to be one of the dramatic highlights of the age. People travelled from all over England and from overseas to witness the event that was to take place just outside Coventry, including King Richard and the entire court.

The hour arrived, and the two dukes took the field. They were supplied with the finest weapons and armour, Henry's brought from Italy, Mowbray's from Germany. Mowbray was the first to enter the arena, his horse dressed in crimson velvet and embroidered with silver. Henry was no less magnificent, on a white horse dressed in blue and green velvet embroidered with golden swans and antelopes. Henry addressed the onlookers, repeating the allegation of treason and asserting that he would kill his opponent. He raised his shield, the red cross of St George on a white background, and then he turned and rode to his tent, adorned in Lancastrian red roses. Mowbray rode forward, declared his innocence and his intention of defending his honour, and then he rode to his tent.

Each donning a helmet and taking hold of a lance, the two men made their way to opposite ends of the arena and turned round, ready to charge. They started to move forward gently. Before either man could dig his spurs into his horse's sides, King Richard stood up and ordered both combatants to return to their tents.

After a wait of some hours, Richard's decision was announced. The two dukes were furious; neither would be allowed to clear his name. Mowbray was banished for life and Henry was banished for ten years, a curious combination of punishments. Anyway, for either to win would have brought problems for Richard. Expelling both adversaries from the country seemed to be the best option; but it was not, for as we have seen it led to Richard's death.

The next attempt to kill Henry occurred after he had been crowned, when supporters of the deposed Richard II stormed Windsor Castle in January 1400, intending to murder Henry and his sons during a great tournament arranged for Epiphany (the end of the twelve days of Christmas, celebrating the arrival of the three wise men). The leaders of the plot were men who had been granted titles by Richard II as reward for supporting him against the Appellants. They were angered when Henry, the last surviving Appellant, reduced the dukes to earls and the earls to barons, principally for involvement in the murder of his uncle, the Duke of Gloucester.

The conspirators planned to restore Richard II, and until he was released they would use a look-alike. They had no difficulty in gaining access to Windsor Castle, as they had been invited to the tournament. But Edward Earl of Rutland (demoted from Duke of Aumale), the oldest son of the Duke of York, revealed all to Henry. So, when Windsor Castle was seized, Henry was no longer there. The would-be assassins fled to the west. They could raise no support, and in time most of them were captured.

Having betrayed his colleagues, the Earl of Rutland was pardoned. Within weeks his father had died, and Edward became the Duke of York.

Henry had won the throne with little spilling of blood, but a great deal of blood would be spilled in keeping the throne. Executing thirty of the Windsor rebels and bringing their dismembered bodies to London in sacks, their heads paraded on poles, did not bring peace.

Rebellion started in Wales, and it had to be put down. In the summer of 1402, Henry marched north-west to deal with the Welsh, and he gathered his forces outside Shrewsbury, where they made camp. On the night of 8th September, Henry was asleep in his tent, with his sword, shield and lance propped up beside him. In the middle of the night, the heavy lance suddenly toppled over and fell directly on to Henry. Fortunately, he was sleeping in full armour, otherwise he would have been killed. The heavy wind was blamed for the incident; or did someone give the lance a push? Was it a murder attempt? Severely bruised and in pain, Henry set out with his forces the next morning, but they were unable to engage the Welsh, so Henry returned to London.

A further problem developed in Wales when a Welsh squire named Owen Glendower became involved in a boundary dispute with his English neighbour, Reginald Grey of Ruthin. Glendower attacked and burned Ruthin. Carried away with his success, Glendower proclaimed himself Prince of Wales, and he seized Conway Castle. Henry sent an army to quell the uprising, and one of the men leading Henry's forces was Sir Edmund Mortimer, uncle of young Edmund 5th Earl of March, the person who should really have been king.

Glendower's support came mainly from northern Wales, and significant allies were his cousins the three Tudor brothers, who had travelled from Anglesey to give their assistance. The uprising became more serious when Glendower defeated Henry's forces, capturing Sir Edmund Mortimer who was held for ransom. Henry, no doubt content that someone with a better right to the throne was imprisoned, refused to pay the ransom. So Mortimer was kept captive by Glendower, later taking his side and marrying Glendower's daughter to seal the alliance.

Henry also married; his second wife was Jean of Brittany, but there would be no children. With the Welsh revolt continuing, another rebellion commenced as one of Henry's most powerful allies, Henry Percy, son of the Earl of Northumberland, took up arms against the King.

The fiery Henry Percy, known as Hotspur, brought the rest of his family with him, the Percy family resentful that lands promised to them for supporting the then Henry Bolingbroke when he returned from exile had been given to others. To make matters worse for King Henry, Hotspur was married to Sir Edmund Mortimer's sister, Elizabeth, the aunt of Edmund

5th Earl of March. The Glendower–Mortimer–Percy alliance was formed.

Undaunted, Henry marched to battle, and he moved so quickly that he was able to engage Hotspur before he had been joined by Glendower and Sir Edmund Mortimer. The Battle of Shrewsbury saw Henry's forces attack Hotspur's inferior numbers. The fighting was savage, with thousands of English longbowmen on either side for the first time, each archer able to discharge twelve arrows in a minute. Casualties were enormous, and Hotspur decided to risk all and win the battle by killing Henry. He charged forward. Henry retired, so drawing Hotspur and his charging knights deep into the royal ranks. In order to confuse his enemies, Henry had taken the wise, if ungallant, step of dressing two of his knights in his suits of armour. Determined to kill the King, Hotspur attacked with his sword again and again. But each time he killed the wrong man. Then, as he raised the visor of his helmet, possibly trying to spot the real Henry, an arrow struck Hotspur in the forehead and killed him.

Henry fought tirelessly in the battle, slaying at least 30 men. Although he avoided a confrontation with Hotspur, others did attack Henry. The assaults on him were not without danger, so much so that Henry was hurled from his saddle three times as his assailants tried to kill him. With great good fortune, each time Henry found himself on the ground and at risk of imminent death, his soldiers came to his rescue.

When Hotspur's death became known, his forces lost their resolve and the battle ended, giving victory to Henry. Hotspur was buried; but there were rumours that he was still alive, so Henry had the corpse dug up and impaled on a spear. It was later beheaded and quartered, each quarter sent for display in a different city, the head being sent to York.

The Earl of Northumberland's life was spared, but he was required to hand over his castles, and he was also obliged to pledge allegiance to Henry in York, having to ride into the city through the gate over which his son's head was fastened. Sir

Edmund Mortimer was taken to Windsor Castle, later escaping to join Northumberland and the Archbishop of York in another uprising. It ended in defeat. Northumberland and Sir Edmund Mortimer rode away, but the Archbishop was captured and executed – an act that shocked the Christian world.

In what was seen as God's punishment, Henry came down with a serious illness, and he became partially paralysed.

The next twist in the rivalry of the Royal Houses occurred in 1406 when Richard Earl of Cambridge, the second son of the late Duke of York and brother of the present duke, married Anne Mortimer, sister of Edmund Mortimer 5th Earl of March, so uniting the Houses of Clarence and York. This union still allowed the two Houses to exist separately, as Anne and Richard were third and second in their respective Houses. Ahead of them in Clarence were Anne's brothers Edmund 5th Earl of March and Roger; ahead of them in York was Richard's elder brother Edward Duke of York. Roger Mortimer died in 1409. Anne died in childbirth in 1411, but her newborn son Richard survived; he was part Clarence/Mortimer and part York. With the death of his mother and her brother Roger, the child Richard was second in Clarence (behind his childless uncle Edmund 5th Earl of March) and third in York (behind the Duke of York and Richard Earl of Cambridge – the child's father).

Matters improved for Henry as the Earl of Northumberland was slain in a skirmish, the King of Scotland was captured, Sir Edmund Mortimer died of plague, and Glendower disappeared never to be heard of again.

Henry's crown was now secure, but he would never enjoy it. Still partly paralysed, he suffered illness after illness, then a mysterious disease said to have been leprosy or syphilis. Worse than physical illness, throughout his reign Henry was haunted by the guilt of having usurped and murdered the anointed king.

Taking advantage of the King's infirmity, Parliament acquired more rights and the Church secured its long-desired privilege of burning heretics.

THE THREE ROYAL HOUSES
after the marriage of Anne Mortimer to the Earl of Cambridge and after the deaths of Anne and Roger Mortimer

1412

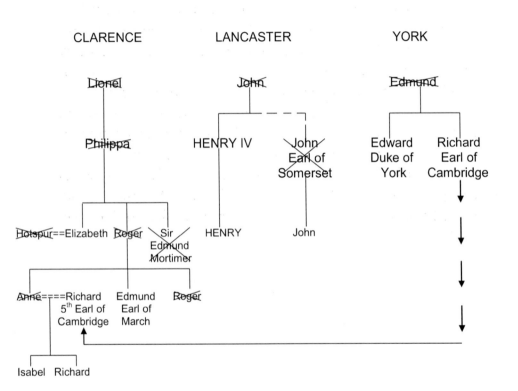

CLARENCE   LANCASTER   YORK

But the Lancastrians would say that Richard did not join the senior House of Clarence; rather Anne married into the junior House of York – so Anne and Richard's children should be moved to the right-hand column.

King Henry's diseases now led to a disfigurement of his body and his face, such that he had to retire from public life. The sight was too shocking and would lose him respect. He also suffered fits, with epilepsy and cardiovascular problems being possibilities. The vacuum was filled when the King's son, also named Henry, but better known as Prince Hal, took effective power.

So, in his early forties, this one-time warrior who had ridden with the Teutonic Knights and had stolen the throne of England, became a neurotic; a physical and mental wreck. However, he was encouraged by a prophecy that he would die in Jerusalem. To him that meant recovery and then death on crusade.

In March 1413, whilst at prayer in Westminster Abbey, the crippled king suffered a violent fit. He was carried away to the abbot's quarters and died in the Jerusalem Chamber.

None of Henry's would-be killers in duel, battle or conspiracy was able to strike a fatal blow. Yet in time Henry must have yearned for the mercy of a sudden and violent death.

****

HENRY V

20 March 1413 – 31 August 1422

(showing the scar under his left eye)

The first attempt to kill Prince Hal was the Epiphany Plot at the beginning of his father's reign. The conspirators intended to restore Richard II to the throne, and it was therefore necessary for them to kill not only Henry IV, but also his four sons. As we have seen, the assassins were betrayed and Henry IV and his sons escaped.

The second attempt to kill Prince Hal came nearer to success. During the rebellion of Owen Glendower, the 16-year-old Hal was nominally in command of his father's army, although Henry Percy (Hotspur) was the true commander. With Hotspur's desertion, Henry IV took charge, and Prince Hal fought alongside his father at the bloody Battle of Shrewsbury.

At a similar stage of the battle, Hotspur and Prince Hal must each have raised the visors on their helmets to survey the battle-scene, or maybe they were gasping for air. Then, random arrows from a shower or aimed by archers with intent to kill a knight struck each of Hotspur and Prince Hal little more than an inch from the eye. For Hotspur it was just above the eye, the arrowhead entered his brain and he was killed. For Prince Hal it was just below the eye. He carried on fighting, and after the battle he was taken away with the arrow still lodged in his face.

The arrow had entered Hal's face below the left eye, close to his nose, taking a diagonal course, continuing below the nose and across his mouth to the right jaw bone. He was fortunate, it was the perfect angle to avoid the central spinal cord, the carotid artery and all brain connections. Any other minimally different angle would have been fatal.

In another piece of good fortune, the arrowhead was not triangular, rather it was a slim heart-shape – so it could be pulled out. The arrowhead had a short tube-like socket at the base, into which the wooden shaft was fitted. As it was being slowly pulled out of Hal's face, the shaft came out of the socket, leaving the arrowhead behind.

Over the course of several days, the royal surgeon crafted a metal tube and screw. The tube was inserted in Hal's face until it slipped into the empty socket at the base of the arrowhead. Next, the surgeon took the long screw; it had a handle at the end, much like a corkscrew. The screw was inserted in the tube and slowly screwed further and further down the tube. Then, another turn of the screw forced the tube to expand slightly within the socket until it was tightly fixed. Now the screw could be pulled out, bringing the tube and arrowhead with it – and all without any form of anaesthetic.

Having been flushed out with alcohol, daily applications of honey allowed the wound to heal. Hal remained scarred for life, but royal painters provided cosmetic improvement.

Hal took the throne on his father's death in 1413 as King Henry V. He was the king's oldest son and was crowned without opposition even though his father was a usurper and Edmund Mortimer 5th Earl of March of the senior House of Clarence had the better entitlement.

All the time, little was made of the child Richard, son of Richard Earl of Cambridge (younger brother of the Duke of

York) and his late wife, Anne Mortimer (the sister of Edmund Mortimer 5th Earl of March). The child Richard was still second in the House of Clarence (behind his uncle the 5th Earl of March) and third in the House of York (behind the Duke of York and his brother the Earl of Cambridge – the child's father).

Henry V started his reign as a popular king. Trouble came from a source that would cause difficulties for many future monarchs: religion. The Lollard movement was gaining strength; these were Christians (followers of John Wycliffe) who sought a purer form of Christianity, adhering strictly to the Bible. They did not believe in confession, they wanted to reduce the powers of priests, and they wanted to do away with the Pope. The Church, supported by the King, dealt with the problem by burning Lollards at the stake for heresy.

Sir John Oldcastle was the leader of the Lollards. Oldcastle was seized and condemned to death, but whilst in the Tower awaiting execution, he escaped. He then assembled a group of conspirators who devised a plot to kill Henry and his brothers. They planned to disguise themselves as mummers (from the Old French *momeur* – wearer of a mask), who were masked actors performing folk plays at festivals. As performers, they could easily gain access to the court at Eltham Palace.

However, their group was infiltrated by Henry's spies, and in the knowledge of what was planned, Henry quietly left Eltham Palace on 8th January. The following morning, the day of the intended assassination, the conspirators were seized. They were tried and executed, apart from Oldcastle. He had escaped again, although not for long; he would eventually be executed along with many Lollards throughout the country.

The memory of Sir John Oldcastle lives on as Falstaff in several Shakespeare plays. In the early versions, the character is actually called Sir John Oldcastle; but following a complaint by one of Sir John's descendants, Shakespeare was forced to change the name to Falstaff (after another knight, Sir John Fastolf who also may have been a Lollard). It was at a cost, for the change from a name with three syllables to a name with two syllables means that references to Falstaff are unmetrical throughout *Henry IV Part I*. In a piece of mischievous revenge by Shakespeare, in Act 1 Scene 2 Prince Hal refers to Falstaff as "my **old** lad of the **castle**".

It was time for action, and that meant restarting the Hundred Years' War by claiming the throne of France, the entitlement of Henry's great-grandfather, Edward III. First Henry listed his demands. Apart from the French crown, he wanted the duchy of Normandy, half of Provence, the hand of King Charles's daughter in marriage, a dowry of two million crowns, and more. The French actually tried to find a compromise, but the English demands would always be too much. Indeed, they were intended to be impossible to accept. In 1415, the negotiations collapsed.

Preparations for war accelerated. Before all was ready, there was yet another conspiracy to kill the King. This plot was led by Richard Earl of Cambridge, the brother of the Duke of York and the father of the child Richard. The replacement king would be Edmund Mortimer 5th Earl of March, brother-in-law of the Earl of Cambridge and uncle of the child Richard. The 5th Earl of March was of course the person entitled to the throne as the senior descendant of the Duke of Clarence; and if he were crowned, then the Earl of Cambridge's son, the child Richard (four-year-old nephew of the childless Edmund), would be next in line.

Apparently, the 5th Earl of March was not involved in the plot. Its participants were those who had a grievance against the House of Lancaster: the Scots, the Welsh, the nephew of the executed archbishop, the son of Hotspur, and the Lollards.

This time Henry's escape was even narrower than with the Lollard plot. Having learned of the plan, the 5th Earl of March revealed all to Henry on the very day of the intended assassination. The conspirators were tortured, tried and executed. With the death of the Earl of Cambridge, his son, the child Richard, was now second to his childless uncle the

5th Earl of March in the House of Clarence, and second to his childless uncle the Duke of York in the House of York. It was all coming together.

Ten days later, on 11th August 1415, Henry set sail with his army. Landing in Normandy, they soon took Harfleur. Then, Henry decided to make for the English possession of Calais. They marched over 100 miles, and when they were 30 miles from Calais, Henry's army was confronted by the army of the King of France, although King Charles VI himself was far off. The absence of their king was a distinct advantage for the French as Charles suffered from periods of insanity, and there was always a risk that he might give battle orders during one of his mad spells.

The battleground was a massive field shaped much like an egg-timer, narrowed in the middle by two woods, one enclosing the village of Tramecourt and the other enclosing the village of Agincourt. Henry's force of knights plus about 900 men-at-arms and 5,000 archers was hugely outnumbered by a French army estimated at anything between 30,000 and 60,000. To limit the enemy's advantage, Henry determined to meet the French in the narrowest part of the field, where with woods to either side the French would be compressed and unable to extend their line and attack the English from the flanks.

Henry stationed his knights and men-at-arms in the centre, with archers to the left and to the right. Despite their numerical superiority, the French held back. So Henry ordered his men to advance in line to within 300 yards of the enemy. Then they planted stakes in the muddy ground for protection. Next, the English archers, a fighting force without equal in Europe, launched continuous flights of arrows, provoking the French horsemen to attack. They did so, but in the muddy ground it was no charge, rather it was an achievement to move at all. Further hails of arrows cut down the French, and then another wave of French knights and men-at-arms attacked, but they struggled to get past the bodies of the dead and dying men and horses and those who had fallen in the first charge and could not get to their feet.

However, some French knights did manage to advance. One was their commander, Duke John of Alençon, and he edged forward, seeking to kill Henry. Having fought his way through the English ranks until he was alongside the King, Duke John raised his battleaxe, lowered it behind his shoulder and then struck out. He hit Henry with a heavy blow to the head, but Henry was saved from death by the strength of his gem-encrusted helmet. Before Duke John could strike again, he was overpowered by Henry's bodyguard and was then killed by one of Henry's Welsh knights, Dafydd Gam.

With the French attacks repelled, the English archers dropped their bows and ran at the struggling enemy wielding their axes, swords and knives, slaughtering incessantly. The victory was enormous, the French losing three dukes, 90 counts, 1,500 knights, 5,000 men-at-arms and thousands of lower ranks. Estimates of the English losses range from 13 to 500.

One of those who died was the Duke of York. Obese and heavily armoured, he perished like so many of the French when he was knocked from his horse (reputedly by Duke John of Alençon), could not get to his feet and was trampled to death. It was another step towards the union of the Houses of York and Clarence, for the fallen Duke's nephew, Richard, was now the Duke of York and second in Clarence after his uncle, Edmund 5th Earl of March.

Returning to a hero's welcome, Henry started preparations for a further invasion of France. After Caen was taken, Normandy submitted, and then Henry advanced to the gates of Paris. In 1420, by the Treaty of Troyes, Henry got most of what he wanted. He was to be Regent of France for the remainder of mad King Charles VI's reign, he was appointed Charles's heir in place of the Dauphin (whose legitimacy his father had already repudiated), and he was given Charles's daughter, Princess Catherine of Valois (younger sister of Richard II's widow), in marriage. However, the southern part of France stayed loyal to the Dauphin, and fighting continued, Henry's further victories being accompanied by grotesque brutality.

THE THREE ROYAL HOUSES
showing the principal members after the Battle of Agincourt

1415

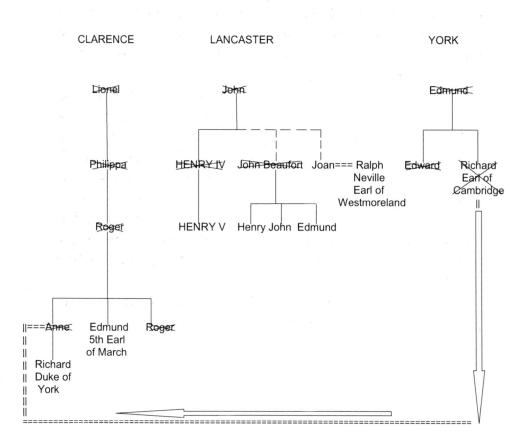

Henry is credited with an invention of more lasting significance than his victories. He introduced a document to help his subjects prove who they were and where they came from when they visited foreign lands. Travellers were generally free to disembark at ports, but to travel inland they had to establish their identity and show that they were from a friendly country before being allowed to **pass** through the gate (French: **porte**) in the city walls. So the necessary document was created: the passport.

News now came to Henry of the birth of what would be his only child, another Henry. Soon afterwards, King Henry V fell ill, and in August 1422 at the age of 35, he died. Henry had survived attempts to kill him by English soldiers, French soldiers, family members, nobles and religious fanatics; yet it was only to suffer the death that was most common amongst English soldiers – dysentery (bacterial inflammation of the colon resulting in severe diarrhoea, fever and pain). He narrowly missed out on inheriting the French throne, for Charles VI died just six weeks later.

Having survived an arrow in the face and a battleaxe to the head, Henry was lucky to have got as far as he did.

****

HENRY VI and EDWARD IV

31 August 1422 – 4 March 1461
and
3 October 1470 – 11 April 1471

4 March 1461 – 3 October 1470
and
11 April 1471 – 9 April 1483

When Henry V died in 1422, he left his nine-month-old son Henry as his only child and heir. Henry VI came to the throne without opposition, the son of a victorious English king and a beautiful French princess. Those were his benefits; the disadvantages came from further back: his paternal grandfather although a king was a usurper, and his maternal grandfather although a king was a madman.

Henry was crowned King of England in London in 1429 and King of France in Paris two years later. A regency council ran England for fifteen years, and during that time most of the French possessions were lost to a French army inspired by Joan of Arc. A more material event for the crown had occurred in 1425, when Edmund Mortimer 5th Earl of March died of plague. He left no children, so his 14-year-old nephew Richard was now Duke of York and Earl of March and therefore the heir of the Houses of Clarence and York. At last, the two Houses were one, with Richard taking his name from his father's House of York and his precedence from his mother's House of

THE PRINCIPAL MEMBERS OF THE ROYAL HOUSES IN THE REIGN OF HENRY VI

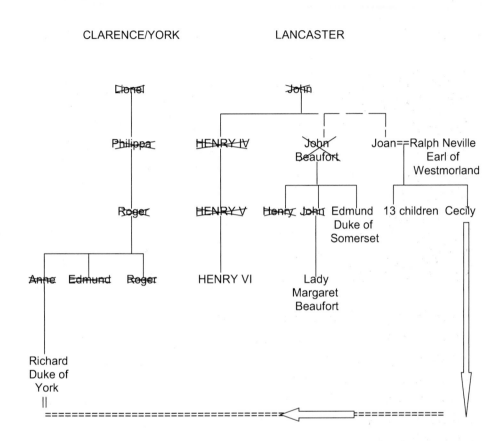

CLARENCE/YORK

LANCASTER

Lionel

John

Philippa

HENRY IV

John Beaufort

Joan==Ralph Neville
Earl of
Westmorland

Roger

HENRY V

Henry John Edmund
Duke of
Somerset

13 children Cecily

Anne Edmund Roger

HENRY VI

Lady
Margaret
Beaufort

Richard
Duke of
York
||

Clarence. He knew, and so did many others, that the House of Clarence, not the House of Lancaster, should be providing the king.

In 1437, Henry VI's mother died and his minority was declared over, although he was still only sixteen years of age. The dowager Queen Catherine had seen little of Henry as he grew up, and she died amidst a scandal when it was discovered that after her husband's death she had given birth to three boys and two girls in a liaison with Owen Tudor, the clerk of her wardrobe (financial controller); he was the son of Mareddud (Meredith) one of the brothers who came to the aid of Owen Glendower. Owen Tudor and two of his sons, Edmund and Jasper (Henry's half-brothers), would be Henry VI's constant supporters.

Although Henry was the king, Richard Duke of York was the wealthiest landowner in England, with inheritances from Mortimer, Clarence and York. He gained important allies when he married Cecily Neville, granddaughter of John of Gaunt and Katherine Swynford. Cecily was the seventeenth of the twenty-three children of the Earl of Westmorland (the eighth of fourteen with his second wife, Joan Beaufort), and she brought with her the political power of the Neville family, many of Cecily's brothers and sisters being married to influential members of the nobility. Most significantly, one of her nephews was Richard Neville Earl of Warwick, the man who would become known as the Kingmaker.

Henry VI also married advantageously, to Margaret of Anjou, niece of the wife of King Charles VII of France. Her early ambitions were for the benefit of France rather than England, although in time her remarkable determination would compensate for some of Henry's weakness.

At first, there was no trouble. The Duke of York was sent to France to command Henry's army seeking to protect the remaining English possessions. It was in France that Richard and Cecily's second son, Edward, was born, their first son having died in infancy.

Henry VI may have been the king, but Queen Margaret was already the real power. Much was to the advantage of France as Margaret, having promised the King of France she would do so, persuaded Henry to hand over Maine and Anjou in 1448. Then Normandy was lost, followed by Aquitaine, which had belonged to England for 300 years. Having dealt with the French territories, Margaret's attention turned to England. Her favourite was Edmund Beaufort Duke of Somerset, who was a grandson of John of Gaunt and Katherine Swynford. It was as a result of Somerset's relationship with the Queen that the Duke of York was removed from his command, which was then given to Somerset himself. The two dukes became deadly enemies, and on the Duke of York's return to England, Somerset saw to it that York was sent to govern Ireland – in Richard's view it was little better than exile.

With a weak monarch, step by step the country, discontented by the failures in France, lurched towards anarchy. A rebellion started in the south-east, and 20,000 men led by Jack Cade marched to London demanding reform, the dismissal of Somerset and the appointment of the Duke of York as chief councillor. The rebels briefly occupied London, but after some looting they were expelled, and they returned to their homes. Nevertheless, Richard Duke of York had heard the call.

Richard asked Henry time and again for high office, but he was always refused. It was clear to Richard that he would get nowhere without a show of strength, maybe more than a show. Critically, with Henry having no son, Richard Duke of York feared that the Queen would bully her feeble husband into declaring Somerset the heir to the throne. So, in 1452 Richard advanced on London with his forces, claiming that he was only opposed to Somerset, not the King. Henry promised that if Richard disbanded his troops, then Somerset would be arrested and put on trial for his failures in Normandy. Richard agreed and sent his men away. But the Queen forced Henry to break his word, and it was Richard who was treated almost as a traitor and compelled to take a public oath of loyalty. He was allowed to leave London only because of a rumour that his son was approaching the city with an army.

It was time to take sides. The simmering feud between Lancaster and York was augmented by the rivalry between the Percys and the Nevilles, the two families who controlled the north of England. With the Percys supporting the King and Lancaster, the Nevilles threw their weight behind York.

In 1453, with defeat after defeat, Calais and the Channel Islands were all that remained of the French possessions, and the title 'King of France' was abandoned. There was an air of dissatisfaction in the country, and then Henry lapsed into insanity, entering a trance-like state, unable to speak. His political position improved slightly when the Queen gave birth to a son, Prince Edward; although given Henry's mental condition and extreme religious behaviour, Somerset was rumoured to be the father. The rumour gained strength when Henry on recovering his sanity joked that the father must have been the Holy Ghost. No one else thought it was funny.

The following year, with Henry relapsing into insanity, the barons took control and ordered Somerset to be imprisoned in the Tower and the Duke of York to be appointed Protector. York's brother-in-law Richard Neville Earl of Salisbury became Chancellor, and Salisbury's son (also named Richard Neville) the Earl of Warwick was appointed to the Council in Somerset's place.

Several months later, just as York and the Nevilles were becoming comfortable with their new-found power, Henry suddenly returned to sanity. Weak as he was, the fact that he was the king forced the barons to back down. Somerset was released from the Tower, and York and Salisbury were dismissed, fleeing north in fear for their lives.

Next, York and Salisbury were ordered to appear before the Council. They came, but knowing what was in store for them, they came with an army; and on 22nd May 1455 at St Albans, the first battle of the Wars of the Roses was fought – the red rose of Lancaster against the white rose of York.[12] The battle lasted less than two hours, but it was enough to give victory to York. King Henry was with his army, and whether it was a random arrow or whether a Yorkist archer took careful aim with the intent of killing the King, we do not know. Either way, Henry was struck in the neck by the arrow and he was wounded, but not seriously. The attempt to kill the King had failed. However, Henry was captured, and Somerset and other royal leaders were killed. Richard and the Nevilles took complete control, although Henry remained king.

Later in the year, Somerset's niece, Margaret Beaufort (the heiress of Somerset's deceased older brother John), was married off at the age of twelve to Edmund Tudor. Within months, Edmund Tudor had been captured by the Yorkists, and he later died in prison of plague. However, he had been married for long enough to provide a Tudor heir. Edmund and Margaret's son, Henry, was born three months after Edmund's death, and Jasper Tudor took his young nephew under his wing.

With the King a prisoner, Queen Margaret assumed the leadership of Lancaster. She assembled an army, and before long the Yorkists were driven out of London, the King was rescued and the Duke of York fled to Ireland. Warwick and the Duke's son, Edward, escaped to Calais, where they formed a new Yorkist army. They sailed for England in June 1460, and marched to challenge Henry's forces. As at St Albans, the brief (this time perhaps no more than half-an-hour) Battle of Northampton resulted in a Yorkist victory, the capture of King Henry, and the death of many of the royalist leaders.

Warwick and young Edward of York returned to London where, just as before, the Yorkists took all the positions of power whilst Henry remained king. There was an uneasy calm, until several weeks later the Duke of York returned from Ireland – and this time he wanted the throne.

The proposal was debated in an unenthusiastic Parliament,

12 The series of conflicts would not be known as the Wars of the Roses until 1829, when Sir Walter Scott used the term in his novel *Anne of Geierstein*.

and in the end a compromise was put forward: Henry VI would remain king for the rest of his life, and when he died he would be succeeded by the Duke of York. Henry agreed, but his strong-willed wife would not abandon the rights of her son, the young Prince Edward (both of them being safe in Scotland). She was supported by Henry VI's half-brother, Jasper Tudor.

Richard Duke of York spent Christmas 1460 at Sandal Castle in Yorkshire. Then, on 30th December, he rode out with his troops and attacked a larger Lancastrian force. At the Battle of Wakefield, Richard's men were overpowered. Richard Duke of York would never be king. He was killed as was Salisbury, and Richard's second son Edmund was captured and executed, the Queen ordering that their heads were to be displayed in York, impaled on spikes.

Young Edward of York, now the Duke, took his late father's army north to confront the Lancastrians led by Jasper Tudor. At Mortimer's Cross, near Hereford, Edward's forces were victorious. Jasper Tudor escaped, but his father, Owen Tudor, was captured and beheaded.

Yet the Tudor name lived on not just in Jasper, but in his late brother Edmund Tudor's young son, Henry Tudor. He was, through his mother Margaret Beaufort, the 2 x great-grandson of John of Gaunt and Katherine Swynford. So the young Henry was the heir of the Tudors and the heir of the secondary illegitimate Lancaster branch through John of Gaunt's third marriage.

As the victorious Yorkist army made its way to London, Queen Margaret's Lancastrian army was ahead of them. Warwick rode out from London with an army to confront the Lancastrians once more at St Albans, but this time the Lancastrians won. Despite her success, Margaret did not advance to London. She held her position in Dunstable, fearing that the Londoners would refuse to open their gates to northern soldiers who had a record of pillaging all towns they entered. That error of judgment allowed Warwick and the Yorkists to retain control of the capital, and days later the 19-year-old Edward Duke of York was proclaimed king.

Edward's position grew even stronger when he and Warwick rode north with an army and confronted the Lancastrians at Towton in Yorkshire. In this bloody battle fought in a snowstorm, both sides suffered heavy losses, and over 20,000 died. The Lancastrians became aware that they were facing defeat, and they made a concerted effort to kill Edward so as to turn the tide. Fighting was man-to-man as one Lancastrian knight after another tried to kill Edward. However, he was strong and brave, an imposing figure over six feet four inches tall; in fact, the tallest ever British monarch. All the attempts to kill Edward failed as he set about his assailants, striking down those who came near.

After victory at Towton, Edward returned to London where he was crowned King Edward IV – at last, a Mortimer had the throne. The new king's brother, George, was created Duke of Clarence; and his other brother, Richard, was created Duke of Gloucester.

So now the senior House of Clarence (with the blood of the Mortimers and the name of the House of York through the marriage of Anne Mortimer to the Earl of Cambridge) took its rightful inheritance from the usurpers of the House of Lancaster. But there was still a problem because Henry VI, his wife and their son were alive and at liberty. Queen Margaret and Prince Edward took refuge in France, leaving King Henry to move from one hiding place to another in the north of England.

Although Edward IV was now king, his crown was far from secure. In 1462, a plot to assassinate him was discovered. Before the would-be assassins could strike they were betrayed, and the leaders, the Earl of Oxford and his son, were executed. Two years later the main threat was dealt with when Henry VI was captured and imprisoned in the Tower.

It was now time to find a queen for the most eligible bachelor in Europe. There were discussions with several foreign royal houses, national alliance being the principal aim. Then, to everyone's surprise and annoyance, Edward (who was infatuated with older women) announced that five months earlier he had secretly married the beautiful but penniless Elizabeth Woodville, a widow whose husband Sir John Grey had been killed fighting for Henry VI at the second Battle of St Albans. Worse than the loss of opportunity for national advantage, she brought with her two sons, five brothers and seven unmarried sisters. The Woodvilles' lust for status and wealth created resentment throughout the nobility. In time, this irresponsible marriage would lead to trouble.

Elizabeth's sisters were married off to Viscount Bourchier, the Earl of Kent, the Earl of Pembroke, Baron Strange, the Earl of Arundel, the Duke of Buckingham and the Duke of Bedford. One brother became the Bishop of Salisbury, another married Baroness Scales, and the 64-year-old Duchess of Norfolk was forced to marry Elizabeth's 20-year-old brother, John.

Warwick the Kingmaker was angriest, because there was no one suitable left for his two daughters to marry. So Warwick suggested that his daughter, Isabel, should marry King Edward's brother, the Duke of Clarence. Annoying his principal ally, Edward refused to allow the joinder of Clarence and Warwick, as he was aware of the power given to him by the joinder of Clarence and York.

Now the Earl of Warwick, so influential in promoting the Duke of York to the throne, could feel his authority waning. His position was further reduced because he was trying to arrange an alliance with France, only to be overruled as the Woodvilles preferred an alliance with Burgundy to whose duke they were related. France was certainly the traditional enemy, but Warwick wanted to end French support of the Lancastrian cause.

When Edward summoned Warwick to court, Warwick refused to come. He would not return while his enemies the Woodvilles were in control. To underline Warwick's fall, Edward arranged the marriage of his sister, Margaret, to the

Duke of Burgundy. So Warwick found a new person to promote in Edward's brother, George Duke of Clarence, the probable heir to the throne as so far Edward and Elizabeth Woodville had produced three daughters but no sons.

High taxation and disappointment in Edward's rule now led to an outbreak of minor rebellions. Some of the uprisings repeated the rumour that Edward was illegitimate, Richard Duke of York said to have been fighting in France when Edward was conceived, the true father being an archer named Blackburn. If that were true, it would make the Duke of Clarence the rightful king. Warwick seemed to be behind this rumour, and he and Clarence quietly slipped away to Calais where Clarence married Warwick's older daughter.

Warwick and Clarence mustered an army, crossed the Channel and made their way to London. Edward's forces were defeated at the Battle of Edgecote Moor, and he fell into Warwick's hands. Nevertheless, Edward continued to reign as king, although he could not prevent the execution of Elizabeth's father and one of her brothers. Yet Warwick and Clarence were unable to sustain their position, and eventually they were forced to flee.

Having failed with Clarence, Warwick moved on. He made his peace with Henry VI's queen, sealing the bargain by marrying his younger daughter, Anne, to Prince Edward, the son of Henry VI.

Warwick now had both his sons-in-law as potential kings, and both his daughters as potential queens. Having joined the Lancastrian side, he returned to England with an army in support of Henry VI, and he was joined by Jasper Tudor and his forces. Edward was unprepared, and without a battle (so keeping his supporters alive for next time), he fled with his younger brother, Richard Duke of Gloucester, to Burgundy where their sister was the duchess.

Henry VI was released from the Tower and reinstated as king. It was not over; by March 1471, Edward and his brother Gloucester had raised an army of 2,000 men, and they were ready to strike back. They landed in Yorkshire, their numbers growing as they marched south. No longer Warwick's choice for king, Clarence rejoined his brother's side with an army of 4,000 men.

Edward was welcomed into London, where he was declared king once more, and where Henry VI again became his prisoner. However, Warwick and his forces still supported Henry. At the Battle of Barnet, Edward's army met and defeated the army of the Earl of Warwick, and Warwick himself was seized and killed. With Warwick dead and Henry VI in custody, the last threats to Edward IV were Queen Margaret and her son, Prince Edward.

Richard Duke of Gloucester led Edward's army against Margaret's forces at Tewkesbury, where the Yorkists won a crushing victory and where Prince Edward was captured and executed, the only Prince of Wales to die in battle (probably after the battle). Before long, Queen Margaret was in the Tower with her husband, the pathetic Henry VI.

The execution of the Prince of Wales changed everything. There had been no point in seeking Henry's death while his son was alive, that would only have increased Prince Edward's status as a rival to King Edward. However, now that Prince Edward had been killed, Henry's death would end the primary Lancastrian line.

The necessary orders were given as soon as Edward was back in London. On that very night, men were sent to the Tower, men who were not afraid of killing a king. Richard Duke of Gloucester was in the Tower, probably ensuring access for the murderers. Shortly before midnight, they burst into Henry's room while he was, as usual, at prayer. Before Henry could protest his innocence, before he could plead for mercy, the first blow struck him from above. Within seconds his skull had been crushed, and another King of England had been murdered.

So the son of the hero of Agincourt, having lost the crown of France, the crown of England, his only child and his sanity, now lost all that was left – his life.

Edward had won. He rewarded his supporters, none more than his brother Richard Duke of Gloucester, whose loyalty and military prowess had been constant and vital. Richard became Constable and High Admiral of England, Great Chamberlain and Steward of the Duchy of Lancaster.

Next, Richard asked for permission to marry Warwick's younger daughter, Anne, the widow of Henry VI's son, Prince Edward. King Edward's other brother, Clarence, objected. Clarence was married to Warwick's older daughter, and he had his eyes on the inheritance when the Countess of Warwick died. In the end a deal was done. Richard married Anne, but Clarence was appointed Great Chamberlain and became entitled to the earldom of Warwick and the bulk of the inheritance, an Act of Parliament being passed declaring that the Countess of Warwick should be treated as legally dead. Surprising reward for Clarence's treachery and Richard's loyalty.

A period of general prosperity followed. By 1475, Elizabeth had borne Edward seven children: five girls and two boys, Edward and Richard. There would be two more girls and another boy, but all three died in infancy.

Clarence's chances of the crown were now remote; yet with his record, he was still the likely centre of any rebellion. After Clarence's wife died in childbirth (the baby dying ten days later), he had her maidservant hanged for poisoning her, and also hanged a man for killing the baby. In retaliation, two members of Clarence's household were charged with plotting to kill King Edward by black magic. Clarence spoke in their defence. Having failed to protect the accused, Clarence started once more to spread rumours of Edward's illegitimacy, and he encouraged riots in Cambridgeshire and Huntingdonshire.

Edward showed his brother no mercy. Clarence was arrested and tried for treason for having put himself above the law by ordering the hangings of two innocent people. He was condemned to death and executed, reputedly by being drowned in a butt of Malmsey wine. The only supporter Edward needed was his brother, Richard Duke of Gloucester, the one person who had never let him down. However, Richard was deeply aggrieved at the execution of his brother Clarence, which he saw as the work of the Woodvilles. He suspected that he would be next, and heavily outnumbered at court, Richard retired to the North, where for thirteen years he loyally ruled for the benefit of Edward.

Only one danger remained for Edward. After the Battle of Tewkesbury, Jasper Tudor had escaped to the Continent with his nephew, Henry. Through his mother, Margaret Beaufort, Henry was the heir of the illegitimate Lancastrian line of John of Gaunt by his third wife, Katherine Swynford. But for the moment, young Henry was not a serious threat.

Much of the rest of Edward's reign was spent in intrigues and alliances against the French, although without success. Then, in March 1483, at the age of forty, Edward suddenly fell ill, and three days later he was dead. Four possible causes were put forward. That Edward caught a chill whilst fishing – the severity of the illness makes that unlikely. That it was an illness contracted eight years earlier in France, yet there is no evidence of previous suffering. That it was an attack of apoplexy suffered when he flew into a sudden rage, infuriated at the signing of the Treaty of Arras under which the French acquired Burgundy – the rage could not have been very sudden as the Treaty had been signed in December of the previous year. Or – poison.

Great efforts were made to display Edward's semi-naked body to prove that there had been no foul play. That in itself suggested foul play. Who could have been the murderer? With Edward having infant children, only two candidates are available. Richard, Duke of Gloucester, who had been Edward's loyal supporter throughout his life, but who was becoming increasingly isolated by the advance of the Woodvilles. Unlikely, as he was far off, and Edward's death left him even more isolated. Or the Woodvilles? That grasping family would have been confident of finally ruling the country through the Prince of Wales who was a child and was, of course, a Woodville himself. And that is exactly what they would try to do.

Of course, violent death was the normal way for men in Edward's family unless they had died in infancy. Not just the crown, but also to be near the crown, risked death.

THE DEATHS OF EDWARD IV's MALE RELATIVES

Paternal grandfather	Richard, Earl of Cambridge	Executed
Maternal grandfather	Roger Mortimer Earl of March	Killed in Ireland at the Battle of Kells
Father	Richard Mortimer Duke of York	Killed at the Battle of Wakefield
Brother	Henry	Died in infancy
Brother	Edmund	Killed after the Battle of Wakefield
Brother	William	Died in infancy
Brother	John	Died in infancy
Brother	George Duke of Clarence	Executed
Brother	Thomas	Died in infancy
Brother	Richard III	Later killed at the Battle of Bosworth
Son	Edward V	Later murdered in the Tower
Son	Richard Duke of York	Later murdered in the Tower
Son	George Duke of Bedford	Died in infancy

****

EDWARD V

9 April 1483 – 26 June 1483

When Edward IV died, his first son, Prince Edward, was twelve years old and the second son, Richard, was nine. They would be the battleground for the rival factions: the Woodvilles led by the Queen and her brother Earl Rivers on one side, and the old nobility led by Richard Duke of Gloucester on the other side.

Prince Edward was living with Earl Rivers, so the Woodvilles had possession of the key to power. In his will, Edward IV appointed his brother Richard Duke of Gloucester as Protector during the Crown Prince's minority. However, a judgment of Solomon did not solve the problem; rather it made it clear to each side that it must destroy the other in order to survive. This was the consequence of Edward IV's irresponsible marriage.

Richard Duke of Gloucester immediately set out for London. While he was making his way from the North, the Woodvilles called a meeting of the Council, where they had a majority. A resolution was passed abolishing the protectorship and replacing it with a Regency Council. Richard would head the Regency Council, but the Woodvilles would dominate its membership. Next, the Woodvilles decided to bring the princes to London and to advance Edward's coronation date. The young king's minority was to end on his coronation, and then Edward V could choose his own advisers. That would give the Woodvilles total control.

THE FAMILY OF EDWARD IV

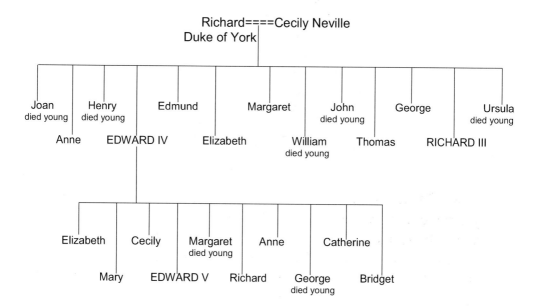

As Richard approached London, it was agreed that Rivers and Prince Edward would meet up with him in Northampton. But when Richard arrived, Rivers and Prince Edward had already moved closer to the capital. Rivers rode back to Northampton and explained to Richard that he had been forced to travel further south because Northampton was too small to cope with both retinues. That was an excuse that did not work.

Later in the day, Richard was joined by a man who would become central to the ensuing events. When Edward III's youngest son, Thomas Duke of Gloucester, was murdered in 1397 on the instructions of Richard II, the House of Gloucester fell out of the battle of the Royal Houses. However, the family of the Duke of Gloucester did not become extinct. Rather, the Duke's descendants lost their prominence and name. The Gloucester title was forfeited on the Duke's death with the accusation of treason, and it had therefore been available to be given by Edward IV to his brother, Richard. Yet the original Duke of Gloucester's family lived on, and his grandson Humphrey Earl of Stafford married Anne Neville (sister of Richard's mother Cecily), and became the 1st Duke of Buckingham. He was succeeded by his grandson Henry. So the present Duke of Gloucester was Richard of the House of York; and Henry 2nd Duke of Buckingham, 2 x great-grandson of Thomas Duke of Gloucester, was the heir of the original House of Gloucester. With all the murders and deaths, Buckingham found himself the premier peer behind Richard and the young princes.

Buckingham hated the Woodvilles, not least because when he was ten years old he had been required to marry one of them – the Queen's sister, Catherine. He wanted revenge for a forced marriage to a commoner, and he explained to Richard that it was time for action. Outnumbered as they were, with inaction matters would only get worse. Richard was convinced. In a matter of hours, Rivers was arrested and Prince Edward was taken into custody.

Once Richard and Buckingham reached London, Richard was confirmed as Protector. Then Buckingham took Rivers's seat on the Council, and he arranged for Prince Edward to be moved from the Bishop of London's palace to 'more spacious lodgings' in the Tower. Of course, the Tower of London, a medieval fortress built at the direction of William the Conqueror, was still a royal residence as well as a prison.

Then trouble arrived as four of Richard's supporters, most importantly Lord Hastings, changed sides, Hastings disappointed at being supplanted as Richard's principal adviser. Richard would not put up with that; Hastings was swiftly executed. The others kept their lives, notably Lord Stanley. But Hastings was not a Woodville, he was of the older nobility. Many of the other peers sensed danger.

It now became clear to Richard that chasing away the Woodvilles was not enough, because Prince Edward was demanding authority and complaining about the treatment of his family. As a first step, the Queen, who was living in sanctuary in Westminster Abbey, was forced to surrender her younger son. He was taken to the Tower to join his brother.

Next, Richard needed a case to show that he was entitled to the throne as of right. There was an old story that before he had married Elizabeth Woodville, Edward IV had contracted to marry Lady Eleanor Butler; it was apparently the only way he could get her to sleep with him. If there had been such a contract, it would have invalidated Edward's marriage to Elizabeth and would make the two princes bastards, thereby nullifying their rights to inherit the crown. As a result, Edward IV's rightful successor would be his brother, Richard Duke of Gloucester (Clarence's retarded son being ignored as the child of a traitor, as was his sister Margaret). The story may well have been true; Clarence had raised it many times and it had been rumoured for years. Of course, neither Edward nor Lady Eleanor was alive to prove or disprove it. Yet it may have explained why Edward married Elizabeth Woodville secretly; for if advance notice of the wedding had been given, then Lady Eleanor might have spoken out.

Buckingham made himself busy, spreading the allegation and warning of the dangers of an infant Woodville king. Then a priest was produced, and he confirmed that there was such a marriage contract, and over-helpfully added that he had actually officiated at the wedding of Edward and Lady Eleanor. Wishing to avoid a child king, hating the Woodvilles and fearful of another civil war, on 25th June 1483 Parliament declared the young princes illegitimate and petitioned Richard to take the throne. He accepted the following day.

Now Richard and Buckingham got to work. Earl Rivers (the Queen's brother), Lord Richard Grey (the Queen's son by her first marriage) and Sir Thomas Vaughan (Chamberlain to young Edward) were executed. On 6th July 1483, Richard

Duke of Gloucester was crowned King Richard III.

What of the two boys in the Tower? They remained there; not in a cell, but in well-furnished rooms. Nevertheless, the Tower was their prison. Soon they were moved to rooms deeper within the building, then they received fewer visitors, then none. Exactly what happened and who did it will never be known for sure. The two boys were not seen publicly again; it is almost certain that they were murdered.

The favoured story is that Richard and Buckingham agreed that Richard's crown and their lives could not be safe whilst the two princes lived. Either the boys must die, or Richard and Buckingham would die. Faced with that choice, they naturally decided that Edward and his brother must be killed.

Forty years later, Sir Thomas More wrote a detailed version of what he was told had happened. Principled as More was, it has to be borne in mind that this version of events was provided at a time when it was mandatory to blacken Richard's name. That blackening is best illustrated by the false description of Richard (which was followed by Shakespeare) as a man with a withered arm, a limp and a hunchback; although there may well have been a problem with one arm.

According to More, Richard summoned one of his most reliable servants, John Green, and gave him a letter to deliver to Sir Robert Brackenbury, who was Constable of the Tower. The letter contained a direct order from King Richard to Brackenbury, requiring him to kill the two princes. Green delivered the letter, but Brackenbury refused to carry out the instruction.

Green told Richard of the response. The furious king complained loudly that those he had favoured could not be relied on to perform a favour for him. On hearing this, one of Richard's pages suggested that the man he could count on was Sir James Tyrrell (remarkably, the same surname as the murderer of William II). Richard immediately summoned Tyrrell and explained to him the duty he was to perform. He accepted the task without demur.

Tyrrell made his way to London bearing a new letter from the King to Brackenbury. It had a different command, it merely ordered the Constable to deliver to Tyrrell all the keys of the Tower for one night so that he might carry out the King's instructions. Although the nature of those instructions must have been obvious to Brackenbury, he had no choice but to obey.

Late the following evening, Tyrrell called on Brackenbury and was given the keys. The princes had known for some time that Richard had taken the crown and that they were in danger. Their low spirits were further depressed as Edward was suffering from osteoangelitis, a bone disease of the jaw that was causing him increasing pain, and which was incurable at the time.

Tyrrell had brought two associates, Miles Forrest who had murdered before, and Tyrrell's horse-keeper, a thug called John Dighton. Having gained entrance to the princes' room, Tyrrell sent Forrest and Dighton inside at about midnight. They rushed in, and as one wrapped the boys in their bed-coverings, holding them down, the other stuffed pillows into their mouths, suffocating them until they died.

The murder of Edward and his brother

Now the murderers called Tyrrell into the room to witness the fact that both the uncrowned Edward V and his brother Richard Duke of York were dead. Tyrrell then arranged their secret burial.[13]

What of the murderers? Forrest was appointed Keeper of the Wardrobe (the spending department) of King Richard's mother. Tyrrell was appointed Master of the King's Henchmen (squires). Amazingly, he was granted a pardon by Henry VII, but was later executed for supporting a failed claimant to the throne.

Of course, Richard's guilt is not certain. The boys were not just a threat to Richard's crown, they were also a threat to Buckingham who aspired to the crown and to Henry Tudor who had some hopes. As to Buckingham, he needed their deaths more than Richard did. Richard had already managed to seize the crown with the boys alive and he would gain little from their deaths other than security. If Richard died, Buckingham would struggle to obtain the crown whilst the boys lived.

But despite Richard's loyalty to Edward IV and his dutiful behaviour in all matters until he saw the possibility of the crown in Northampton, he remains the likeliest, if not the certain, person responsible for the murder of Edward V.

****

---

13 In 1674, the skeletons of two children were found under a staircase during renovation work to the White Tower. They were re-buried in Westminster Abbey.

RICHARD III

26 June 1483 – 22 August 1485

King of England at last, Richard had a number of advantages and a number of disadvantages. On the plus side, he was the brother of the previous king (or uncle if young Edward was counted), he was from the senior House of Clarence/York, he was of good age for a king, he had an impressive record of military leadership, he was popular in the country and his wife had already produced a son.

On the minus side, he was a usurper, he had apparently organised the murder of the true heir, he had ordered the execution of nobles without trial, and apart from Buckingham he had no major allies.

Yet one problem can always override many advantages. In the end, it would be the deaths of three children that united Richard's enemies and lost him support.

Having accepted the throne by acceding to Parliament's petition engineered by Buckingham, and having in all likelihood disposed of the rightful heir, Richard was comfortable in his position. A usurper on taking the throne certainly, but after the deaths of the two princes he was actually the first adult male in line. The only possible better claim was that of the son of Richard's older brother, Clarence.

But that son was an eight-year-old mentally retarded child whose father had been attainted (convicted of treason by parliament and without trial). The attainder also barred issue – although attainder could be reversed. His sister Margaret was also barred by the attainder.

Now Richard travelled the country on a royal progress, impressing his subjects and receiving their genuine approval. But in time, news of the murder of the two princes galvanised the Woodvilles and the Lancastrians. However, their candidates for the crown had all been killed; they needed a new one who could be supported by both factions.

Edward IV's two sons had been murdered and a third had died in infancy. He also had seven daughters, and five of them were still alive. The best choice was the oldest, Elizabeth of York, and she was unmarried. Certainly there was little chance of her being accepted as queen to rule alone. Yet she carried the royal blood of the House of York, and so would her son. If a suitable husband could be found, each would improve the other's position.

When Henry VI and his son, Prince Edward, were killed, it meant that no legitimate issue of Henry IV, V and VI were still alive. That was really the end of the House of Lancaster. What of the secondary illegitimate Lancaster line through John of Gaunt's marriage to Katherine Swynford? Their grandson and heir, John Beaufort, had left a daughter Lady Margaret Beaufort as his sole heiress, and she had married Edmund Tudor, the son of Owen Tudor and Queen Catherine (the widow of Henry V).

The son of Lady Margaret Beaufort and Edmund Tudor was Henry Tudor – and he was as good as was available for a Lancastrian heir. Henry was 27 years old and safe in Brittany, having been smuggled there by his uncle Jasper Tudor after the Battle of Tewkesbury.

Next came a major development – Buckingham, Richard's main ally, changed sides. An agreement was made between Buckingham, the Woodvilles and Henry Tudor. Henry promised to marry Elizabeth of York, and Buckingham agreed to support Henry's claim to the throne. The Duke of Brittany would supply the finance and the army, and they would invade England in October. Why did Buckingham change sides? Very possibly he was scheming to become king when Richard was dead.

But too many people were involved and too many knew of the plot. Richard found out, and he assembled an army to defend his crown.

Buckingham was to raise forces on the mainland, but incessant torrential rain made travel difficult and many did not arrive at the rallying points. Most of those who did arrive soon left, and Buckingham fell into Richard's hands and was executed. Richard then marched west, and the Woodville forces scattered in disarray. Henry Tudor's fleet with 5,000 men on board was caught in a storm, and the few vessels that came near the English shore abandoned the venture and returned to Brittany. It had been a complete farce.

Richard was more secure than ever. Then came the disastrous death of another child. Richard's only son, 10-year-old Edward Prince of Wales, died after a short illness. Queen Anne (one of Warwick's daughters did become queen) had not given birth for ten years, and there would clearly be no child to replace Edward.

Now the succession was not assured. After years of civil war, the country yearned for an automatic and peaceful change of monarchs – it was one of the things that Richard had brought to the throne. He needed to nominate a successor. Clarence's son and daughter were not options, so Richard selected another nephew, John de la Pole Earl of Lincoln, the son of Richard's sister Elizabeth and her husband the Duke of Suffolk. Lincoln was, in law, next in line; nevertheless, Richard's position had been seriously harmed.

Of course the real danger was the fact that Henry Tudor was still at liberty. Richard's first move was to make a deal with Brittany, supplying them with archers in return for a promise that they would take Henry Tudor into custody. Then Richard offered the Treasurer of Brittany (the effective ruler during the Duke's mental illness) the revenues of the earldom of Richmond if he would hand Henry over. Somehow, Henry, who had adopted his father's title of Earl of Richmond (although titles were not inherited without the King's consent), discovered the offer, and he escaped to the court of the King of France.

For both Henry and Richard, it was now time to settle the issue. In December 1484, Richard was almost pleased to learn that Henry was planning to invade in the following summer.

Henry Tudor landed with his army at Milford Haven in south-west Wales on 7th August 1485. His 2,000 soldiers were all French convicts who had been promised a pardon if they fought for Henry. He also brought his uncle Jasper Tudor, plus the Earl of Oxford and very few others. They should have had no chance.

As Henry marched through Wales, thousands joined his army, all eager to fight for a Welsh-named claimant to the throne, although Henry and his parents were born in England and just one of his grandparents was Welsh. When Henry moved into England, his army's numbers continued to grow as he neared Richard's fortress base in Nottingham.

Richard prepared for battle. Then, while he was still gathering his forces, he was hit by treachery. Lord Stanley had been an ally of Edward IV, but when Warwick invaded in support of Henry VI, Stanley changed sides. He was forgiven when Edward regained power. After Edward's death, Stanley backed Richard, only to join the Hastings group who switched to the Woodville side. Although arrested, Stanley was again forgiven. He supported Richard once more, yet he would be the first to defect if he thought that the other side was likely to be victorious. This time there was an added motivation, for Stanley had married Lady Margaret Beaufort, the widowed mother of Henry Tudor. Now Stanley refused to bring his force of 3,000 men to join Richard, even though Richard had taken the precaution of holding one of Stanley's sons as hostage.

Preparing to move out to battle, having already lost Stanley's men and having lost to Henry the Welsh contingent he was expecting, Richard heard that Henry was heading for London. Richard had to act, and he left Nottingham at the head of 10,000 men; still larger than Henry's forces.

The two armies approached each other near Watling Street, the road to the capital. Here, on Redmore Plain (later renamed Bosworth Field), they took their positions, Richard's army being better placed on the 400 foot high Ambien Hill.

Richard sent a message to Lord Stanley, warning him that failure to join the King's army would result in the execution of his son. Stanley replied saying that he could afford the loss as he had other sons; but Richard did not carry out his threat. Yet Lord Stanley did not ride to join his stepson Henry's army. Instead he kept his men to one side of the battle, with his brother, Sir William Stanley, keeping his men to the other side. Both of them were waiting to see who was the certain winner before riding to support the victor.

Henry's army advanced under the command of the Earl of Oxford. Having no experience of warfare, Henry remained at the rear. As Henry's men reached Ambien Hill, part of Richard's forces led by the Duke of Norfolk ran down the slope to meet them. But Norfolk was slain, and his troops began to retreat.

Then Richard ordered the Earl of Northumberland to move forward with his 3,000 soldiers to engage Henry's advancing men. Northumberland refused, saying unconvincingly that he needed to stay at the rear in case of an attack by Lord Stanley.

All of a sudden, Richard's numerical advantage had gone. His senior nobles told him to flee, but Richard rejected their advice. He decided to risk all and charge with his remaining loyal knights and squires. Richard led eighty of them, storming down the hill. He knew that killing Henry was now the only way to survive. So Richard rode with his supporters in a wild attack around the right-hand side of the battle, circling the fighting armies and galloping towards Henry, who was waiting behind his army.

Having reached the soldiers surrounding Henry Tudor, Richard and his companions fought their way forward. Slowly, they edged nearer their target, but their numbers were reduced as they advanced. Now Sir William Stanley knew what to do to be sure of ending up on the winning side, and he rode with his men to attack Richard's small group from the rear.

Eventually, King Richard, having got as near to Henry Tudor as slaying his standard bearer, was isolated and surrounded by the enemy. Richard continued to wield his axe in all directions, shouting out "Treason!", "Treason!", until he was cut down and butchered; so joining Harold as the two English monarchs to die in battle.

Not remembered as such because of the antipathy of Tudor historians and playwrights, Richard died more gallantly than any other English king before or since.

Killed by traitors, Richard's naked body was thrown on a horse and taken to Leicester, where it lay exposed for two days before being buried without ceremony in a friary. It is said that years later, his bones were dug up and thrown into the River Soar. A cruel fate for a murdered king who had probably procured the murder of a king himself.

****

HENRY VII

22 August 1485 – 21 April 1509

Henry Tudor shrewdly claimed the throne not by inheritance, but by conquest. Shrewd, because on any view of inheritance his claim was bettered by others.

Who was really entitled to succeed on Richard III's death? As Richard left no issue, it would be the heir of Richard's oldest brother, Edward IV. With the two princes dead, the answer is clear: Edward IV's oldest surviving daughter, Elizabeth of York, sister of the murdered princes, who actually had a better right to the crown than Richard.

If it had to be a man (or if Edward or his children were illegitimate and therefore disqualified), it should have been Clarence's son Edward; but he was the son of a traitor, he was a child and he was said to be mentally retarded, so he could be ruled out. The next male in line was Edward IV's and Richard III's sister Elizabeth's son, John de la Pole Earl of Lincoln, nephew of two kings. Lincoln had been appointed successor by Richard III, but he seems to have had little support in the country. Anyway, he did not promote his claim. Instead, he pledged his allegiance to Henry immediately after Bosworth.

Henry Tudor had no right to be king. His father, Edmund

RICHARD III and HENRY TUDOR
(relevant personnel only)

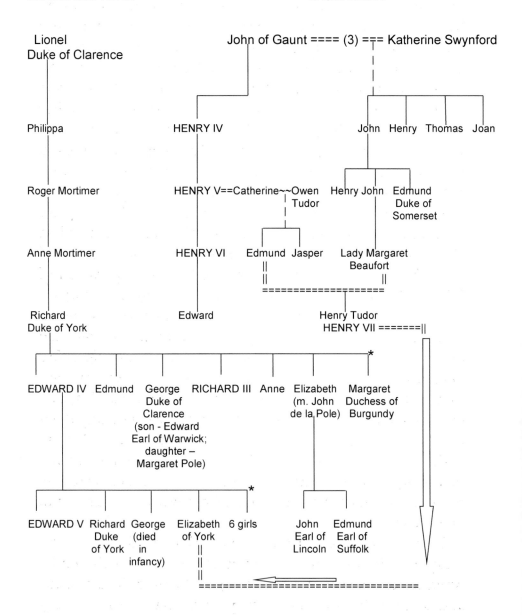

CLARENCE/YORK   LANCASTER

Lionel
Duke of Clarence

John of Gaunt ==== (3) === Katherine Swynford

Philippa   HENRY IV   John   Henry   Thomas   Joan

Roger Mortimer   HENRY V==Catherine~~Owen   Henry John   Edmund
                           Tudor   Duke of
                                            Somerset

Anne Mortimer   HENRY VI   Edmund   Jasper   Lady Margaret
                                          Beaufort
                            || ||
                            || ==================== ||

Richard   Edward   Henry Tudor
Duke of York   HENRY VII ======||

EDWARD IV   Edmund   George   RICHARD III   Anne   Elizabeth   Margaret
                     Duke of   (m. John   Duchess of
                     Clarence   de la Pole)   Burgundy
                     (son - Edward
                     Earl of Warwick;
                     daughter –
                     Margaret Pole)

EDWARD V   Richard   George   Elizabeth   6 girls   John   Edmund
            Duke   (died   of York   Earl of   Earl of
            of York   in || Lincoln   Suffolk
                     infancy) ||
                               ||
                    ===================================

* Sons before daughters (see page141 for order of birth)

Tudor, was the son of Owen Tudor and Henry V's widow, Queen Catherine. Owen Tudor had been a page at Henry V's court, and had distinguished himself at the Battle of Agincourt, later rising to the rank of squire in the Queen's household. When the scandal broke that the former Queen had given birth to five children in a relationship with her servant, the Council forced Catherine and Owen to separate, and Catherine was sent to Bermondsey Abbey where she died several months later. Of course, Owen and Catherine were not married, so their son, Edmund Tudor (the father of Henry), was illegitimate, that being confirmed when it was found necessary for an Act of Parliament to be passed in 1452 declaring his legitimacy. So, through Henry's father there was not an ounce of entitlement to the throne.

It was only through Henry's mother, Lady Margaret Beaufort, who was only thirteen years old and a widow when she gave birth to Henry, that Henry could make any sort of case, the case being that he was the 3 x great-grandson of Edward III. Margaret Beaufort was the great-granddaughter of Edward's son John of Gaunt and his mistress Katherine Swynford, who later became his wife. Their children, the oldest being Margaret's grandfather, were called Beaufort after Beaufort Castle in France where they were brought up, and they were all illegitimate. They were later legitimised by Act of Parliament, but only on condition that it gave neither them nor their descendants any right to the crown, Henry IV having added the phrase '*excepta dignitate regali*' to make it clear that their disqualification through illegitimacy was unaffected by the Act. So Henry Tudor's descent from Edward III gave him no rights at all.

There was no alternative; Henry claimed the crown by conquest. He was only too aware that taking the throne by conquest established a precedent for others to do the same, and that would always be Henry's fear. But it was his only way to become king.

The coronation took place on 31st October 1485, Henry

insisting on being crowned before he married Elizabeth of York, so as to show that he had not needed to rely on her royal blood to take the throne. Nevertheless, the fact remains that the true right of all their descendants in their claims to the crown runs not from Henry but from Elizabeth of York, the oldest child of Edward IV.[14]

In January 1486, Henry married Elizabeth, thereby joining York and Lancaster (albeit the illegitimate line) via the Tudors, combining their symbols in the red and white Tudor rose, and ending the Wars of the Roses. Henry and Elizabeth had been living together for some time, and Elizabeth was already pregnant. Later in the year, she gave birth to Arthur; so the Tudor line was assured and the country celebrated.

Although there would be many plots to overthrow Henry, the real attempt to kill him was Richard's desperate charge at Bosworth Field. Technically it was an attempt to kill the King, because Henry enacted that his accession was to be backdated to 21st August 1485 (the day before Bosworth) so that all those who had fought with Richard could be declared traitors for taking up arms against the King, even though nobody knew at the time that Henry was the king – not even Henry himself. It was another shrewd move, because with Richard's supporters being attainted as traitors, it meant that Henry could seize their property and lands.

Lashing out at all within reach, Richard and his men made deep inroads, getting ever closer to Henry Tudor. In front of Henry, Richard saw Sir William Brandon holding Henry's standard. Brandon was in the way, in between Richard and Henry. Richard struck him down. Then Richard shouted to Henry, challenging him to personal combat as he manoeuvred his horse closer to his rival. Henry ignored the challenge, and he turned his horse, trying to move away.

---

14 Elizabeth's father, uncle, brother, husband, son and grandson were Kings of England; and two granddaughters were Queens of England. She is said to be rewarded by her likeness being used for the Queen of Hearts in a standard deck of cards.

Richard had insisted on wearing a crown over his helmet, resolved to fight as a king no matter the consequences. So when Sir William Stanley saw from a distance that it was Richard leading such a small force, he knew that if he and his men charged from behind, Richard would be trapped. Now Stanley was certain to be on the victorious side.

Stanley and his men rode forward and attacked Richard's group of knights. Undaunted, Richard was determined to kill Henry. Richard raised his sword high, moving in to strike the vital blow. At that very moment, when Richard was almost within a sword's length of Henry, Sir William Stanley's men, having cut through Richard's followers, reached the King. They dragged Richard from his horse. Thrown to the ground, he got to his feet and continued to fight; but he was alone and completely encircled. Richard was attacked from all sides, the assault continuing beyond his death until his corpse was totally mutilated. Only a few yards from each other; one king nearly killed, the other killed – and it was just seconds from being the other way round.

Henry was now the king, but he was worried. After all, he had taken the crown after invading with an army of only 2,000 men. Henry's first step was to ban all the barons from having private armies; disobedience was treason.

Next, it was time to deal with his main rival. The new king gave orders for Clarence's son, the sickly and retarded Edward Earl of Warwick, to be confined in the Tower. Impossible as it was for this 11-year-old child to be king, he had a far better right to the throne than Henry, and he had to be locked away.

Before long, to Henry's annoyance, news arrived that Edward Earl of Warwick had escaped and was raising support, demanding to be crowned as the true king. It was a deception; Edward was still in the Tower. The so-called true king was in fact Lambert Simnel, a joiner's son, who was impersonating Edward. Arrangements were made for the real Edward to attend a service at St Paul's so as to show himself, but it made no difference. Even John de la Pole Earl of Lincoln was convinced, or pretended to be convinced, that the child was his cousin. The hope was that with foreign aid Henry could be removed, after which Edward or Lincoln himself would take the throne. Either way, it would be the House of York.

Foreign support came from Margaret of Burgundy, who was the sister of Edward IV and Richard III and aunt of Lincoln and Warwick. She helped Lincoln to recruit 2,000 German mercenaries. They sailed to Ireland, and on their arrival Lambert Simnel was crowned King Edward VI in Dublin Cathedral.

Lincoln's army then made for England. They landed on the Lancashire coast and set out for Yorkshire; but unlike Henry Tudor's forces before Bosworth, their numbers did not increase significantly as they advanced. Henry confronted the rebels at Stoke Field in Nottinghamshire. Although initially the rebels had the upper hand, in the end Henry's greater numbers triumphed. John de la Pole Earl of Lincoln, the adult male with the best legal right to the crown, was killed. Lambert Simnel was seized and sent to work in the King's kitchen, and in later years he was promoted to falconer.

The next extraordinary threat to Henry's crown came in 1491. A Breton ship arrived in Cork harbour with a cargo of silks and fine clothes. On board was 17-year-old crew member Perkin Warbeck (originally spelled 'Werbecque'), the son of a boatman from Tournai. One of Warbeck's duties was to 'model' the silks and other finery to potential customers. Many of those who saw him thought that he must be high-born, so much so that the Mayor stated that he was probably Clarence's son, Edward Earl of Warwick, who had escaped from the Tower. Others thought he was Richard Duke of York, the younger of the two princes murdered in the Tower whose bodies had never been produced.

In Dublin the leading citizens decided to go with Richard Duke of York, as the King was in a position to produce the real Warwick. Warbeck was told to take on the Duke's identity, he was taught English and he was trained to behave like a duke.

Warbeck's supporters soon included the King of France,

the King of Scotland, Margaret of Burgundy and Holy Roman Emperor Maximilian, all of them happy to cause Henry trouble. After a while, even Henry himself wondered if it might be true. He sent agents to Ireland to investigate, and they reported back that it was all utter nonsense. However, Henry's agents also discovered the names of those in England who were supporting Warbeck. The supporters were arrested, the most senior being the Lord Chamberlain Sir William Stanley, the very man whose attack on Richard III had been so instrumental in securing Henry's victory at Bosworth Field. It appears that Stanley's guilt was based solely on his comment that if the young man really was the Duke of York, then he could not take up arms against him. It was enough; Stanley could not be trusted, so he was executed.

Then Warbeck landed on the south coast with a small force. In a brief skirmish, most of his men were killed or captured – the English to be hanged, the foreigners to be ransomed. Warbeck and the others escaped and sailed back to Ireland. Henry's forces were waiting for them, so they carried on to Scotland. Warbeck was welcomed by King James IV, treated as the duke he was not, and then married off to James's distant cousin, Lady Catherine Gordon, the daughter of the Chancellor.

In return, Warbeck promised to surrender English territory to Scotland if he became king, so James decided to incite unrest by sending his army to make an incursion into northern England. Now Henry had to levy taxes in order to raise an army for a Scottish campaign. This provoked great discontent, and in no time at all 15,000 rebels from Cornwall made their way to London, claiming that only northerners should pay for protection from the Scots. They were routed by Henry's men, 2,000 rebels being killed. Then Henry's army marched north and forced the Scots back over the border.

Undeterred, in 1497 Warbeck landed in Devon with only 120 men, and he was proclaimed King Richard IV. By the time he laid siege to Exeter, his supporters numbered over 8,000. However, their weaponry was inadequate for a siege, so they moved on to Taunton. With Henry's army approaching, Warbeck took fright, and one night he and sixty of his followers ran off. Most of them were captured, and Warbeck surrendered. Of course, Warbeck was not English so he was not guilty of treason. He was not executed; not even tried. Warbeck and his wife were merely forced to live at Henry's court. A few months later, Warbeck ran away. He was captured, and this time he was sent to the Tower.

Incredibly, in early 1499 another phoney Warwick appeared. This one was Ralph Wilford, the son of a London shoemaker. He was hanged straight away. Now Henry had had enough; it was time to deal more firmly with all rivals.

Later in the year, a so-called plot was said to have been hatched to rescue Warbeck, Warwick and other Yorkists from the Tower with the intent of overthrowing the King. Almost certainly the plot had been instigated, probably invented, by Henry's agents so as to provide justification for killing everyone who was a threat to Henry. Warbeck, Edward Earl of Warwick and others were executed for involvement in the 'plot'.

After all the executions, there should have been no one left to cause problems for Henry. But there would always be someone else. Lincoln left no issue, so his heir, the new Yorkist claimant, was his brother, Edmund de la Pole Duke of Suffolk. He started negotiations on the Continent, and found some support; but in time his followers (including Sir James Tyrrell, who had organised the murder of Edward V) were seized and executed, and Edmund fled to the court of Emperor Maximilian.

Now Henry could deal with the next issue: the succession. It was agreed that Prince Arthur would marry the youngest daughter of Ferdinand and Isabella, the King and Queen of Spain, and in late 1501, Crown Prince Arthur married Catherine of Aragon. Everything was now in place: King Henry secure, the Tudor dynasty established, Arthur advantageously married, and the King's second son, the 10-year-old Henry, destined for the Church.

In the following March, the country suffered an epidemic of influenza. Both Catherine and Arthur fell ill. Catherine recovered within weeks, but Prince Arthur was not that lucky and five months after the wedding he was dead. It was a devastating blow for Henry and Elizabeth. However, they did have a second son, Henry, and two daughters, Margaret and Mary; their two other children, Elizabeth and Edmund, having died in infancy. Queen Elizabeth became pregnant again, but having given birth, both mother and child died a few days later.

Then King Henry lost the company of his daughter, Margaret, when at the age of thirteen she married King James IV of Scotland in a union that would be of overwhelming importance in British history.

Prince Henry was next. It was agreed that he would marry his brother's widow, Catherine of Aragon. So, the young man who had been destined for the Church and a life of celibacy agreed to take the first of his six wives, although the wedding would not take place for some considerable time.

Marrying a deceased sibling's spouse was not an unusual step. It maintained the strategic purpose of the marriage, and it meant that it was not necessary to return the dowry. In this way, Catherine's oldest sister Isabella had married King Alfonso of Portugal. When Alfonso died, Isabella married his brother, King Manuel. Then, when Isabella died, Manuel married her sister Maria – completing the substitution of both spouses.

Henry VII now looked for a new wife. At first he had favoured his widowed daughter-in-law Catherine of Aragon, but her mother had objected. Next he considered Catherine's cousin, the widowed Queen of Naples, but she brought no wealth. Then there was Archduchess Margaret of Austria, the daughter of the Holy Roman Emperor. That proposal advanced when in early 1506 a ship was driven on to the Dorset coast in a storm. On board were Philip Duke of Burgundy, the son of the Emperor, and Philip's wife Joanna of Castile; they were travelling from the Netherlands to Spain. Philip was Archduchess Margaret's brother, and Joanna was a sister of Catherine of Aragon.

Philip and Joanna became 'guests' of Henry for a month, before being allowed to continue their voyage. During their stay, Philip agreed an alliance with Henry, signing for himself and for his father, Emperor Maximilian. Henry was in a strong negotiating position, and he extracted a supplementary agreement requiring the delivery of Edmund de la Pole Duke of Suffolk on condition that he received a full pardon. Edmund was promptly returned, pardoned and sent to the Tower. Another agreement provided for Henry's marriage to Archduchess Margaret, for Henry's daughter, Mary, to marry Philip's son, Charles of Ghent, and for Crown Prince Henry (despite the agreement for him to marry Catherine of Aragon) to marry Philip's daughter, Eleanora (Catherine's niece).

Within months, Philip was dead. So Henry turned his attention to Philip's widow, Joanna. He had been much taken with her when she was his guest, despite rumours that had led her to be known as 'Mad Joanna'. It was justified. Joanna would not permit the burial of her husband; instead, she set out on a second honeymoon with Philip – Joanna travelling in a bridal gown and Philip travelling in a coffin. She was locked up for the remaining 50 years of her life.

None of the marriages agreed by Henry and Philip took place.

Having given up on marriage, Henry became increasingly worn out. Then his eyesight began to deteriorate, and his fear of being overthrown was replaced by fear of blindness. He turned into a recluse, and in April 1509, Henry VII died at the age of fifty-two.

A king who had nearly been killed by a king, and whose forces or executioners had killed a king, two men entitled to be king and two bogus kings, Henry VII died miserable and alone, unloved by his people. Yet the narrow failure to kill him at Bosworth Field gave England a line of succession that would in future be departed from only because of religion.

****

CHILDREN OF HENRY VII

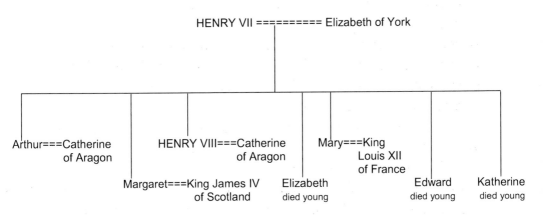

HENRY VII ========== Elizabeth of York

Arthur===Catherine
of Aragon

HENRY VIII===Catherine
of Aragon

Mary===King
Louis XII
of France

Margaret===King James IV
of Scotland

Elizabeth
died young

Edward
died young

Katherine
died young

HENRY VIII

21 April 1509 – 28 January 1547

As the second son, Henry had not been trained to be king. In fact, he had been a spoilt child, even having a 'whipping boy' who was punished when Henry misbehaved. But on Prince Arthur's death, everything changed. Henry VII virtually imprisoned the new heir.

Young Henry's bedroom had one door, so he was unable to leave without passing through his father's room. He was only allowed to go outside into a private garden, and even then only if accompanied by his tutors or guards. Henry was rarely permitted to attend state functions, and when he did attend he was not allowed to speak to anyone; and he certainly could not see Catharine of Aragon, even though they were betrothed.

After being crowned king at the age of seventeen, Henry soon made up for the years of repression. Having married Catherine within two months of his accession, Henry spent most of his time enjoying his favourite pastimes: eating, hunting, jousting and music.

Henry's joy was completed when in 1511 Catherine gave birth to a boy, named Henry. Sadly, two months later the young prince was dead.

When the French challenged the authority of the Pope, Henry decided to go to war against France. Before he left, he dealt with the last threat to the Tudor crown. The man who (if Clarence's issue were excluded) was probably the rightful king, Edmund de la Pole Duke of Suffolk, had been a prisoner in the Tower for seven years after being handed over by Emperor Maximilian. As part of the deal, Henry VII had promised that Edmund would not be harmed. Henry did not consider himself to be bound by his father's promise, so he had Edmund executed.[15]

The war against France was a disaster. However, Henry was not one to give up. He tried again, and this time Henry came home having won some French territory. While Henry had been in France, James IV of Scotland (to whom Henry's sister Margaret was married) had taken the opportunity to invade England. Henry dealt with him forcefully. The Scots were soundly beaten at the Battle of Flodden, and James was killed along with 10,000 of his countrymen, leaving him famous as the first recorded player of golf. He was succeeded by his son, the infant James V, and Henry's sister was appointed regent.

Henry returned to his pleasures, and he left control of the country in the hands of Thomas Wolsey, who became Chancellor and cardinal. Wolsey, the son of an Ipswich merchant, would prove to be as ruthless and unscrupulous as his master.

After some years of peace, Henry joined Holy Roman Emperor Charles in war against France. Charles was the winner, and he secured much of France and the Vatican. Henry would come to regret giving assistance to Charles.

The mood in England was hostile, as the war gained England little, it had cost a fortune, and Wolsey's constant raising of

---

15 Edmund left a young daughter, so his brother Richard declared himself Earl of Suffolk, and the Yorkist claimant to the crown. With French support, he spent years preparing to invade England; but he was killed in 1525 at the Battle of Pavia while commanding the French infantry against a Spanish/Imperial army. He left no legitimate issue; and that was the end of the Yorkist cause.

taxes was resented. Then a greater problem arrived. Henry had grown tired of Catherine, who had failed to produce a male heir. It was not for lack of trying. In 1510 she had given birth to a still-born daughter; in 1511 a healthy son who died within weeks; in 1513 a son who died immediately; in 1515 a stillborn son; and finally, in 1516 a healthy child – but it was a girl, Mary. Several pregnancies followed, but there were to be no more children.

Yet Henry did have a son. In 1519, Henry's mistress, Elizabeth Blount, a lady-in-waiting to Catherine, gave birth to a healthy boy: Henry Fitzroy. However, an illegitimate son could not be the heir to the throne.

Henry began to wonder why he could not have a healthy son with Catherine. She could produce a child, he could produce a son; why not both together? He found the answer in the Bible. In Leviticus it was written: "Thou shalt not uncover the nakedness of thy brother's wife." Presumably this only applied to a living brother's wife, but it did not say so. That was why papal dispensation had been needed for the marriage in the first place, and it had been granted on the basis that Catherine's marriage to Arthur had not been consummated.

There was soon an added complication. A young woman whose mother was the daughter of the Duke of Norfolk had become the King's mistress. Her name was Mary Boleyn, said to have formerly been the mistress of King Francis II of France amongst others, and known as 'the English mare'. She later arranged for her sister, Anne, to become a lady-in-waiting to Queen Catherine. Henry immediately showed a keen interest in Anne, but she refused to become his mistress – it was wife and queen or nothing.

So Henry had to dispose of Catherine. He demanded an annulment of his marriage, claiming that Catherine and Arthur had indeed consummated their union. Over the centuries, a pope's agreement could be obtained in some sort of negotiation; but Pope Clement VII was the prisoner of Emperor Charles. Unluckily for Henry, Charles was Catherine's nephew; so nullifying the marriage would make Catherine's daughter Mary, who was Charles's cousin, illegitimate. There was no way he would allow that.

Predictably, the Pope refused the annulment. It was a popular decision as the people of England were all for Catherine the foreign queen, Anne and her sister being regarded as whores. Nevertheless, Henry would not relent; he wanted to be rid of Catherine, he wanted a legitimate son and he wanted Anne Boleyn. Now Henry was angry; Wolsey had failed him, so he was dismissed, later having the good fortune to die on his journey to London for trial and the inevitable execution.

Angry or not, Henry was always happy to be jousting. On 10th March 1524 it almost cost him his life. Henry had designed a flamboyant suit of armour, and as soon as it was delivered he ordered a joust so that he could show off his new outfit.

Henry's opponent was Charles Brandon Duke of Suffolk (son of Henry VII's standard-bearer who had been killed by Richard III at the Battle of Bosworth). Both men sat astride their horses at either end of the tilt, the long barrier along the middle of the arena that had been introduced to change jousting from a battle to the death to merely an extremely dangerous sport. Each contestant acknowledged the crowd and welcomed the cheers. Then each took hold of a shield in one hand and a lance in the other.

An official approached Brandon and said: "Sir, the King is come to the end of the tilt." Brandon replied: "I see him not, by my faith, for my headpiece blocks my sight." Then the official told Brandon: "Sir, the King is coming." It was the instruction to proceed.

Both men charged along the tilt from opposite ends. The onlookers were shouting particularly loudly, but Henry could not decipher their words. They were not shouting encouragement, they were shouting "Hold! Hold!". All of them could see that Henry had forgotten to lower his visor, and his face was unprotected.

The two men rode on, and as they closed, Brandon's lance

struck the King on the brow under the guard of the headpiece, right on the basinet to which the visor was hinged. That basinet was not strongly made, as it was meant to be covered by the visor when it was lowered. Brandon's lance pushed Henry's unlowered visor so far back that Henry's face was quite naked. The end of the lance disintegrated, with a host of sharp splinters flying into Henry's face.

Although his face was badly cut and bruised, by sheer good fortune Henry had not been blinded or killed. An accident? Did Brandon have to aim for Henry's head? Surely he could see that Henry's visor had not been lowered. Surely Brandon could have ridden away from the tilt. Strangest of all was Brandon's premature defence, saying in advance that he could not see Henry.

Mary and Charles Brandon

The answer may lie in the succession. If Brandon had killed Henry, the first in line to the throne was Henry's only legitimate child, Mary. She was eight years old; a long regency to be followed by a young queen was not an inviting prospect. The second in line was Henry's sister Margaret, the widow of the King of Scotland; she was effectively ruling Scotland as chief councillor to her son, the king. That son, the twelve-year-old King James V, was therefore third in line to the English throne. Of course, the chief councillor and the child monarch of a neighbouring and hostile country were not acceptable candidates for the English throne. So the fourth in line was the most realistic successor; that was Henry's younger sister, Mary – and she was married to Charles Brandon Duke of Suffolk (her first husband the King of France having died). Although a close friend of Henry's, they had fallen out when Brandon married Mary without obtaining Henry's consent. Brandon was only saved from a charge of treason by paying Henry £24,000 plus Mary's recovered £200,000 dowry from her first marriage, together with all her plate and jewels. The motive was there; perhaps the joust offered Brandon the opportunity. Possibly another attempt to kill the King of England.

Henry's new Chancellor was Sir Thomas More, a lawyer. To his considerable annoyance, Henry would learn that although More was not a cleric, he would not countenance disobedience to the Pope.

Yet even though Henry would eventually break with Rome, he always regarded himself as a good Catholic. Indeed, Henry had written a book opposing the views of Luther, and as a reward the Pope had granted Henry the title 'Defender of the Faith'. That title has been assumed by all subsequent English monarchs, 'FD' (*fidei defensor*) appearing on current coins, even though the title was for Henry alone and not available to be inherited.

However, the annulment was paramount. There was little sympathy for it in England, although there was plenty of backing for an attack on the power and privilege of the Roman Church, which owned one-third of all the land in England, and was constantly imposing taxes so as to acquire more.

Henry started to make his moves, and they were all against the impious behaviour of priests: holding multiple positions, engaging in commerce, not visiting their parishes and so on.

But nothing improved the chances of an annulment until Henry found a new ally, a young don (fellow or lecturer) at Cambridge University named Cranmer. He advised the King to collect opinions from learned men to aid his case. Henry loved the idea, seeking help throughout Europe from scholars, clerics, doctors, lawyers and even rabbis.

Many of these experts came out in favour of Henry's case. However, others found a problem, for moving from Leviticus to Deuteronomy it was written that "If brethren dwell together, and one of them dies and shall have no son, the wife of the deceased shall not be married abroad unto one not of his kin; her husband's brother shall go in unto her, and take her to him to wife ...". Now it was clear that the prohibition in Leviticus only applied to two living brothers; Henry's marriage to Catherine was valid, in fact the Bible had required it. In 1530, the Pope issued a bull (a papal decree to which a lead seal (*bulla*) was attached) prohibiting anyone from writing or speaking against the marriage. Henry's case was hopeless.

Then Henry found someone who would look for new ways to cast Catherine aside. This man was Thomas Cromwell, an ambitious young lawyer who had formerly been Wolsey's assistant. Cromwell used Parliament to pass laws attacking church rights, declaring that the Church's authority derived from the sovereignty of the King. Unable to countenance such a proposition, Sir Thomas More resigned as Chancellor.

A new urgency arose at the end of 1532 when, despite her stance of wife and queen or nothing, Anne became pregnant. Perhaps a promise of wife and queen was enough. Anyhow, a son was a possibility; he must not be illegitimate. In January 1533, Henry secretly married Anne Boleyn.

Later that year, Thomas Cranmer became Archbishop of Canterbury, and he dutifully declared that Henry and Catherine had never been man and wife and that Henry's marriage to Anne was valid. Next, Catherine's daughter, Mary, was declared illegitimate. The people did not approve. Nevertheless, the link with Rome was broken, although there was no desire to adopt any new religious beliefs or practices. It was to be the Roman Church without rule from Rome.

At last, in September 1533, Anne gave birth – to a girl, Princess Elizabeth. Henry did not even bother to attend the christening.

Now Henry wanted blood, despite the problem with Catherine having been resolved. Henry was declared head of the English Church, and everyone was required to acknowledge Henry's supremacy on oath. Many refused, and hundreds of priests, monks and bishops were executed and the same fate befell Sir Thomas More.

In 1536, Henry and Anne rejoiced when it was announced that Catherine had died. Strangely, she had made a will, something that was unlawful for a woman whose husband was still alive. It was Catherine's only implicit acknowledgement of the annulment, or perhaps she was unaware of the rule. Henry had waited for six years to be freed from Catherine; if he had waited another three years for her death, the breach with Rome would not have been necessary.

Catherine died after suffering stomach pains and nausea. Poison was suspected by many. If it was poison, probably the culprit was not Henry, it was Anne. After all, in the same year Anne's brother had tried, no doubt on her behalf, to poison another of Anne's rivals, Henry's illegitimate son, Henry Fitzroy. He survived only because he shared the bottle of poisoned wine with others.

On the day of Catherine's funeral, Henry celebrated by going jousting. He entered the 'lists' at Greenwich Palace; not some sort of document, but the name of the barrier enclosing the jousting arena. It was generally advisable to allow the King to win, although not too obviously. However, on this day Henry's opponent would not be trying to lose. The two men charged, and they clashed, simultaneously unhorsing each other. Henry's opponent's lance had caught Henry full and square in the midriff and knocked him flying from his horse. He crashed to the ground in full armour, and the horse (also wearing heavy armour) fell on top of him. Henry lay motionless, the crowd silent. At first it was feared that the King had been killed. It was over two hours before Henry regained consciousness. Was this a murder attempt? Was his opponent trying to kill Henry to avenge Catherine? If he was, he could hardly have done a better job. Mysteriously, despite the notoriety of the event, the name of Henry's opponent is not known – while all attention was focused on the injured Henry, his opponent had remounted and ridden away without removing his helmet. Henry survived, but many believe that his brain was damaged, as he suffered increasingly from insomnia, headaches and a terrible temper. He never jousted again, and his personality seemed to have changed.

News of the accident was brought to Anne. Within hours she went into premature labour and miscarried a boy. She blamed Henry, but he had no time for excuses. Henry had moved on; he was now interested in one of Anne's ladies-in-waiting, Jane Seymour. He told Cromwell to deal with the matter, adding that Anne was cursed, the evidence being a sixth finger on one hand and (never proved) a third breast. Cromwell's 'enquiries' produced a list of adulteries; and with confessions extracted by torture, Anne was duly found guilty of treason and beheaded, as were four of the alleged adulterers. The day before Anne's execution, Cranmer annulled her marriage to Henry, but without giving any reason. Perhaps it was because Anne's sister had been Henry's mistress. Now both princesses were illegitimate.

The moment Henry was told of Anne's death, he set off to see Jane Seymour; the next day they were betrothed and ten days later they were married. Henry had great hopes for a son. However, a son would take at least a few months to arrive, and Henry's brush with death had led him to think once more about the succession. So an Act was passed giving Henry the right to appoint his successor for so long as Jane had no children. It is likely that the person Henry had in mind was his illegitimate son Henry Fitzroy, who was now the Duke of Richmond and

Somerset. Clearly Henry was very fond of Fitzroy; although he did chastise Fitzroy and his friends when on a visit to France with Henry they had placed rotting corpses in the beds of the ladies of the French court to give them a fright.

If Fitzroy's succession was indeed Henry's plan, he failed yet again. Within weeks of the passing of the Act, Henry Fitzroy died of consumption.

Next, Henry and Cromwell saw to the dissolution of the monasteries and the acquisition of their wealth by the Crown and, upon a payment to Henry, by the nobility. There were uprisings, but nothing came of them except several hundred executions.

Henry was at last in control of both the country and the Church, he was rich and he had a new bride. All he needed was a son and heir. In October 1537, Henry was living in Esher to the south of London so as to escape the plague, having left the pregnant Jane at Hampton Court. Henry rushed back when he heard that Jane had given birth to a son. Everything seemed to be perfect. Unfortunately, the 'surgeons' who cut out the child, Prince Edward, took little care of Jane. Twelve days later she died of septicaemia. She was probably 29 years old, as 29 women walked behind the coffin at her funeral – one for each year of her life, as was the custom.

The disconsolate Henry continued with his attack on the Church, horrifying the Pope. In particular, the Pope was enraged when he learned of the confiscation of jewels and other valuables from the shrine of St Thomas Becket, and in December 1538 he excommunicated Henry. The breach was now final.

For his next move, Henry decided to deal with the remaining potential rivals to his new son as claimants to the throne. His attack was on the family of George Duke of Clarence (brother of Edward IV and Richard III). Henry VII had already executed George's son, the Earl of Warwick, so Henry turned to George's only surviving child, his daughter. He executed the 67-year-old Lady Margaret Pole Countess of Salisbury and her first son, Henry Pole[16], the Poles not to be confused with the de la Pole Yorkist claimants who were descendants of Clarence's sister, Elizabeth.

Lady Margaret's second son was in Italy; he was a cardinal who would be the Pope's agent in raising opposition to Henry. The third son was left to wander about Europe, having saved his life by giving Henry evidence of treason by the rest of his family; the fourth son was already dead. Cousins, friends and children were executed or imprisoned.[17]

Now a widower, it was time for Henry to look for a bride; one bringing a foreign alliance would be best. The artist Holbein was sent out on missions to paint portraits of prospective spouses, and his paintings hanging in galleries today are no more than medieval photographs for matchmaking. Cromwell recommended Anne of Cleves, a princess "of incomparable beauty". Henry accepted the recommendation, but he had been misled; the portrait was too flattering. When Anne arrived in England in January 1540, Henry was horrified at the sight of what he called "this Flanders mare".

However, Henry did not wish to offend his German allies, so the wedding took place – but not much else. Seven months later, Anne had confirmed the non-consummation of the marriage, and she retired to the English countryside where she spent the rest of her life; the divorce was finalised in July. Henry did not blame Holbein; the victim would be Cromwell, who was later executed.

Turning to his former source, Henry was now taken with one of Anne's ladies-in-waiting, 16-year-old Catherine Howard, niece of the Duke of Norfolk. She made herself very available,

---

16 Pole had some posthumous revenge when his great-grandson signed Charles I's death warrant.

17 If the royal line should have run through the Duke of Clarence (which it should have done if Edward IV or his children, in particular Elizabeth of York, were illegitimate) then despite the executions the line would have run through Lady Margaret Pole and then through her first son Henry's daughter Catherine so that Michael Abney-Hastings Earl of Loudoun would now be king. He is an avowed republican, living in Australia.

flirting with the aged king as she had already flirted with so many others. Within days, Henry had married Catherine. But this young girl married to a fat old man with legs covered in suppurating ulcers soon found numerous lovers. She was as promiscuous after her wedding as she had been before it. In early 1542, just like her cousin Anne Boleyn, Catherine was executed, several of her lovers having already gone to the block. As a precaution for the future, it was made a treasonable offence for an unchaste woman to marry the King without having first declared her unchastity.

It was time again for war. Before attacking France, their ally Scotland had to be controlled. The English attacked, and the Scots retaliated and were defeated. Henry's nephew, King James V of Scotland, who suffered from bouts of severe depression, died in total despair at what he thought was the end of the Stewart dynasty when his wife gave birth to a girl. He left the throne to his one-week-old daughter, Mary (later known as Mary Queen of Scots).

Next it was war with France. Henry made some territorial gains before peace was agreed. But the cost of the war had depleted the royal and national treasuries, and the king who had been one of the richest and most magnificent in Europe was now an invalid and virtually bankrupt.

If it was not war, it had to be marriage. Having taken an eighteen-month break, Henry returned to his domestic pastime, and in July 1543 he married for the sixth time. His new wife was Catherine Parr. She was 31 years old and had already been widowed twice. Henry would make her a widow for a third time, and then she would take a fourth husband. So, England's most married king married England's most married queen.

King Henry was now a complete wreck; often in pain, usually suffering a fever, always immobile. Henry had known that death was approaching, but his physicians could not give him a prognosis because to forecast the death of the king was – like so many other things – treason. It is possible that Henry in fact died of syphilis. However, his demands for wives were largely to have sons, not because of any heightened sexual appetite.

Perhaps in the end Henry was killed by three of his passions: jousting damaging his legs and his brain, food resulting in obesity and strokes, and women resulting in anxiety and possibly syphilis.

So died the king who had been desperate to create a family that would prolong the Tudor dynasty, in the process casting off two wives, killing two wives, bastardising two children, and never having grandchildren. Yet all his wives were part of Henry's family even before he married them; all of them descended from Edward I, just like Henry himself.

Death at the joust, the scene of the two attempts to kill him, would have spared Henry his grotesque old age, but it would have deprived him of his greatest claim to fame – the six wives.

****

HENRY VIII and his wives

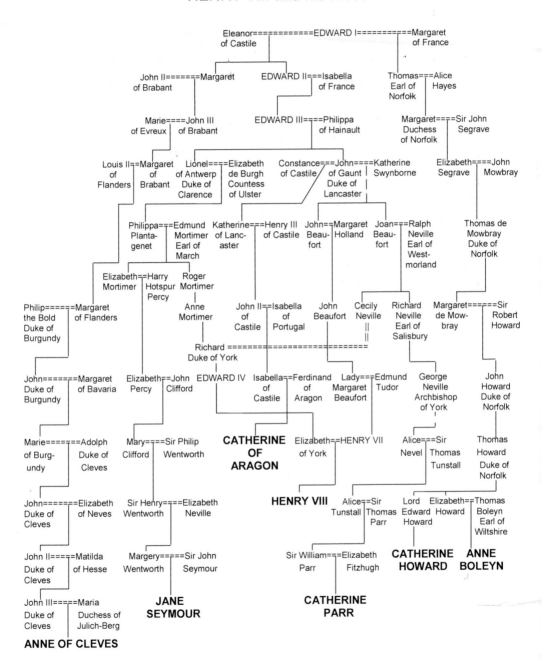

EDWARD VI

28 January 1547 – 6 July 1553

Apparently, Henry VIII had been so concerned to ensure a successful birth after all the disappointments that he ordered the physicians to deliver Jane's baby by Caesarean section. It resulted in the death of Queen Jane and the survival of a baby who became a sickly child.

In his will, Henry established a Regency Council of sixteen men to govern the country during his son's minority. But when Edward succeeded to the throne at the age of nine, his uncle, Edward Seymour, the brother of Queen Jane, took control and was appointed Lord Protector by the Council. He immediately granted himself the title of Duke of Somerset, and then he began the construction of his own palace in London: Somerset House.

It had been Henry's wish that Prince Edward should marry Mary Queen of Scots, so uniting England and Scotland. However, Mary's mother, the French Mary of Guise, would not agree to the marriage. In response, Somerset marched into Scotland with an army, and he defeated the Scots at the Battle of Pinkie, killing over 10,000 of the enemy. It did not help, because Mary Queen of Scots was smuggled out of the country and taken to France where she was betrothed to the Dauphin, whom she later married.

With his foreign policy in ruins, Somerset dealt with religious matters at home. It was in this reign that England became a Protestant country, adopting the beliefs of followers of the reaction against Catholic doctrines and practices, although much of the population remained Catholic. Somerset was a strident Protestant, keen to make compulsory changes in observance. The Mass, regarded by Protestants as idolatry, was prohibited, as was the use of Latin in churches. Chantries where Masses were said for the dead on receipt of payment were closed down, and their funds were confiscated. Much of the seized money was used to fund universities and to establish schools, and that is why there are now so many King Edward VI schools in England.

Only 13 years old, Edward joined the attack on Catholics, even summoning his 34-year-old half-sister Mary to court so that he could order her to cease Catholic observance. Hearing of this, Mary's cousin, King Charles V of Spain, threatened war, so the Council backed down and allowed Mary to continue attending Mass in private. When the Council overruled Edward, he burst into tears.

Then, Somerset's over-ambitious brother, Thomas, started to cause trouble. Six months after Henry VIII died, Thomas Seymour had married the King's widow, Catherine Parr, who had become one of the wealthiest women in the country. Within a year, Catherine died in childbirth, and Thomas inherited her entire estate. Now a rich man and Lord High Admiral, Thomas set his eyes on Princess Elizabeth. Maybe he thought that with Princess Mary being a Catholic, Elizabeth was only one step from the throne.

On 16th January 1549, Thomas Seymour, accompanied by two servants, travelled to Hampton Court Palace, arriving in the dead of night. Armed with pistols, they climbed over a wall and made their way across the Privy Garden. They broke open a door, and then crept along the corridors and up the staircases. Finding the King's living quarters, they headed straight for Edward's bedroom. All was dark, there was no one about. Perhaps the guards were absent, perhaps they were asleep. Seymour reached for the handle of the bedroom door. It was unlocked. Slowly and quietly, Seymour opened the door. It all seemed too easy.

Unluckily for Seymour, Edward had pet spaniels. One of the dogs stirred. It raced forward to challenge the intruders. Not recognising Thomas, the dog began to bark incessantly. Next, the dog made for Seymour's leg. The spaniel would not be shaken off, nor would it be silent. Panic took over as Seymour grasped his pistol and shot the dog. Guards came running and Seymour was arrested.

Seymour said that he had come to protect the King from a plot. It was unconvincing, and he was accused of attempting to kidnap the King. But why kidnap him? Certainly not for ransom. If it was to force some kind of deal, it was bound to end in Thomas's execution. Probably he wanted to kidnap and then kill Edward so that his prospective bride, Elizabeth, would become queen and he would become king.

Very likely the yapping dog thwarted the murder of the King. Thomas Seymour was convicted of treason and executed. His powerful brother could not save him.

Thomas Seymour

Religious change accelerated. Archbishop Cranmer produced a new compulsory prayer book, and paintings, stained glass windows and statues in churches were destroyed, only English could be used in prayer, and priests were allowed to marry.

In London, the changes were readily accepted. Elsewhere people were bemused; why was all this was being done, what did it mean? Worst of all was the situation in Devon and Cornwall. People there complained that they could not understand church services in English as most of them spoke only Cornish. In 1549, they took up arms, demanding the return of Latin. However, there would be no exceptions. Somerset sent an army to the West Country, and the slaughter of thousands followed by multiple hangings subdued the uprising.

Next there was trouble in East Anglia. This had nothing to do with religion. The problem was that landlords were enclosing their lands, evicting tenant farmers and replacing corn with sheep, and sheep needed fewer workers than crops. In July 1549, a rebel force seized Norwich, the country's second largest town. Somerset was sympathetic to their plight. He prohibited further enclosures and taxed the ownership of sheep. Having won concessions, the rebels wanted more.

The Council treated Somerset's leniency as weakness. They empowered John Dudley Earl of Warwick to deal with the rebellion. He set out for Norwich with an army of mainly foreign mercenaries, and they killed thousands of the rebels, hanging their leaders.

With the rebellion over, the discredited Somerset was sent to the Tower, and was later executed. Warwick, the new power in the country, gave himself the title of Duke of Northumberland. He then set about acquiring wealth, and he became the most hated man in England. Turning his attention to religion, Northumberland stepped up the rate of Protestant reform, and the new orthodoxy was strictly enforced.

Overall it was a difficult time for the English. The fighting against the Scots and the French went badly, with territory lost. Then the economy collapsed, crippled by the cost of the unsuccessful wars. The country was riven by dissent, hatred and fear.

King Edward's health had always been poor, and now it deteriorated. In 1552, he contracted smallpox and measles. In itself measles was not life-threatening, but the measles virus suppresses host immunity to tuberculosis (called consumption in those times), and eventually the incessant coughing up of blood started.

Northumberland was desperate. If Edward died, the next in line was his half-sister Mary, a staunch Catholic. Northumberland would be unlikely to escape with his life. He had to find a Protestant successor, preferably one he could control.

Mary Tudor was Henry VIII's younger sister, and she had a 15-year-old granddaughter, Jane, who was a Protestant. Northumberland quickly arranged for his fifth son, Lord Guilford Dudley, to marry Jane Grey. Then he instructed King Edward to sign a will (although legally too young to do so) declaring that as his half-sisters were bastards, they were excluded from the succession, and his cousin Frances having waived her rights, her daughter, Lady Jane Grey, was his heir.

Needing more time to further his plans, Northumberland put Edward in the care of an 'expert'. The arsenic she administered brought temporary relief and enabled Edward to sleep, but it began to poison the King. Edward's legs and arms swelled, his skin darkened, his fingers and toes became gangrenous, his hair and his nails fell out, and he coughed incessantly. All because his dog had saved him from being murdered.

On 6th July 1554, Edward died in agony. Killed as a consequence of disease inherited from Henry VIII or poisoned by arsenic? Either way, the end could not come too soon.

****

JANE GREY

10 July 1553 – 19 July 1553

Why did Northumberland select Jane Grey for Queen? Edward VI had no children, so his siblings were next in line. He was survived by two half-sisters, Mary and Elizabeth. Mary was a Catholic; Northumberland could exclude her because she had been declared illegitimate. Elizabeth was a Protestant, but she would not be easy to control; anyway she too had been declared illegitimate, so Northumberland could exclude her as well.

It was therefore necessary to go back one generation to Henry VIII and look for a successor among his siblings who survived infancy and their issue. The only brother, Arthur, had died childless in 1508. Next came Henry's sisters. The older sister, Margaret, had married King James IV of Scotland. She had died in 1541, so her children were next in line. Three of her sons had died young, the fourth had become King James V of Scotland; but he had died in 1542. Next came his children: a son who died young, and a daughter, Mary Queen of Scots. So, accepting the illegitimacy of Mary and Elizabeth, it was Mary Queen of Scots who was clearly entitled to be queen. But Mary Queen of Scots was a Catholic, was living in France and was betrothed to the Dauphin. The English would never accept the King and Queen of France as their rulers, so it was easy to exclude Mary.

DESCENDANTS OF HENRY VII
– showing in red those alive on the death of Edward VI

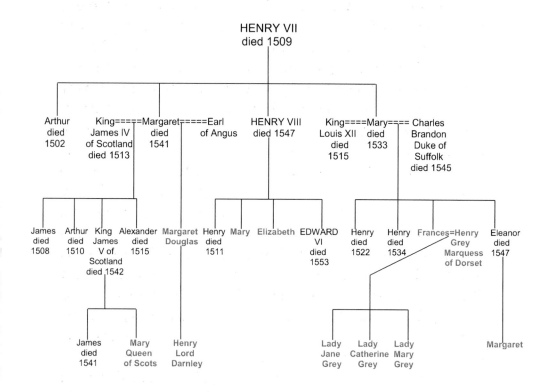

After her husband King James IV had died, Margaret Tudor (Henry's sister) had married the Earl of Angus, and they had a daughter, Margaret Douglas, who lived at the English court. She was a Catholic, so she was unacceptable to Northumberland. Fortunately for him, Margaret Douglas was also inappropriate for the English because of her misalliances (affairs). First she had a misalliance with Anne Boleyn's uncle, Lord Thomas Howard. They were both sent to the Tower. Howard was sentenced to death, but died before his execution. Margaret was forgiven, but then she had a misalliance with Howard's nephew, Sir Charles Howard, the brother of the Queen. Margaret Douglas was dismissed from court. So she could be excluded by Northumberland, particularly as Henry VIII had declared her illegitimate on the spurious grounds that her mother Margaret Tudor's marriage to the Earl of Angus was unlawful[18]. The next in line was Margaret Douglas's son (she had later married the Earl of Lennox), but Henry Lord Darnley was only seven years old and was the son of the leading Catholic Scottish noble, who had sworn to guard the Grand Alliance of Scotland and France against England. So, Darnley could easily be excluded as well.

Then came Henry VIII's younger sister, Mary. She had married King Louis XII of France, who had died before they had any children. Mary later married Charles Brandon, Duke of Suffolk. Brandon had been brought up as a favourite at the court of King Henry VII, as his father was Henry's standard-bearer who had been killed by King Richard III at the Battle of Bosworth.

Mary had died in 1533, and her sons had died childless. So next came Mary's older daughter, Frances. She had married Henry Grey, Marquess of Dorset (the great-grandson of Elizabeth Woodville and her first husband, Sir John Grey). They had three daughters: Jane, Catherine and Mary. Therefore, accepting the illegitimacy or unsuitability of Princess Mary,

---

18 Unwilling on principle to accept the divorce granted by the Pope, but wishing to free Margaret from the faithless Angus, Henry relied on Margaret's earlier desperate claim that James IV (whose body was not found after Flodden) may have been alive when she married Angus.

Princess Elizabeth, Mary Queen of Scots, and Margaret Douglas and her son, it was Frances Brandon who was entitled to the crown. She waived her rights in favour of her oldest daughter, Jane, whom she had sent away at the age of nine to be brought up by Catherine Parr. Most importantly for Northumberland, Jane was Protestant and single; it meant that she was available to marry Northumberland's son, who would become king. Jane married Lord Guilford Dudley on 21st May 1553.

In truth, Jane was seventh in line, and almost everyone knew that Princess Mary was the rightful heir; her illegitimacy was not genuine.

Conscious of the widespread support for Mary, Northumberland suppressed the news of the King's death while he tried to capture her. However, Mary was warned of his plans, and she escaped to Framlingham Castle in Norfolk, the stronghold of the Catholic Howard family. With Mary out of the way, Northumberland had his 16-year-old daughter-in-law proclaimed queen.

Now everything went wrong for Northumberland. First he told Jane to declare his son, Guilford Dudley, the king; but Jane refused, regarding Guilford as an arrogant bully. Next, Mary advanced on London with her forces, and Northumberland raced to confront her. Northumberland was hugely outnumbered, and in his absence the Council, accepting the inevitable, declared Mary the queen.

Northumberland surrendered. He was imprisoned, tried, convicted of treason and executed. After a reign of just nine days, Jane and her husband were sent to the Tower, never to meet again. They were convicted of treason, but Queen Mary would not consent to their execution.

Some months later, plans were being made for Mary to marry Philip, the only son of King Charles V of Spain. There was widespread opposition to the marriage, and this led to a rebellion that was only narrowly defeated. The rebellion had not been in Jane's name and she took no part in it, but one of its leaders was Jane's father, the Duke of Suffolk. Hundreds of the rebels were executed, Suffolk included.

Now all prominent Protestants were in danger. When she refused to accede to Mary's demand to convert to Catholicism, Jane's fate was sealed. Mary ordered Jane's execution. On 12th February 1554, Jane watched from a window as her husband was led away. A few hours later, Jane was standing at the same window as the horse-drawn cart returned with her husband's body, the attendants carrying away the headless corpse and the head wrapped in cloth.

Jane had already been told that she was to be executed that day. She had dressed for the occasion, and had prepared herself. The guards called at her door, and Jane was led to the scaffold that had been erected on the green by the White Tower. She walked calmly to her place of execution, all the time reading from a book of prayers. Having climbed to the scaffold platform, she stepped forward to address the few people who had been allowed to attend.

"Good people, I am come hither to die, and by a law I am condemned to the same," she announced in a firm but nervous voice. "The fact, indeed, against the Queen's highness was unlawful," she continued, "and the consenting thereunto by me. But touching the procurement and desire thereof by me or on my behalf, I do wash my hands thereof in innocency…"

She knelt down and read Psalm 51, starting with the words, "Have mercy on me God … forget that I did not obey You." When she had finished, she rose to her feet and gave her gloves and handkerchief to her lady-in-waiting, and her prayer-book to a soldier. It was the executioner's job to blindfold Jane, but she stopped him and took the piece of white cloth in her hands. The executioner knelt before Jane and asked for her forgiveness, which she gave.

Then he told her to step forward, and she turned white as she saw the block. Jane said to the executioner, "I pray you to despatch me quickly." She covered her eyes with the blindfold and tied a knot at the back of her head. Jane had prepared for this moment, determined to reach her end with dignity. But as Jane was about to kneel down and place her head on the block, panic took over as she became disorientated. She cried out, "What shall I do? Where is it?"

One of the attendants took hold of Jane's arm and guided her; then he told her to kneel. As she rested her head on the wooden block, she stretched her arms forward and said quietly, "Lord, into Thy hands I commend my spirit."

The axe was raised, and immediately came down. Nine days a queen, her death at the age of sixteen was the only memorable result. Killed by order of Queen Mary; but responsibility for Jane's death lay firmly with her father-in-law and her father – they as good as murdered her.

The execution of Jane Grey

****

MARY I

19 July 1553 – 17 November 1558

Mary came to the throne with the support of the vast majority of the population. Even Protestants, with some exceptions, supported her as the rightful heir almost as a matter of principle – they would come to regret it.

Queen Mary's maternal grandparents were Ferdinand of Aragon and Isabella of Castile, who united their kingdoms to become King and Queen of Spain. They were enthusiastic supporters of the Inquisition, the persecutors and murderers of thousands of Muslims and Jews. In England there were no Muslims or Jews; Mary's victims would be the Protestants.

Her hatred of Protestants began early in life, as she grew up to believe that anyone who did not share her strict Catholic faith must be killed, preferably burned alive. When Henry VIII attacked the authority of the Pope, the Protestants sided with him. Nevertheless, Henry continued to burn Protestants as heretics, also burning Catholics who would not deny the supremacy of the Pope.

For Mary it was different, as she was not motivated by anger. In her case it was pure hatred, and that hatred was enflamed by the annulment of her mother's marriage and the declaration of her own illegitimacy.

After Henry's decision to seek the annulment, Mary was separated from her mother, and later forbidden even to write to her. Then Mary was forced to give her jewellery to Anne Boleyn, and ordered to give precedence to Anne Boleyn's daughter, Elizabeth, whom she was required to serve as lady-in-waiting. Everything conspired to turn Mary into an even more vengeful and nasty person.

Her first brush with death came in 1535. Henry and Parliament required everyone to swear the Oath of Succession recognising Anne Boleyn's children as the heirs to the Crown, and implicitly that Mary was illegitimate. In addition, all those taking public or church office had to swear the Oath of Supremacy acknowledging that Henry was the supreme head of the Church, and implicitly that the Pope had no authority in England. Refusal to swear the oaths was treason, and that meant death.

Catherine of Aragon and Mary had agreed that they would not swear any such oath, and they fully expected to be executed. However, the Holy Roman Emperor Charles V was the son of Catherine's sister and therefore Mary's cousin. He was also King of Spain and Naples, Archduke of Austria and Duke of Burgundy. Charles was England's natural ally against the French, and being Duke of Burgundy he ruled the Netherlands, which was the chief market for English wool. As a result, neither Catherine nor Mary was asked to take any oath.

Mary's situation improved with the death of her mother and the execution of Anne Boleyn. Cranmer had annulled Anne's marriage to Henry, so Elizabeth was now illegitimate and it was no longer necessary to protect her from Mary's claims.

At Mary's request, the Spanish ambassador sought an audience with Thomas Cromwell, the man with the greatest influence over the King. The ambassador asked Cromwell to speak to Henry, explaining that Mary wanted to be a faithful daughter and wished to return to court. Henry eventually agreed, but only on condition that Mary first signed a document repudiating the Pope's supremacy and admitting that her mother's marriage had been unlawful. Mary had fallen into a trap. Would she betray her mother?

A group of councillors travelled to see Mary with the document. She refused to sign it. The councillors were taken aback. They argued with Mary, they threatened her; but still she would not sign. As the councillors returned to court, they must have feared the effect of the King's temper on messengers bringing unwelcome news. They were right about the temper, Henry flew into a rage. This time the messengers were spared; Henry's anger was directed at Mary.

Treason, disloyalty, refusal to obey the King; any of them would have been enough. Henry knew only one way to deal with such behaviour – he sent Mary to the Tower. That was almost as good as a sentence of death, it only needed one more explosion of the royal temper.

The members of the Council were horrified; they feared war with the Emperor. Naturally, they did not dare to argue with Henry. Cranmer had more courage than the others, and he agreed to speak to the King. Diplomatically, Cranmer did not question Henry's decision or pass on the Council's views, he merely asked the King if Mary could be given a second chance to sign, and the exasperated Henry agreed.

Henry was furious with Cromwell for having suggested the reconciliation, and Cromwell wrote to Mary begging her to sign, otherwise both of them would be executed. The Spanish ambassador also urged Mary to sign, even if she was insincere. In the end Mary signed, at the same time writing to the Emperor asking him to obtain a dispensation for her from the Pope, allowing her to break her word. Six months later, Mary was back at court. Yet she would hardly have been nearer to death if the axe had been raised above her neck.

When her half-brother, Edward, succeeded to the throne, Mary retired to the countryside to avoid compliance with the new Protestant practices and prohibition of the Mass (the central act of Catholic worship). Mary's insistence on continuing to celebrate Mass led to imprisonment for her servants, but Mary herself was not touched.

In later years, Mary would not reciprocate such merciful conduct to Protestants. She regarded her privilege not as a favour, but as a message from God that she was right and therefore all the more reason to burn the heretic Protestants.

After Edward VI's death, the support of the people enabled Mary to overcome the Duke of Northumberland and his daughter-in-law, Lady Jane Grey. Mary took the throne thirteen days after Edward's death, Jane Grey's father proclaiming Mary as queen to the joy of all Londoners.

Now that she was queen, an early consideration for Mary was the succession, and that meant marriage. As a princess, there had been several possibilities, but none had proceeded because of her father's refusal to provide a large dowry, Mary's reluctance and the fact that she had been declared illegitimate. Soon to be formally legitimised, and now a wealthy woman, she was, however, 37 years old and no great beauty. Fortunately, Emperor Charles's son Prince Philip of Spain was available, as his wife (and cousin on both sides) had died shortly after giving birth to a deformed son (inbreeding meant that Philip had only six great-great-grandparents instead of the usual sixteen). Mary had no interest in a man eleven years younger than her, nor indeed in any man as she found the idea of sex abhorrent. But despite her feelings, she was prepared to do her duty, and she was eager to provide an alternative successor to her Protestant half-sister, Elizabeth.

First, Mary wanted to deal with religion. Edward's anti-Catholic laws were still in force, and Protestant preachers were taking full advantage. So Mary started to arrest them. Next, Protestant refugees from the Continent were expelled from England. Mary added her own particular piece of nastiness by sending the Emperor details of the vessels on which the refugees would be returning, so that they could be seized immediately on disembarking with everything that was bound to follow.

All married priests were sacked, and those who had been monks were ordered to separate from their wives and children and were prohibited from ever seeing them again. Then the Mass was restored, and it was made illegal to attend a Protestant service.

Much of this took place without trouble as the English hated foreigners even if they were of the same faith, and few people accepted the notion of married priests. The only issue was Mary's proposed marriage; the English did not want a Spanish king.

In January 1554, a Protestant rebellion broke out. The plan was for simultaneous uprisings in Kent led by Sir Thomas Wyatt, in Wales led by Sir James Croft, in Devon led by Sir Peter Carew and in the Midlands led by Jane Grey's father, the Duke of Suffolk. They were all to march on London. Their ambition was never made clear; certainly to prevent the Spanish marriage, probably to depose Mary, perhaps to kill her. Wyatt moved first, and his supporters took to the street in Maidstone. The Duke of Norfolk was sent with a force to confront them. When Norfolk's men reached Rochester and saw the size of Wyatt's army, most of them joined him and the others retreated.

Within a week the rebel army was at Southwark, on the south bank of the Thames. Mary was advised to flee, but she stood fast. At the Guildhall she addressed the aldermen, demanding support in a war against traitors. It led to 20,000 men taking up arms to defend Mary against Wyatt and his 7,000 supporters.

Wyatt's army advanced and they crossed the Thames during the night, making their way to the Palace of Westminster. Killing the Queen would bring immediate victory, end the threat of a Spanish king and make further bloodshed unnecessary. In the early hours of the morning Wyatt's forces attacked the Palace, shooting arrows at the windows. If enough arrows were fired, perhaps a lucky shot would kill the Queen. Mary was awoken and warned of the likelihood that the Palace would be stormed. She hurried to the main chamber where she found the ladies of the court crying hysterically as arrows clattered against the outside walls, smashing the windows and then flying into the room; but despite the efforts of the rebels, Mary was not harmed.

Courtiers advised Mary to leave by a secret passage and escape in a boat, for to stay meant certain death. Again, she refused to run. Her response was prayer. In the end, Wyatt's men made no attempt to breach the walls, completely overestimating the strength of the forces in the Palace. They moved on and marched to the City, where they were surrounded by Mary's troops. Wyatt and his men surrendered without a fight. All the other uprisings failed for lack of support. The Duke of Suffolk hurried to his estates. He was found hiding in a tree, and was taken to join Wyatt in the Tower.

Thomas Wyatt

Mary had survived. Now she would wield the axe and light the flame, promising to "strike terror into all those who ventured to do evil"; that is, all who were not orthodox Catholics.

Within days, Jane Grey and her husband had been executed for treason, as were Wyatt and Suffolk. Cranmer was not to be executed for treason, Mary wanted to have him convicted of heresy – that would mean burning. However, Henry's Heresy Act had been revoked in Edward's reign, so Cranmer would have to wait for new legislation.

Hundreds were put to death, and corpses were displayed throughout London. Sir Nicholas Throgmorton, the man who had warned Mary of her impending arrest by Northumberland, was charged with treason for complicity in Wyatt's rebellion. He was acquitted, so Mary ordered his imprisonment together with all members of the jury.

Finally, in July 1554, Mary married Philip of Spain. Now it was time to reinstate the Pope's authority in England. The legate sent by the Vatican was Cardinal Pole, son of the aged Countess of Salisbury who had been executed by Henry VIII. Pole was a grandson of George Duke of Clarence, the executed brother of Edward IV and Richard III. Cardinal Pole now advised Mary and Parliament in the name of the Pope. So, one of the senior survivors of the House of York became the most powerful man in England.

The Act of Supremacy was repealed and a new Heresy Act was passed, as was an Act for the Burning of Heretics. Now the burning could begin, supervised by the Lord Chancellor Bishop Gardiner and Cardinal Pole, who would be the last Catholic Archbishop of Canterbury. However, the most vigorous burner was Mary herself. All Protestant bishops were burned, including Latimer, Ridley and Cranmer. The fact that Cranmer had saved Mary's life did not help him; Mary would not even read his letter professing that he had converted to Catholicism and pleading for mercy. She said it was a sin to read a letter written by a heretic.

Generally, heretics were burned in public on market days. Many were preachers, others had read the English Bible; but the most common heresy was denial of transubstantiation – the Catholic belief that the bread and wine used at communion become the body and blood of Christ. Friends of heretics were still allowed to tie small bags of gunpowder around the condemned person's neck so that his or her head might be blown off rather than suffer the agonising burning process, but Mary ended the policy of pardoning heretics who recanted and promised to be good Catholics. For her, it was too late.

Mary apart, an heir was a more important issue than Mass. In late 1554, Mary informed the Council that she was pregnant, in April 1555 it was announced that a son had been born, later that a baby was due. But it was all wishful thinking. Then, in October 1555, Charles V abdicated, and Mary's husband Philip became King of Spain. Philip left for his kingdom. Mary realised that she would never produce an heir and that Elizabeth would succeed to the throne.

Two years later, Philip returned briefly to England in order to prepare for a Spanish/English invasion of France. For England, the only meaningful outcome was the loss of Calais after 200 years. It was the last English territory on the Continent.

In the spring of 1558, Mary became seriously ill with dropsy (the accumulation of fluid below the skin or in a bodily cavity), and it may have been such a swelling that had led her to believe that she was pregnant. Alternatively, she may have been suffering from a tumour. Mary became extremely depressed; Philip was gone, Calais had been lost, despite the burnings there were more heretics than ever, she would never have a child, and Protestant Elizabeth would succeed her. It had all gone horribly wrong. Then, on 17th November, Mary died. The date was celebrated in England for hundreds of years.

One of the most popular English sovereigns on her accession, she became the most hated. Mary is the only English monarch not to be commemorated with a statue; rather, she is remembered as Bloody Mary. It would have been so much better if Henry had gone through with Mary's execution, or if one of the arrows shot by Wyatt's forces had found its intended victim. Better not just for the Protestants, but for the English Catholics who would suffer centuries of persecution, first inspired by the desire to avenge Mary's burnings.

****

ELIZABETH I

17 November 1558 – 24 March 1603

Wyatt's Revolt had threatened the lives of three queens. It was very likely the rebels' intention to kill Mary, it resulted in the execution of Lady Jane Grey, and it nearly sent Elizabeth to the block.

As soon as the rebellion started, Mary assumed that the rebels were planning to replace her with Elizabeth, so Mary ordered Elizabeth to come to London where she could be closely watched. However, Elizabeth was unwilling to be a prisoner; so she declined, claiming that she was too ill to travel. After the rebellion was over, Mary sent soldiers to bring her half-sister to London.

Certainly some of the rebel leaders had visited Elizabeth, certainly they had written to her; but Elizabeth had wisely always replied orally, never in writing. Under torture Wyatt implicated Elizabeth, then on the scaffold he spoke publicly denying her involvement. Despite that denial, Mary was convinced of Elizabeth's treason, and she sent Elizabeth to the Tower.

For two months Elizabeth remained in prison while Mary tried to summon up the courage to put her on trial. But all the witnesses had already been executed, and Mary had seen a jury acquit Throgmorton. Even worse, Elizabeth was hugely popular in the country, a trial would risk further rebellion. Elizabeth's life lay in the balance. Finally, Mary gave up. She had come as close as she dared to killing her half-sister. Elizabeth was sent to Woodstock Palace to live under house arrest. When Mary believed that she was pregnant and would be producing an heir, Elizabeth was allowed to return to court.

Later it became clear that Mary would never have a child, and on the urging of Philip, Mary accepted that she had no choice and she named Elizabeth as her successor. The next in line after Elizabeth was Mary Queen of Scots, and she was betrothed to the Dauphin. If she became Queen of England, then Philip's enemy the King of France would be King of England in Philip's place. Fanatical Catholic though he was, Philip preferred an English Protestant monarch to a French Catholic one.

Elizabeth's accession was widely welcomed. The death of Bloody Mary meant no more Spanish influence, no more burnings of Protestants, and no more Cardinal Pole – the man who had even ordered the exhumation of heretics so that their corpses could be publicly burned. He died a few hours after Mary, and the nation rejoiced.

Religion was dealt with first. England returned to Protestantism; church attendance became compulsory, Catholic practices were banned and the Pope's authority in England was once more abolished. The new order was not as severe as it had been under Edward, Catholics were only burned if they threatened Elizabeth's throne. Some Protestants, like the Calvinists, were also proscribed as Elizabeth did not want religious extremists of any persuasion.

As with Mary, the second matter to be considered was marriage and an heir. Suitors or their representatives came from foreign courts, but probably Elizabeth had already decided that she would never marry a foreigner, perhaps that she would never marry anyone. Quite possibly she had been put off the idea by Thomas Seymour, who had euphemistically been accused of forcing his attentions on Elizabeth when she was a ward of his wife, ex-Queen Catherine Parr. She sent Elizabeth to live elsewhere when she caught her in an embrace with Seymour. However, it is more likely that Elizabeth's reluctance to marry was simply because she was unwilling to share power.

Nevertheless, for a time there seemed to be possibilities for several Englishmen. The front-runner was Lord Robert Dudley, fourth son of the Duke of Northumberland who had been executed by Mary for putting Jane Grey forward as queen. Dudley's hopes were hindered by the fact that he was already married. Then, in late 1560, Dudley's wife was found dead with a broken neck at the foot of the stairs at their home. It was apparently an accident, she had been seriously ill. But there was too much talk, and Dudley had to leave court. He would soon be back, later created Earl of Leicester, and there was plenty of flirting, but marriage was no longer an option.

In 1562, Elizabeth contracted smallpox and became gravely ill. She recovered, although her face was pitted with scars, requiring heavy make-up. Parliament, to the Queen's annoyance, was now more anxious than ever that she should marry and provide an heir.

Without a new heir, there were six leading claimants. The situation had changed little from the time of Lady Jane Grey. Again, the first route was through Henry VIII's older sister, Margaret Tudor. Her marriage to James IV of Scotland produced a son, James V, who died leaving a daughter, Mary. So Mary Queen of Scots was clearly the first in line if Elizabeth died. Mary had married the Dauphin, and on his accession she became Queen of France. Francis II died 17 months later at the age of 16, and Mary returned to Scotland, then ruled by a council of Protestant lords.

Margaret Tudor's second marriage was to the Earl of Angus. Their daughter was Margaret Douglas, and she was therefore second in line. Margaret Douglas had married Matthew

Stewart Earl of Lennox, and their sons, Henry Lord Darnley and Charles, were third and fourth in line.

These claimants were all Catholics. The Protestant claimants were the descendants of Henry VIII's younger sister, Mary. Her older daughter Frances Brandon had died in 1559, so this would have led to Frances's oldest daughter, Lady Jane Grey, being a genuine potential successor. With Jane's execution, her sisters Catherine and Mary were fifth and sixth in line. Elizabeth did not welcome such a threat, so she kept Catherine and Mary at court under her close watch. Then both sisters married without Elizabeth's permission; it was the only way, because the Queen would never consent to the Grey sisters getting married. Catherine 'married' the son of the former Protector, the Duke of Somerset. They were both sent to the Tower, and as there was no documentary proof of their marriage, their sons were declared illegitimate. Mary Grey married the son of a servant; they were parted, and she was placed under house arrest until her husband died eight years later. Elizabeth had her way; the Grey sisters would never produce legitimate heirs.

In July 1565 Mary Queen of Scots married her cousin, Henry Stewart Lord Darnley. Before long, Mary discovered that Darnley was a drunkard and a violent bully. She took up with her Italian secretary David Rizzio. Darnley would not put up with that, and with assistance from some colleagues he murdered Rizzio in Mary's presence.

Three months later, Mary Queen of Scots gave birth to a son, James Stuart. Mary used the spelling of the surname she had adopted during her time in France so that it would be pronounced properly by the French. They kept pronouncing Stewart as 'ste – wart'.

Mary soon found a replacement for Rizzio; it was the Earl of Bothwell. He dealt with Darnley. Having survived the blowing up of the house where he was living, Darnley was found strangled in the garden. Now Mary married Bothwell, but the Scottish lords had had enough of her. They forced Mary to abdicate, and her 13-month-old son was crowned

King James VI of Scotland, to be brought up as a Protestant. Mary was imprisoned. She escaped eight months later and fled to England, where she was held in Bolton Castle.

Mary's presence in England had a destabilising effect. Catholic lords could see a way to topple Elizabeth, marry Mary and take power. They would somehow have to deal with Mary's husband, Bothwell (who lived until 1578, when he died insane in a Danish prison where he had been chained to a pillar for ten years). Perhaps the marriage could have been declared a nullity as it had been performed according to Protestant rites.

The greatest threat to Elizabeth came from the North, still controlled by the Percys and the Nevilles, the Catholic Earls of Northumberland and Westmorland. They planned to start an insurrection and invite the King of Spain to send an army to aid them. Westmorland's brother-in-law, Thomas Howard Duke of Norfolk, would marry Mary, and Elizabeth could be deposed and in all likelihood executed.

When the earls gathered their forces, Elizabeth immediately arranged for Mary Queen of Scots to be brought further south to Coventry. The rebels set out for London, but on learning that Elizabeth's army was approaching, they took fright and retreated. With the onset of a severe winter, many of the earls' soldiers deserted, and the leaders fled to Scotland. A force led by Leonard Dacre of the third major northern family did engage Elizabeth's army, but he was heavily defeated.

As a result, the centuries-old power of the Nevilles and the Percys in the north of England was ended, their lands being confiscated and redistributed. About 750 of the earls' supporters were executed, and anti-Catholic legislation that would stand for over 200 years was enacted.

Norfolk was taken to the Tower, but he was the most senior English noble and her second cousin, so Elizabeth spared him and sent him to live in the country under house arrest. Yet he was still able to conspire with a Florentine banker called Roberto di Ridolfi to devise another plot, supported by the Pope and Philip, to rescue Mary Queen of Scots with the aid of a Spanish army that would land at Harwich and unite with Norfolk's forces. The combined armies were to march to London and assassinate Elizabeth, Norfolk would marry Mary and she would take the throne.

It was all so straightforward. But the plot was discovered; Ridolfi's messenger was seized, and he revealed all under torture. Ridolfi was fortunate enough to be in Paris at the time, and he was able to return to Florence. Norfolk's luck had run out. This time there would be no leniency; he was beheaded. Yet despite pressure from Parliament, Elizabeth could not bring herself to have Mary executed – she was a queen, and queens were appointed by God.

Throughout these years, the main threat was from Spain. Philip had conquered Portugal, so giving Spain command of the seas, he was acquiring vast territories in the New World and beyond (including the Philippines – named after him), and he still controlled the Netherlands. The only challenge to Spanish supremacy was Francis Drake's constant plundering of Philip's treasure-laden vessels returning from the Americas.

Mary Queen of Scots was a more immediate problem, and the longer Elizabeth failed to marry and produce an heir, the more dangerous a problem Mary became. As a Catholic, Mary was championed by the Pope, who absolved Catholics from allegiance to Elizabeth and declared that anyone who assassinated her would go to heaven where treasure would be awaiting him. This turned all Catholics into potential traitors.

It now became urgent to root out actual and potential plotters. As a result, a nationwide spying and intelligence network far ahead of its time was developed by Sir Francis Walsingham, who had already uncovered the Ridolfi Plot. Some did not need spies to catch them. In 1583, John Somerville boasted that he was going to shoot Elizabeth with a pistol and parade the streets with her severed head at the top of a pole. He was arrested, and was later found hanged in his cell. Then Francis Throckmorton devised a scheme under which Mary's French cousin, the Duke of Guise, would invade with an army, capture and execute Elizabeth and set Mary on the throne. The plot was discovered by Walsingham's men, and it all came to nothing save for Throckmorton's execution.

A Welsh doctor, William Parry, became involved with Catholic conspirators when he was sent abroad to spy on them. He revealed everything to Elizabeth, and she rewarded him with a pension and a seat in Parliament. Parry then suggested to Sir Edmund Neville that they should ride up alongside the Queen's coach and shoot her. Probably he wanted to create another plot so that he could again disclose the plan to Elizabeth and obtain a further reward. He moved too slowly; Neville told Walsingham first, and Parry was hanged.

Flushed with success, Walsingham's spies and double-agents kept busy. A Catholic named Gilbert Gifford returned from exile in France, and when he was searched he was found to be carrying a letter of introduction to Mary. Faced with the alternative of death, he agreed to become Walsingham's man. As instructed, Gifford made contact with the French ambassador and told him that he could arrange for correspondence with Mary to be smuggled in and out of her castle prison in beer barrels. The ambassador fell for it, and the correspondence started. Walsingham allowed the correspondence to continue unobstructed for seven months until at last he intercepted a letter to Mary from Anthony Babington, who became devoted to Mary when he was a page in the service of her former custodian, the Earl of Shrewsbury. The letter set out details of a scheme to assassinate Elizabeth and put Mary on the throne.

"We ... will undertake the delivery of your royal persons from the hands of your enemies ... For the despatch of the usurper ... six noble gentlemen, who, for the zeal they have for the Catholic cause ... will undertake that trajical execution."

Then a letter arrived from Spain confirming that assistance was coming from Philip, whose forces would invade England. Still Walsingham did not act; he wanted more. He allowed the letters to be delivered after having been copied. Walsingham was waiting to see if there was a reply from Mary.

And eventually there was. Mary wrote to Babington giving her approval and advising him how to proceed.

> "When all is ready, the six gentlemen must be set to work, and ... when it is accomplished, I maybe in some way got away from here ... then we will await foreign assistance."

After 18 years of imprisonment, Mary had in effect signed her own death warrant. Yet the crafty Walsingham still held back. He arranged for Mary's letter to be returned to the beer barrel, but only after a sentence was added in Mary's handwriting, and that sentence contained a request asking Babington for the names of his associates. Over-excited at the development of his plot, he duly obliged. Now Walsingham acted. Mary was moved to Fotheringhay Castle in Northamptonshire, and the conspirators were seized and executed. Even though she was not English, Mary was convicted of treason. Yet despite more pressure from Parliament, Elizabeth still hesitated to allow the execution of a queen. Then, after weeks of dithering, Elizabeth found a way to proceed and deny responsibility. She signed the execution warrant, saying that the seal should not be affixed without her further instruction. Fearing that the further instruction would never be given, or perhaps they received a nod and a wink, the Council proceeded.

It was a unique event; a queen executing a queen, a monarch executing her heir. However, it was not without elements of black farce. With Mary's head on the block, the executioner swung the axe down, but he missed and struck her on the back of the head. The second attempt nearly cut Mary's head off; a third effort completed the job. As was the custom, the executioner took hold of the severed head by the hair to hold it up to the onlookers, shouting out, "Behold the head of a traitor!". Unfortunately, Mary was wearing a wig, so the executioner held up the wig as the grey-haired head rolled on the floor. Even then it was not over. All of a sudden, from under Mary's petticoat her Skye terrier ran out and sat obediently beside his mistress' head.

Next there was trouble in Europe. With the Spanish having occupied Brussels and Antwerp, the Dutch turned to England for help. An army under the leadership of the Earl of Leicester was despatched, but he was unsuccessful.

Antwerp (the second largest town in Northern Europe) was the centre of all international trade, and it had therefore been England's main trading port with the world. Now it was closed to English merchants, as was Lisbon and its spice market. So the English were forced to trade directly with distant countries. It was the best thing that ever happened. Trade with Russia (formalised in a treaty between Bloody Mary and Ivan the Terrible) had begun in the previous reign. Now the Barbary Company started to trade with West Africa, the Levant Company with the Ottoman Empire, and William Adams journeyed to Japan, the beginnings of the Dutch East India Company. With the benefit of the crafts of the thousands of Huguenot, Dutch and Walloon refugees, England's arms stretched out to the world. London became a major international port, and the country prospered.

After the Dutch intervention, the execution of Mary Queen of Scots and Drake's attacks on Spanish ships, war with Spain could not be far off. In 1587, Philip decided on invasion. With their new-found confidence, the English would not sit back and wait to be attacked. Drake led a violent assault on Cadiz, sinking 40 Spanish ships, pounding fortresses and destroying supplies. As a result, Philip was forced to postpone the invasion. The delay saw the death of the Admiral of the armada. His replacement was the Duke of Medina Sidonia, a man with absolutely no naval experience.

At last, on 12th July 1588 the *Armada Invencible* (the Invincible Navy) set sail with 130 ships, 8,000 sailors and 18,000 soldiers. Two weeks later, the armada anchored off Calais. Then, before the 30,000 Spanish troops waiting on the coast could board the vessels, the English sent fire-ships to drift blazing into the armada. The only way for the Spanish to avoid the fire-ships was to set out to sea. They had to move quickly, so rather than slowly raising their anchors, the Spaniards cut the anchor cables and set off. The English fleet was waiting for them and engaged the armada, gaining the upper hand and sinking several Spanish vessels. Victory was achieved with the revolutionary tactic of long-range guns with salvo firing, and without making any attempt to go alongside and board the enemy. Not a single English ship was lost.

Sidonia had had enough. With English warships holding the Channel, he decided to sail around the British Isles and back to Spain. During the journey many of his vessels were wrecked in storms off the western coast of Ireland, unable to hold position in sheltered areas as they no longer had their anchors. When he finally reached Spain with his remaining 67 vessels, Sidonia was delirious, thousands of his men had been killed, and many more had died from typhus or scurvy.

It was a great victory. Now the English, despite having one-third the population of Spain, half that of France, knew their power. Protestants everywhere treated it as a sign from God. However, Elizabeth's joy turned to grief when Leicester died. She locked herself in her room until the door was broken down four days later. Her mood changed when Leicester's stepson, Robert Devereux Earl of Essex, came to court to seek his fortune. He was the great-grandson of Elizabeth's aunt, Mary Boleyn.

Although aged 56, and 34 years older than Essex, Elizabeth succumbed to his flattery. She needed her final paramour, for the previous one, Sir Walter Raleigh, had been sent to the Tower for seducing and marrying one of Elizabeth's maids of honour, and Drake would die of fever whilst unsuccessfully raiding the Spanish Main (the coastline of the Spanish territories bordering the Caribbean Sea).

Yet the fear of assassination was still present. In 1594, the royal physician, Dr Rodrigo Lopez, was accused of trying to poison the Queen. When the Inquisition reached Portugal, Jews were given the choice of converting to Christianity, emigrating but leaving their children behind, or being killed. Lopez chose conversion. Then the Inquisition started to kill converts, claiming that they were not sincere. So, Dr Lopez fled to England where he enjoyed great success, becoming the physician to Leicester, Walsingham and then the Queen. Essex was jealous of Lopez's popularity with Elizabeth, and he became Lopez's enemy.

On Walsingham's urging, and so as to obtain information, Lopez joined a Spanish plot to kill Don Antonio, the claimant to the Portuguese crown, who was living in exile in England. When some of the conspirators were seized, one of them disclosed Lopez's involvement. Essex saw his opportunity. He had Lopez tortured on the rack until he admitted that the Spanish had asked him to poison the Queen.

At his trial, Lopez denied the charge, saying that he had joined the plot against Don Antonio at the request of Walsingham, who had chosen him because he was fluent in Spanish and Portuguese. But Walsingham had died, and Lopez was not believed. He was convicted of treason. Elizabeth refused to sign the warrant for three months; then she gave in, and Lopez was hanged, drawn and quartered.

The trial had been a sensation, and it produced outbursts of anti-Semitism in the streets and in literature. As the only Jew most Englishmen had ever seen, Lopez is referred to in Marlowe's *Doctor Faustus*, in Dekker's *Whore of Babylon*, in Middleton's *Game at Chess*, and is probably the model for

Shakespeare's Shylock in *The Merchant of Venice* – first staged a few weeks after the execution; again with a trial, with a Jew as the villain, with an intended victim named Antonio, and with a hero (Antonio/Essex) supported by a woman (Portia/ Elizabeth).

In 1596 it was time for more action. Raleigh was released from prison and allowed to join the fleet under the joint command of Lord Howard and Essex. All the Spanish galleons in Cadiz harbour were destroyed, and the city was seized. Philip sent what was left of his fleet to attack England, but he failed again as his vessels were damaged in a storm and forced to limp home. Essex took all the credit for the victory. He was the idol of the country.

With Spain quiet, rebellion broke out in Ireland. It was therefore necessary to send an army to subdue the rebels. First, a Lord Deputy had to be appointed to take charge of Ireland. Elizabeth and Essex favoured different candidates. The matter was to be decided at a meeting of the Council. At the meeting, Elizabeth expressed her view, and then Essex put his case with considerable force, dismissing all that the Queen had said. The argument continued, and it became increasingly heated, the other members of the Council remaining silent. Essex's voice grew louder, exasperated that his judgment was not being accepted. For her part, Elizabeth's anger at the lack of respect shown to her was clear to all.

Elizabeth had had enough, her candidate would be appointed. While Elizabeth was still speaking, Essex turned his back on her to show his contempt. He was not going to stand there meekly and accept being overruled on a military matter by a woman. Essex had gone too far. Elizabeth took a step forward, raised her hand and slapped him across the side of the head. Even as his ear was turning red, Essex spun round. "This is an outrage that I will not put up with," he shouted in the presence of the stunned members of the Council. "I would not have borne it from your father's hands" – not that he was alive when Henry was king.

Essex's hand reached for his sword. It seemed that in his uncontrollable fury, he was about to strike down the person who had publicly insulted him, regardless of rank or gender. It was a natural reaction, nothing less could have been expected of him.

Grasping the hilt, Essex half-drew the sword; but before he could raise it to strike, other councillors had taken hold of him from both sides. Who knows what might otherwise have happened. It cannot be said that in his rage, Essex would not have killed Elizabeth there and then before he was able to realise the consequences. Very possibly those councillors saved Elizabeth from an attempt to kill her.

Forced to return his sword to its scabbard, Essex shrugged himself loose and walked away as Elizabeth and the other councillors stood speechless. Essex retired for several days to Wanstead. When he returned to court, nothing more was said of the incident, and Essex was given command of the army to be sent to Ireland.

It was not a good idea. Once in Ireland, Essex behaved as if he were the king, granting knighthoods and ignoring his orders. He lost several battles, made a truce and then returned to England contrary to his instructions. Full of confidence, and covered in mud, he burst into Elizabeth's bedroom at Nonsuch Palace in Surrey to address her even before she had changed from her nightclothes or put on her wig. It was asking for trouble. Essex was deprived of public office and banished from court.

Elizabeth had not finished. She refused to renew Essex's only source of income, the lease on the duty on sweet wine. Impoverished and humiliated, Essex, supported by ambitious hotheads, decided to seize the crown. The most popular man in England sent Elizabeth a message: he paid the actors at the Globe Theatre to put on Shakespeare's *Richard II* – a monarch who was deposed, murdered and replaced by a warrior. Elizabeth understood it all too clearly. She sent men to bring Essex to court; but they were imprisoned by

Essex's supporters. Then Essex and 200 followers (over half the knights in England owed their knighthoods to Essex) rode into the City with swords drawn; Elizabeth was their target. Yet again Essex had overestimated his position. The Londoners remained loyal to their Queen, and Essex was arrested. Arrogant to the last, at his trial Essex welcomed the death sentence, informing all who were present that the Queen could not be safe while he was alive. He went to the block without asking for mercy; the last person to be beheaded in the Tower.

Robert Devereux, Earl of Essex

In the later years of the reign, the economy suffered with attacks of plague, poor harvests, high taxation and the cost of further fighting in Ireland and with Spain. By now Elizabeth was old and frail, but death would not come from another plot to kill her.

It was the fashion for women to have a white complexion with red cheeks. To achieve a snow-white skin, women of the nobility used ceruse – a paste made of white lead and vinegar.

With her pock-marked face and lines from age, and with public appearances nearly every day, Elizabeth used ceruse in ever-increasing quantities.

Unfortunately, ceruse is toxic; it withers the skin and causes sores, and that made the user apply even more. Worse than that, the poison from the ceruse rots the teeth (Elizabeth suffered from violent toothache, lost several teeth and in the end her speech was almost incomprehensible), it makes the hair fall out (Elizabeth's hairline retreated halfway across her head, so that high foreheads became the fashion) and it damages the internal organs, particularly the lungs.

Elizabeth may also have used kohl (black eye make-up made of powdered antimony), and cinnabar (a red compound of mercury and sulphur for her cheeks and lips), and drops of deadly nightshade to make her pupils larger (therefore called *belladonna*, 'beautiful lady' in Italian); all poisonous.

She ended up lying on the floor speechless for four days, refusing to allow her doctors to examine her. Then, on 24th March 1603, in those times the last day of the year[19], she died in her sleep at the age of 69. She probably died of blood poisoning; killed by cosmetics – the original fashion victim.

Elizabeth left a country changed in stature. England had

---

19 Although 1 January was popularly treated as the beginning of the year, from the twelfth century until 1752 when England adopted the Gregorian Calendar, the English legal year began on 25 March. That is why even today leases of property commonly have quarterly rent payment dates of 25 March, 24 June, 29 September and 25 December. Both the Julian and the Gregorian calendars allow an extra day in every fourth year. However, unlike the Julian Calendar, the more accurate Gregorian Calendar introduced in Catholic countries in 1582 does not have the extra day in three of every four century years. So when England changed from the Julian Calendar in 1752, in order to correct the position 11 days had to be missed (the day following 2 September was 14 September) and then a twelfth day in 1800. As a result, the first day of the legal year moved from 25 March to 6 April; still the first day of the tax year in the UK.

With both Shakespeare and Cervantes having died on 23 April 1616, 23 April was chosen as World Book and Copyright Day. But in 1616 Spain had already adopted the Gregorian Calendar; England, unwilling to follow a ruling of the Pope, was still on the Julian Calendar. So, in fact they did not die on the same day, merely on the same date – Cervantes died 10 days before Shakespeare.

become a major trading nation exploring distant lands, with Drake circumnavigating the world and Raleigh promoting colonisation in North America, the first permanent colony being named Virginia after the Virgin Queen. It was the country of Edmund Spenser, Christopher Marlowe, Sir Francis Bacon, John Donne, John Webster, Sir Philip Sidney, Ben Johnson and William Shakespeare.

Elizabeth is remembered as 'Gloriana', England's greatest royal leader. What a different country it would have been if Queen Mary had signed her half-sister's death warrant, or if one of the many assassination conspiracies had succeeded. And what if the councillors had not taken hold of Essex?

****

JAMES I

24 March 1603 – 27 March 1625

The family called the Stewarts (changed to Stuarts by Mary Queen of Scots) were descendants of Alan FitzFlaad, whose ancestor was a Breton knight who had come to England in the army of William the Conqueror. Alan's second son, Walter Fitzalan, fled from England with other supporters of Matilda (the rival of King Stephen) in the twelfth century, and he was appointed the first Hereditary High Steward of Scotland by King David I. The Scottish royal family took the surname Stewart in the fourteenth century when Marjorie, the daughter of Robert the Bruce, married the sixth High Steward, and on the death of Marjorie's half-brother King David II without issue her son became King Robert II. His 6 x great-granddaughter was Mary Queen of Scots, and James was her only child. He became King James VI of Scotland at the age of 13 months when his mother was forced to abdicate.

At the age of thirteen, James had formed a romantic attachment with Darnley's 37-year-old French cousin, Esmé Stewart Sieur d'Aubigny (later to become the Duke of Lennox).

From this first experience, homosexual relationships would be a constant theme of James's life. Nevertheless, James had to secure the succession, and in 1589 (after the Scottish nobles had forced James to banish Esmé) he married Anne, the 14-year-old daughter of the King of Denmark. They went on to have seven children, but only three, Henry, Elizabeth and Charles, survived infancy.

James's long-time obsession was his fear of witchcraft. So it was no surprise that when Shakespeare wrote his Scottish play, the first scene of *Macbeth* concerned a meeting of three witches.

Maintaining his throne was difficult for James because of a Scottish king's lack of power. James had no standing army and he was confronted by hostile earls. One of those earls was the Earl of Bothwell; not the Bothwell who was Mary Queen of Scots' third husband – his title had been forfeited shortly before Mary was forced to abdicate. The new Earl of Bothwell was Frances, the son of James V's illegitimate son John Stewart (Mary's half-brother), the man who might have been king but for his father's illegitimacy. James believed that Bothwell had employed witches to kill him.

The first violent incident occurred when Bothwell and his supporters broke into Edinburgh Castle and raced through the building, seeking the King. James ran away and locked himself in a small room. Bothwell found the room, but he could not break down the door, so he set it on fire. Before the door had burned down, help arrived, and Bothwell and his men were chased away.

In 1592, Bothwell came with 300 men to besiege James at Falkland Palace in Fife. This time they brought a battering ram to break down the gates, but the next day they gave up and left. The following year, James was awoken in Holyrood Palace early one morning by loud noise, and he rushed from his bedroom. Bothwell had seized the palace, and he approached James, sword in hand. James turned and ran to the Queen's bedroom, but it was locked. The King was trapped; all he could do was stand there shouting "Treason!". Bothwell came up to James, who challenged Bothwell to kill him. Surprised at the proposal, Bothwell hesitated, and then he offered his sword to James inviting James to kill him. Negotiations began, and they led to a deal under which Bothwell agreed to stand trial for witchcraft. In 1594, having been acquitted of witchcraft, Bothwell and his men once more went on the attack, ambushing James and his retinue and pursuing them until they reached the safety of Edinburgh. After further failed conspiracies, Bothwell gave up and left Scotland for ever.

Next there was trouble from the Ruthven family, headed by the Earl of Gowrie. According to James, when he was out hunting, Gowrie's brother, the Master of Ruthven, invited James to Gowrie House to see a pot of gold. When James entered the room where the supposed gold was kept, the Master drew a dagger and held it to James's throat saying that the Earl would join them and that James was to do as he was told. Again, James shouted "Treason!" repeatedly, and his retainers rushed to rescue him. In the melee, the Earl and the Master were killed.

The assassination attempt at Gowrie House

James's final years in Scotland passed without further attacks. However, as a precaution, in future he would always wear a heavily padded doublet – his own version of a bullet-proof vest.

When Queen Elizabeth died in 1603, James (who had already been King James VI of Scotland for 36 years) was accepted by the English as the rightful heir. He was the great-grandson of Henry VIII's older sister Margaret, he was Protestant and he already had two sons. Crucially, James's succession was supported by Elizabeth's chief minister, Robert Cecil (later the Earl of Salisbury), who had been in secret correspondence with James for several years. There was no opposition. On the contrary, men seeking office rushed to Scotland to ingratiate themselves with their new sovereign – 300 of them received knighthoods.

James adopted the title of King of Great Britain, although it was without authority as the English Parliament would not agree to a union of the two countries. James was King of England and, separately, King of Scotland.

From the start of his English reign, James disappointed his subjects because he was not interested in showing himself and seeking their favour. Also, he was at odds with the Puritans, being unwilling to accept their religious demands; and he was in constant conflict with Parliament and its claimed exclusive right to levy taxation. As for the Catholics, James was not in favour of persecution, and he promised them toleration. However, resistance from the Puritans meant that he did not deal with the issue as quickly as the Catholics expected.

The Puritans and Parliament would act in the next reign; the Catholics did not wait. Not only were they disappointed at the broken promise, but James had made peace with Spain. Paradoxically, the Catholics were unhappy at the signing of peace with the leading Catholic state; it meant that there was no chance of Spain invading and supporting them.

Unlike persecutions in continental Europe by Catholics, in England the Catholics were not maltreated merely for belonging to their faith. Rather, they faced numerous restrictions: they could not celebrate Mass, have their children baptised in the Catholic manner, marry in a Catholic service, or receive extreme unction (annointing with oil) when approaching death. They were also forced to attend Protestant services. The vast majority obeyed and were safe and could even attain high office, but those who disobeyed were heavily fined or imprisoned.

The Catholic reaction began in 1603, when a group led by Father Watson conspired to seize the King and his Council, intending to imprison them until every item of anti-Catholic legislation had been repealed. One of the conspirators feared retribution against all Catholics, and he informed the authorities. Watson and two accomplices were executed before the plot, known as the Bye Plot, could be put into operation. As a result, Catholic priests were ordered to leave England.

Later in the year, participants in another conspiracy, the Main Plot, sought to kill James and his children and put Lady Arbella Stuart (James's cousin) on the throne. She was believed to be sympathetic to Catholics. These conspirators were not all Catholics; some were Protestants, including Sir Walter Raleigh, many of whose privileges had been withdrawn by James who disliked the dashing 'lady's man'. The plotters were betrayed by Arbella, and the leaders were arrested; some were executed, others were imprisoned. Raleigh was sentenced to death, but was instead confined in the Tower.

The fact that the Bye Plot had been revealed by a Catholic helped, particularly with James. It did not help with the Puritans (Protestants who believed that the Reformation had not gone far enough), so the chances of toleration were over.

Of course, some Catholics were not interested in mere toleration; they wanted a Catholic state.

When Essex made his ridiculous attempt to seize the throne from Elizabeth, most of the men who had supported him were fined and allowed to return to their homes. Some of them were Catholics, for Essex had been in favour of toleration. Among the hotheads had been Catholics Robert (also called Robin) Catesby, Francis Tresham, Jack Wright and John Grant. They had believed in James's promises of toleration, not least because James's parents were Catholics and his wife, Queen Anne, was believed to have converted to Catholicism. But Catesby was not just disappointed, he was angry.

Another angry man was a Catholic from York named Guy Fawkes. He had been fighting for Spain against the Protestants in the Spanish Netherlands. Fawkes then travelled to Spain, begging the authorities to invade England and enforce compulsory Catholicism. The only outcome was that he changed his first name from Guy to Guido.

With the 1604 Parliament increasing the level of fines payable for Catholic observance, it was clear that matters were only going to get worse. Catesby decided to act. He was a tall, good-looking man with a powerful personality, most of the conspirators later saying that for love of him they would do all he asked.

Catesby knew that not only the king had to be changed, but also the Council and much of Parliament. He told his second cousin Tom Wintour and Jack Wright of his plan to blow up Parliament and kill the King (and incidentally the Queen and Prince Henry), as well as his ministers and many lords and members of parliament, and both of them agreed to join him. Wright introduced his former schoolmate, Guy Fawkes, to the conspiracy. He was a useful addition, as his face was not known to the authorities because of his long absence abroad. Next to join was Wright's brother-in-law, Thomas Percy.

On 20th May 1604, at the Duck and Drake Inn just off the Strand in London, the five original conspirators agreed to carry out Catesby's plan. By October, they had a sixth member – Robert Keyes. He was to take charge of Catesby's house in Lambeth where the gunpowder was to be stored. Catesby's servant, Thomas Bates, became the seventh conspirator.

In March 1605, the group increased to ten with the addition of Tom Wintour's brother Robert, Wright's brother Kit, and the Wintours' brother-in-law, John Grant. Further details of the plan were now agreed. It was assumed that Prince Henry would be killed in the explosion. Prince Charles might or might not be in attendance, but he was only four years old, so it mattered little. Eight-year-old Princess Elizabeth lived outside London; the plan was to seize her and crown her queen under the regency of the Earl of Northumberland, who although a Protestant had sympathy for the Catholics. He was the second cousin once removed of Thomas Percy. The plotters believed that a nationwide Catholic uprising would come to their aid, possibly with assistance from Spain.

Next they rented a small house next to Parliament. This house had a storeroom on the ground floor that extended under the House of Lords. By 20th July, 36 barrels of gunpowder had been brought from Lambeth. Now a little more time as the final traces of plague led to a postponement of the opening of Parliament until the fateful day – 5th November. This gave Catesby time to recruit three more conspirators: Ambrose Rockwood (married to a cousin of Robert Keyes), Catesby's cousin Francis Tresham and Sir Everard Digby – the man assigned to capture Princess Elizabeth.

Eight of the Gunpowder Plotters

With so many conspirators and such a long period of preparation, it is likely that a number of people knew something of the plot, perhaps wives, relatives, friends and priests. On 26th October, an anonymous letter was delivered to Lord Monteagle, whose wife Elizabeth was the sister of Frances Tresham. The letter included the advice:

"My Lord, out of the love I bear to some of your friends, I have a care of your preservation. Therefore I would advise you, as you tender your life, to devise some excuse to shift your attendance at this Parliament ... yet I say they shall receive a terrible blow this Parliament; and yet they shall not see who hurts them ... "

Monteagle had his servant, Thomas Ward, read the letter out aloud. Then Monteagle took the letter to the King's chief minister, the Earl of Salisbury.

Who wrote the Monteagle letter? Obviously someone who cared for Monteagle. Tresham, Catesby, Robert Wintour, Thomas Wintour and Grant's wife were related to Monteagle's wife. Lord Monteagle had been one of Essex's hotheads, so Catesby, Tresham, Jack Wright and Grant had been his colleagues. Many of them, and others, are suspects; yet the identity of the author remains a mystery.

But another relationship was also relevant: Thomas Ward's brother was married to the Wrights' sister, and Ward's sister was married to Kit Wright – Ward knew the conspirators and he knew of the plot. He rushed off to tell the plotters of the letter and of its delivery to Salisbury. Yet, despite objections from his associates, Catesby refused to abandon his plan.

Aware of what was intended, Salisbury decided to let matters develop so that he could catch the conspirators in the act. On 4th November, Fawkes (the man appointed to light the gunpowder) remained in London as the others headed for the Midlands, ready to start the uprising. Shortly before midnight, a search was carried out in Parliament and the surrounding buildings, and the searchers stumbled upon a man in a dark cloak and hat, holding touchpaper and matches. He called himself John Johnson, but it was Guy Fawkes. Next the gunpowder was found; it was enough to have blown Parliament sky-high, everyone within 100 yards would have been killed. Bonfires were lit across the country to celebrate the King's deliverance.

Now that the game was up, Fawkes admitted that he had intended to blow up Parliament and the King. But he did not reveal his true name or the names of his colleagues, hoping to give them time to escape to the Continent. Yet Catesby took no advantage of Fawkes's heroism, believing that an insurrection could be initiated despite the failure in London. The others knew that there was no hope, but still they followed Catesby.

After two days of torture, Fawkes's body was broken on the rack, his arms and legs stretched until they were dislocated, and he revealed his name and the names of the others. The remaining conspirators were tracked down to Holbeche House in Staffordshire. Catesby and Percy were shot (killed by the same ball), and the Wright brothers were also killed. The others were captured and taken to the Tower, as were many of their friends.

Catesby and Percy were buried. Their bodies were later exhumed and the heads were cut off. Francis Tresham died in the Tower; his corpse was nevertheless executed. The surviving conspirators were tried and sentenced to death. It was the customary sentence for male traitors: to be hanged, drawn and quartered.[20]

First, to be tied to a horse and dragged backwards through the streets to the place of execution, the victim's feet not being fit to tread on English soil, and face down so as not to breathe English air. The practice developed of dragging the condemned man on a wicker mat, so that he should not arrive unconscious, unable to make a speech or provide the necessary drama.

Second, the victim was hanged; suspended between heaven and earth, being unworthy of both. He was to be cut down before he was dead (friends sometimes managed to pull his legs so that he did die), the length of time hanging often depending on the contrition shown in his speech on the scaffold.

Third, to have his private parts cut off and burned in front of him so that he could not produce another generation. Fourth, to have his bowels and organs, where the evil had been harboured, cut out (withdrawn or drawn) and burned before his eyes. Fifth, to have his head, where the evil was conceived, cut off. For sure he was now dead. Yet it was still not over. Next his body was cut in quarters, and the four quarters and the head were sent for display in different towns to be devoured by the fowls of the air.

But Guy Fawkes, the last to stand on the scaffold, jumped from the gallows as soon as his head was in the noose. The fall broke his neck, so he died without suffering the further torments. Keyes had tried the same trick, but the rope broke.

During the trial, the Attorney General had quoted part of a psalm to the court, "Let his posterity be destroyed, and in the next generation let his name be quite put out." For one of the conspirators, nothing could be further from the truth. With Catesby killed before trial and Guy Fawkes having been the man to light the gunpowder, his name is remembered as well as anyone else in English history.

Every 5th November, bonfires are lit throughout England in

---

20 Women traitors were burned, later changed to hanging; except in the Isle of Man where they were, as far as possible, treated in the same way as men.

commemoration of the discovery of the Gunpowder Plot, and an effigy of Guy Fawkes is set atop of the flames. Children raise money to purchase the customary fireworks[21] by displaying their 'guy', begging for "a penny for the guy" – Fawkes's first name having become part of the language (originally a 'guy' was a strangely dressed man, but now it is any man or an effigy of Guy Fawkes).

Unlike the Battle of Hastings, Magna Carta and other notable historical events, the day and the month, but not the year, of the Gunpowder Plot are remembered by everyone: "Remember, remember the fifth of November, gunpowder treason and plot; there is no reason why gunpowder treason should ever be forgot."

At first the anti-Catholic feeling was controlled. King James wanted retribution to be limited to the conspirators, but as more details emerged and more Catholics were arrested, the anger increased. As a result, further anti-Catholic laws were introduced, some lasting centuries.

The Catholics having been dealt with, James and the court busied themselves with grandeur and pleasure. It was now that James found a new favourite, Robert Carr, a handsome young Scotsman whom James insisted on kissing in public. Carr soon became Viscount Rochester, and then Earl of Somerset.

In order to pay for his pleasures, James raised money by selling peerages and then secured further funds by inventing the concept of hereditary knighthoods (baronets). It was not enough, and James's demands for more money led to conflict with Parliament. The relationship deteriorated when the Commons insisted on debating the extent of the King's powers, infuriating James who believed that God-given rights were not for discussion.

Although it was not the subject of debate, James was concerned with ensuring the succession for his older son,

---

21 One of the principal manufacturers of fireworks to this day being Pains, founded by Charles Pain who manufactured the gunpowder used (unknown to him at the time) in the Gunpowder Plot.

Prince Henry. There were no real rivals, but there was another possibility. That was Lady Arbella Stuart, James's cousin, the daughter of Darnley's younger brother. So James kept her at court and forbade her from marrying. When she married William Seymour (the grandson of Lady Catherine Grey), James sent Arbella to the Tower where she remained until she starved herself to death.

It did not help Prince Henry. He died of typhoid in 1612. James's younger son, Charles, became the heir. However, the royal lineage was more radically affected when James married off his daughter Elizabeth to Frederick the Protestant Prince-Elector of the Palatinate of the Rhine. That marriage would provide the succession six monarchs later, introducing German blood to the monarchy.

Another decision would also have a long-term effect. James granted to Protestant English and Scottish settlers most of the lands in Ulster (in the north-east of Ireland) that had been confiscated from the Catholic Irish lords defeated at the end of Queen Elizabeth's reign. It would lead to perpetual Catholic/Protestant conflict in Ireland, as well as several attempts to murder future sovereigns.

Unpopularity with the Catholics was not all. A foreign-born ruler who believed that he had been appointed by God, and who was the leader of a debauched court, became hated by his subjects. It did not help that James had a tongue too large for his mouth and walked with a limp.

In 1615 James fell out with Somerset and found a new favourite, a new love: George Villiers, who became Sir, then Earl, then Marquess and finally Duke of Buckingham. James referred to Villiers as his "sweet child and wife". Under the influence of Villiers, royal expenditure soared. To add to the problem, monopolies giving control of trades were handed out to James's cronies, particularly Villiers and his family.

There was another apparently minor event that would become hugely significant: the voyage of the Pilgrim Fathers in the Mayflower. They were non-conformists, most of whom had fled

England for the toleration of Amsterdam and Leiden, and were then financed by English investors to settle in North America. Others followed, establishing English settlements in North America, South America, the East Indies and India. One venture did not fare well; after 13 years in prison, Sir Walter Raleigh had been released to search for El Dorado (the city of gold) in Venezuela. He failed, but took the opportunity to destroy a Spanish settlement. To placate Spain, on Raleigh's return to England, the death sentence passed 15 years earlier was carried out.

The disputes with Parliament about finance were aggravated by James's dealings with Spain. Foreign policy was still the King's prerogative, and in 1623 an agreement was made for the marriage of the Infanta Maria Anna (sister of King Philip IV) to Prince Charles. A secret addendum promised the lifting of various restrictions on English Catholics. But the Spanish smelled a trick. They knew that the English Protestant Church regarded itself as the Catholic Church freed from rule by the Pope; the English might later say that the reference in the addendum to Catholics ('Catholic' from the Greek for 'universal' – *katholikos*) meant followers of the Church of England. So to make it clear, the Spanish changed the reference from 'Catholics' to 'Roman Catholics'; and that term, peculiar to England, came into common use. In the end, the Infanta was not allowed to leave Spain, and the marriage plans were abandoned.

Facing increased opposition from Parliament and struggling with debt, in early 1625 James suffered a stroke. He lingered on until he died on 27th March. Prince Charles and Buckingham were accused of having poisoned the King, but there was no evidence against them other than their desire for power.

However, as will be seen in the following century, it was not through Charles, but through Princess Elizabeth that the line of English sovereigns would eventually run. It was what the gunpowder plotters had wanted; but perversely, it would be solely to avoid a Catholic monarch.

****

HENRY VII to CHARLES I

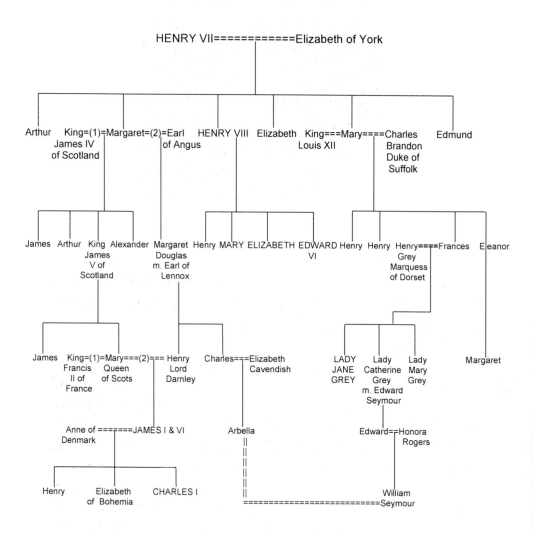

Margaret Tudor took as her third husband Lord Methven, and Mary Queen of Scots took as her third husband the Earl of Bothwell; but neither marriage produced children.

CHARLES I

27 March 1625 – 30 January 1649

Charles was born in Scotland three years before his father was crowned King of England. Twelve years later, Charles became heir to the throne when his older brother, Henry, died. Charles grew up to be an arrogant little man with a stammer; obstinate and not at all clever.

When he succeeded to the throne, Charles was as dominated by George Villiers Duke of Buckingham as King James had been. The problem was not so much Buckingham's lust for wealth, rather it was his combination of power and stupidity.

Angry at the failure of the Spanish marriage proposal, Buckingham and Charles had demanded war against Spain. Parliament resisted, only agreeing to grant funds for a naval war, and totally forbade Buckingham and Charles's proposed expedition to recover the Palatinate for his sister Elizabeth's husband. Frederick had accepted the crown of Bohemia at the request of the Protestants (the majority of the population), as a result of which the Catholic Habsburgs seized not just Bohemia (making Catholicism compulsory), but also Frederick's own lands.

Putting the Spanish failure behind him, six weeks after succeeding to the crown Charles agreed to marry the 14-year-old

Henrietta Maria, sister of King Louis XIII of France – the wedding taking place hurriedly by proxy in Paris before Parliament could object. As part of the agreement, Charles lent Louis several ships, and Louis used them to attack the Protestants in La Rochelle. Charles also undertook to grant concessions to Catholics in England. At the same time, Charles agreed to Parliament's proposals for increased persecution of Catholics.

Buckingham, jealous of the new Queen and irritated by her French courtiers, now demanded war against France. He led a force to relieve the Protestants of La Rochelle, but he was driven back to England. Parliament was against war with either France or Spain, and refused to provide finance unless Buckingham was removed. Charles treated the refusal as a personal insult. He told Parliament to remember that parliaments were for him to call and dismiss; adding that he was not threatening them, as he scorned to threaten anyone but his equals.

Without sufficient funds from Parliament, Charles exercised his prerogative powers. He demanded loans from landowners, he billeted troops with townsfolk and he made those living in seaports pay for the fleet. Having lost the support of Parliament, Charles now started to lose the people. But he did not care; there was no need for his subjects' approval – just like his father, he had been appointed by God.

In 1628, Buckingham was murdered by a former officer who had been wounded in one of the failed wars. That led to peace with Spain and France. With foreign problems solved, domestic issues took over as the tension between Parliament and the King centred on an argument about the right to make religious appointments. Parliament would not accept Charles's claim that they were not entitled to interfere. So Charles dissolved Parliament. He decided to rule alone.

Queen Henrietta Maria (after whom Charles named the American colony of Maryland) became his principal adviser. She was no cleverer than Buckingham. At least she produced seven children, two of whom would become sovereigns of England, as would three of her grandchildren.

No Buckingham, no war, no Parliament; for some time absolute rule stifled dissent. It was known as the Eleven Year Tyranny, the peace being maintained by unlawful taxation, confiscations and the use of the law courts and torture to silence opposition. However, the absence of Parliament meant that Charles became increasingly out of touch with the people. It was not just the English. When Charles tried to force the Scottish Church to adopt the English prayer-book, it led to riots and the creation of the National Covenant under which Scots swore to resist to the death.

So Charles led an army north to quell the Scots. He accomplished little except the unification of the Scottish and English opposition. At last, Charles realised that he needed assistance, so he recalled the iron-fisted Thomas Wentworth from Ireland. In 1640 Wentworth advised Charles to recall Parliament. Wentworth believed that Parliament would be willing to provide the finance for a further attack on the Scots in exchange for Charles abandoning the right to levy ship money – a tax on people in coastal areas to support the navy in times of war, which Charles had imposed throughout the country as a general money-raising exercise.

Wentworth was wrong, very wrong. The recalled Parliament threw up a new leader, John Pym, a brilliant parliamentarian, who led the House of Commons in opposition to the King's demands. When Charles realised that Wentworth's plan had failed, he again dissolved Parliament. That caused anger throughout the country, and there were outbreaks of disorder, as well as rejection of royal appointments and refusal to pay tax. With the administration collapsing, the Scots marched into England and seized the northern counties.

Desperate to raise more forces, Charles summoned a new Parliament; but the members were in no mood to help. Instead, they impeached Wentworth and sent him to the Tower and then the scaffold; other ministers fled the country. So Charles sought advice from the Queen, and she told him to rely on his absolute powers – it would prove to be fatal.

An apparently minor event occurred in 1641 that would turn out to be almost as important in the future as his sister's marriage to Frederick; Charles's daughter Mary married William, the son of the Prince of Orange. Critically for the succession, both marriages were to Protestants.

Having failed to raise an English army to fight the Scottish opposition, Charles decided to travel north to raise a Scottish army to fight the English opposition. But he was an absolute ruler, so he left no one in London to govern in his place. Parliament filled the vacuum.

Charles achieved nothing in Scotland. Ireland would become more important as the Catholics went on a killing spree, murdering thousands of the Protestant settlers. As a result, it was necessary to send an army to Ireland to restore order. However, both Parliament and Charles feared how the other might use such an army after the Irish had been dealt with – perhaps before.

Predictably, Charles insisted that control of the army was his royal prerogative. In response, Pym demanded that Parliament should control the army and have the right to veto Charles's appointment of ministers. After again seeking the Queen's advice, Charles made his way to Westminster and stormed into the House of Commons with an armed guard.

Charles sat on the Speaker's chair and demanded the arrest of Pym and four other leading members. He ordered the Speaker to point them out. The Speaker, William Lenthall, fell to his knees and replied: "May it please Your Majesty, I have neither eyes to see nor tongue to speak in this place but as the House is pleased to direct me, whose servant I am here ..." From that moment, the Speaker became the protector of the Commons, no longer the monarch's overseer. In any case, Pym and the others had already fled.

The King left the chamber to cries of "Privilege!"; although the privilege (immunity) of freedom from arrest in the House only applied to civil matters – so they must have been referring to the privilege of freedom from interference. No monarch has entered the House of Commons since that day. As the King travelled home, the cries of "Privilege!" were repeated in the streets. The city was on the verge of an uprising. Six days later Charles and his family fled as Pym and his colleagues returned to Westminster in triumph. Charles moved to York with Princes Charles and James. The Queen and the younger children (with the Crown Jewels) went to the Netherlands.

Now Charles made yet another error of judgment; he ordered the loyal members of parliament to join him in York. This gave Pym and his supporters unopposed control of Parliament and the capital, a city of over 300,000 people; no other town had 30,000. Then, on 22nd August 1642 (the 157th anniversary of his 3 x great-grandfather's victory at Bosworth), Charles issued a call to arms; the matter would be decided by war. Wales, the North and the West were behind the King, the South and the East were with Parliament.

Charles marched for London. After the first major battle, at Edgehill in the Cotswolds, the Parliamentary Army fell back, and four weeks later Charles and his forces reached the outskirts of the capital. Again a mistake, as Charles hesitated and then returned to Oxford for the winter.

The battles in 1643 were indecisive. Then Parliament suffered a setback when Pym died. By then, he had negotiated a treaty with the Scots, and several months later, at the battle of Marston Moor just outside York, the military genius of one of the Parliamentary Army's commanders together with the assistance of the Scots brought a decisive victory. The name of the commander was Oliver Cromwell. Despite victory, Parliament still wanted an accommodation with the King, but Charles rejected the opportunity to negotiate. He was counting on help from abroad.

In 1645, at the Battle of Naseby, the New Model Army led by Fairfax and Cromwell won the Civil War after Charles, making yet another mistake, had divided his forces. Although Charles still retained considerable military support, he decided to surrender to the Scots. He hoped to keep his crown by persuading them to assist him against the English. After all, he was a Scot himself. But when Parliament paid the Scots £500,000, said to be for their military assistance, the King was handed over.

With the war having apparently ended, Parliament ordered the army to disband, but they refused. Charles saw an opportunity to play the army off against Parliament. The army put forward a scheme that would allow Charles to remain king; so did Parliament. Charles rejected both proposals.

In fact, matters were moving the other way. One group, the Levellers, demanded a democratic parliament and the abolition of the monarchy; but that had never been Parliament's ambition, the majority only wanted to restrict the powers of the king.

Although he was confined to Hampton Court, Charles still lived as a king. He was lightly guarded as he had given his word that he would not try to escape. But a word given to inferiors did not have to be kept. Charles fled south to the Isle of White (one step from the Continent). He surrendered to the Governor, whom he mistakenly believed was sympathetic to the Royalist cause.

Charles now started intrigues in all directions. He offered to give up control of the army for the duration of his reign, at the same time he proposed terms to the Scots under which they would invade England and restore his powers, and so it went on. Then Charles incited Royalist uprisings across the country; in effect, a second civil war. It took several months for the Parliamentary forces to subdue the uprisings.

This second civil war increased the sentiment against Charles. He seemed to care nothing about spilling his subjects' blood; he was only concerned to secure his own power. Now the army was determined to deal with 'the man of blood'.

Negotiations between Charles and Parliament continued, the main issue being control of the army. It had become academic; no one controlled the army, it was the army that would control Parliament and the King. In December 1648, the army returned to London, having removed Charles to Hurst

Castle on the mainland. The Commons complained that the King had been taken without their consent, and they voted to continue discussions with Charles.

The next day, in Pride's Purge, Colonel Thomas Pride led a regiment to Westminster where he arrested or sent home all members whose views differed from those of the army. These were principally the Presbyterians, opponents of the King who were willing to restore him provided he handed over control of the army and abolished bishops. The Independents (their numbers swollen by members returning from the war) were of a similar view, but unlike the Presbyterians who wanted command of a uniform religion, the Independents favoured religious toleration within the limits of Anglicanism with each parish being independent and deciding on its own form of worship. Their leader was Cromwell, and the army was with them.

Now the Independents were in charge. Cromwell, by sheer force of personality, would decide the way forward.

The army demanded justice for the deaths of more than 300,000 people (over 5% of the population) in a war for the benefit of one man. Yet Cromwell was not motivated by revenge, rather he was guided by religion.

On 13th December, the Commons voted to bring the King to trial. The charge was that "… Charles Stuart, the now King of England, not content with those many encroachments which his predecessors had made upon the people in their rights and freedoms, hath had a wicked design … to introduce an arbitrary and tyrannical government and … he hath prosecuted it with fire and sword … whereby the country hath been miserably wasted, … thousands of people murdered and infinite other mischiefs committed …" The House of Lords (only 12 peers turning up for the debate) did not agree; so the Commons proceeded on its own.

It would not be a secret trial; it was going to be held in one of the most public places in the country, Westminster Hall, a vast chamber divided by high screens into the principal courts of law. For this trial, the screens would be removed to create a giant single court.

A total of 135 Commissioners were appointed to act as a jury. They were mayors, Scottish and Irish peers, baronets, members of parliament, merchants, army officers, aldermen and gentry. Some lived far from London, others disagreed with the trial or were frightened, so 55 of the Commissioners did not attend any part of the hearings.

The chief justices of England, although mostly anti-Royalist, all refused to participate. Many politicians and lawyers were concerned that the proposed trial would be unlawful; the decision had been taken by a purged Commons, the Commons had acted without the Lords, and a court could not try the King. Cromwell's answer was clear: "We will cut off his head with the crown upon it."

John Bradshaw, a little-known Welsh judge, was chosen to preside. Fearing some sort of violence, he sat throughout the trial wearing a hat lined with metal and with armour beneath his robes. The Attorney General failed to attend, claiming illness (they checked; apparently it was true). So John Cook, a barrister of Gray's Inn, agreed to prosecute.

At two o'clock on Saturday 20th January, the trial began. The King was summoned. Dressed in black with a cloak bearing the silver star of the Garter, he took his seat, keeping his hat on to show his contempt for the Court.

Bradshaw addressed the King, "Charles Stuart, King of England, the Commons of England assembled in Parliament, being sensible of the great calamities that have been brought upon this nation, and of the innocent blood that hath been shed … which are referred to you as the author of it … you are to hear your charge upon which the Court will proceed."

John Cook took over. "My Lord, in behalf of the Commons of England and of all the people thereof, I do accuse Charles Stuart here present of high treason…" Cook started to read the indictment. Charles ordered him to stop, rapping him on the shoulder with his silver-headed cane so forcefully that the top fell off. Charles instructed Cook to pick it up. When Cook ignored the command, Charles was nonplussed; he would have to pick up the top himself.

The indictment set out Charles's position as trusted with limited power to govern according to law. Next, it detailed Charles's breach of that position by upholding himself as entitled to rule according to his will with unlimited power, in support of which he had traitorously levied war against Parliament and the people, seeking support from abroad. Therefore he was charged with responsibility for the resultant treasons, murders, rapes and burnings. On behalf of the people of England, Cook impeached Charles Stuart as a tyrant, traitor and murderer, and an enemy to the Commonwealth of England.

Charles's response was to laugh out loud.

Bradshaw told Charles that the Court now expected his answer. "I would know by what power I am called hither," Charles replied. "I would know by what authority. I mean *lawful* ... Remember I am your king ... I have a trust committed to me by God ... I will not betray it to answer a new unlawful authority."

To that, Bradshaw responded, "In the name of the people of England, of which you are elected king."

With some justification, Charles countered, "England was never an elective kingdom, but a hereditary kingdom for near these thousand years."

Bradshaw had had enough. "Your way of answer is to interrogate the Court, which beseems not you in that condition."

Charles continued, "I do not come here as submitting to the Court. I will stand as much for the privilege of the House of Commons ... as any man here...", conveniently forgetting his attempt to arrest Pym and his colleagues. "I see no House of Lords here that may constitute a Parliament."

After further sparring on the same issue between Charles and Bradshaw, the proceedings were adjourned.

Nowadays, if an accused refuses to plead, a plea of not

guilty is entered, and the trial proceeds. However, until 1827 a refusal to plead was treated as a plea of guilty. This meant that according to legal practice, Charles would now be convicted, and after sentencing the proceedings would end. That was not what his accusers wanted. They were intent on a public trial at which witnesses would be called to show Charles's guilt, a conviction on its own was not enough.

The Court reconvened on the Monday. Cook said that if the accused refused to plead, he should now be declared guilty. Charles told the Court that no jurisdiction could try a king.

"Sir, you are not to dispute our authority," shouted Bradshaw. And so it continued until Charles completed the circle by saying, "I will answer so soon as I know by what authority you do this…"

"It is not for prisoners to require," answered Bradshaw.

"I am not an ordinary prisoner," parried Charles, unnecessarily adding "the king is not suffered to give his reasons for the liberty and freedom of all his subjects."

This allowed Bradshaw to reply scornfully, "How great a friend you have been to the laws and liberties of the people!"

"… I never took up arms against the people, but for the laws," declared Charles, showing how much better he had been doing by refusing to deal with facts.

That was how the second day of the trial ended. The next afternoon, the trial recommenced. Cook again asked for judgment, but Bradshaw offered Charles one more opportunity to plead. Yet again, Charles refused to recognise the Court, and the session moved nothing forward.

Now a way was found to hear testimony as to Charles's guilt, a committee was set up to hear the prosecution evidence. Witnesses told of Charles's call to arms in Nottingham so as to wage war on his subjects, of his encouragement of plunder after victory, of correspondence with foreign powers inviting them to invade, of the abuse and murder of prisoners, and of how when a Royalist officer had tried to stop the stripping and cutting of captured soldiers, Charles had intervened and ordered the continuation of the mistreatment saying, "I do not care if they cut them three times more for they are mine enemies."

On 27th January, the Court reassembled. The Commissioners had made their decision. First, Bradshaw gave Charles another opportunity to speak in his defence provided he did not challenge the jurisdiction of the Court. Of course Charles did challenge that jurisdiction. Before Bradshaw could interrupt, Charles asked for permission to address Parliament. Bradshaw saw this as a delaying tactic, but there were murmurings amongst the Commissioners, so Bradshaw adjourned the proceedings for further consideration of the request.

The Commissioners were nervous. Outside the army, the passage of time had cooled anti-monarchist feelings, and people now recoiled from killing the King; they wanted a way out. Some of the Commissioners hoped that if he were allowed to address Parliament, Charles might propose a compromise that all sides could accept. But Cromwell was well aware that any deal would eventually be disowned by Charles. Anyway, if he had something to offer, why not tell the Court what it was? Cromwell silenced the doubters by the power of his oratory.

The Court reconvened. Bradshaw told Charles that the Court would suffer no further delaying tactics; Parliament would not be summoned. It was time to announce the verdict.

Charles repeated his request to address Parliament, adding, "I so require you as you will answer it at the dreadful Day of Judgment". Bradshaw would not be threatened, and he delivered the Court's judgment. He stated that the King was subject to the law, and he held his office in trust. Contrary to his coronation oath to call parliaments for the protection of the people, Charles had subverted the laws of the land.

Then Bradshaw reached the charge of which Charles was indeed guilty, although it was hardly a criminal offence. "There is a … bargain between the King and his people … the one bond is the bond of protection that is due from the sovereign, the other is the bond of subjection that is due from the subject. Sir, if this bond be once broken, farewell sovereignty …"

Bradshaw was right. From early times, the subject accepted the rule of his lord not from fear or divine right, but in return for protection. Charles had never been concerned with the protection of his subjects, only protection of his own rights. For that he made war on his people.

Bradshaw declared Charles guilty, and the clerk read out the sentence: "that the said Charles Stuart as a tyrant, traitor, murderer and public enemy ... shall be put to death by the severing of his head from his body." The Court kept to the established practice that although traitors were to be hanged, drawn and quartered, for royal traitors beheading was the method of execution.

Charles asked for permission to address the Court, but it was impossible. Once sentence of death had been passed, the condemned prisoner was treated in law as being already dead. Bradshaw was astonished that Charles did not know this. Charles was led away, pausing only to direct condescending insults at those about him who were shouting "Execution!", "Justice!"

A scaffold was erected outside the Royal Banqueting House, which was part of Whitehall Palace. On the morning of 30th January 1649, Charles prepared for his execution. He put on two shirts as it was a cold day and he did not wish to shiver with onlookers saying that he was shaking from fear. Now a brief delay as the Commons hurriedly met to pass an Act making it illegal for anyone to proclaim a new king, for they had not yet abolished the monarchy.

At about two o'clock, Charles made his way along the banqueting hall, through one of the windows and on to the scaffold. The executioner and his assistant were already there, masked as was customary; but for this execution they also wore wigs and false beards.

Unusually, the block was only ten inches high, with staples hammered to the floor to fix ropes to in case Charles struggled and had to be tied down. Charles realised that the public, being kept some distance from the scaffold, would not be able to hear anything he said, so he took out some notes and addressed those on the platform.

He said that he spoke as a good king and a good Christian. Charles denied having started any war against Parliament, and he denied the justice of his sentence. However, he accepted his fate as God's justice for an unjust sentence he had authorised. He was obviously referring to the death warrant he had signed at Parliament's request for the execution of Wentworth. Charles made no mention of the 300,000 people who had perished in the Civil Wars.

Next, he prayed that those guilty of his murder would repent for the great sin they were committing, but he forgave everyone and prayed for the peace of the kingdom. Then at great length he gave advice on how to run the country, ending by declaring himself a martyr. Charles took off his jewels and doublet, put his hair under a cap, removed his cloak and rested his head on the block, having complained that it was too low. He stretched out his hands, and with one blow his head was off.

The execution of Charles I

The people as a whole did not rejoice. It was the army that had demanded Charles's execution. The royal grudge has lasted to this day; it is the Royal Navy, the Royal Air Force, the Royal Marines – but 'the Army'.

****

THE INTERREGNUM

30 January 1649 – 29 May 1660

Not a king, but eventually a sovereign in all but name, Oliver Cromwell was born in Huntingdon in 1599. By a strange coincidence, Oliver's mother's maiden name was Steward, but she was no relation to the Stewards who became Stewarts and then Stuarts. Oliver's father, Richard Cromwell, was a gentleman, the second son of a knight.

There may have been no relationship to the Stuarts through his mother, but Cromwell was related to the Tudors through his father. Owen Tudor's son, Jasper Tudor (uncle of Henry VII), had an illegitimate daughter called Joan Tudor. She married William ap Yevan, and their son was Morgan ap Williams.

He was the Morgan Williams who married Katherine Cromwell, the sister of Henry VIII's chief minister Thomas Cromwell; and Morgan and Katherine's great-grandson was Oliver Cromwell. Seeing an easy advantage, Morgan and Katherine's sons used their mother's maiden surname of Cromwell. The family called themselves 'Cromwell alias Williams' in legal documents, as Oliver did in his marriage contract.

So, even if he did not know it, Oliver Cromwell was the 5 x great-grandson of Owen Tudor, as was Charles I. That made them sixth cousins.

Oliver went from a local school to nearby Cambridge University (a Puritan-controlled institution), although he had to leave when his father died. In time, his mother was able to send Oliver to London to study law at Lincoln's Inn. While in London, Oliver met and later married Elizabeth, daughter of wealthy leather merchant and landowner Sir James Bourchier, after which they returned to live in Huntingdon.

In 1628, Cromwell was elected to Parliament as his father had been before him, but he made little impression. Everything changed when King Charles raised his standard in Nottingham. The 43-year-old Cromwell was one of the first to react. Within a week he had recruited a troop of horse in Huntingdon.

In the first major battle, at Edgehill, Prince Rupert (son of Prince-Elector Frederick and Charles's sister Elizabeth Stuart) led the Royalist Army ('the Cavaliers'); the Earl of Essex (son of Queen Elizabeth's former favourite) led the Parliamentary forces ('the Roundheads'). Cromwell's cavalry played a small but successful role late in the battle. However, there was no victory, and Cromwell returned to London to enlist more men, enlarging his troop to a regiment. With that came promotion to Colonel.

Cromwell's choice of personnel was revolutionary. He had seen the Royalist Army with its cavalry of young nobles, and he saw no hope in using rabble to fight them. So Cromwell concentrated on recruiting believers, men committed to the cause, led by officers with ability, appointed regardless of class. Soon he had a force of 2,000 disciplined men, and when they made their way through towns and villages, the sight of the trained and smartly-uniformed troops encouraged others to enlist. This was the origin of the New Model Army, full-time professional soldiers rather than part-time local militia.

At the next major battle, at Grantham, although heavily outnumbered, the charge of Cromwell's horsemen (later to be named 'the Ironsides') secured victory, and it halted the Royalist Army's march on London. Cromwell was thanked by Parliament, and he proceeded to win several minor engagements, always tactically superior to his opponents. He had learned from Prince Rupert's mistake at Edgehill that when cavalry set men to flight, they should not charge after them for miles in the hope of easy slaughter, but should return to the main battle. It was the same mistake as had been made by the Anglo-Saxons (on foot) at Hastings and by Prince Edward at Lewes. Cromwell's tactical genius was all the more remarkable because he had no military experience. He put it down to God's will.

Cromwell was then sent north to serve under the Parliamentary commander, Lord Fairfax. He saw Cromwell at his best during an engagement at Winceby. Leading the cavalry charge, Cromwell's horse was killed beneath him. Cromwell got to his feet, but was knocked to the ground; scrambling up again he found another horse and continued the assault. Fairfax led the second charge and secured victory.

Now Cromwell was Lieutenant-General and one of the Parliamentary leaders. His rise in both arenas was irresistible. The Battle of Marston Moor in 1644 saw a massive conflict, with the advantage going first one way and then the other. In the heat of the battle, Colonel Marcus Trevor, Commander of one of the Royalist regiments, spotted Cromwell and manoeuvred until he was almost alongside him. Riding as close as he could get to Cromwell, Trevor thrust his sword at Cromwell's head and stabbed him in the neck. But the wound was minor; the attempt to kill Cromwell had failed. Nevertheless, Trevor was rewarded when Charles II became king; he was created Viscount Dungannon.

Cromwell left the action to have his wound dressed. He quickly returned to the fray, and he led his cavalry in a charge that scattered Prince Rupert's horsemen. Contrary to all practice, Cromwell held his men in formation, not allowing them to chase the fleeing Royalists. Imposing his iron discipline, he ordered his men to turn and charge the other Royalist regiments, and a significant victory giving Parliament control of the North was secured. It was Cromwell's secret: having cavalry that could make a second charge, in effect doubling the numbers under his command.

The Royalist Army re-formed, but Cromwell halted their advance with a series of successes. It was now decided that all officers who were members of parliament would leave the army and return to London. However, at Fairfax's request and to the delight of the army, Cromwell was asked to continue as Lieutenant-General of the Horse at the Battle of Naseby.

Having superior numbers, the Parliamentary Army, with the benefit of Fairfax's tactics and Cromwell's genius, not just in leading the cavalry but also in directing the dragoons, gained a decisive victory. Once again, a vital element was Cromwell's control of his horsemen, calling the majority back after routing the Royalist cavalry so that they could attack the Royalist infantry. As if to underline the difference, at the vital moment Prince Rupert and his cavalry were plundering the Parliamentary baggage train in continuation of a successful charge – they ended up two miles from the battle; when they returned, it was too late.

After the Second Civil War ended, Pride's Purge gave control of Parliament to the Independents led by Cromwell.

The first task was to put Charles on trial. Every step Cromwell had taken in war and in Parliament had been successful, confirming to him that all he did was God's will. The execution of the King was no different.

With the King dead, it was said that Cromwell ordered the head to be sewn back on so as to limit the horror suffered by any relatives viewing the corpse before burial. But this is not confirmed. If true, the favour would not be reciprocated; quite the opposite.

Next, the monarchy was abolished, followed two days later by the House of Lords. Then the Privy Council went, as did various courts, the Lord Chancellor, the Chancellor of the Exchequer and the Secretaries of State. All that was left was the House of Commons and the common law courts. Government was put in the hands of a council of 41 elected members. This was the new republic: the Commonwealth.

Two hostile groups faced the Commonwealth. The Levellers complained bitterly about the lack of social reform and the position of Cromwell as a quasi-monarch. More violent opposition came from Royalists in Ireland. Now Commander-in-Chief, Cromwell took an army to Ireland. Nine months of sieges and battles led to the bloody destruction of most of the Royalist strongholds, accompanied by massacres of Royalists and Catholics in towns that had refused to surrender. With Catholicism suppressed, more Protestant settlers were sent to Ireland. Cromwell was welcomed back to London as a hero.

It was time to deal with Scotland where King Charles's oldest son, Charles, had landed and been proclaimed King. Taking his army north, Cromwell (now Lord-General) was faced with a problem: the Scots would not confront him in battle.

That did not make the situation safe. Cromwell advanced with a party of senior officers to reconnoitre near Coltbridge. They were spotted by a group of Scottish soldiers hiding in the undergrowth. One of the Scots stood up, raised his musket and fired at Cromwell, narrowly missing him. Cromwell shouted at the man, saying that if he had been under his command he would have had him cashiered for wasting a random shot from distance. The Scotsman shouted back that it had been no random shot; he had fought at Marston Moor and, having recognised Cromwell, he was taking the opportunity to kill him. With that, he ran off.

After some minor skirmishes, the Scottish Army moved forward, trapping Cromwell's army at Dunbar. Having a two-to-one advantage, the Scots lay down to sleep, expecting victory in the morning. Early on 3rd September 1650, Cromwell attacked, and the Scots were routed in Cromwell's most brilliant triumph.

Nearly a year later, while Cromwell was still in Scotland, Prince Charles marched at the head of a new Scottish army into England, advancing as far as Worcester. Many English supported him, but few would join an army of invading Scots. Cromwell followed with his troops, and was soon only 15 miles away. He held fast until it was to the hour exactly one year from his attack at Dunbar. A pincer movement led to an overwhelming victory: 2,000 killed and 9,000 taken prisoner for the loss of 200 men. Prince Charles hurried back to Paris, and Cromwell retired from the battlefield undefeated.

It was time for a fresh start. Treason in the past by word alone was forgiven, and penalties on Catholics were reduced. Although the Mass was still prohibited, it was no longer compulsory to attend Protestant services. However, there was little social reform and no change in the administration of justice other than abolition of the use of Latin.

Then a new problem arose: there was tension between the army and Parliament over the fact that an election was long overdue. After protracted argument, everything was agreed for a new election. The very next day, 100 members of parliament turned up at the Commons and voted on their own prolongation. When he was told, the deceived Cromwell stormed down to Westminster and addressed the House in fury at their treachery, ending, "You have been sat too long here for any good you have been doing. Depart I say, and let us have done with you. In the name of God, go!" He summoned soldiers, who removed the Speaker and cleared the chamber.

That was the end of the Rump Parliament (the rump that was left after Pride's Purge) to general public satisfaction. A Council headed by Cromwell was established to govern the country until suitable arrangements had been made. The Council nominated 140 members for a new parliament from lists supplied by cities and counties. Within weeks, arguments about tithes (the tax payable to the Church) compelled Cromwell once more to send in the army and dissolve Parliament. This time, power passed to Cromwell.

He rejected the title of king, and agreed to be called Lord Protector; so the Commonwealth became the Protectorate. The position was to be elective, with a governing council and a new parliament in every third year.

The Protectorate produced a period of liberalism when compared to Puritan rule. Cromwell allowed dancing and theatre, even opera; literature flourished with Milton, Dryden, Lock, Isaak Walton and Marvel; and hunting and sport were encouraged. Cromwell himself smoked tobacco and drank alcohol, and he is said to have introduced port drinking to England. All a far cry from his stern reputation, although he did maintain the prohibition of Christmas festivities introduced by the Puritans who disliked their boisterous nature and the connection with Catholicism.

An example of Cromwell's toleration was his attitude towards the Jews, Cromwell being only too aware of their contribution to the intellectual and economic prosperity of the Netherlands. When Cromwell's secretary John Thurlow visited The Hague, he met with Manasseh ben Israel, a leader of the Jewish community, and, presumably on Cromwell's instructions, advised Manasseh to apply to the English government seeking permission for the re-admission of Jews. Tolerant individuals and Puritans seeing an opportunity for conversion were in favour; merchants and most of the populace were against. The matter was argued in the Council and elsewhere, and in view of the opposition the matter was put aside. However, it was made clear that Jews already in England (mainly descendants of refugees from the Spanish Inquisition) were allowed to stay and follow their faith undisturbed, the Chief Justice having declared that the expulsion order of 1290 only applied to the Jews living in England in 1290. It was in effect an informal re-admission.

Toleration did not satisfy everyone. With one man holding so much power, assassination was always an option.

In early 1654, a group of Royalists plotted to assassinate Cromwell as he travelled to Hampton Court, a journey he made almost every Saturday with a troop of only thirty horsemen. After the assassination, the plan was for an army of 10,000 men led by Prince Rupert and James Duke of York (Charles I's second son) to land in Sussex and proclaim Charles Stuart as king. The plot was discovered, and three of the principal conspirators, Peter Vowell, John Gerard and Summerset Fox, were seized and charged with treason. Vowell was hanged, and Gerard was beheaded. As he had confessed, Summerset Fox's life was spared, he was transported to Barbados – it was the first time in English legal history that anyone had pleaded guilty to a charge of treason; it would only happen one more time.

Some of the Levellers also plotted assassination. A former Leveller officer, Edward Sexby (who had been court-martialled for executing a soldier and withholding his men's pay), met in the Netherlands with another former Leveller soldier, Miles Sindercombe (who had fled after a failed mutiny), and they decided to murder Cromwell. They opposed his elevation to Lord Protector; they wanted a genuine republic.

Sexby would supply money and weapons, Sindercombe would gather more men and would carry out the assassination. Back in England, Sindercombe recruited renegade soldier John Cecil, petty criminal William Boyes and John Toope, who was one of Cromwell's guards.

They decided to shoot Cromwell as he travelled through Westminster in his coach. Sindercombe rented a house in King Street, from which they would be able to see Cromwell's coach as it went past. They quickly realised that it would be difficult for them to escape after the shooting, so they abandoned the plan.

Then they sought to shoot Cromwell with an arquebus as he left prayers in Westminster Abbey before the opening of Parliament. The arquebus was a lightweight predecessor of the rifle, capable of firing a shot that could pierce armour. On 17th September 1656, the conspirators met in the house of a Royalist, Colonel Mydhope, which was located next to the exit door of the Abbey. The first floor window would give a clear view of Cromwell as he left. Boyes was to do the shooting. He held the arquebus at the window, waiting for Cromwell to appear. As he waited, a large crowd gathered in the street below. The assassins would not be able to run through the crowd to get away. Boyes panicked, threw down the firearm and ran off.

Next, they decided to shoot Cromwell as he made his weekly journey to spend the weekend at Hampton Court. Sindercombe rented a house in Hammersmith from the coachman of the Earl of Salisbury. The house had a dining room that overlooked the narrow street along which Cromwell's coach always passed, so narrow that the coach travelled at walking pace. Toope, as one of Cromwell's guards, agreed to let Sindercombe know when Cromwell would be passing. All was prepared. Then, for some reason, Cromwell decided that on this occasion he would travel to Hampton Court by boat.

Still persisting, Sindercombe formulated a new plan. Cromwell often went for a walk in Hyde Park. So, the proposal was that Cecil would ride towards Cromwell, shoot him and then ride off. But as Cecil came near, Cromwell walked right up to him and complimented him on his horse. Cecil could not cope with the situation; he lost his nerve and galloped off, later telling Sindercombe that the horse had caught a chill and he would not have been able to ride away.

Finally, they decided to plant explosives in the chapel in Whitehall Palace where Cromwell often prayed. Toope helped them gain access, and they planted a device made of gunpowder, tar and pitch. Then Toope took fright and informed the authorities, and the explosives were removed. Boyes ran off, but Cecil and Sindercombe were caught. Sindercombe avoided a traitor's death. A letter was delivered to him in prison, and the guards watched bemused as Sindercombe rubbed the letter on his hands and nose (or what was left of it after most had been cut off in the struggle when he was arrested); then he held his hands to his nose and mouth, inhaling and licking his fingers. The paper had been soaked in arsenic, and

Sindercombe collapsed and died. Sexby was later arrested, but died of a fever before his trial.

Once more it was proposed that Cromwell should be crowned king. The Royalists were not altogether against the idea, at least it would re-establish the principle of monarchy; there would just be a contest between two families: the Cromwells and the Stuarts. Cromwell agonised on how to respond. After ten weeks of indecision, Cromwell said that he could not take the title of king, but he would be prepared to nominate his successor.

Now in his sixtieth year, Cromwell fell ill, probably malaria, possibly septicaemia. He struggled on, straining for an extra few days until he reached the anniversary of his famous victories at Dunbar and Worcester. Then, on 3rd September 1658, he died without nominating his successor.

Memories last for generations, statues of Cromwell being the main bone of contention. Queen Victoria refused to open the new Manchester Town Hall, because there was a statue of Cromwell outside. The Irish Nationalist Party forced Parliament to abandon a proposal to erect a statue of Cromwell in the House of Commons. Instead, it was erected outside Parliament, paid for by Prime Minister Lord Rosebery and his wife, Hannah de Rothschild.

****

CHARLES II

30 January 1649 (de jure) or
29 May 1660 (restoration) – 6 February 1685

Charles I left six legitimate children: Charles, Mary, James, Elizabeth, Henry and Henrietta. Of course, on Charles's execution in 1649 there was no coronation; first it was the Commonwealth, then the Protectorate.

After Naseby, Prince Charles fled first to the Isles of Scilly, then to Jersey[22], and after that he joined his mother in exile in Paris, spending the following years in idleness and debauchery. He later moved to the Netherlands where he was informed of his father's execution when his chaplain entered the room and addressed Charles as "Your Majesty"; nothing more had to be said. Not long afterwards, Charles started an affair with an English exile, Lucy Walter, and she bore him an illegitimate son, James, later to be the Duke of Monmouth.

Despite the excesses, Charles was determined to recover the throne, and he realised that it would be easier to gain it through Ireland or Scotland where the execution of his father had been unpopular. The Scots offered Charles support on condition

---

22 In gratitude, after the Restoration Charles granted to the Governer of Jersey, George Carteret, land in the American colonies called New Netherlands, which Carteret naturally renamed New Jersey.

that he adopted Presbyterianism and promised to enforce its observance in England and Ireland. So Charles decided to forget about Scotland and instead go to Ireland. Whilst he was in Jersey (the only Royalist stronghold never taken by Parliament) waiting for a ship, he learned that Cromwell had arrived in Ireland with an army. Charles immediately changed his plans and went to Scotland, forced to accept the terms the Scots had demanded; though he had absolutely no intention of keeping to the bargain.

After Cromwell's victory at Dunbar, Charles was crowned King of Scotland and was given a new army, but he was utterly defeated at Worcester. Charles had been watching the battle from Worcester Cathedral's tower, but when he learned that the Duke of Hamilton's head had been blown off, Charles joined the fighting, taking command. Seizing the opportunity, Cromwell's forces made every effort to kill Charles, so much so that two horses perished under him. But Charles survived the attempts to kill him, and in defeat he managed to escape.

He left in such a hurry that he failed to pay £453 and 3 shillings to Worcester Clothiers for the uniforms they had supplied for his army. The present Prince Charles paid off his ancestor's debt in June 2008, but he declined to pay interest, which at 5% p.a. compounded annually amounted to £15,643,542,841.

Charles fled with Lord Wilmot, Colonel Giffard and others, and they raced to Giffard's Boscobel Estate. There they met the five Pendrell brothers, who were tenants living on the estate. They gave Charles old clothes to wear, and they cut his hair short.

Once it was dark, Richard Pendrell rode off with Charles, heading for Wales where Royalist support was strong. They reached the River Severn, only to discover that the riverside was being patrolled by Parliamentary troops. So they returned to Boscobel where they met another fugitive, Colonel Carlis.

Suddenly, a man came running into the building shouting that Parliamentary soldiers were approaching. Charles and Carlis were taken into the woodlands (Boscobel from the Italian *bosco bello* – beautiful woodland), and they were helped to climb high up a large oak tree. There they hung on, crouching motionless all day. Having found no fugitives in the houses on the estate, the troops began a search of the grounds. If caught, Charles would either have been killed (there was £1,000 on his head, dead or alive), or arrested and taken to London for trial. Charles had invaded England with an army from another country, so a conviction for treason would be automatic. His life literally hung in the balance as the soldiers searched the undergrowth below, but finding no one, they moved on.

Late the next day, the Pendrells took Charles to Moseley Old Hall, where Lord Wilmot was waiting for them. Charles was given food and wine by a Catholic priest, Father John Huddleston, who was chaplain to Thomas Whitgreave, the owner of the Hall.

Charles rested for two days, and again a warning was received that soldiers were approaching. Huddleston and Charles were hidden in a priest hole, the secret room built in many Catholic homes to hide those in danger. Fortunately, the soldiers were not looking for Charles; they had come to arrest Thomas Whitgreave, who was suspected of fighting for Charles at Worcester. However, Whitgreave had not fought at Worcester because he had been ill. When the Parliamentary soldiers were convinced of his innocence, they left without searching the building.

Lord Wilmot had planned to escape from England by acting as servant to Jane Lane, who had a pass (as was required by a Catholic) for herself and a manservant to travel to Bristol to visit a friend. Wilmot suggested that Charles should take his place. So Charles and Jane set out, and after five weeks of adventures and near capture they reached Shoreham on the south coast. Charles boarded a coal boat, The Surprise, and for £60 he was taken to France.

After the Restoration, Jane Lane received £1,000 – the sum on Charles's head. The Pendrell brothers were granted a pension of £200 a year in perpetuity; it is still being paid, although now divided amongst many descendants. As for the oak tree, it is commemorated in the name of 626 pubs called 'The Royal Oak'.

Charles travelled around Europe, gaining the reputation of a wastrel. He left Lucy to die in abject poverty, having already taken their child from her. Charles's future seemed hopeless.

Then, in 1658 Cromwell died, and his son, Richard, was appointed Lord Protector. Richard Cromwell had neither the ability nor the desire for the position; and he was not a soldier, so the army did not support him. Besides, the mood in England was for the restoration of the monarchy. General Monck marched to London with an army and reinstated Parliament, and this time it was controlled by Royalists. Charles immediately announced a pardon for his enemies, his intention to uphold the Anglican Church, his desire for liberty of conscience for all Christians and his promise to leave all difficult questions to Parliament. In response, Parliament sent a ship to collect him with a gift of £50,000. Richard Cromwell escaped to France, and Charles returned to England, reaching London on 29th May 1660 (his 30th birthday) amid wild celebrations. Once crowned King Charles II, the Restoration saw the encouragement of sport, theatre (women being allowed to act on stage for the first time), music, the arts and the sciences.

Later in the year, it was time for retribution. Of the 59 regicides who had signed Charles I's death warrant, 20 had already died. Those who were still alive were pursued; 9 were executed and 3 died before execution, 14 were sentenced to life imprisonment, 12 escaped abroad and just one was pardoned. Of the Commissioners who did not sign the warrant, 6 were imprisoned for life, one was murdered, and most of the others suffered fines and confiscations. Many others involved in Charles I's trial, such as clerks and guards, suffered similar fates; although only John Cook the prosecutor, one officer and a preacher were hanged, drawn and quartered – but the identity of the executioner of Charles I was never discovered.

Charles had had enough: "… I am weary of hanging, except

upon new offences." It was not enough for everyone. On the anniversary of Charles I's execution, the bodies of Cromwell, his son-in-law Henry Ireton and Bradshaw were dug up, dragged along the streets of London from Holborn to Tyburn, hanged all day and then executed[23]; although it may be that in anticipation of revenge Bradshaw's son had taken his father's corpse to Jamaica for burial and replaced it with another. The heads were stuck on poles at the top of Westminster Hall, where they remained for over 20 years. Cromwell's head was then blown down in a gale, picked up and sold from person to person until in 1960 it reached his old college, Sidney Sussex at Cambridge University, where it now lies buried – the precise location remaining secret for fear of mischief by Royalists.

There was still one problem; Charles had not produced an heir. He married the Catholic Catherine of Braganza, daughter of King John IV of Portugal and Luisa of Medina-Sidonia. So the great-granddaughter of the Admiral of the Spanish Armada became Queen of England. Her dowry included Bombay, Tangier and £300,000; and the chance acquisition of Bombay became the base from which colonial India and the British Empire developed.

Mistresses and illegitimate children multiplied in the scandalous court, with honours and titles heaped upon them. Charles eventually acknowledged that fourteen illegitimate children were his, but there would be no legitimate children – Catherine was barren. However, she did make two lasting contributions to English life. One was making tea-drinking fashionable. Although it was the favourite drink of the Portuguese court (brought from Portuguese possessions in the Far East), until Catherine's arrival in London, tea was a rarity in England. The other was the introduction of the fork at dining tables, previously regarded as an effeminate south-European custom.

Now Charles's easygoing life was about to be interrupted. He wanted religious toleration for all Christians, the Council

---

[23] Colonel Pride was to suffer the same fate, but his corpse was too decayed.

having already formalised the re-admission of the Jews on Charles's urging. However, Parliament wanted further restrictions on Catholics and Puritans. Charles wanted peace, Parliament wanted war against the Netherlands, now England's greatest rival in foreign trade. On both issues Charles was overruled.

The war would make official the fighting that was already taking place between the two nations. In North America, the Dutch towns of New Amsterdam and Fort Orange were taken. Senior members of the Royal Family had to have at least two titles, one English and one Scottish. Charles's brother James was accordingly Duke of York in England and Duke of Albany in Scotland. So, in his honour, New Amsterdam was renamed New York and Fort Orange became Albany. New York was later divided into twelve counties, including 'Queens' named after Catherine and 'Kings' named after Charles.

All the joys of life came to a halt in June 1665, when plague struck London, killing over 100,000 people, later moving on to other parts of the country. It was believed that dogs and cats spread the disease, so the Lord Mayor ordered their destruction. The killing of 40,000 dogs and 200,000 cats allowed rats (the true culprits) to reproduce in ever greater numbers. By September 1666, the plague had gone, never to return. In its place another disaster arrived as the Great Fire of London destroyed most of the town, although only nine people were killed. St Paul's Cathedral was made of stone and unlikely to catch fire. Unfortunately, it was being renovated and was covered in wooden scaffolding, so it burned to the ground.

After the fire, it was planned to rebuild London in a geometric pattern with avenues and gardens, much like Paris in later years. But in the aftermath of the plague and the fire, it was impossible to trace all the property owners in order to buy their land, so the rebuilding kept to the original haphazard pattern.

The war with the Netherlands appeared to be a stalemate, until another year brought another disaster. A Dutch fleet sailed up the River Medway (to the south of the Thames) as far as Chatham, fired on riverside towns, captured Sheerness on the North Sea coast, destroyed English vessels and towed away the navy's flagship. England quickly entered peace negotiations with the Netherlands.

Better times came in 1669, with Sir Christopher Wren leading the rebuilding of London, and Charles becoming absorbed in horse racing at Newmarket; it therefore became known as 'the sport of kings'. In the meantime, the court continued totally out of control; debauched, drunken and with the occasional murder. One of the court's beauties was Frances Stewart. Charles had Jan Roettiers paint her in profile dressed as Britannia, holding a trident and shield. That image has appeared on English medals and coins ever since.

Charles's latest mistress was the actress and (possibly) former prostitute, Nell Gwynne. When she produced an illegitimate son for Charles, she is said to have insisted on calling him 'Little Bastard', complaining that he had no other name; so Charles made him Earl of Burford and later Duke of St Albans. Another four bastards became dukes; two became earls.

Although Charles and his siblings living in England had been brought up as Protestants, his mother had managed to bring up her youngest child, Henrietta (called 'Minette'), in Paris as a Catholic. Minette had been married off to King Louis' brother, Philip Duke of Orleans, a homosexual and a brute. Living virtually alone, Minette became very close to Charles, and it was with her assistance (possibly at her instigation) that Charles negotiated the secret Treaty of Dover with her brother-in-law, King Louis XIV, who was also Charles's and Minette's cousin.

Under the terms of the treaty, Charles promised to join Catholic France in war against the Protestant Netherlands, to convert to Catholicism at a time of his choosing and to impose Catholicism in England. In return, Charles was to be paid £200,000 for each year of war against the Netherlands, plus £140,000 for imposing Catholicism. Was it greed, or was it plain stupidity? If the details became public, his crown would be gone within days.

Perhaps Charles's friendship with the French should have been no surprise; he was after all half-French and half-Scottish, he had lived in exile in France, and the English had killed his father. The treaty was signed, but Charles's conversion was put on hold when Minette died three weeks later, said to have been poisoned by her husband's long-time lover, the Chevalier de Lorraine.

To cheer Charles up, Louis sent him a lady-in-waiting, Louise de Kerouaille, to be his next mistress; and the descendants of their illegitimate son, Charles Lennox Duke of Richmond would include the past and present wives of the current Prince Charles and Prince Andrew: Diana, Camilla and Sarah; so when the present Prince William becomes king, he will be the first descendent of Charles II to do so. Suitably cheered, Charles was ready to deal with his treaty obligations. Without consulting Parliament, Charles issued a Declaration of Indulgence, allowing Catholics to worship in private and allowing Dissenters (Protestants who had separated from the Church of England) to worship together if they obtained a licence. Two days later, he declared war on the Netherlands, foreign affairs still being a royal prerogative. Taxation to provide funds for war was for Parliament, but ever since Charles signed the secret Treaty of Dover, Parliament had agreed to his periodic requests for money to enlarge the army and the navy in ignorance of the true purpose.

War with the Netherlands had mixed results. The English Navy was comprehensively defeated by the Dutch. However, the French Army drove into Dutch territory. In desperation, the Dutch opened their dykes to flood the countryside so as to halt the French advance, and they gave leadership of the provinces to William of Orange, Charles's nephew.

The politicians were angry. Charles's war had been a failure, the English now favoured the Protestant Netherlands not Catholic France, and the revocation of statutes relating to religion was for Parliament, not the King.

"I am resolved to stick to my Declaration," was Charles's defiant response. In retaliation, Parliament refused to supply Charles with more money. He withdrew the Declaration.

That encouraged Parliament to go further. They passed a Test Act; every holder of office under the Crown had to confirm acceptance of the beliefs of the Anglican Church. Several members of the Council had to resign; so did Charles's brother James (a recent convert to Catholicism), who was also the heir to the throne and Lord High Admiral.

Still Charles kept the Treaty of Dover a secret. He told Parliament: "I assure you, there is no ... treaty with France not already printed ..." It was concealed for 140 years.

Without sufficient money, Charles had to abandon the war against the Netherlands, so breaking his promise to Louis. He then dissolved Parliament. Charles's stupidity and duplicity brought England to the verge of another civil war. Like father, like son. At least he did not abandon London and raise his standard.

Instead, Charles put Thomas Osborne (later to be the Earl of Danby) in charge of the Council, and Danby succeeded in managing the country and the economy with a combination of intelligence and bribery. The bribery gave him control of Parliament, such that his supporters became the court party insultingly called 'Tories' by their opponents, a contraction of 'Toraidhes' – the name given to Irish thieves. The opposition formed their own party, insultingly called 'Whigs' by their opponents – the name given to Scottish outlaws. The Whigs wanted to exclude Catholic heirs to the throne; the Tories were against exclusion. Even though staunchly Protestant, the Tory gentry disliked anything that upset the accepted rules of heredity. They had gained their titles and wealth by those rules, and they feared anything that might challenge them.

In late 1677, William III of Orange, champion of the Protestants, arrived in England to a hero's welcome. Charles humoured his people with what he thought was a small gesture; he gave his 15-year-old niece Mary (his brother James's daughter, but a Protestant) to his nephew William (therefore Mary's cousin) in marriage.

By mid-1678 the mood in the country was extremely nervous. Would France attack? Who would be the next monarch? Despite all the illegitimate children with mistresses, Charles had no children with Queen Catherine; and now that Charles had venereal disease, he could never produce an heir. His Catholic brother, James, was next in line. Could he be excluded? Charles was determined not to allow it. The country was on the edge.

It was 13th August 1678, and Charles was taking his daily walk in St James's Park. Christopher Kirkby, a man who was known to the King, came up to Charles, "Sire, your enemies have a design against your life ... you may be in danger in this very walk."

"How may that be?" asked Charles. "By being shot at," was the reply. Charles waved the man away and continued his walk. With all the Stuart failings, cowardice was not one of them. Nothing happened.

Kirkby had been put up to it by two men, Israel Tonge and Titus Oates. Tonge was a biologist and a cleric, a man devoted to discovering supposed Catholic plots. Oates was a perjurer, a man willing to give false evidence at a price, having been expelled from two Cambridge colleges, falsely claimed a degree, been ordained a Protestant priest, then imprisoned for perjury and escaping, later appointed a naval chaplain and been expelled for buggery, converted to Catholicism, then expelled from two Jesuit colleges, now once more a Protestant.

These two scoundrels had decided to invent the story of a Catholic conspiracy to murder Charles following which his Catholic brother James would take the throne. As it was exactly what much of the country feared, people readily believed it, even though it was wholly untrue.

Rebuffed by Charles, they took their lies to the anti-Catholic Earl of Danby, who took them seriously. He put the two liars in front of the Council, where in the presence of the King they disclosed the names of the principal Catholic conspirators. They included the Pope, King Louis, the General of the Jesuits, the Archbishop of Dublin and five leading Catholic lords. Charles was to be seized by Irish thugs and stabbed by Jesuits, Oates later claiming that Charles would also be shot with silver bullets (said to make healing impossible) or poisoned by the Queen's doctor. Next, Catholics would murder thousands of Protestants in London and then burn the city to the ground. Charles treated it as a joke and left for Newmarket.

Two very real events now occurred, and they gave Oates's story credibility. The secretary of James's wife (whose name was on Oates's list of conspirators) was found to have written in code to prominent Catholics in France seeking funds and looking forward to the time when power would be in the hands of James and the English Catholics. Next, the magistrate to whom Tonge and Oates had given their evidence was found murdered on Primrose Hill. Londoners took fright. Catholic homes were ransacked, Catholic books were burned, Catholic priests were sent to prison. Oates was now the saviour of the nation, and he was given a troop of soldiers with which to arrest Catholics.

There is a story that one blameless Catholic confessed under torture to involvement in the plot. Forced to name his non-existent accomplices, he cried out "Greenberry Hill!" – Primrose Hill had formerly been called Greenberry Hill. The story goes on to say that in Somerset House (where the Queen had a Catholic chapel) there were three Catholic servants named Green, Berry and Hill. Although completely innocent, they were arrested and hanged.

Many Catholics were executed in the lust for blood. Charles knew that it was nonsense, but he signed the death warrants nonetheless. "Let the blood lie on those that condemn them," was his lame defence.

However, when the Commons started to debate the exclusion of James as his successor, Charles fought back. He dissolved Parliament. So the country found a Protestant hero who might take the crown: the Duke of Monmouth. Dashing, ambitious and son of the King, even if he was illegitimate. But the nobility and the gentry opposed him; if an illegitimate son could inherit the crown, who might turn up to claim their inheritances?

Charles was tireless in his opposition to the Exclusionists. Then Oates overstepped the mark and denounced James as a traitor. Oates was sent to prison for sedition (undermining the authority or peace of the state), and the anti-Catholic hysteria calmed down.

The calm did not last very long. In June 1683, Charles was at Newmarket, enjoying his horses and the racing. The entertainment was halted when a fire destroyed many of the buildings, including Charles's house. As a result, he returned to London early, travelling with his brother James.

Unaware of that early return, supporters of Monmouth had gathered at a property owned by Richard Rumbold, a former officer in Cromwell's New Model Army. It was known as the Rye House, in Hoddesdon in Hertfordshire, located on the road from Newmarket to London. The plan was to conceal 100 men in the grounds of the Rye House, overturn a cart on the road so as to halt the royal carriage and then ambush the royal party, killing Charles and James, after which the Duke of Monmouth would be proclaimed as king. They prepared the cart, and then they waited and waited; still the look-outs did not report the approach of the royal party. The Newmarket fire had saved both Charles and James from being murdered. They had travelled past the Rye House before the would-be assassins had blocked the road.

The conspirators were worried; were their names known to Charles's spymasters? They rushed to be the first to inform on their colleagues so as to save their skins. Some left the country, some were arrested, and several were executed. Monmouth, no stranger to the plot, fled to the Netherlands, as did Rumbold.

Now the only problems for Charles were the rift with his son, Monmouth, and ensuring the succession of the Catholic James. Then a bigger problem arrived. On the morning of Monday 2nd February 1685, Charles suffered a fit and collapsed. Two days of medical treatment, mainly bleedings and potions, led to a gradual deterioration in the King's condition. It was clear that death was approaching.

James was at his brother's side. Charles sent James to find a Catholic priest (or perhaps James did it of his own volition). He brought Father Huddleston, who had been given a position in the Queen's household as reward for helping Charles in his escape after the Battle of Worcester.

Huddleston heard Charles's confession and reconciled him to the Roman Church. On Friday morning, 6th February 1685, Charles died a converted Catholic. The suddeness of his death led to allegations of poison; although a kidney dysfunction is now considered more likely.

The Rye House Plot, not Titus Oates's evil lies, had been the real conspiracy to murder Charles and James; but the nearest Charles came to a violent death was at the Battle of Worcester. As they waited in Hoddesden, the Rye House assassins would not have known that just down the road (four miles away) in Cheshunt, lived a man in constant fear of assassination. He used the name John Clarke. It was in fact Richard Cromwell, for a short time Lord Protector of the country, who had returned to England in 1680. Richard Cromwell lived on another 27 years, dying in 1712 at the age of 85; the longest-lived ruler England ever had.[24]

And perhaps he, and not Elizabeth I, was the last Tudor to rule England as the 6 x great-grandson of Owen Tudor.

****

---

[24] Queen Elizabeth II overtook him on 29th January 2012.

JAMES II

6 February 1685 – 11 December 1688

Imprisoned with his brother Henry and sister Elizabeth after the fall of Oxford, Royalists helped the 14-year-old James escape to the Netherlands dressed as a girl. He was taken to the court of his mother and older brother in Paris.

After years of exile, James achieved his ambition to attain high military rank. He was commissioned in the army of the King of France, fighting against the Spanish. James acquitted himself well, earning promotion to Lieutenant-General. Then, in 1655, Cromwell agreed to send some of his Ironsides to assist the French. One of the terms of the agreement was that Prince Charles, James and seventeen other prominent Royalists were to be expelled from France. James's response was to change sides and join the Spanish Army.

Now James fought against the French in Spain's attempt to relieve the siege of Dunkirk. Almost 18,000 French troops and 2,000 Ironsides faced a Spanish army that included 2,000 English and Irish Royalists, hoped by many to be the core of an army that would invade England and restore the monarchy. The French attacked in what would be known as the Battle of the Dunes because of the fierce assault by one of the Ironside regiments up a 50 metre-high sand dune.

James led his troop of horse, charging several times, but they were outnumbered and endured heavy casualties. In the melee, the French singled out James as the leader of the cavalry. He was struck with blows that would have killed most men, but the attempts to kill him failed. James was saved by the high quality of his armour. The Spanish were defeated. Only 700 of the Royalists survived, and that ended the prospect of an invasion of England.

After his brother was crowned King Charles II, James returned to England. James was a strict, dour man; his interests being confined to warfare, hunting and women. In 1660, to general disapproval, James married the pregnant Anne Hyde[25], daughter of the Chancellor. Disapproval, because Anne was a commoner and James was, for the time being at least, heir to the throne. Soon after the child was born, a wave of smallpox struck London, and the baby died as did James's brother Henry and his sister Mary.

It was at about this time that James found a new mistress, one of his wife's ladies-in-waiting, Arabella Churchill. She would give birth to four of James's illegitimate children, all called 'Fitzjames' – from *fiz*, Norman for 'the son of', used in England for the surnames of illegitimate children of kings and princes (most of the King's bastards were called 'Fitzroy'). Arabella was the daughter of Sir Winston Churchill, an impoverished cavalry officer in Charles I's defeated Royalist Army who had been heavily fined during the Commonwealth. Churchill was rewarded on the Restoration with a seat in Parliament, a place at court for Arabella and a post for her brother John, who became a page in James's household. Arabella's grandfather, John Churchill, had married Sara Winston. Wishing to perpetuate her family name, rather than adopting a double-barrelled surname, they used 'Winston' as a first name for their son; so 'Winston' was converted into a forename and became a

---

25 She was the last English woman to marry an heir presumptive or apparent to the Crown until Diana.

traditional name for Churchill boys.

In time, young John Churchill joined the army, James's influence assuring him of a favourable position. Churchill's rise would be meteoric. A hero in just about every action in which he took part, he climbed to ever higher rank and greater wealth, spurred on by his naked ambition and later aided by the grasping aspirations of his wife.

James's responsibility was the navy. He had been appointed Lord High Admiral, and in the 1665 war against the Dutch, James commanded the fleet. The navies met at the Battle of Lowestoft, sailing in line past each other, guns ablaze. Then both fleets turned and sailed past one another in line once more. Next, James decided to seek out and attack the ship of the Admiral of the Dutch fleet. He found it, and the two vessels exchanged broadsides.

During the attack, James was standing on the deck of the Royal Charles accompanied by several senior officers. Seeing them all standing together on the English flagship, the Dutch let fly with chain shot. It was a recent invention in which two cannonballs were linked by a short chain, so that when fired they spun, forming a massive projectile, and it proved to be hugely effective for bringing down masts and massacring sailors. The English officers stood transfixed as the spinning weapon hurtled towards them. It struck the group, all in their finest naval uniforms. Several of them were decapitated. The chain shot also took off half of the Earl of Falmouth's head; it was unkindly said that it was the first proof ever provided that he had any brains – it was also the last.

James was covered in the blood of his colleagues. However, he had been lucky, he was one of the few not to be harmed. Another attempt to kill him had failed. Even luckier for James, a random English shot hit the magazine of the Dutch flagship, and it blew up. This was the opportunity to seize a decisive victory. James gave the order to pursue the Dutch fleet, and then he went below for a sleep. While he slept, the order was mistakenly countermanded, and the Dutch escaped. After the disaster when the Dutch sailed up the Medway humiliating the English Navy, peace was agreed.

Once more at court, James secretly converted to Catholicism, his wife having converted some time before. Then Charles's Declaration of Indulgence led to the Test Act, and James was compelled to resign his naval office, so announcing his conversion. James suffered another blow in 1671, when Anne died, leaving him with two daughters, Mary and Anne, six other children having died in infancy. Two years later a new wife was found for James; the Catholic Princess Mary of Modena.

Having weathered the anti-Catholic hysteria resulting from Oates's lies, the efforts to bar James from the succession and the failed attempt to murder him in the Rye House Plot, James recovered his status in the last years of his brother's reign. The Test Act was ignored and James was restored to the Council, assisting Charles in ruling the country.

Yet despite the fears of James's Catholicism, when Charles died, James was readily accepted as king. Many people looked forward to a disciplined, hard-working man instead of the duplicitous, lazy Charles. The only drawbacks with James were his desire to impose Catholicism, and belief in his divine right to absolute power.

Titus Oates was dealt with straight away. He was convicted of perjury and sentenced by Judge Jeffries. After two days in a pillory, he was stripped, tied to a cart and whipped as he was dragged a mile from Aldgate to Newgate. Then he was imprisoned for life.

More importantly, in Amsterdam the Duke of Monmouth (the Protestant son of the last king, but illegitimate) was preparing to make his move. He would land in the Protestant south-west and at the same time the Duke of Argyll (with the former owner of the Rye House, Richard Rumbold, as his second-in-command) would raise his Campbell clan and the Covenanters in Scotland. Argyll failed, and many of his supporters were branded and sent to the West Indies as slaves.

Both Argyll and Rumbold were executed, and part of the former Leveller's speech from the scaffold would be much-quoted when the American Constitution was being framed: "… none comes into the world with a saddle on his back, neither any booted and spurred to ride him…"

There was initial success for Monmouth in south-west England, where he was proclaimed king. But he had struck too early; hatred of James II had not yet had time to develop. James's army, led by the Earl of Feversham, defeated Monmouth's forces at the Battle of Sedgemoor. Feversham's second-in-command was John Churchill (now Baron Churchill).

Monmouth was later captured and condemned to death. The public executioner, Jack Ketch, completely botched the beheading. Five strikes of the axe were not enough to sever Monmouth's head, and Ketch had to finish the job with a knife. His reward is that the hangman in Punch and Judy shows is named Jack Ketch. It is said that after the execution, it was discovered that there was no official portrait of Monmouth (he was, after all, the son of a king). So his head was sewn back on, and Monmouth sat motionless while his portrait was painted, and then he was buried.

Victory was not enough for James. Monmouth's soldiers were relentlessly pursued, and those who were caught were killed. Next, James decided to teach the people a lesson. Three hundred Monmouth supporters were hanged, drawn and quartered following the Bloody Assizes, supervised by Judge Jeffries – the Hanging Judge. Dozens more were whipped to death, and a thousand were transported as slaves to the West Indies. Some who had money were merely fined, including Daniel Defoe who would later write *Robinson Crusoe*. The country was subdued, parts of the quartered men displayed in just about every town and village in south-west England.

James now appointed Catholics to senior posts in the army and the Council. This was at a time when a flood of Huguenot (French Protestant) refugees was arriving in England. They brought stories of their persecution following King Louis' revocation of the Edict of Nantes, which had granted rights to Protestants and guaranteed their safety in specified towns. Hundreds of Protestants were killed, and over 400,000 left France. This filled English Protestants with fear of what James might do.

Full of confidence, James demanded funds from Parliament to strengthen the army, an army commanded largely by Catholic officers. The refugees had told of how Louis had used the army to force Huguenots to convert to Catholicism. Many politicians voiced their unease at the prospect of an enlarged army in James's hands, so he dissolved Parliament.

James then gathered his forces outside London, where Catholic officers made a point of publicly celebrating Mass. Next a commission was given the power to suspend or discharge Protestant clergymen. Protestants could almost feel the noose tightening. The expectation was that the Jesuits (a Catholic anti-Protestant order with a military-style organisation) would soon take control.

For some time, fear of another civil war and the power of James's army kept the population's discontent peaceful. Probably the Protestants were biding their time. James was now 54 years old; of the 13 English kings since Edward III, only one (James I) had reached his 56th birthday, and even he died at 58. James's heir was his Protestant daughter Mary, and she was married to the hero of Protestantism, William of Orange. Surely there would soon be a Protestant monarch to undo all that James had done.

It was a solution for the Protestants, but for the Catholics it was a problem. They wanted a law enacted that would provide for the succession to bypass James's daughters, Mary and Anne, and his nephew William. James's niece, Marie Louise (daughter of the Catholic Minette), was next in line. That would not have been a good solution because she was already Queen Consort of Spain. Anyway, the proposal made no progress because James was against it; just as Charles would not exclude his brother, so James would not exclude his daughters – it was contrary to the divine plan.

Besides, James had a better idea. He had a young wife, so he was going to pray for the birth of a son who would lawfully take precedence over older sisters, and that son would be brought up as a Catholic. It worked; a few weeks later the Queen became pregnant, and James was certain it would be a boy. Not just a boy, but a strong healthy boy; this despite the fact that Queen Mary had so far had two miscarriages, three children who died before the age of one, and one who died aged four.

James now ordered that in all churches the terms of his Declaration of Indulgence should be read from the pulpit on four successive Sundays, thereby announcing the return of Catholicism. Seven bishops refused, so they were sent to the Tower.

Then, several weeks earlier than expected, the Queen gave birth to a healthy boy. It seemed too convenient. People were suspicious. Had the Queen really given birth? If so, had it been a girl, swapped with someone else's baby boy? James ordered an enquiry, which proved nothing. Rumours spread, and the public mood was not helped when James asked the Pope to be the baby's godfather.

With a Catholic male heir, James felt stronger than ever. He ordered the seven bishops in the Tower to be tried for treason. To widespread public celebration, they were acquitted. James had misjudged the situation, his new son had not made his position stronger, it had made it weaker because Protestant complacency towards an ageing Catholic king with a Protestant heir had been replaced by horror at the prospect of a line of Catholic monarchs. Who was the alternative? After James's new-born son, the first in line was James's Protestant daughter Mary; the first male in line was James's Protestant nephew William of Orange – and he was married to Mary.

Protestant refugees who reached the Netherlands told William of the disaffection in England and the longing for a Protestant monarch. William was encouraged when he was sent promises of support by prominent Englishmen, including Danby and Lord Churchill (still smarting at being only second-in-command at the Battle of Sedgemoor). Then, William received a letter signed by Danby, the Bishop of London and others inviting him to invade.

As William gathered his troops, James did nothing in the belief that William was preparing for war against France. When James finally realised that England was the target, he panicked. He started to undo some of his work, dismissing Catholic office-holders and replacing them with Protestants. It was too late.

James prepared his forces, but he had to spread them across the south and east of the country as he did not know where William would land. On 19th October 1688, the invasion fleet left the Netherlands. Of the 20,000 troops, 4,000 were English and Scottish soldiers who had been stationed in the Netherlands and had refused to return.

The weather was against William, and a storm sent the fleet back to port. James, with his naval background, was sure that William would not try again until winter was over. He did not know his son-in-law/nephew well enough. On 1st November, the fleet set out once more. They sailed along the Channel, landed at Brixham in south-west England, and then moved on to Exeter without meeting any resistance. The people in the south-west remembered the horrors of the Bloody Assizes only too vividly, and they hastened to support William.

James's forces marched to confront the invaders. William held his position; James's army was larger. Then, both sides moved forward, with William leading his army to Axminster and James's army (again commanded by Feversham) advancing to Salisbury. They were only 50 miles apart. Several towns declared for William, and then James's friend, the second-in-command of his army, Lord Churchill, went over to William, taking many officers and most of the cavalry with him. The entire navy followed.

Not knowing what to do, James scuttled back to London. He discovered that his daughter Anne and her close friend Sarah,

Lord Churchill's wife, had left to join William. It was all falling apart. After vacillating for two weeks, James decided to flee, the Queen and her son having already been sent to France.

Travelling at speed through country lanes, James reached the coast. A vessel was waiting to take him across the Channel. He boarded and they set sail, but immediately ran aground. It did not take long for three boats to come alongside. Those on board were searching for fugitives, seeking reward for their capture; dead or alive. They were not sure whether James was a fugitive, and they definitely did not know who he was; so they took him to the coastal town of Faversham. There he was recognised, and he was returned to London.

With William's forces still far to the west, James carried on as king, living in Whitehall Palace and holding audiences. It was an unreal situation. Then a contingent of Dutch troops arrived to watch over James, and he was told that he should leave London for his own safety and go to Ham. He asked to go to Rochester on the northern Kent coast instead, making his intentions obvious. That suited William, who had been angered when James's first attempt to flee had been foiled. In Rochester, James was lightly guarded. There was no desire to keep him in England, far less to put him on trial or execute him; he was, of course, William's uncle and his wife's father. James was allowed to escape to the river, where a ship was waiting to take him to France.

He later tried to regain the throne through Scotland and Ireland, but he failed and returned to exile. In truth, James's first flight from London was his abdication. It was the act of a man who had lost his courage. The brave soldier fighting for France and then for Spain, the Admiral directing the English fleet, a man nearly killed in battle on two occasions, was a distant memory.

The end of the Stuart kings; two were given the crown and two gave away the crown. Not one clever man among them.

****

WILLIAM III and MARY II

13 February 1689
– 8 March 1702

13 February 1689
– 28 December 1694

From the tenth century the Laurenburg family ruled the county of Nassau in what is now Germany as self-appointed counts. Their scattered possessions were in time divided between two brothers, Otto and Walram.

In 1403, Otto's descendant, Count Engelbert, married Johanna of Polanen, who brought lands in the Netherlands and through whom their son inherited the barony of Breda. It was 112 years later that his descendant, Count Hendrik III of Nassau-Breda married Claudia of Chalon-Orange, and their son René eventually inherited the principality of Orange from Claudia's brother, Philip.

Far from being in the Netherlands, the tiny principality of Orange was in Provence in southern France, not far from Avignon. When René died childless in 1544, his lands passed to his cousin William who became Prince William of Orange (a place he never visited), the founder of the House of Nassau-Orange. He was called William the Silent, possibly because he had for a time managed to keep his Protestant allegiance secret from the Spanish rulers of the Netherlands.

William led the Dutch revolt against the Spanish, and he was appointed stadholder (lieutenant, in effect head of state) of Holland, the first province to rebel. He is known to the Dutch as 'Father of the Fatherland'. William was shot by a Spanish agent in 1584 (the first person to be assassinated with a firearm), and was succeeded in turn by three of his sons, Philip, then Maurice and then Frederick.

In 1647, Frederick was succeeded by his son, William II of Orange; and the following year, after 80 years of struggle, the Netherlands (being the Protestant northern provinces of the Spanish Netherlands) became an independent state. William married Mary, the oldest daughter of King Charles I of England and sister of Charles II and of James II.

When William died of smallpox at the age of 24, he was succeeded by his son, William III of Orange, who was born a week after his father died. On his birth, William was, through his mother, fifth in line to the English throne after his (so far) childless uncles Charles, James and Henry and their sister (William's mother) Mary.

Years later, William's leadership in resisting the French led to his appointment as Captain-General of the army for life and stadholder of Holland, although governmental rule of the country still lay with the States General (in Dutch, *Staten Generaal* – hence Staten Island, which kept its name unlike New Amsterdam (New York), Fort Orange (Albany) and Nassau (Long Island)). Small as the Netherlands was, it had become the leading trading nation in Europe, and had the highest level of literacy and the freest press in the world.

The Netherlands was a republic, but William's thoughts were not focused on the crown; they were, and they would always be, dominated by the need to resist French aggression. For that, William needed support. Against the Catholic French, his best ally should have been his Protestant uncle, King Charles II of England. But Charles favoured his French cousin, Louis XIV.

As a result, the war with France went badly, and the States General was reluctant to provide further funds for hopeless fighting. So, in 1676 William journeyed to England; his plan was to marry the heir of the heir, his cousin Mary, the daughter of James, the King's brother. William hoped that the marriage would encourage the States General to believe that England might join the war against France. Also, there was a chance that one day William would be consort to Mary, a position that would enable him to ensure English assistance.

Admittedly, Charles might have a legitimate child or James might have a son who would take precedence over Mary, but there was still hope – after all, the Nassaus had gained their main Dutch lands through marriage, and had also gained their title of 'Prince of Orange' through marriage. It could happen for a third time.

The marriage was quickly agreed, although the 15-year-old Mary was less than happy to leave home to marry a 27-year-old ugly man with a hunched back and asthma who was five inches shorter than her. However, she had no choice, and the Protestant union was very popular in England.

As soon as Mary and her husband reached the Netherlands, William was off to war. He loved military campaigning and the company of men. Nevertheless, Mary and William became devoted to one another, the relationship smoothed by Mary's acceptance that she should not interfere in politics and matters of state.

Over a short period of time, William saw to it that his rivals in the Netherlands were murdered, and he assumed increased power as the French were driven back. Peace was negotiated in 1678, but four days after the treaty was signed, and before the two armies were aware of it, William's forces attacked the French at the Battle of St Denis near Mons (in what is now Belgium).

Leading the attack, William exposed himself to danger without hesitation as he had always done. Then, in the heat of the battle, a French soldier found himself face-to-face with William. He reached out and held his pistol to William's chest. Seeing the Frenchman about to shoot, Hendrik Ouwerkerk

Count of Nassau, William's second cousin, swung round and shot the French soldier before he could pull the trigger. The attempt to kill William, just seconds from certain success, had been thwarted. With 2,000 men killed on either side, the battle ended in a stalemate.

William was extremely annoyed that the States General had signed a peace treaty with France, especially as French aggression continued. Even worse, Louis seized the principality of Orange, which had become a refuge for Protestants. William was powerless to do anything about it, as he had no support from the States General or from England.

In 1685 Charles II died and James II was crowned king. William's position was now more hopeful; his wife Mary was first in line and William himself was third in line after Mary and her sister Anne. William was content to wait.

The events of 1688 changed everything. James's second wife was pregnant and a son was expected. The Queen's pregnancy was believed by both William and Mary to be a trick to cheat Mary of the succession. In addition, James's deteriorating relationship with Parliament and the English people made William fear a revolution in England that would see the abolition of the monarchy. Matters were urgent, William would have to act.

After James's son was born, there was only one option. Asked to invade in a letter from seven senior Englishmen, William decided to secure the throne for Mary; and more importantly, to take the steps that would bring England on to the Netherlands' side against France.

It had been William's intention to land on the north-east coast, but an easterly wind blew the invasion fleet through the Channel. That meant landing in the Protestant south-west, miles from James's forces, most of whom had been deployed to defend the expected landing in the east.

Before any fighting started James fled to France, and William was left as the only power in the country. But he was not entitled to the crown. With contorted reasoning, Parliament declared

JAMES I to ANNE

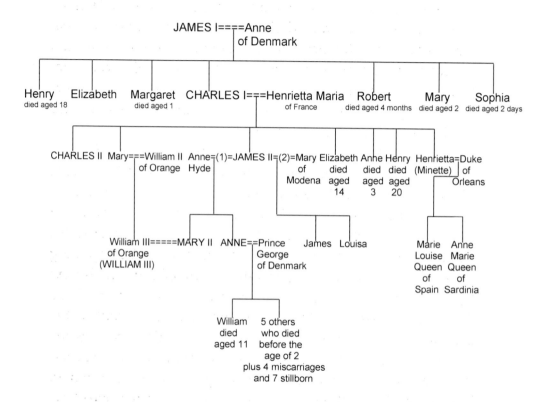

that by fleeing, James (and his infant son) had abdicated, and therefore his daughter Mary was entitled to the crown. Neither William nor Mary would accept this, so instead Parliament had to offer them the throne jointly, with Anne nominated as heir if William and Mary had no children. In February 1689, William and Mary were proclaimed King and Queen of England, and later of Scotland (the Scots having announced that James had forfeited the throne; someone with a divine right could not abdicate, it offended God's order). However, apart from matters concerning the Church, Mary took a subordinate role, and William acted almost as sole monarch.

One of William's principal supporters was Hendrik Ouwerkerk Count of Nassau, the man who had saved William's life at the Battle of St Denis. Having changed his surname to Overkirk, he was rewarded for his services with a house in London that he called Overkirk House. Some years after his death, Overkirk House was incorporated with the adjoining terraced house and cottage, and the combined building is now known as 10 Downing Street. The terrace had been built by Sir George Downing. Born in Dublin, Downing went to the colonies to live in Massachusetts Bay where his uncle was the Governor. Downing was one of nine students in the first class to graduate from Harvard University. He then returned to England and fought with Cromwell, later becoming one of his main spies, tracking down exiled Royalists in the Netherlands. After the Restoration, Downing confessed his 'errors' and changed sides. He stayed on in the Netherlands, where he saw to the arrest of three of the regicides (his former colleagues), who were returned to England to be hanged, drawn and quartered. Diarist Samuel Pepys called Downing 'a perfidious rogue' and 'an ungrateful villain'. With the rewards of spying and informing, Downing built the terraced houses in what is now Downing Street as a property speculation.

Finding themselves in a strong negotiating position, those in Parliament took the opportunity to extract all they wanted when offering William and Mary the throne, and William was happy to agree to it all as he was totally unconcerned with 'divine rights'. By the end of the year, the Bill of Rights had been enacted. This confirmed the succession, and stated that no Catholic or spouse of a Catholic could become king or queen of England. Other provisions included the rules that in time of peace a standing army might only be raised with the consent of Parliament, that parliamentary debates and elections were to be free, that Parliament should meet regularly and that Protestants had the right to bear arms. This was one of the most important enactments in English history, giving the people more than most countries gained by bloody revolution. Although William's invasion was called the 'Glorious Revolution', arguably it was the Bill of Rights that was entitled to that name. In time, the US Constitution would draw heavily on the Bill, not least the right to bear arms contained in the Second Amendment.

Yet true parliamentary rule only arrived when Parliament refused to provide William with income for life. From now on, the monarch would have to rely on periodic grants. He was beholden to Parliament; the balance of power had changed.

Titus Oates was released from prison and given a pension of £5 a week. But he had insulted Mary's father, so she had his pension cancelled. It was reinstated after Mary died. Fortunes also changed for Judge Jeffries; he was captured whilst trying to flee the country and was sent to the Tower where he died.

Despite all his concessions, almost from the start of his reign William was unpopular. Any gratitude for saving the English from enforced Catholicism was clouded by the fact that they had never intended that William should be king. They only wanted his help; they certainly did not want a foreigner as monarch. The feeling was mutual; William hated London and the court, and despite surrounding himself with Dutchmen, he was homesick. To William's disappointment there was no time to visit his homeland; he was pressed into action in Ireland.

Ex-King James II had incited a futile uprising in Scotland.

Although there was victory at the Battle of Killiecrankie, Viscount Dundee the leader of the Jacobites (as supporters of James and his successors were called) was killed. Defeat followed at Dunkeld, and the Jacobite army disbanded. James's position improved when William declared war on France – always his ambition. In retaliation, King Louis XIV agreed to support James's attempt to regain the throne through Ireland.

With the settlement of Protestants in Ireland and the confiscations, by 1660 the Catholic majority owned less than 10% of the land. Under James II the position had been reversed, and the Catholics recovered much of the land and all the power; it was the Protestants who were being driven out. The Catholics, led by the Earl of Tyrconnel, saw a chance to finish the job and destroy the position of the Protestants for good before the new Protestant monarchy was ready to move.

In March 1689, James arrived in Ireland with a 20,000-strong army. He was joined by Tyrconnel's ragged troops. However, there would be no Catholic soldiers deserting from William's army. He had wisely sent them to Hungary to support the Emperor in his war against the Turks.

James was welcomed into Dublin. He marched with his forces to Protestant Londonderry and stood with senior officers outside the besieged town as a message was sent demanding its surrender. The reply was instant; a shot rang out as a soldier fired at James from the town's walls. He escaped death yet again, as the shot killed the officer standing next to him. James returned to Dublin.

A few days later, James presided over a parliament that ordered the dispossession of 2,400 Protestant landowners. Over the sea in England, preparations for war commenced, and in June 1690, William landed in Ireland with his army. As soon as he learned of William's landing, James advanced with his forces to the River Boyne north of Dublin. The English moved forward to confront him.

William, accompanied by several officers, rode out to

reconnoitre the likely battlefield among sporadic fire from each side. He was spotted. William stopped to discuss the lie of the land, the stationary target was inviting. One of James's soldiers, a marksman, came forward. He took careful aim, and fired. The ball pierced the gun holster of the Prince of Hesse, who was alongside William. Before William's party could ride off, there was a second shot. William was hit, and he fell to the ground. A great cheer rang out from James's army, but it was only William's right shoulder that had been struck, and he was helped back to his camp.

The wound was not serious; it drew blood, but it was merely a graze. The attempt to kill William had failed. William rode along the line of his troops to show them that he was fine.

Now it was time for action. William ordered a third of his army upstream to attempt a crossing of the Boyne. Seeing the movement, James took fright, thinking that William was preparing to attack from the rear, perhaps intending to cut off James's line of retreat. So James sent two-thirds of his army upstream to resist the crossing.

Next, William ordered the rest of his infantry to cross the river. William's numbers were greater, but James had a strong defensive position. With William sending one-third upstream and James sending two-thirds upstream, the difference in numbers was accentuated. Despite facing withering fire, William's infantry managed to cross the river, forcing the Irish to retreat. Then William led his cavalry across, and the Irish cavalry fled in disarray. James, who had kept a safe distance from the fighting, raced back to Paris. His angry Irish supporters remembered him as *Seamus an chaca* – James the shit.

For James it was all over, although it still took more than a year for the English forces to subdue the whole of Ireland. William wanted toleration and no revenge against Catholics. The result was quite the opposite. Confiscations, banishment of clergy and numerous anti-Catholic laws followed.

Mary had ruled alone while William was in Ireland, and

she ruled alone again when he visited the Netherlands in 1691. She was in general a popular queen, but she had her enemies who condemned her for having broken the Fifth Commandment: Honour thy father. During William's absence in the Netherlands, on the night of 10th April, Mary was asleep in Whitehall Palace when a fire suddenly broke out, spreading rapidly until it engulfed much of the building. Mary managed to escape in her nightclothes. An accident or the act of an enemy? The carelessness of a maid was blamed.

One matter that troubled Queen Mary was the strong influence on her not very clever sister, Princess Anne, of the scheming Sarah Churchill. Both William and Mary were annoyed when Sarah's husband, John Churchill, now the Earl of Marlborough (his reward for changing sides after William invaded), used his influence to persuade Parliament to grant Anne £50,000 a year, out of which Anne gave Sarah £1,000 a year.

As usual, when any position or financial reward was obtained by the Marlboroughs, they set about finding the next opportunity for increased status and moneymaking. Marlborough demanded command of the English Army, complaining that there were too many foreign officers. William was not interested. First, Marlborough was of low birth. In the alliance between England, the Netherlands, the Holy Roman Empire, German states and Spain against France, most of the commanding officers were princes; they would not deign to speak to anyone so socially inferior. Second, William was disgusted at the way Marlborough had deserted his king and changed sides. As far as William was concerned, Marlborough was a traitor. Even worse, he was now in contact with James, seeking forgiveness for changing sides in case James was restored to the throne. So William terminated all Marlborough's commands and offices.

Then Anne brazenly appeared at court with Sarah. Mary was furious with her sister. She ordered Anne to dismiss Sarah, but Anne refused. Anne was told to leave court. Apart from a brief visit after Anne gave birth, Mary never saw her sister again.

Having dealt with James, William could concentrate on his main interest: war against France, trying to halt Louis XIV, who was determined to create a Catholic French empire across Europe. William was happy to be with his army once more, commanding the Grand Alliance. Initially the French won several battles, but the tide turned, and after William won his great victory at Namur, Louis was forced to agree to a peace treaty.

In December 1694, Mary fell ill. It was smallpox. Within eight days she was dead, aged only 32. The whole country mourned. William was devastated, and he turned to religion. He made up with Anne, and Marlborough was restored.

With no wife and no war, William was constantly miserable; his only joys were riding and hunting. He never remarried. In fact, he became increasingly attached to one of his pages, a young Dutchman called Arnold van Keppel. The long-standing rumours of William's homosexuality became louder. They were encouraged when William created Keppel the Earl of Albemarle. He is the 8 x great-grandfather of Camilla, Duchess of Cornwall, the wife of Prince Charles.

William's misery increased as Parliament became hostile. The Whigs were against the Catholics and gave some support to William, but he did not trust them; they were revolutionaries who had deserted their former king. William identified more with the Tories, the gentry; but for them William was a usurper.

In 1696, Sir George Barclay, a Scottish army officer, plotted with others to ambush William and kill him at Turnham Green (to the west of London) as he was returning from a hunt. They were betrayed, and nine of the conspirators were executed, although Barclay escaped to France.

A few months afterwards, another plot to assassinate William was discovered. The leading conspirator was Sir John Fenwick, the assassin was to be Robert Charnock. Several of the conspirators were captured and executed. Fenwick, a long-time Jacobite, hated William for having publicly reprimanded him when Fenwick was serving with the English forces in the Netherlands. Fenwick was executed for treason. As a traitor, his property was confiscated by the Crown. One item seized was his favourite horse, called White Sorrel. William took the horse for his own use.

It was now clear that Anne would succeed William. Then, in 1700, Anne's last surviving child, the Duke of Gloucester, died. Who would follow Anne? James, her father, was still alive, and so were his children by Mary of Modena. But they and the children of Charles II's and James II's sister Minette (that is, all Charles I's surviving descendants other than William and Anne) were Catholics.

In June 1701, Parliament passed the Act of Settlement. It enacted that Anne would be succeeded by Sophia the daughter of Elizabeth Stuart, sister of Charles I, who had married Frederick the Elector Palatine of the Rhine. Although Frederick and Elizabeth had thirteen children, by 1701, nine of them, all Protestants, had died without leaving issue. A tenth, Edward had died leaving issue, but he had converted to Catholicism. Another son, Charles, had died leaving a daughter, but she had converted to Catholicism on marriage. That left two daughters who were still alive; Louise who had converted to Catholicism, and the twelfth child, Sophia. She was the only living Protestant child and the only child with Protestant children. Sophia had married the Prince-Elector of Hanover. The House of Hanover would be the succession.

Later in the year, James II died in France. He left not just the son born in 1688 (James Francis Edward Stuart), but also a daughter, Lousia Mary, born in 1692 in France. So Mary of Modena giving birth in 1688 was credible after all.

On 21st February 1702, William went riding in Richmond Park. It was now the nearest he could get to his beloved military campaigning. As he rode along, there were no dangers in view. There were no dangers in view for his horse either. However, there was a tiny mammal making its own progress under the surface, an animal to be found throughout Europe, except in Ireland. It was a mole. William's horse stumbled on the molehill. The horse staggered forward, and William was thrown. He fell to the ground, breaking his collarbone.

William was carried to his bed. He seemed to be recovering, but there must have been some other damage because his condition suddenly deteriorated. William stopped eating, he developed a fever, and on 8th March 1702, he died.

Buried privately without any ceremony, William's death caused no sorrow. In fact, many Jacobites drank a toast to the little gentleman in the velvet coat who had killed the King. But another animal was involved: the horse that had thrown William was White Sorrel, taken from Sir John Fenwick. So Fenwick had his revenge after all.

****

ANNE

8 March 1702 – 1 August 1714

Born the younger daughter of the King's brother, Anne had little realistic chance of becoming queen. Yet as time went by and Charles II died without legitimate issue, then James fled the country, and then William and Mary produced no children, Anne's succession to the throne became more and more likely. Finally, it was decreed by Act of Parliament.

That Act was significant, because it meant that for the future the monarch would be monarch solely because of Parliament; the doctrine of divine right, and consequently absolute power, disappeared for ever.

While still a child, Anne became infatuated with, and was later dominated by, the younger sister of one of Anne's mother's ladies-in-waiting. Sarah Jennings was five years older than Anne, and she quickly took advantage of the relationship, which would last long into Anne's reign. Anne was quiet and self-conscious; Sarah was vivacious and domineering. The friendship was barely affected when Sarah married John Churchill.

In 1680, it was time for Anne to find a husband. Her second cousin, Prince George of Hanover, was invited to court, but Anne did not interest him, and anyway his family had other plans. Offended by the snub, Anne would always hate George and the Hanoverians. The next visitor was more favourably inclined, and in 1683 Anne married another Prince George. This one was Prince Jørgen, the brother of the King of Denmark.

Despite marriage, first place in Anne's affections continued to belong to Sarah, the two women writing to each other for years using the names Mrs Freeman (for Sarah) and Mrs Morley (for Anne). Nevertheless, Anne and George became very close, with George never interfering in politics and only wanting a quiet life. The marriage produced seventeen pregnancies; but just one child, William Duke of Gloucester, lived to be over two years old.

After William and Mary became joint monarchs, Anne's relationship with her sister started off well. Later, the bitter argument about Anne's parliamentary allowance and issues caused by Anne's bond with the Churchills led to increasing friction. When Anne refused to be separated from Sarah, she was forced to leave court, going to live in Syon House to the west of London.

Then Mary died, and William was obliged to recognise that Anne was his heir (and really with a greater right to the throne than he had), so Anne was recalled to court. Her priority was the care of her only surviving child, William, who had been sickly from birth. In 1700 he died at the age of eleven. As a result, the Act of Settlement was passed, decreeing that after Anne the throne would pass to her nearest Protestant relation, the widowed Sophia of Hanover.

On King William's death in February 1702, the nation rejoiced at the accession of the Protestant and English Queen Anne. Her first step was to appoint Marlborough the Commander-in-Chief of the English army stationed in the Netherlands. Marlborough was also given the lucrative post of Master-General of the Ordnance. Sarah was not left out; she was appointed Groom of the Stole, Keeper of the Privy Purse and Mistress of the Wardrobe (administering Anne's finances). These were the highest offices available for a woman; all well paid.

Sarah took control, forbidding Anne new clothes and arranging for her to hire rather than buy jewellery. An exception was made for the coronation, when Anne, considerably overweight and suffering from gout, was so heavily dressed and jewelled that she had to be carried to the throne on a chair.

Two weeks later, Anne declared war on France. The issue was the inheritance of King Carlos II of Spain. He was a Habsburg, and like all the Habsburgs he suffered from generations of inbreeding. Carlos's father had married his niece, so Carlos's mother was also his cousin and his grandmother was his aunt. He had the Habsburg large lower lip, which with an oversized tongue made him drool, and he also had the Habsburg jaw. In fact, Carlos's jaw was so large that his upper and lower teeth could not meet. As a result, he was unable to chew food, and this led to intestinal problems. Carlos was also lame, epileptic, impotent and mentally deficient. Obviously, he had not produced an heir.

The problem was that a united Spain and France under one monarch was unacceptable to the Alliance (England, Austria, the Dutch Republic, Savoy, Prussia and Portugal). That seemed to be a distinct possibility on Carlos's death, and it had to be prevented.

The next in line after Carlos had been his half-sister, Maria-Theresa. She had married King Louis XIV of France. But Maria-Theresa had died in 1700, so the heir to the Spanish crown was her son, and he was also the Dauphin, the heir to the French crown. Looking to the next in line was no help, as the Dauphin's elder son, Louis, was also likely to become King of France in the future. France and the Alliance agreed a compromise; the Dauphin's second son, Philip of Anjou would share Carlos's titles and lands with Archduke Charles of Austria, Carlos's cousin.

However, when Carlos died, angered to have seen others dividing his lands while he still reigned, he left everything by will to Philip. Despite the agreement with the Alliance,

Louis XIV immediately sent his forces to the Spanish Netherlands to support Philip in securing the entire Spanish inheritance.

The War of the Spanish Succession began, the Alliance being opposed by France, Spain, Bavaria and Hungary. In the Earl of Marlborough, the Alliance had a commander who started as he would continue, capturing Venlo, Stevensweert, Roermond and Liege. Anne rewarded Churchill by elevating him to Duke of Marlborough, the highest rank she could bestow. Sarah was unimpressed; the title brought no extra revenue. So Anne offered Sarah £2,000 a year out of the Privy Purse (the sovereign's private income). Sarah was disappointed with the amount, and rejected the offer. Nine years later, Sarah changed her mind and claimed the annual payment and all the arrears.

The year 1703 brought a setback for the Marlboroughs when their only surviving son died of smallpox at the age of seventeen. Sarah was overcome with grief; Marlborough's solace was his military campaigning.

In 1704, Marlborough realised that it was not the Netherlands but the Emperor who needed support, as the French were threatening to take Vienna. Marlborough told no one of his new plan of action, pretending to the French and to his allies that the defence of the Netherlands was England's main concern. He marched his troops to the west as if he was about to attack Lorraine or Alsace. Then he suddenly moved to the south-east. Now Marlborough informed his allies of his intentions, and he was joined by the Emperor's army led by Prince Eugene of Savoy. On 13th August, the two most gifted commanders of their day led the attack against the French and Bavarian armies near the Bavarian village of Blindheim (called 'Blenheim' by the English), securing a brilliant victory and the destruction of the French Army. Belief in the invincibility of Louis' forces was ended. Louis even issued an edict making it a crime to speak of Blenheim.

All England rejoiced in the country's greatest victory for almost 300 years. Marlborough was the national hero. The navy's equally important capture of Gibraltar went almost unnoticed.

The Emperor created Marlborough the Prince of Mindelheim, a prince of the Holy Roman Empire; the title giving Marlborough royal status on a par with most of the other commanders. Anne had nothing more to grant him; 'duke' had been as much as was available. However, Sarah was dissatisfied with being Princess of Mindelheim. It brought little money (£1,500 per year and Marlborough's investiture ceremony cost him £4,500) and she said that she could not even find Mindelheim on a map. Sarah had a better idea; she complained to Anne that the Marlboroughs' mansion in St Albans was inadequate for their elevated status. They needed something grander. So Anne gave the Duke and his heirs the Manor of Woodstock in return for the annual presentation to the monarch of a replica of the French colours – still being delivered to this day. On the land, at huge expense to Anne, the State and Marlborough, the massive Blenheim Palace was built over a period of 17 years.[26]

Next there was a problem with Scotland. Ever since James I, the monarch had not been King or Queen of England and Scotland, but King or Queen of England and King or Queen of Scotland. The countries were not united, because neither parliament had wanted union. As a result, although the Act of Settlement promised the crown of England to the House of Hanover, that promise did not bind Scotland.

North of the border there was no rush to deal with the succession. The Scottish Parliament decided that they would leave the selection of the next monarch of Scotland until after Anne had died. They agreed that it would be a Protestant in the Scottish royal line, but said it would not be the same person as the new English sovereign unless the English granted freedom of trade to Scottish merchants. The English were worried; there was a real danger that when Anne died, the Scots might choose

---

26 The only case in England of a palace that is not or was not the residence of royalty or a bishop.

James Francis Edward Stuart (son of James II) if he converted from Catholicism. That would enable his ally, Louis XIV, to use Scotland as a base from which to attack England.

In retaliation, the English threatened economic sanctions. It was an opportune time, as Scotland was virtually bankrupt following the failure of the Darien Scheme to establish a colony in Panama. Hundreds of Scottish colonists died, hundreds of Scots were ruined. Negotiations began.

On the Continent, despite Blenheim, the war in Europe continued. It soon produced another victory for Marlborough, this time at Ramillies in Flanders. The new French army was destroyed, and the Spanish Netherlands was freed from French control.

There had to be a new reward, but there were no honours left to bestow on Marlborough. However there was something that could be done for him. The Marlboroughs now had two daughters but no son; on Marlborough's death, the dukedom would become extinct. So a special Act of Parliament was passed allowing the dukedom to descend through the female line.

The year 1707 saw the parliaments of England and Scotland agree to the union of the two nations, and Anne became the first monarch of Great Britain. Naturally, the union was hated by the Jacobite Scots, and Louis saw his chance. In 1708, he sent James II's son, James Stuart, to Scotland with French troops to claim the throne. The invasion was a disaster. James contracted measles, and when his fleet reached the Firth of Forth on the east coast of Scotland, it was chased away by the British Navy. Without having set foot on Scottish soil, James returned to France.

More success as Marlborough (supported by Prince Eugene and Count Overkirk) won a famous victory against the French at Oudenarde. The Alliance cavalry led by Danish General Rantzau included a Hanoverian unit commanded by George, Duke of Brunswick-Luneburg, the oldest son of Sophia of Hanover. As the French vanguard advanced, they were attacked by Rantzau's horsemen who charged, destroying much of the vanguard and forcing the survivors to retreat. Rantzau's cavalry pursued them, but then found themselves confronted by the French cavalry. Now heavily outnumbered, Rantzau ordered his men to withdraw. Taking the last opportunity, the French aimed their guns, each man selecting a target, and fired. The shot aimed at the officer alongside George found its target, the officer was killed outright; the shot aimed at George was less accurate, it narrowly missed him and killed his horse. Falling to the ground, George managed to mount a riderless horse, and he withdrew with the rest of his squadron. The attempt to kill him had failed. By the end of the day, the Alliance had gained a decisive victory, later forcing their way into France and capturing Lille, the strongest fortress in Europe, then taking Bruges and then Ghent. Arrangements were made for a victory celebration at St Paul's Cathedral.

St Paul's was being prepared for the ceremony, and workmen were clambering around, completing their tasks and checking that all was in order. Suddenly, one workman looked at the beams directly over the area where Anne would be sitting. Then he looked closer. The screw-bolts holding the beams were loose, very loose. What had happened? Had they not been screwed in properly or had someone unscrewed them? Either way, something was seriously wrong. The screw-bolts were immediately tightened so as to secure the beams and the chandelier attached to them.

What was it all about? The point was that the Whigs were the 'war party', and Whig supporters were making a fortune out of the conflict. Marlborough alone was receiving a 2.5% commission from providers to the army, including £64,000 from the suppliers of bread and £230,000 from the payment for foreign troops. Peace would end their income. According to the Tories, the so-called 'Screw Plot' was a Whig attempt to assassinate Tory-supporting Anne, with the beams and chandelier crashing down on her, so that she would be replaced by a Whig-supporting pro-war monarch. According to the Whigs, the loose screws were no more than negligence by some workmen, and it was being used by the Tories to turn Anne even further against the Whigs and to lower the Whigs in public esteem. Anyway, with the screws tightened, the ceremony took place without incident. The attempt to kill Queen Anne, if that is what it was, failed.

The ceremony led to a rift between Anne and Sarah when Sarah publicly chastised Anne on the steps of the cathedral for not wearing the jewels Sarah had laid out for her. When Anne tried to explain what had happened, Sarah told her to keep quiet. Sarah was now falling out of favour, although Marlborough was still needed. His next victory was at Malplaquet, but it was at the cost of 20,000 lives.

The French rejoiced briefly in the mistaken belief that Marlborough had been killed. A song was quickly written, mockingly telling of how news of Marlborough's death was brought to his wife: "Your beautiful eyes will weep at the news I bring; Monsieur Marbroug is dead." An English wit took the tune and wrote new words congratulating Marlborough: "For he's a jolly good fellow", and in time it became the second most popular song in the English language.

In late 1708, Anne's husband, Prince George, died. Anne was heartbroken. Sarah was no help at all, only complaining of her own mistreatment. Further rows between the two women led to Anne finally dismissing Sarah from all her positions.

Like William before her, Anne relieved her loneliness by horse riding. One day, when riding out from Windsor Castle, she came upon an area of open heath that she said was suitable for "horses to gallop at full stretch". It was near the village of 'Eastcote', at times called by the similar-sounding name of 'Ascot'; and shortly afterwards, Ascot Racecourse was opened.

Suddenly, peace became more desirable, even to the Whigs, when Archduke Charles succeeded to the crown of Hungary and the Holy Roman Empire on the death of his brother. The Alliance had been opposing a French King of Spain who might join Spain with France. Their preference had been Archduke Charles, a man with only minor territories. Now that had changed; if Charles became King of Spain it would join Spain with his newly inherited central European territories. The Austrian Habsburgs with Spain would be as great a threat as the French Bourbons with Spain.

Terms were agreed for the division of King Carlos's inheritance. After the deaths of 400,000 soldiers, it was very much on the lines of what had been agreed before Carlos died. Philip could have Spain provided he abandoned his succession rights to the French throne, and Charles was given most of the Spanish territories in Italy as well as the Spanish Netherlands (what is now Belgium).

The treaty also confirmed various conquests, and the British took the opportunity to secure territories and rights around the world. Britain was granted a thirty-year monopoly of the Spanish-American slave trade, ownership of Gibraltar, Nova Scotia, St Kitts, Minorca, Hudson Bay territories and Acadia (French north-east America, Canada and Newfoundland). However, Mindelheim was returned to Bavaria, and Orange was confirmed as part of France. In addition, Savoy took Sicily and part of Milan, and Portugal's sovereignty over Brazil was agreed. Finally, Louis undertook to recognise the Protestant succession in Britain, and he promised not to give further aid to the Jacobites. The terms of the peace were contained in the Treaty of Utrecht.

With peace agreed, there was no need for Marlborough, so Anne relieved him of his command. He thanked her for the great honour of being dismissed by her own hand, and then threw the dismissal letter into the fire.

By now, Anne's physical condition was deteriorating. She became very ill, and although she recovered, the shape of her face had changed and it had become discoloured. Her death was expected at any moment. The succession of Sophia of Hanover was considered a foregone conclusion, even though she was 34 years older than Anne. On 8th June 1714, Sophia was taking a walk in her gardens, when it suddenly began to rain heavily. Sophia ran for shelter, but at the age of 83, the strain was too much. She collapsed and died. Now her son, George, was the heir. Unfortunately he could not visit England to facilitate a smooth succession, because after the insult when George rejected marriage, Anne had ordered that no member of the House of Hanover could set foot in England while she was alive.

In late July, Anne collapsed, trembling, feverish and bleeding from the nose. If she was ill now, her doctors would ensure that it got worse. She was bled again and again in line with the belief that fever was caused by having too much blood rushing round the body. Hot irons were placed all over her so that she would blister, they gave her drugs to make her vomit, they covered her legs with garlic, and then they shaved all her hair off. She must have regretted the discovery of the loose screw-bolts. If anyone killed Anne, it was her seven doctors, and on 1st August 1714, Queen Anne died. It was probably a relief.

****

THE LINE TO GEORGE I

showing the order of entitlement after Anne without the Catholic exclusion
(those dead by 1 August 1714 in square brackets; Protestants in **heavy script**)

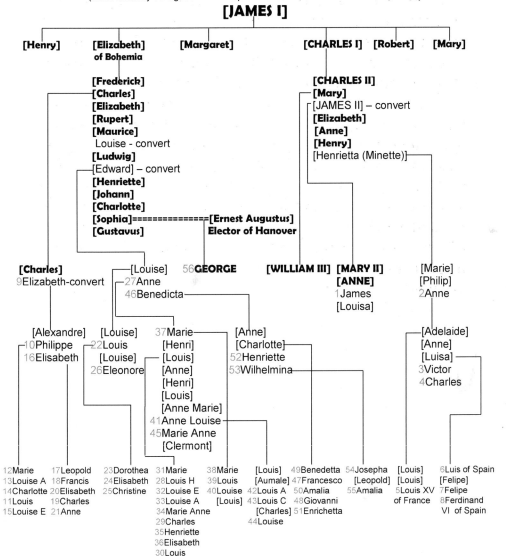

The rules of entitlement (without the Catholic exclusion) being: (1) only legitimate persons; (2) in the same rank males in age order before females in age order; (3) for each person, go down through all descendants applying rules (1) and (2) before moving to the next person in the rank; (4) go first to the children of the deceased monarch, on exhaustion go to the monarch's parent's children, on exhaustion one generation further back, and so on.

GEORGE I

1 August 1714 – 11 June 1727

As decreed by the Act of Settlement, when Queen Anne died the House of Hanover took the throne. Sophia had missed out by six weeks. She had wanted the crown. Her son, George, was not in the least interested in England or its crown; he never would be. His interests were confined to horses, hunting, women and Hanover. In truth he was 56th in line, but because the 55 ahead of him were Catholics, he became the first King of Great Britain.[27]

Hanover was a north-German state in Lower Saxony, to the south of Denmark. It was not really the state of Hanover, it was the Duchy of Braunschweig-Lüneburg ('Brunswick-Luneburg' in English). However, when Hanover became the main town, the English and others called the duchy 'Hanover'.

---

27 If Sophia had failed to provide an heir or had converted to Catholicism or married a Catholic, in order to find a Protestant monarch it would have been necessary to go back to Henry VIII's younger sister, Mary. Her two sons died young, her daughter Frances' three daughters left no legitimate children, so the line would have run through Mary's younger daughter, Eleanor. As a result, her 3 x great-granddaughter Margaret Brydges (daughter of Lord Chandos) would have become queen, and her heir Lady Caroline Ogilvy (née Child Villiers) would now be queen; although there are other views on the descent.

The ruling family traced their descent from the Guelphs, a branch of the House of Este from Lombardy, themselves claiming Saxon ancestry. George Ludwig (George Lewis in English) was the oldest son of Duke Ernest Augustus and his wife, Duchess Sophia of the Rhineland Palatinate. Sophia was the twelfth child of Elizabeth Stuart (sister of King Charles I) and Frederick the Elector Palatine (the Palatinate of the Rhine being a small state in mid-west Germany) and for a short time the King of Bohemia. The electors each had a vote in the election of the Holy Roman Emperor. There were for a long time seven electors, then eight, and George Lewis would become the ninth.

Although Elizabeth Stuart was the daughter of a king of England and the sister of a king of England (both born in Scotland), there was little English in her. She was Scottish, and all of her parents, grandparents and great-grandparents were Scottish, German, Danish or French. Just one great-great-grandparent was English (Henry VIII's sister, Margaret Tudor). And through that one great-great-grandparent, Elizabeth was a 7 x great-granddaughter of John of Gaunt and Katherine Swynford, and an 8 x great-granddaughter of Philippa of Clarence and Edmund Mortimer 3rd Earl of March. It was the thread that led to the crown for her grandson, George; although he was even less English than Elizabeth, none of his other grandparents having any English blood at all.

In England, the oldest son inherited his father's titles and lands. Under the law of most German states, the titles and lands were divided amongst all the sons. That is why Germany was split into over 350 states and mini-states.

During the sixteenth century, the ruler of the duchy was Duke William, and he had seven sons. He did not want to see his duchy disintegrate into seven small territories. However, he accepted that each of his sons was entitled to inherit part of the duchy. So he devised a plan; he declared that all of his sons could inherit, but only one son would be allowed to marry. Then on the deaths of the six unmarried sons, their lands would pass to the married son (or if he had died, then to his heirs who

297

would have to be bound by a similar arrangement) and the duchy would be reconstituted. They drew lots, and the sixth son, George, won. In time it went just as Duke William had planned, and the territories were re-united.

George himself had four adult sons. The oldest, Christian, had married, but he had no sons. That left the unmarried George William, John Frederick and Ernest Augustus. The family decided that the oldest of the three must marry and produce a male heir to preserve the family's rule over the duchy. As a result, George William was betrothed to Sophia, daughter of Elizabeth Stuart. But when it came to the wedding, George William changed his mind, he just could not face matrimony. So he made an agreement with his youngest brother, Ernest Augustus: if Ernest agreed to marry Sophia, George William would never marry and on his death his lands would pass to Ernest or his heirs. Ernest agreed, and so did Sophia.

John Frederick complained bitterly; he was next in line, not Ernest. But it was too late. In time, both Christian and John Frederick died without leaving male heirs[28]. Years later, George William, now Duke of Celle, broke his promise and married his mistress so as to legitimise their daughter, Sophia Dorothea. It was not a great problem for Ernest Augustus, because under the Salic Law females could not inherit territory or titles.

However, in order to acquire the Duke of Celle's rights of income that were not covered by the Salic Law restriction, Ernest Augustus insisted that his oldest son, George Lewis, should marry his cousin, Sophia Dorothea. In the same year, Ernest Augustus established the right of primogeniture in the English style, so that George Lewis and his descendants would not face the same problem.

At first George Lewis and Sophia Dorothea disliked each other; within a short time they hated each other. Nevertheless, a son, George, was born and later they had a daughter.

---

28 John Frederick later converted to Catholicism and married, and his daughter Charlotte married the Duke of Modena who was the brother of James II's wife Mary of Modena.

When the call of war came in 1683, young George Lewis led the Hanoverian troops, part of the Christian alliance against the Turks. The Battle of Vienna, won by the Polish-Austrian-German forces led by King Jan III Sobieski of Poland, reversed the Turkish advance into Europe. The story is that to celebrate the victory, Viennese bakers created a new design for their *kipferl* pastry (itself possibly a descendant of the ancient Jewish *rugelach* rolled up dough pastry), shaped like the crescent on the Turkish flags. It was introduced to France when a former Austrian officer opened the Boulangerie Viennoise in Paris. Over time, it was developed in France into a rolled up buttery flaky bread still in a crescent-shape, and therefore known as a *croissant* (French for 'crescent'). To this day, croissants and similar baked foods are called *Viennoiseries* in France.

rugelach, kipferl, croissant

Another story from the victory is that the Austrians found a huge store of coffee that had been abandoned by the fleeing Turks. Holy Roman Emperor Leopold tried the coffee, but found it too bitter; so one of his advisers, a Capuchin friar called Marco d'Aviano, added milk and honey to sweeten the coffee – he had invented the *cappucino*.

George Lewis returned to Hanover, and he soon acquired a mistress. When the dashing Swedish Count Philip von Konigsmark was appointed Colonel of Dragoons at court, he too acquired a mistress; he started an affair with Sophia Dorothea, and he made no effort to keep it secret. That could not be allowed. The Count was murdered, and George Lewis divorced Sophia Dorothea on terms that she was forbidden to re-marry and could never see her two children again. Only 28 years old, she was (with the agreement of her father) confined in Ahlden Castle for the rest of her life, not allowed to have any visitors other than her mother. Still confined, she died there 32 years later.

In 1693, George Lewis again led his forces, this time supporting the English and the Dutch against the French. At the Battle of Neerwinden, King William had taken up a defensive position. After protracted canon-fire, the French attacked. William ordered a counter-attack, but was forced back by the superior numbers of the enemy. In order to support his flanks, William decided to move troops from the centre. The French commander saw what was happening, and he ordered his cavalry to charge the weakened centre of William's line. Before George Lewis and his cavalry could call for reinforcements, the French were upon them. Suddenly, George Lewis found himself detached from his men and surrounded by French horsemen. His fate was clear, the French moved in for the kill. But General von Hammerstein had seen his commander's plight and, without a thought for his own safety, he immediately galloped through the French horsemen directly to George Lewis. At the very moment when the French came up to George Lewis and swords were swung at him, von Hammerstein arrived. He snatched the reins from George Lewis's hands and led him to safety. The battle was lost, but the attempt to kill George Lewis had failed.

On the death of his father in 1698, George Lewis became Duke of Brunswick-Luneburg. Seven years later, on the death of the Duke of Celle, George recovered his uncle's lands, thereby enlarging the duchy. There was still time to serve in the War of the Spanish Succession; but now that he was nearly 50 George resigned from active service, for which he was later rewarded with appointment as a Prince-Elector.

When Queen Anne was approaching death, the Tories were in power. Many of them were uncomfortable that the true royal line had been subverted, even though James II (who had died in exile in 1701) and his son were Catholics. They believed that James II's son, James Stuart, would convert to Protestantism and the Act of Settlement could be repealed. However, James Stuart was dominated by his mother, the devoutly Catholic Mary of Modena. James would not convert, and he even refused to guarantee the right of worship to Protestants should he become king as a Catholic. Like his father and his grandfather, each of whom lost the throne, it was all and everything without compromise.

So, on Anne's death in 1714, the 54-year-old George Lewis was proclaimed King George of Great Britain and Ireland. The Ludwig/Lewis was dropped. Mirroring William of Orange's prime motive for taking the crown, George was content to be king as it would benefit the security and power of Hanover.

With a marked lack of eagerness, George landed in England seven weeks after Anne's death, accompanied by his son George, soon to be the Prince of Wales. King George's ministers were almost all Whigs, their leaders being Viscount Townshend, James Stanhope, Lord Sunderland and Robert Warpole. Their first problem was that Jacobitism was still alive, and nowhere more so than in Scotland. The Scots resented the Act of Union, most of them supported the Scottish House of Stuart and many Highland chiefs were Catholics.

In September 1715, the Earl of Mar raised the Jacobite standard, proclaiming James II's son, James Francis Edward Stuart ('the Pretender'), as king. Mar's forces captured Perth, but hopes of support from France ended abruptly when Louis XIV died. After a month of indecision, part of Mar's army marched into England, and they were joined by the forces of several Catholic Northumbrian lords. The Jacobites advanced to Preston where they were surrounded by a royal army to whom they surrendered. On the very same day, at Sheriffmuir in Scotland, Mar's remaining troops returned to their homes after they had failed to defeat forces loyal to George.

A month later, the Pretender landed in Scotland. He was unimpressed with Scotland and the Scots, and he made no secret of his views. The feeling was mutual, the Scots disliked him, a leader who had no respect for his supporters – men who were willing to die for the cause. But James was a Stuart, believing that he was appointed by God and that Scots and English were duty-bound to lay down their lives for him, there was no need to curry favour with them. He returned to Paris. The French Regent forced him to move to the papal city of Avignon, and James later travelled south to spend the rest of his life in Rome under the protection of the Pope.

Retribution was mixed; in Scotland there were confiscations and lootings, but no hangings. English rebels were more harshly treated; 26 officers were executed and 700 captured soldiers were sent to the West Indies as convicts. In addition, seven lords were sentenced to death, of whom two were executed and three were pardoned. That left two in the Tower awaiting execution. Lord Winton sawed through the bars of his cell and escaped to the Continent. Lord Nithsdale would be saved by his wife, Winifred.

The night before her husband's execution, Winifred went to the Tower to say goodbye, accompanied by two other ladies. They were dressed in bulky dresses on top of which they wore cloaks with hoods. The three women made a great commotion going down the stairs to Nithsdale's cell, two of them finding an excuse to go back upstairs, and then going down again.

After all three entered the cell, they dressed Nithsdale in a spare dress and a cloak with a hood, which had been hidden within one of the women's dresses. The guards were totally confused as to how many people had entered the cell. They did not realise that three went in, but four came out, and they did not for some time go to the cell to check, because Winifred had asked the guards not to disturb Nithsdale as he was saying his final prayers. Lord and Lady Nithsdale lived out the remainder of their lives in Italy.

The position of the Hanoverians was hugely enhanced by the Jacobite defeat. Now they could settle down to enjoy their good fortune. With his ex-wife imprisoned, George had brought his two mistresses to London; one tall and skinny, the other fat. The English called them the Maypole and the Elephant. They and the other Hanoverians would now exercise vast power through their influence over George, who spoke hardly a word of English. Any decision or appointment to be made by the King would involve the bribery of one or more mistresses and Hanoverian ministers.

George was regarded as stupid, dull and lazy. All true, but exaggerated because of his total lack of interest in England and the English. It was all a bore for him. The luckiest man in the world: his grandfather inherited by drawing lots, his father inherited by taking over his brother's fiancée, George inherited the crown despite being 56th in line, he had been saved from certain death in battle, and the wife he hated had been locked up for life.

His son, George Prince of Wales, had similar good fortune when he visited the Theatre Royal Drury Lane in 1716. A man armed with several loaded pistols tried to enter the royal box. He was stopped, and then he drew one of the pistols and shot at George, the bullet just missing the Prince's shoulder. The assassin, a man called Freeman, who was known to be mad, was taken away as ladies screamed and tried to climb out of the box. George remained calm in his seat.

The King's relationship with the Prince of Wales had never been good. It deteriorated after a row over who should be appointed godfather to the Prince's second son. The Prince and his wife were banished from court, being allowed to see their children once a week. A consequence of the rift was that the Prince was banned from attending Cabinet meetings as the Council was now called, 'cabinet' being the collective noun for a group of ministers. The Prince had been his father's interpreter at those meetings; so, no longer having an interpreter present, the King stopped attending as well. This created a vacuum that resulted in one minister dominating the Cabinet in place of the King; he would become known as the 'Prime Minister'. The influence of the monarch was forever reduced. But George did not care, he was content to rule Hanover as a despot, never wanting to be involved in ruling a country together with a parliament.

An economic catastrophe arrived with what became known as the South Sea Bubble. The Government granted exclusive trading rights (mainly slave-trading) in South America to the South Sea Company. Then the Government convinced holders of government debt securities to exchange them for South Sea Company shares, the National Debt having hugely increased to fund Marlborough's battles. In addition, the South Sea Company was to be paid £500,000 a year, which the Government expected to recover from duties on the company's imports from South America. The arrangements were accompanied by massive corruption of ministers, George's mistresses and others, all of whom were given free shares with the right to sell them back to the company at market price, so encouraging them to drive up the share price.

A frenzy developed as the share price rocketed from £128 to £1,050, with people eager to buy shares regardless of the cost; and the frenzy spread to shares in other companies, many of them without any substance. Then a similar scheme in France collapsed, as did numerous fraudulent companies in England. The market plummeted. Thousands were ruined; only a few got out in time. One was Sarah Churchill; another was publisher and printer Thomas Guy, called by some the meanest man in England, who made a fortune from selling his shares. At least he used £20,000 of his profit to build the hospital in London that still bears his name.

Walpole had retired to the country, keeping out of the allegations of corruption. He lost money, but he was saved from financial disaster by following the advice of his banker, Robert Jacomb of Gibson, Jacob and Jacomb. Walpole was called back to London. He put forward schemes devised by Jacomb, and with limited compensation (funded by property confiscated from the directors of the South Sea Company), rescheduling of debts and the transfer of South Sea stock to the East India Company and the Bank of England, the economy was saved and stability gradually returned. After a stressful debate on the scandal in the House of Lords, Stanhope collapsed and died, and Sunderland resigned. The success of the schemes he had proposed led to Walpole's appointment as First Lord of the Treasury and Chancellor of the Exchequer. He became in fact the first Prime Minister, although it was not an official position, the premier title being First Lord of the Treasury[29]. With Walpole controlling Parliament and the Cabinet, the Hanoverian cronies lost their power.

Recognised as the supreme politician and master of bribery ("Every man has his price" – his own saying), Walpole continued as Prime Minister for 30 years. He is immortalised as Macheath (highwayman and captain of thieves) in John Gay's *The Beggar's Opera*; and as Mack the Knife in Bertolt Brecht and Kurt Weill's adaptation, *The Threepenny Opera*.

One of Walpole's interests was art. George had repeatedly said that he hated poets and painters, so there would be no royal art collection. It was left to Walpole to create one of the world's great collections, buying Poussins, Rubens, Rembrandts, Raphaels, Titians and so on. Unfortunately, his grandson had to sell the collection in order to pay off his debts. The British

---

29 Even today, the inscription on the brass plate on the door of 10 Downing Street reads 'First Lord of the Treasury' rather than Prime Minister, as it is the official residence of the First Lord of the Treasury, not of the Prime Minister. Nowadays the Prime Minister takes both positions, but as recently as the beginning of the twentieth century when Lord Salisbury was Prime Minister, he was not First Lord of the Treasury and had to live elsewhere.

Government would not meet the asking price, so the collection was sold to Empress Catherine the Great of Russia. It became the basis for the collection at the Hermitage in St Petersburg.

For all the country's new-found prosperity, George never became popular. He still could not speak English, he spent as much time as possible in Hanover and he held only a limited court in St James's Palace. George used just two rooms; one for sleeping and eating, the other for audiences. In the evenings, he spent his time with one of his elderly mistresses, usually cutting pieces of paper into interesting shapes.

Yet unsophisticated as the King was, Britain was still the country of Vanbrugh, Wren, Newton, Gay, Swift, Defoe, Pope, Fielding and Handel.

In 1727, now aged 67, George was preparing for another trip to Hanover, when he suffered a fit. Undeterred, he left on 3rd June. Having crossed the North Sea and reached the Netherlands, George stopped for the night in the village of Delden. For dinner, he ate a huge meal ending with plate after plate of melons. Resuming his journey the next morning, within one hour George had collapsed. After recovering consciousness, he insisted on proceeding, later reaching his brother's palace in Osnabruck. He lived through the following day, but died during the next night in the room in which he had been born.

It was said that he died of a fit of apoplexy brought on by severe indigestion. Another story is that Sophia Dorothea (who had died seven months earlier) had written to George just before her death, cursing George and denying adultery with Konigsmark, although her correspondance with Konigsmark (if genuine) suggests otherwise. As George was leaving Delden, the letter was delivered to him. He read it while the journey started, the contents leading to his fit.

Perhaps Sophia Dorothea had her revenge. Did she posthumously kill George? Maybe she had more success than the French cavalry at the Battles of Oudenarde and Neerwinden.

****

GEORGE II

11 June 1727 – 25 October 1760

When King George I died, his first-born child George Augustus took the throne as King George II. It was the natural succession, yet it was anything but usual. Since the death of Henry V, this was the first time a crowned English king succeeding on his predecessor's death had been that predecessor's first-born child; and after George II, it would happen only once more (George IV) until today.

Few people in England, certainly not his son, mourned George I's death. There was little interest in bringing his body back for burial in Westminster Abbey. In Hanover they waited for three months, and then they gave up and buried him there. George II's first act as king was to take out a hidden portrait of his mother, Sophia Dorothea (whom he had not been allowed to see since the age of ten), and hang it in a prominent position.

Initially, George wanted to dismiss Walpole, whom he considered his father's man. George had decided to appoint Sir Spencer Compton as First Minister, and George instructed him to write the King's inaugural speech. But Compton took fright and asked Walpole to write the speech for him. George had married his aunt's former ward, the orphaned Caroline of Brandenburg-Ansbach. When Queen Caroline, always Walpole's greatest supporter, found out about the speech (perhaps Walpole told her), she convinced George to keep Walpole on, aided no doubt by Walpole's promise to increase George's Civil List payment to £800,000 a year. More significantly, although George could understand and speak English, albeit with a heavy accent, he continued the practice developed during his father's reign of leaving government largely in the hands of his ministers.

George was a bad-tempered, arrogant man. However, he loved music, particularly opera. He was the patron of Handel, who had been his father's court musician. At a performance of Handel's *Messiah*, as the Hallelujah Chorus began, George suddenly, and for no apparent reason, stood up and remained standing until the end of the second act. With the King standing, everyone had to stand. Since then, it has been the tradition for the audience to stand during every performance of the Hallelujah Chorus, whether or not the monarch is present.

Later in his reign, George was involved in the establishment of the British Museum. Royal physician Sir Hans Sloane left his library and collection of curiosities (over 70,000 items) to the nation on payment of £20,000. In order to house the bequest, to which George added the Royal Library, the British Museum was founded; and to house the botanical items, the Natural History Museum was established. When Sloane had been in Jamaica, he tried a local drink made of cocoa and water. Not liking it, he added milk, so inventing drinking chocolate. Sloane brought his new concoction back to England, where it was sold by apothecaries as a 'pick-me-up'. It was in the nineteenth century that the Cadbury brothers started to sell tins of Sloane's Drinking Chocolate. The Cadburys were Quakers, and they saw drinking chocolate as an alternative to alcohol – Cadbury's Bournville estate is still alcohol-free.

Just as George had argued with his father, so George and Queen Caroline argued with their oldest son, Frederick Prince of Wales, banishing him and his family from court in 1737. Later in the year, Queen Caroline died when gangrene set in following a hernia operation. George had her buried in a coffin with a detachable side, so that when he died he could be buried in a similar coffin alongside her and they could lie together.

With Caroline's support, Walpole had been able to restrain George's warlike intentions. Without Caroline, George would not be stopped. The British had been exercising the trading rights in South America granted by the Treaty of Utrecht. However, the Spanish were later given the entitlement of boarding British merchant ships to check that they were not abusing their rights. Suspecting piracy, the Spanish boarded the brig 'Rebecca' as it was sailing from Cuba where Spain had a trading monopoly. The captain, Robert Jenkins, was tied to the mast, and the Spanish captain drew his sword and sliced off Jenkins' ear, telling him (presumably in the remaining ear) that the same would happen to his king if he dared to do the same.

The Government demanded that the boarding of British ships should cease, and in retaliation the Spanish seized all British vessels in Spanish harbours. In 1738, Parliament held an investigation, and called for evidence. Jenkins arrived and told his story, and then he dramatically produced a jar containing his ear. Against the advice of his ministers, George declared war on Spain.

Britain gained a notable victory at Porto Bello in Panama, destroying Spain's major naval base. The victory was celebrated with a new patriotic song first performed as the finale to a play about Alfred the Great: "Rule, Britannia!"; the phrase being an instruction whose meaning is lost by the omission of the exclamation mark. The next line: "Britannia rule the waves!" was also an instruction to the nation; it later changed when Britain did rule the waves and no further instruction was needed. Consequently, the Victorians added an 's' to turn it into a statement: "Britannia rules the waves". Other victories followed, but defeat in Colombia saw the mood in England change, and it led to the downfall of Walpole. Then, in 1742, the War of Jenkins' Ear merged in the larger War of the Austrian Succession as the belligerents turned their eyes to central Europe.

The War of the Spanish Succession had ended with a negotiated peace when Archduke Charles became Holy Roman Emperor. His only son died in infancy, so when Charles died (after eating poisonous mushrooms) he left two daughters. Charles had foreseen the problem, and he obtained the agreement of all the major European states to the succession of his older daughter, Maria Theresa, in the Pragmatic Sanction of 1713. As had been agreed, on Charles's death Maria Theresa claimed the crowns of Hungary and Bohemia and the rule of Austria. The Prussians saw an opportunity; they reneged on the Sanction and invaded Silesia, claiming that the Salic Law made Maria Theresa's claims unlawful. Anxious to diminish the power of the Habsburgs and increase their own, the French supported Prussia.

Britain joined the Austrian side so as to challenge any increase in French dominion. For George the prime motive was to protect Hanover. The King and his third son, William Duke of Cumberland, took the British army into Europe, and at Dettingen, George II became the last British monarch to lead his forces into battle. The British-Hanoverian-Austrian troops lined up, ready to attack. George rode out in front of his army. He drew his sword and waved it in the air as he proceeded, shouting to his men: "Now boys! Now for the honour of England!". The soldiers responded with loud "Hurrahs!", but George's horse, which had a history of being unruly, was startled and maddened by the din. It reared and plunged and then ran straight towards the enemy lines, George struggling to hold on.

The horse galloped faster and faster. For sure George was about to be killed by the French as he unwillingly charged them on his own. A young ensign, Cyrus Trapaud, was the only one to react. He dug his spurs into his horse's sides and raced after

George. Gaining ground on the crazed animal as the French opened fire trying to kill George, Trapaud drew alongside the King and managed to grasp the bridle of George's horse; then he swung the beast round and brought it to a halt.

Trapaud led George out of range of the French guns and back to the British lines. Whoever was about to kill George – the horse or the French – Trapaud had saved the King's life. George was helped to dismount. "Now that I am on my own legs, I am sure I shall not run away," said the King.

The French attacked, and they were thrown back by George's forces, which he led sword in hand, having decided it would

Cyrus Trapaud saving George II at Dettingen

be safer to fight on foot. Inspired by the strategic advice given by the Scottish Colonel Agnew, first instructing his troops not to shoot until they could "see the whites of the e'en", and then adding, "lads … kill them afore they kill you", the battle was won. As for Cyrus Trapaud, he was immediately promoted; and George saw to it that he received further promotions in later years.

Maria and Elizabeth Gunning were two Irish beauties who were taken to London by their mother to be presented at court. In order to fund the journey, Mrs Gunning agreed to act as chaperone to the rich and beautiful Catherine Plaistow, who also wished to be presented at court. When they reached London, the three young women caused such a sensation that George had to provide them with an armed guard. Maria married the Earl of Coventry, Elizabeth married the Duke of Hamilton; but Catherine Plaistow preferred the hero, Cyrus Trapaud, who ended his military career as Britain's most senior General.

However, the war was unpopular in England, seen as only for the benefit of Hanover. The Jacobites saw their chance, and so did the French. The Pretender was now an old man and regarded as a failure. He had married Maria Sobieska, daughter of the Crown Prince of Poland who was the son of King Jan III Sobieski the victor of the Battle of Vienna. Unfortunately for her, although both her father and her husband had been heirs to a throne, each of them was usurped. The Pretender's older son was now 25 years old, and in July 1745, Charles Edward Stuart – Bonnie Prince Charlie – landed in Scotland with seven followers and a promise of 12,000 French troops to follow him.

Many Scots, Catholic and Protestant, answered the call to arms, but the troops promised by Louis XV did not arrive. Nevertheless, British forces were defeated at Prestonpans. That defeat led to the singing of a new song in England, "God save the King". In later years it arguably became the world's first national anthem. For a time the tune was used for the anthems of Germany, Russia, Switzerland and Sweden. It is still the national anthem of the United Kingdom, several Commonwealth countries and Liechtenstein[30], and it is also the royal anthem of Norway.

Having proclaimed his father as king, Bonnie Prince Charlie led his army into England. The intention was to take London and capture the Hanoverian Royal Family. George was to be

---

30 It caused bewilderment when England played Liechtenstein in a football match (a qualifier for Euro 2004) and the band played the tune twice.

tried as a traitor for usurping the throne and would then be executed. Yet knowledge of the intention to kill him did not cause George any concern. He said that he would gladly chase the Scots back to Scotland himself.

Few English rallied to Charles's side; and although his army reached Derby, news of an approaching British army (false news as it happens) moved the invaders to turn round and make for Scotland. Fearful that his Highlanders would not accept a command to retreat, Charles ordered the return to Scotland to start before dawn so that they would not realise that they were marching north.

The Duke of Cumberland and his troops pursued the Scots and drove Bonnie Prince Charlie's disheartened followers into the Highlands. In the last battle to be fought on British soil, the Jacobite army was destroyed at Culloden, where Bonnie Prince Charlie had foolishly positioned his men on open land in front of the British Army's guns, although he sensibly kept to the rear. When asked for instructions after the battle, Cumberland wrote 'no quarter' on the back of a playing card, the nine of diamonds – a card still known as 'the curse of Scotland'.

As a result, the slaughter continued after the battle was over, with Scots fighters and many of their supporters being massacred. Assisted by Scottish patriot Flora MacDonald, Charles made his way to the Scottish Islands disguised as a lady's maid, and then he returned to France. It was the end of Jacobite hopes.

Three years later, a treaty ended the War of the Austrian Succession with Maria Theresa recognised as Archduchess of Austria and Queen of Hungary and Bohemia, her husband having been elected Holy Roman Emperor. Under the terms of the treaty, Prussia, led by Emperor Frederick the Great (whose mother was the daughter of George I and Sophia Dorothea), was allowed to keep Silesia. It was a concession that showed the Prussians how to enlarge their country. German nationalism had been triggered.

All enemies having been dealt with, the succession to the

British crown was now secure; then it changed. Frederick Prince of Wales had been won over by the game of cricket, the country's most popular sport. He became a player, and even formed his own team. Apparently, whilst attending a game as a spectator, he was said to have been hit on the head by a cricket ball, leading to an abscess or septicaemia. He died at the age of 44, and his 13-year-old son, George, became the heir to the throne.

Now Maria Theresa showed her true colours. Despite having been supported by the British, as a Habsburg and therefore a Catholic, Maria Theresa regarded them as Protestant heretics, and she wanted nothing more to do with them. Catholic France would be a more acceptable ally. That decision to befriend France would in time lead to the execution of Maria Theresa's daughter, Marie-Antoinette.

Anyway, in signing the 1748 peace treaty, Maria Theresa had only been playing for time; she wanted Silesia back. She improved and enlarged her army. The Prussians saw what was happening, and in 1756 they launched a pre-emptive attack and invaded Saxony. Now it started all over again, although this time Austria was allied to France, Russia and Sweden. Fearing a French attack on Hanover, Britain supported Prussia.

The Seven Years' War saw every participant winning and losing battles. The conflict spread to Canada, America, India and the Caribbean, as the British challenged French and Spanish colonies in the first global war. Under the direction of William Pitt, Britain's efforts outside Europe were increasingly successful. His genius was to finance allied armies on the Continent so as to tie down and drain French resources there, so enabling Britain to concentrate on acquiring territories in Canada, the West Indies and India.

George was now 78, and had lost interest in war and government. On 25th October 1760, George rose at 6 o'clock in Kensington Palace and drank a cup of hot chocolate. Then he went to the toilet, suffering as always from constipation[31]. The effort was too much; he collapsed on the floor. Hearing the loud crash, his valet came running, and George was carried to his bed, where he died.

It was an undignified end for a man who had been so courageous on the battlefield, where he had narrowly escaped death. At least he was granted his dearest wish: he was buried next to his wife with one side of each of their coffins removed so that their remains could mingle.

****

---

31 So maybe haemorrhoids was the reason he stood up during the Hallelujah Chorus.

THE GEORGES

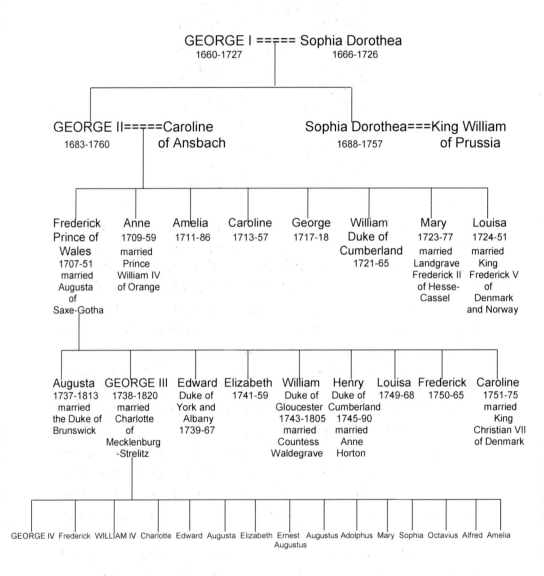

GEORGE I ===== Sophia Dorothea
1660-1727 · 1666-1726

GEORGE II=====Caroline of Ansbach
1683-1760

Sophia Dorothea===King William of Prussia
1688-1757

| Frederick Prince of Wales 1707-51 married Augusta of Saxe-Gotha | Anne 1709-59 married Prince William IV of Orange | Amelia 1711-86 | Caroline 1713-57 | George 1717-18 | William Duke of Cumberland 1721-65 | Mary 1723-77 married Landgrave Frederick II of Hesse-Cassel | Louisa 1724-51 married King Frederick V of Denmark and Norway |

| Augusta 1737-1813 married the Duke of Brunswick | GEORGE III 1738-1820 married Charlotte of Mecklenburg-Strelitz | Edward Duke of York and Albany 1739-67 | Elizabeth 1741-59 | William Duke of Gloucester 1743-1805 married Countess Waldegrave | Henry Duke of Cumberland 1745-90 married Anne Horton | Louisa 1749-68 | Frederick 1750-65 | Caroline 1751-75 married King Christian VII of Denmark |

GEORGE IV Frederick WILLIAM IV Charlotte Edward Augusta Elizabeth Ernest Augustus Adolphus Mary Sophia Octavius Alfred Amelia
Augustus

GEORGE III

25 October 1760 – 29 January 1820

King George III succeeded his grandfather at the age of twenty-two. In the early years of his reign, George was firmly under the thumb of his widowed mother, Augusta of Saxe-Gotha Princess of Wales and her alleged lover the Earl of Bute (George's former tutor), who was appointed Prime Minister. They arranged for George to marry Duchess Charlotte of Mecklenburg-Strelitz, whom he first met on their wedding day. In 1762, their son, George, was born. Anticipating many more children, the new king bought Buckingham House in London for £21,000 as a private residence. He was right; there would be a total of fifteen children.

The signing of the Treaty of Paris ended the Seven Years' War. Pitt's determination to pursue Britain's enemies and their colonies outside Europe brought extraordinary rewards. Britain was confirmed in the conquest of Canada, various Caribbean islands plus huge territory in India, and also gained Senegal, Florida and Minorca. In Europe, Prussia (which retained Silesia) was now the dominant force; but Britain became the major colonial power across the world. Nevertheless, in the light of so many victories, in England the treaty terms were considered inadequate, and the unpopular Bute was forced to resign.

New Prime Minister Grenville found a novel way of raising money that would cause no problems with the electorate. He decided to tax the American colonists; all legal documents, newspapers and pamphlets would require a revenue stamp. Grenville's justification was that the colonists should pay for the cost of their protection. In truth, little protection was needed; the French had been defeated and the colonists felt able to defend themselves against any hostile Indian tribes. Also, the legality of taxing those living outside Britain was questionable.

It did not go down well. Rioting started in the American colonies, followed by a boycott of British goods. Parliament was forced to reconsider the tax. Fortunately, Grenville had been replaced by Lord Rockingham, and the Stamp Act was repealed.

Pitt, 'the Great Commoner', a man who represented the people not the monarch, now became Prime Minister. However, he was not the success he had been when directing the war. He suffered a breakdown, and Charles Townshend, the Chancellor of the Exchequer, led the Government during Pitt's absence. Having learned nothing from the failed Stamp Act, Townshend decided to tax the colonists' imports of glass, paper, lead, paint and tea. The tax revenue would help to pay the cost of maintaining the freedom of the seas, from which the colonists benefitted. Before he had any more bright ideas, Townshend died.

When Pitt recovered, he found out that the French had been allowed to take Corsica. It seemed a trivial matter at the time; but if Corsica had belonged to Britain, the great Corsican military leader (born just a year later) might one day have been directing British troops against the French rather than the other way round. It was only one of many matters that had gone wrong, but worst of all, Pitt's mental health was damaged, and he had to resign.

As so often happened, the real culprit was rewarded; the Duke of Grafton became Prime Minister. It quickly became clear that he was not up to the job, and he was replaced by Lord North, a man who not only thought like the King, he even looked like the King.

Next, there was a serious personal problem for the King. George's sister, Caroline, had been married off at the age of 15 to her cousin, King Christian VII of Denmark (his mother Louisa was a daughter of George II), despite concerns as to his mental state. Christian had to be persuaded to have intercourse with Caroline, which produced a son. He then took up with a prostitute, bringing her to court. Christian's behaviour deteriorated by the day, involving low-life brothels, perversion and self-mutilation. Caroline was continually in distress at her husband's preference for prostitutes and boys. Then Christian appointed a German doctor as his new physician. The physician, Johann Struensee, became Caroline's lover. After little more than two years, Struensee had acquired such influence over the King that he exercised absolute power.

In January 1772, Struensee and Caroline were arrested. Struensee was executed, and George feared that Caroline would suffer the same fate. The navy prepared to attack Denmark. Then a deal was negotiated. Caroline was divorced and taken by a British ship to Hanover where she was confined for life in the Castle of Celle, much like her great-great-grandmother, Sophia Dorothea. At the age of twenty-three, Caroline conveniently died of scarlet fever in her castle prison.

More serious trouble was literally 'brewing' in America. North had repealed all Townshend's import duties other than the tax on tea. In fact, the tax would raise little more than £3,000 a year, but it became a matter of principle for both sides. In December 1773, a tea ship belonging to the East India Company was attacked in Boston harbour by colonists disguised as Mohawk Indians, and the cargo was destroyed. North's response to the Boston Tea Party was to close Boston harbour and put the Massachusetts Council under Crown control. That drove the other colonies to support Massachusetts. In England, initial sympathy for the colonists was diminished by what was seen as a criminal act.

Fighting started on a small scale between local militias and the British Army after soldiers had been sent to seize munitions at Concord. The war had begun. Pitt (who considered taxation of colonists to be unlawful) was for reconciliation, but he and his supporters were now in the minority.

It became increasingly difficult for Britain to cope with such a large area from so far away; instructions from London arrived in America weeks after the situation in the colonies had changed. Even worse, the hostilities polarised the two sides; the colonists' resolve grew, and objection to taxation developed into a demand for independence. North wanted to resign in favour of Pitt, but the King was aware of Pitt's sympathies and would not allow it; and then Pitt died (having given his name to Pittsburgh).

A General Election increased North's majority. However, the election's real significance lay in the entry to Parliament of Pitt's second son, also named William Pitt, and therefore known as 'Pitt the Younger', at the age of twenty-one. From the day of his first speech, Pitt the Younger was destined to become one of the most brilliant of all members of parliament.

Meanwhile, problems were mounting in America. After several successes for British forces, the war started to go badly, with the colonists inspired by a man who had fought for Britain in the French and Indian War: George Washington. Then, with French support in troops and equipment, the colonists trapped Cornwallis and his army at Yorktown, and he surrendered. In England, support for the war collapsed.

North was compelled to resign; he was replaced by Lord Rockingham, who was a supporter of American independence. In July 1782, Rockingham died, and the Earl of Shelburne became Prime Minister with Pitt the Younger appointed Chancellor of the Exchequer. By the end of the year, American independence, already a reality, was formally accepted. Thousands of colonists who had stayed loyal to the Crown had to be brought back to Britain for their own safety. Among them was Flora MacDonald, the Scottish woman who had helped Bonnie Prince Charlie to escape after Culloden. She had gone to live in America, and was a staunch Loyalist, her husband being a British officer.

Shelburne resigned, to be replaced by the Duke of Portland. After eight months he was replaced by Pitt the Younger. This was a man who had gone to Cambridge University at the age of 14, graduated at 17, been called to the Bar and become an MP at 21, been appointed Chancellor of the Exchequer at 23, and was now Prime Minister at 24.

Pitt had taken every opportunity to speak out against the American War, against corruption, for a reduction in taxation and for parliamentary reform. George would benefit from Pitt's popularity.

George's only problem was the hostility of the Prince of Wales, who always supported George's enemies in Parliament. That problem became worse when the Prince announced that he had secretly married the twice-widowed Maria Fitzherbert, a Catholic. However, after the King's brother, Henry Duke of Cumberland, married a commoner, George had insisted on the passing of the Royal Marriages Act, which provided that no descendant of George II (other than issue of princesses who had married into foreign families) could marry without the consent of the monarch; but if consent is refused to a person over the age of 25, that person may marry after giving the Privy Council one year's notice unless both Houses of Parliament disapprove[32]. Consequently, the 'marriage' of the Prince of Wales was unlawful and ineffective.

In the country, the economy improved with the peace and all seemed well. It was 1778, and George's carriage was arriving at his official residence, St James's Palace. The carriage came to a halt, and a footman lowered the step so that George might climb down. As usual, there was a small crowd of onlookers

---

[32] No application for consent has ever been refused; although there have been occasions when consent has not been sought in anticipation of refusal – the children were therefore illegitimate.

hoping to catch sight of the monarch, maybe even to cheer him. Suddenly, a woman, Rebecca O'Hara, rushed forward holding a knife in her outstretched hand. Before she could stab George she was grabbed by two soldiers. On questioning the woman, it emerged that she believed that George had usurped the throne, to which she was entitled; although she could not explain the basis of her claim. She said that if she were not crowned queen, England would be deluged in blood for a thousand years. Sent to Bethlehem Hospital for the mentally ill[33], she remained there for the rest of her life.

A similar incident occurred eight years later. Again, George was returning to St James's Palace. His coach halted at the Garden Entrance. Without causing any disturbance, a woman manoeuvred her way to the front of the crowd. In her hand she had a rolled-up petition. After King George stepped down from the coach, he walked towards the woman to receive the petition. She held it out to the King. Then, with her other hand, the woman raised an ivory-handled knife and stabbed George. Fortunately, the weapon was a table knife of such poor quality that rather than plunge through George's waistcoat and into his chest, the knife simply bent, causing no wound. It was snatched from the woman's grasp, and she was held fast by a yeoman and a footman. George remained calm. In fact, his main concern was for his assailant's safety. "The poor creature is mad. Do not hurt her; she has not hurt me," he shouted.

George was right; Margaret Nicholson was quite mad. She was a needlewoman from Stockton-on-Tees. At the age of twelve she had been sent to work in a series of respectable households, ending up in the home of Sir John Sebright. Later, she was found to be having an affair with a footman, and was dismissed. Having lost her livelihood and her lover, she descended into poverty and insanity. She petitioned the King

---

[33] Originally a priory, a hospital was attached to it in about 1329. In 1377 it was designated a hospital for 'distracted patients', who were chained to the wall and ducked in water or whipped when they were violent. It became a lunatic asylum in 1547 when the priory was dissolved.

twenty times, begging for assistance, but received no reply. So she had gone to St James's Palace to remonstrate with him. Asked what she wanted from the King, she replied: "That he would provide for me, as I want to marry and have children like other folks." She was not prosecuted, instead she was sent to Bethlehem Hospital for life under the Vagrancy Act by order of the Home Secretary, even though the Act gave him no power to make such an order. Locked in a room, she was chained to the wall for five years. The chains were then removed, but she remained at Bethlehem until her death 37 years later.

The attack and his sympathetic reaction to Margaret

Margaret Nicholson attempting to assassinate George III

Nicholson increased George's popularity. However, trouble of a different kind was coming. In June 1788, George suffered a painful gastric attack. His doctor blamed it on too much sauerkraut, and sent George to take the waters in Cheltenham. George recovered, but in October he suffered another attack, which caused him great pain and left him speechless. He developed a rash, his eyes became yellow and his urine turned very dark. When George regained the power of speech, he talked drivel for hours without stopping, constantly repeating bizarre remarks. It was even claimed that he had approached an oak tree, shaking one of its branches as if it were a hand, and talking to the tree in the belief that it was the King of Prussia.

After a brief period of calm, on 5th November George once more began to speak nonsense at great speed, foam coming from his mouth. He attacked the Prince of Wales, attempting to smash his head against a wall, and the constant rambling speech continued day after day.

George was in effect imprisoned in his palace at Kew. He was forced to swallow drugs, and was tied up sitting on a chair during the day and lying down on a bed during the night. Starved as a punishment for any misbehaviour, when he objected he was gagged. Then the doctors blistered George's body to draw out the evil, causing him excruciating pain.

It is now believed that George was suffering from porphyria – an excess of the pigment that gives the blood its red colour. That excess turns the urine dark, and in extreme cases it poisons the nervous system and the brain. Unfortunately, throughout his life George was given medicine containing antimony for his various maladies. Antimony contains arsenic, and arsenic triggers porphyria attacks.

Despite all the Hanoverian inbreeding, porphyria was probably a Stuart defect that was inherited by George from his 3 x great-grandmother Elizabeth Stuart, through whom the Hanoverians gained the crown. Evidence of the disorder can be found in James I (who suffered periods of delirium) and his mother, Mary Queen of Scots, who had attacks of hysteria. Despite the 'treatments', George began to recover, and by March 1789 he could return to Windsor. But porphyria was, and still is, incurable.

Some generations can escape porphyria attacks. After George, the first descendants we know for certain suffered from the disease were Princess Charlotte of Prussia (daughter of Queen Victoria's daughter, also called Victoria), who often tore her clothes and who suffered constant ill health, and then her daughter Princess Feodora of Saxe-Meiningen who committed suicide in a sanatorium in 1945 – recent tests on their remains evidenced the porphyria. In England, it was the present Queen's cousin Prince William of Gloucester; he was diagnosed with the disease shortly before he died in 1972, when the plane he was piloting in an air race crashed after takeoff. A bachelor, he was ninth in line to the throne.

There may have been others who were not diagnosed, such as Prince Henry, oldest son of James I, who suffered from delirium; Princess Henrietta (Minette), sister of Charles II, who married the Duke of Orleans and died aged 26, suffering incontinence and vomiting; Queen Anne, who suffered hysterical fits; and Queen Caroline of Denmark, George III's sister, said to have died of scarlet fever.

Despite a Prime Minister in favour of reform, a reaction set in following the French Revolution in 1789. Although there was shock at the execution of Louis XVI and his wife Marie-Antoinette (daughter of Maria Theresa), there was some satisfaction that the French ruling classes were receiving their deserved retribution for supporting revolutionaries in the American War of Independence.

For a time, the French were occupied in war against Austria and Prussia, who had tried to come to the aid of Louis XVI. Then France declared war on Britain. At sea, Britain was victorious. The army, sent to the Netherlands under the command of George's second son, the Duke of York, suffered a series of defeats, and he would forever be mocked as:

The grand old Duke of York,
He had ten thousand men.
He marched them up to the top of the hill
And he marched them down again.

Back in England, the Prince of Wales continued to be a problem, and he was still unmarried. Parliament offered to pay off his debts of £630,000 over a period of years if he took an acceptable wife. George selected for his son the fat and ugly Caroline of Brunswick. Even though Caroline was the Prince's first cousin (her mother was George III's sister), he had never met her. Having met her, he asked for brandy. He had to get drunk in order to go through with the wedding ceremony. It was not just her looks and vulgar behaviour, Caroline rarely washed or changed her underclothes. Apparently, the smell was nauseating. George and Caroline had a daughter, Charlotte, and then they separated. It was probably worth it for £630,000; a vast sum at the time.

Elsewhere it was all bad news. The first coalition against France broke up when the French Army led by Napoleon forced Prussia and Spain to submit to his terms. In England, the failing war and poor harvests damaged the economy. Living standards plummeted and discontent grew. Perhaps the French Revolution suggested that killing the monarch was the solution. On 29th October 1795, George travelled to Westminster by coach to open a new session of Parliament. He must have become aware of the hostility in the streets. As he neared the Houses of Parliament, George heard the chants of the people demanding bread, demanding peace and demanding "No King!". George's coach turned into Old Palace Yard where protestors attacked the coach; then one of them drew a gun and fired. The ball flew through the window of the coach. Usually, George's head would have been at the window, as he waved to his cheering subjects. This time, in view of the crowd's demeanour, George was sitting back in his seat – it saved his life. The assassin escaped.

The attempt to assassinate George III at Old Palace Yard

In 1800, the second coalition against France collapsed following further victories for Napoleon. Britain was left to fight alone. France now controlled most of Europe; but the British Navy, inspired by Nelson, ruled the seas. Nevertheless, Britain prepared for the expected French invasion. On 15th May 1800, George went to Hyde Park to watch a field exercise of the Grenadier Guards. During the exercise, blanks were to be fired. Suddenly 'by accident' a live shot was fired in George's direction, missing him by a few feet. William Ongley, a clerk in the navy pay office, was hit in the thigh. Following an investigation, it emerged that amongst the blanks distributed to the soldiers there were nine live cartridges disguised as blanks. Maybe it was not a coincidence that the Guards had recently had their beer allowance withdrawn. Possibly it was another attempt to kill the King.

The day was not yet over. In the evening George went to the Theatre Royal Drury Lane, where (in the former theatre building) an assassin had tried to kill his grandfather in 1716. He went to see the comedy, *She Would and She Would Not*. George made his way to the royal box. Entering the box, he walked to the front to receive the applause of the audience.

George stood there smiling as everyone got to their feet and cheered the King, celebrating his escape in Hyde Park.

All eyes were on the King. In the second row, a man stepped up on to his seat and aimed a pistol at George. But David Moses Dyte leaned over from the third row and struck the assassin on the arm as he fired, so the shot narrowly missed the King's head. The would-be assassin was seized and taken away. George was advised to leave, but he would have none of it. He insisted that the performance should continue, and sat quietly enjoying the play. Two assassination attempts in one day; and he still fell asleep during the interval. Dyte's reward was the patent for selling opera tickets.

The failed assassin was James Hadfield, a former soldier in the 15th Light Dragoons. He had been wounded at the Battle of Tourcoing, struck eight times on the head with a sabre, and had been discharged from the army because of the state of his mind. Hadfield generally appeared to be normal, but at times he was convinced that he had conversations with the Almighty who had told him that the world would come to an end unless he sacrificed himself for its salvation, thereby procuring the second coming of Christ. Hadfield had also been warned that he must not destroy himself. He worked out that killing or attempting to kill the King would ensure his lawful execution.

At his trial for high treason, Hadfield surprisingly pleaded 'not guilty'; it was contrary to his supposed plan to be executed. Doctors, former army colleagues and family members gave evidence that he was mad. The Court declared Hadfield insane and acquitted him. Persons found to be insane by the criminal courts were treated in the same way as other lunatics, and were released to their families; only the family could commit them to a madhouse. To release a man who had tried to murder the King would have caused outrage. So Hadfield was sent to prison for four days while Parliament rushed through the Criminal Lunatics Act. That Act gave the courts power to order the indefinite detention in a madhouse of persons accused of crimes who had been declared insane. Hadfield was then sent to Bethlehem Hospital ('Bedlam' for short), where he died of tuberculosis 41 years later.

That was not George's only eventful visit to the theatre. The following year, he went to see a play when visiting Weymouth on the south coast. At the end of the performance, a man suddenly ran towards the royal box and tried to climb in. He was quickly seized and taken away. It was only the next morning that a knife was found embedded in the door next to the royal box. Urban Metcalf was a 25-year-old lace and garter hawker from London, who had already spent five years in asylums. He believed that he was the true king, and that was why he had repeatedly tried to enter royal palaces. Metcalf had travelled down from London to throw his knife at George. As no one had noticed the knife being thrown, the authorities decided to do nothing. Then Metcalf created a disturbance outside the King's Lodge, demanding to be allowed inside. He was locked up in a madhouse. Although released after several years, he ended up in an asylum in York.

Next the French started to foment trouble in Ireland. So Pitt decided to abolish the Irish Parliament (where membership was restricted to Protestants), and instead have Irish members of parliament at Westminster. In 1801, by a further Act of Union, the Kingdom of Ireland was joined to the Kingdom of Great Britain to create the United Kingdom of Great Britain and Ireland. Pitt promised legislation to enable Catholic Irish members to sit in Parliament. That would involve a change in the oath of membership, which included denials of the principal tenets of Catholicism.

A Bill only became an Act and therefore the law after approval by both Houses of Parliament and receipt of the monarch's assent. George was outraged; he believed that assenting to such an Act would be a denial of his coronation oath to protect the Protestant faith, and would make him undeserving of the throne in God's eyes. Also, George was well aware that the crown had been given to the House of Hanover because

James II and his descendants were Catholics, whereas the Hanoverians had sworn to protect England from Catholicism. If George failed to do so, on his death the Stuarts would have a better right to the crown than the Hanoverians. Bonnie Prince Charlie, the Young Pretender, had died a drunken old man without children. His brother was a cardinal. So the throne could be claimed by the Cardinal or the man who became the Jacobite heir on the Cardinal's death in 1807, the senior descendant of Charles I's daughter Henrietta (Minette) and her husband the Duke of Orleans, and that was King Charles Emmanuel IV of Sardinia[34] – 3 x great-grandson of Charles I.

George lined up the Church, the judiciary and much of Parliament against the proposed legislation. Pitt admitted defeat, he resigned and was replaced by his friend Henry Addington (the son of Pitt's doctor).

Within a short time, the King's illness returned. Addington and George's doctors had him taken to Kew House and kept there as a prisoner, drugged and in solitary confinement. He was rescued by the Lord Chancellor, Lord Eldon. Freed from his doctors, George's condition improved.

A greater threat to George was said to have come from Colonel Edward Despard. He had been appointed superintendent of what is now Belize in Central America, and, contrary to instructions, granted land to colonists regardless of colour. Following complaints by white settlers, Despard was ordered back to England. After an investigation, he was exonerated and told that he would have been reinstated, but unfortunately his position had been abolished. Pursued by his enemies, Despard was bankrupted and spent two years in debtors' prison. He then took up the cause of political reform, and with 30 others was seized and imprisoned for three years without trial on suspicion of being revolutionaries. Six months after his release, Despard and 32 colleagues were arrested and charged with treason for conspiring to kill the King and start a

---

34 See Appendix A to find his heirs and the present Jacobite pretender.

revolution. The only evidence against them was the testimony of government spies. They said that Despard's plan was to fire a canon at George's coach as he made his way to Parliament. The army had conveniently put a captured French canon on display in St James's Park. It was alleged that Despard planned to use that canon to blow George's coach sky-high.

Despite Nelson appearing as a character witness, Despard and nine of his co-conspirators were convicted, the jury recommending mercy because of Despard's previous good character and service to the nation. The judge ignored the

Despard making his speech on the scaffold

recommendation. Despard and his colleagues became the last to be sentenced to be hanged, drawn and quartered. However, the Government feared public dissent, so the condemned men were merely hanged and beheaded.

Then, in June 1803 the French occupied Hanover. Soon Napoleon had installed himself as Emperor of France, ready to invade England. George decided to lead his troops into battle, but in early 1804 his illness returned. Addington and the doctors tried to take control of the King, but they were unable to do so as two of George's sons, the Duke of Cumberland and the Duke of Kent, stopped them from entering Buckingham House. As a result, George recovered and Pitt was reappointed Prime Minister.

George now had to contend with the Prince of Wales, who was becoming increasingly impatient for power, showing constant animosity towards his father. Then Queen Charlotte became hostile. After over 40 years of fairly happy marriage, the Queen, who had become old, fat and ugly, decided that she wanted nothing more to do with her husband; she was disgusted by his mental state.

The porphyria now led to blindness in one eye and poor sight in the other. George was ignored by his family other than his daughter Amelia and his granddaughter Princess Charlotte, the only child of the Prince of Wales. Charlotte was George's favourite, and he took control of her education, expecting the royal line to pass through her.

The chances of invasion were reduced as rule of the seas was secured at Trafalgar off the south-west coast of Spain in Britain's greatest naval victory, won by Britain's greatest sailor – Nelson, a man who suffered throughout his life from chronic seasickness. However, the war in Europe went badly. The Russian and Austrian armies were defeated at Austerlitz, and yet another coalition against France collapsed. Napoleon ruled continental Europe. The setback proved too much for Pitt, who died at the age of 46.

An added problem for the King was that he was bedevilled by problems with his children. The Prince of Wales had always been antagonistic with his persistent support of his father's enemies; George's second son, Frederick Duke of York, was found to have allowed his mistress to sell commissions and promotions in the army; George's third son, William Duke of Clarence, was living with an actress and their ten illegitimate children and spoke out against the war with France; the fourth son, Edward Duke of Kent, was detested throughout the country for his brutal treatment of soldiers; George's fifth son, Ernest Augustus Duke of Cumberland, had claimed that he was the victim of an assassination attempt after which his valet committed suicide by cutting his throat – it later seemed more likely that the valet had found out about the Duke's homosexual activities and that the Duke had murdered him, inventing the assassination attempt and suicide as a cover-up, and he was also suspected of incest with one of his sisters; the sixth son, Augustus Duke of Sussex, married without permission and had his marriage annulled; the seventh son, Adolphus Duke of Cambridge, surrendered command of the Hanoverian Army and fled when Prussia invaded; the eighth son, Gustavus, had died at the age of four; the ninth son, Alfred, died at the age of one.

As for George's six daughters, Charlotte had married but produced only a stillborn child. Augusta, Elizabeth, Mary, Sophia and Amelia had not married. At least George had one grandchild, Charlotte, the daughter of the Prince of Wales.

Then George's favourite daughter, Amelia, died. It seemed to be the last straw for an old man who had reigned for 50 years, only one of which had so far involved madness. Now George became deluded; he believed that Amelia was still alive. He was put in a strait-jacket and bled by having leeches placed on his forehead. May 1811 was the last time the King was seen in public.

George spent most of his remaining time talking nonsense and obscenities. The Prince of Wales was at last appointed Regent, and George was left to the devices of doctors who believed that physical punishment would cure insanity. However, George continued to have lucid intervals when he could understand news of Napoleon's defeat in Russia followed by abdication and exile in Elba. Most of all George was cheered by news of the recovery of his beloved Hanover.

It got worse. Already blind, George now went deaf. Having grown a long white beard, George spent his days wandering around his rooms in Windsor Castle wearing a dressing gown. So he was never aware of Napoleon's escape from exile, or his attempt to recover his empire, ended by Wellington's victory at Waterloo; nor of Hanover's elevation from an electorate (irrelevant now that the Holy Roman Empire had ceased to exist, and there was no Emperor to elect) to a kingdom.

The Queen no longer visited George, and in 1818 she died. George never knew of his wife's death. Nor did he know of the death of his fourth son, the Duke of Kent, who died in delirium, said to have been the result of pneumonia caused by not changing his wet socks after a long walk in the rain. Curiously, he had written to George complaining of attacks "the severity of which is, I believe, not unknown to Your Majesty" – so was it porphyria?

Christmas 1819, and George had a final surge of strength. He talked rubbish without stopping for 58 hours and then fell into a coma for a month. He died on 29th January 1820, aged 81.

Remembered for his madness and for losing America, his reign also saw the acquisition of Canada and much of India, the beginning of the Industrial Revolution and the defeat of Napoleon. As to America, he just could never understand why he should suffer disloyalty or how a nation could exist without a monarch.

People recalled that at the banquet following George's coronation, one of the largest jewels had fallen out of his crown. In retrospect it was seen as an omen.

****

GEORGE IV

29 January 1820 – 26 June 1830

Although George IV's reign began in 1820, he started to act almost as king when he was appointed Regent in February 1811.

It was a time when Britain was isolated. With brilliant victories year after year, Napoleon controlled most of Europe. Fortunately, the navy still ruled the oceans. When the Secretary for War was asked to assure Parliament that there would be no invasion, he responded: "I can give no such assurance, but they will not get here by sea."

Nevertheless, there was great discontent in the country. On 11th May 1812, John Bellingham, a bankrupt commercial agent who had a grudge against the Government for not coming to his aid when he was imprisoned in Russia and for not compensating him when he was released, shot Prime Minister Spencer Perceval (who as Attorney General had prosecuted Edward Despard) in the lobby of the House of Commons. Far from being appalled by the assassination of a man who left a widow and 12 children, the public rejoiced. There were calls in the streets to do the same to George. Bellingham was hanged, and a public appeal raised far more money for Bellingham's family than the amount of compensation he had been seeking.[35]

Ignoring the discontent, George pursued his personal interests. Apart from alcohol, food and older women, his loves were new buildings, furniture and silver. However, his taste was ostentatious to the extent of vulgarity, leading to the Regency being remembered as a time of excesses.

A new conflict started in June 1812 when America declared war on Britain. It was for several reasons: Britain restricting trade with France, seizing British-born American sailors for service in the navy, and supporting Indian tribes into whose lands the United States was trying to expand. With British forces busy fighting the French, the Americans were able to take part of Canada and gain victories over Indian tribes.

Still in 1812, the Tsar refused to join the trade boycott of Britain, and then Napoleon received intelligence that the Russians were considering an attempt to recapture Poland. He marched into Russia with 650,000 troops. The French took Moscow, and according to the rules of war the Russians should have formally surrendered and submitted to Napoleon's terms. They did not, because the Russians had deserted the city, and there was no one of seniority left behind. Critically, there were insufficient buildings to garrison the French troops, and there was no food. In order to survive, the soldiers killed and ate their horses; as a result, the French cavalry ceased to exist. With no shelter, no food and no Russian surrender, the situation was hopeless. In the severe Russian winter, the French Army started the long march home. Thousands froze to death, thousands starved and thousands were killed by the Russians, then the Prussians and then the Austrians. Only about 27,000 fit soldiers made it back.

Undaunted, Napoleon raised a new army, and he won further victories, although at heavy cost. He had not been

---

35 Bellingham's descendant, Henry Bellingham, was elected a Conservative MP in 1983; but he lost the seat in 1997 as a result of votes won by the Referendum Party candidate Roger Percival who claimed to be a descendant of the murdered PM. Bellingham regained the seat in 2001.

destroyed by the Russian campaign, but it showed that he was not invincible. The pendulum had swung. Defeated in Spain and outnumbered on all sides, Napoleon retreated as British forces moved through south-west France, and Britain's allies progressed from the east. By March 1814, the Prussians had reached Paris. Napoleon abdicated and was exiled to Elba.

With Napoleon defeated, the British turned to the American War, taking Washington and burning the White House. Further American invasions of Canada ended in defeat, as did further British invasions of the United States. It ended in a stalemate and a treaty under which each side abandoned its gains. The only losers were the Indian tribes who lost land and any hope of securing their own autonomous territory; the only winners were about 3,000 slaves who escaped to Canada. The US protested at Britain's refusal to return the slaves. The matter went to arbitration, and the arbitrator, the Tsar, ordered Britain to pay the slave-owners compensation of $1.2M.

Then, in February 1815, attention returned to Europe where the victors were meeting in Vienna to carve up the continent. While they were busy talking, Napoleon escaped from Elba where he had been allowed to reign as sovereign, and by May he once again ruled France. He advanced with his army, intending to attack before the coalition forces could combine.

Command of the British-German-Dutch Army was given to Arthur Wellesley, created Duke of Wellington for leading the British Army to a series of victories that had expelled the French from Spain. The victories were gained with the aid of Spanish forces who harassed the French in minor attacks known as 'little wars', or in Spanish, 'guerrillas' – the name later given to such fighters.

Napoleon forced Wellington back towards the Channel. Wellington took his position on an escarpment near the village of Waterloo, not far from Brussels. Now Napoleon prepared to attack, eager for victory before Blücher's Prussian troops could march to Wellington's side. On the morning of 18th

June 1815, Napoleon delayed, waiting for the ground to dry after overnight torrential rain. He was unconcerned, certain of victory with his greater numbers, and holding Wellington in low regard – but Napoleon had never faced him in battle before and critically, Wellington had selected the battlefield. At last the French advanced, but the delay had been too long; as the French attacked, the Prussians arrived and they immediately charged, breaking through the flank of the French Army. At this vital moment, Napoleon was resting at his headquarters, having handed command to Marshal Ney. Wellington directed a minimal withdrawal; Ney thought it was a retreat and ordered his 9,000 strong calvary to take the escarpment without waiting for artillery support. Thirteen British batallions in defensive squares were waiting for them. Wellington knew he had won. After twelve failed French cavalry charges, Wellington counter-attacked, and following savage fighting, the remains of the French Army fled. Fatally, Napoleon had underestimated his opponent; it cost him his empire.

Napoleon returned to Paris, but he had no support. He surrendered to the British, sending a letter to the Regent asking for asylum. Instead he was taken to St Helena in the middle of the south Atlantic, more than 1,000 miles from the nearest land. He remained there until his death six years later.

The map of Europe had changed: Russia was in ruins, Austria and Prussia were enlarged, the German states were in recovery, France was defeated, Spanish power was gone, and the Holy Roman Empire and Poland no longer existed. Britain (having acquired Cape Colony in South Africa and Ceylon) was the most powerful country in the world.

Now the Regency moved into its richest phase. George had already overseen the rebuilding of Windsor Castle and the building of the Royal Pavilion in his beloved Brighton. He became the patron of John Nash, who rebuilt the Pavilion in Indian style with Oriental onion-shaped turrets. Nash also redesigned part of London, principally Regent's Park, Regent's Street and the surrounding areas, building Regency terraces covered in painted plaster with Greek columns and entered through Roman arches. The focal point of Regent's Park was the Royal Menagerie to which the King's collection of animals was moved from the Tower of London (other than the ravens because of the traditional belief that if they ever leave the Tower, the kingdom will fall). It later became London Zoo.

Culture also flourished; this was the time of Wordsworth, Scott, Austen, Shelley, de Quincy, Lamb, Sheridan, Keats, Coleridge, Byron, Constable, Turner and Kean.

Next the country's attention turned to the Regent's daughter. George's marriage to Caroline had been a disaster. According to George, he was able to overcome his aversion only three times: twice on his wedding night and once the following night. Princess Charlotte was born nine months later. Then the royal couple separated. Although he had many mistresses, for most of his adult life Mrs Fitzherbert was the Regent's companion, regarded by him as his wife despite several periods of estrangement.

In 1814, Princess Caroline had left for the Continent, where she lived a merry, not to say scandalous, life. The Regent had written to her saying that he would not have 'relations' with her again, and she could do as she liked – she certainly did. Princess Charlotte, the Regent's daughter, felt deserted by her mother, growing up a lonely woman. Charlotte had been told that she was to marry the Prince of Orange, but she refused. Then she found someone she was prepared to marry. On 2nd May 1816, Charlotte married Prince Leopold of Saxe-Coburg-Saalfeld.[36]

There were great celebrations at the wedding of the ultimate heir, but George was not allowed to share in Charlotte's popularity. He had become increasingly disliked because of his opulent lifestyle, spending enormous sums on lavish entertainment at a time when millions faced unemployment and starvation, the situation exacerbated by the Corn Law that

36 It became Saxe-Coburg and Gotha in 1826 when Saxe-Coburg acquired Gotha and transferred Saalfeld to Saxe-Meiningen.

prevented the import of cheap foreign corn.

Throughout the world, 1816 was known as 'The Year without a Summer'. There had been a number of massive volcanic eruptions in Indonesia, and the dust blocked the sunlight for months. Crops failed, there were food shortages, prices rocketed and riots broke out. On the positive side, Turner painted the extraordinary sunsets, and some writers holidaying in Switzerland were forced to remain indoors, so they held a competition to see who could write the most frightening story: Mary Shelley won with *Frankenstein*.

On 16th January 1817, a ball was held for the Tsar's brother at which 100 dishes were served in nine courses (the new idea of having courses, instead of everything being served at once, had been introduced by the Russian ambassador in Paris, and was therefore known as eating *a la Russe*). Twelve days later, the Regent was travelling in his coach along the Mall towards his home at Carlton House. He soon became aware of protestors in the street shouting abuse at him. George had seen all this before; he no longer appeared in public unless he was surrounded by soldiers. The coach continued at its usual calm pace as the shouts became louder and louder. All of a sudden, a stone hit the coach. More stones were thrown, some hitting the side of the coach with considerable force. Then a shot, as a bullet broke through the window and flew across the chamber. Fortunately, just like his father 22 years earlier, the Regent was sitting well back in his seat, keeping out of sight, so the shot did not find its intended victim.

The driver cracked his whip, and the coach sped away as the protestors dispersed. No one was apprehended. George was outraged at the attempt to kill him. The following Sunday, prayers were offered in churches throughout the country, seeking the Almighty's protection of 'the Royal Person'. It worked; there were no further assassination attempts.

All the joys of Charlotte's pregnancy and the expected birth of an heir were shattered when her child, a boy, was stillborn. Charlotte died a few hours later. Two generations of future monarchs had been lost within a day. The nation shared the Regent's grief; shops were closed for two weeks. It became known as 'the triple obstetrical tragedy', as the obstetrician, Sir Richard Croft, later shot himself. Having lost the chance to be consort in Britain, Charlotte's husband Leopold refused the crown of Greece, and later became the first King of the Belgians when Belgium gained independence.

Now the situation regarding the succession was disastrous. Certainly the Regent was the heir to the elderly George III, but who would succeed the Regent? His only child had died, and he was 55 years old and estranged from his wife. He would not have any more legitimate children.

The Regent had eight younger brothers. Therefore the succession would go to the oldest of them living at the Regent's death otherwise to that man's issue, failing which to the next brother, then his issue, and so on; and then the sisters. However, so far none of them had any legitimate children. Although George III had fifteen children, of whom twelve aged from 40 to 55 were still alive at the end of 1817, following the death of Princess Charlotte he had not one legitimate grandchild.

The Regent's six surviving brothers suddenly woke up to the realisation that one, perhaps more, of them would inherit the throne, and the oldest to produce a child would provide the line of royal descent. It was not just a matter of personal glory, the heir and the father of the eventual heir could each expect a considerable increase in his annual allowance from Parliament. Of course, all six brothers were hopelessly in debt. Could the married ones produce a child? Could the unmarried ones find a wife?

Certainly the bride would have to be Protestant and of royal birth. Fortunately, there were plenty of German candidates around. Unlike Hanover, most German territories still split the inheritance amongst all the surviving sons, so the daughters of all of them were princesses. The race was on.

The first brother, Frederick Duke of York, had married his cousin Princess Frederica of Prussia, but they had separated before having any children. Anyway, he and his wife were now in their fifties. So Frederick was first in line after the Regent, but would not provide the succession.

The second brother, William Duke of Clarence, quickly married Princess Adelaide of Saxe-Meiningen in 1818. They had two daughters, but both died in infancy. So William was second in line after the Regent, but would not provide the succession.

The third brother, Edward Duke of Kent, quickly married Princess Viktoria of Saxe-Coburg-Saalfeld in 1818. She was the sister of Charlotte's widower, Prince Leopold. In 1819, Viktoria gave birth to a daughter, Alexandrina. So Edward was third in line after the Regent, and had provided the succession.

The fourth brother, Ernest Augustus Duke of Cumberland, had already married his cousin, Frederica of Mecklenburg-Strelitz. They quickly produced a son, George, in 1819. So Ernest had provided a secondary royal line should Alexandrina die.

The fifth brother, Augustus Duke of Sussex, had married without the King's permission. His marriage was annulled. Nevertheless, he continued to live with his 'wife', so there would be no legitimate children.

The sixth brother, Adolphus Duke of Cambridge, quickly married Princess Augusta of Hesse-Cassel in 1818 (after all, at that time his older brothers had no legitimate children), and they later produced a boy and two girls.

CHILDREN OF GEORGE III

GEORGE IV====m====Caroline of Brunswick ——————————Charlotte=m==Leopold of Saxe-
Prince of Wales   (daughter of George III's sister Augusta)   1796-1817   Coburg-Saalfeld
1762-1830

Frederick======m=====Frederika of Prussia
Duke of York and Albany   (George II's sister Sophia Dorothea was her
1763-1827   great-grandmother on both sides)

WILLIAM IV====m=====Adelaide of Saxe-Meiningen
1765-1837

Charlotte======m=====King Frederick I of Wurttenberg
1766-1828   (he was 6ft 11in, and weighed 31½ stone/200kg)
                            (great-grandson of George II's sister Sophia Dorothea)

Edward=======m=====Viktoria of Saxe-Coburg-Saalfeld ———— ALEXANDRINA VICTORIA
Duke of Kent
1767-1820

Augusta
1768-1840

Elizabeth======m=====Frederick of Hesse-Homburg
1770-1840

Ernest Augustus==m===Frederika of Mecklenburg-Strelitz————George
Duke of Cumberland   (daughter of her mother-in-law
Later King of Hanover   Queen Charlotte's brother)
1771-1851

Augustus Frederick   twice unlawfully married
Duke of Sussex
1773-1843

Adolphus======m=====Augusta of Hesse-Cassel——————————George, Augusta, Mary (mother
Duke of Cambridge   of Queen Mary, George V's wife)
1774-1850

Mary=========m=====William Duke of Gloucester
1776-1857   (son of George III's brother William)

Sophia 1777-1848

Octavius 1779-83

Alfred 1780-82

Amelia 1783-1810

The Regent's sisters had no realistic prospect of the crown for themselves or for any children they might have. Anyway, Queen Charlotte kept her daughters close to her and would not allow them to marry until they were over thirty. That made it difficult to find husbands for them. Charlotte married at thirty but had died without leaving issue; Elizabeth and Mary married at forty, too late to have children. The other three daughters never married.

So the line of descent after the Regent was his first brother Frederick Duke of York, then his second brother William Duke of Clarence, then his third brother Edward Duke of Kent, and then the first of the next generation, the Duke of Kent's daughter, Alexandrina. She was acknowledged as the ultimate heir should she survive and should her parents not have a son. The possibility of a son disappeared in 1820, when the Duke of Kent died. There would be no brother to precede Alexandrina, and she moved up to fourth in line behind her three oldest uncles, the Regent, Frederick Duke of York and William Duke of Clarence.[37]

Throughout this time, the Regent's wife, Princess Caroline, continued to break all boundaries of accepted behaviour. She lived with one of her servants, an Italian called Bartolomeo Pergami. Caroline travelled with him and a retinue to Constantinople, Jerusalem and Jericho, posing for portraits 'much exposed', later driving through Genoa in a very low-cut top and a short skirt, dancing in Geneva stripped to the waist, and generally behaving outrageously.

However, England had more serious problems as mass demonstrations calling for electoral reform were held across the country. In St Peter's Fields in Manchester at the 'Peterloo Massacre' the cavalry charged 80,000 protesters, and fifteen

---

37 If none of his brothers had produced legitimate issue, then after the death of the last of George IV's siblings, the royal line would have descended through George III's sister Augusta Duchess of Brunswick (the mother of the Regent's wife, Caroline), so that today Prince Michael Benedikt Georg Jobst Carl Alexander Bernhard Claus Friedrich Prince of Sachsen-Weimar-Eisenach (senior agnate of the House of Wettin) would be king; but he is in fact 558th in line.

were killed and over 700 injured. Laws were quickly passed limiting free speech and peaceful demonstration.

Finally, the great wait came to an end; on the evening of 29th January 1820, King George III died, and on 31st January the Regent was proclaimed King George IV. He immediately suffered a serious attack of pleurisy (inflammation of the lining of the cavity surrounding the lungs). On 1st February, his doctors announced that he was on the verge of death. It was expected that the longest reign would be followed by the shortest reign. Despite the doctors draining 5¾ pints (over 3¼ litres) of blood from his body, George recovered.

Different trouble was on the way. Informed that her husband was King, Caroline returned to England. George wanted a divorce, but proceedings in the customary manner before the ecclesiastical court would entitle Caroline to produce evidence about Mrs Fitzherbert and George's other mistresses. That could not be allowed. The solution was an Act of Parliament ending the marriage, and it would have to pass through both Houses of Parliament by vote. It started in the House of Lords. Caroline could attend, but she had no right to speak or to produce evidence about George. All that was to be debated was whether Caroline had committed adultery with Pergami and whether the Act should be passed. According to Caroline, she committed adultery only once, and that was "with the husband of Mrs Fitzherbert".

In the House of Lords, Caroline's sex-life was investigated and discussed for eleven weeks. It was unjust, it was public and the evidence given by Caroline's servants was sordid. The Lords voted in favour of the Act by a majority of only nine. Clearly it would fail in the Commons, so the whole sorry procedure was dropped. There was rejoicing in all major cities. Caroline was provided with a residence and an annuity, and everything calmed down.

It was time to crown the new king. George was lucky that his father had insisted on the passing of the Royal Marriages Act. George's failure to obtain the King's consent to his marriage to Mrs Fitzherbert meant that the marriage was invalid. If the marriage had been valid, then having married a Catholic, George would have been disqualified from the succession and George III's second son, the Duke of York, would have been crowned King Frederick.

The long-delayed coronation took place in July 1821. Caroline was not invited. Nevertheless, she turned up at Westminster Abbey, only to be refused admission because she was unable to produce an invitation. Caroline created a scene, and then the waiting public turned on her. Having had her victory, she should not spoil everyone's day. Caroline hastily returned to her home, where she immediately fell ill, complaining of having been poisoned. The problem of the 'unconventional' queen was resolved when Caroline died 19 days later. Very convenient and rather suspicious.

A king at last at 59 years of age, George's patronage of the arts continued. In 1824, he talked the Government into purchasing for the nation the art collection of the late John Julius Angerstein, a Jewish refugee from Russia who had become a successful Lloyds underwriter and philanthropist. To house Angerstein's collection, the National Gallery was created. It is ironic that the mistake of not buying the art collection of an Englishman (Walpole), so enabling it to become the basis for the principal Russian art gallery, was in part remedied by buying the art collection of a Russian (Angerstein), so enabling it to become the basis for the principal English art gallery.

New buildings were still a passion, as John Nash was commissioned to convert Buckingham House into a palace, although he was dismissed from the project when George IV died. Nash also designed Marble Arch, which was, until it was moved in 1851, a gateway to the Palace.

Much as he loved new buildings, George had a greater passion – his appetite. He just would not control his eating and drinking. His waist was over 58 inches, his weight over 25 stones (350 pounds or 160 kilos), and with pain from gout, he could barely move. Gout is aggravated by red meat, seafood and alcohol. George was unrestrained. His doctors prescribed laudanum, an alcoholic preparation containing opium and morphine. Unfortunately, it is addictive, and it was given to George in ever-increasing quantities to ease the pain. Laudanum is also dangerous – as little as a teaspoonful can cause death.

For the last three years of his life, George was hardly ever seen in public. In fact, he spent most of his time in bed, drinking cherry brandy and eating without reserve. It was in bed that George appointed Wellington as Prime Minister, Wellington soon forcing George to agree to Catholic emancipation, giving them almost full civil rights. It was also in bed that George learned of the death of the heir, his brother Frederick Duke of York. So William Duke of Clarence moved up to first in line, followed by the daughter of the late Edward Duke of Kent, young Alexandrina.

On 26th June 1830, George IV died from a ruptured blood vessel, perhaps the result of heart disease, perhaps high blood pressure; or maybe his doctors killed him by prescribing so much laudanum. Whichever it was, in the end he was a physical mess. He had been too ashamed of his grotesque appearance to allow Mrs Fitzherbert, his only true love, to visit him. She was one of the very few to mourn his death.

And the man who tried to kill George in the Mall remains anonymous.

****

WILLIAM IV

26 June 1830 – 20 June 1837

On the death of George IV without surviving legitimate children, the throne passed to his second brother, William Duke of Clarence, the first brother Frederick Duke of York having already died without leaving legitimate children.

As a child, William had not been expected to become king, so at the age of thirteen his education was halted and he was sent to serve in the navy, which is why he was known as 'the Sailor King'. Naval life plus natural arrogance resulted in William's appalling social conduct and foul language; although his constant spitting in public seems to have been regarded as eccentricity.

When he was twenty-five, William retired from the navy with the rank of Rear Admiral. To his annoyance, on the outbreak of war with France, William was not given a command. So in 1813 he travelled to the Low Countries to watch British forces who were besieging Antwerp. To get a better view, William climbed up a church steeple. William stood there, calmly surveying the scene, oblivious to the danger. He had been spotted; someone took aim and fired. A shot rang out and the bullet went straight through William's coat; fortunately he was uninjured. Having avoided death by a few inches, he returned to England.

In 1791, William had taken up with the leading comic actress of the time, Dorothea Jordan. Although she had never married, Dorothea already had three daughters from previous relationships. She moved in with William, and over the years produced five boys and five girls – the Fitzclarences.

Dorothea's real surname was Bland; she biblically adopted Jordan as a stage name after she crossed the waters from Ireland. She continued with her acting career for a time in order to provide for her three older daughters, as William was always short of money.

After struggling with debt for 20 years, William decided that the only solution was for him to marry a rich woman. As a first step he threw Dorothea out, agreeing to pay her £2,900 a year plus a further £1,500 a year on condition that she did not return to the stage, which she had left some years earlier. If she did start acting again, then the £1,500 a year was to be forfeited and she would lose custody of the Fitzclarence daughters.

However, Dorothea needed more money to provide for her older daughters, and she also wanted to help one of her sons-in-law who was in financial difficulties. So, she returned to the theatre. The £1,500 a year was immediately cancelled, and the Fitzclarence daughters were taken away. Then another of her sons-in-law defrauded Dorothea, and she found herself penniless. Having asked William for help, she fled to France to escape her creditors. William did nothing, and Dorothea died a year later, totally destitute.

After having marriage proposals rejected by several rich Englishwomen, William set his sights on the Tsar's sister. She was not interested, finding William awkward and unpleasant. Besides, he was the third son of the King, and not likely to succeed to the crown.

He gave up the chase. Things changed when his brother George's daughter, Princess Charlotte, died. The Queen told

William that he must marry, but he had lost his enthusiasm. Anyway, it would have to be a minor German princess who would bring a small dowry. He pleaded that with heavy debts, ten illegitimate children and now in his fifties it would be madness.

The Queen and the Prime Minister were not put off. Lord Liverpool promised to raise William's annual allowance to £40,000 if he married. Finally, after further rejections, it was arranged for William to marry the 26-year-old Princess Adelheid (Adelaide in English) of Saxe-Meiningen. When it was put to Parliament, they would only increase William's allowance by £6,000 a year. William rejected it in disgust. Nevertheless, William and Adelaide married in July 1818, and to save money they went to live in Hanover.

In 1820, George IV became king. William was now second in line. He only had to survive his two older brothers to take the crown.

Adelaide's first child, a daughter, died after one day. When Adelaide became pregnant again, William decided that they should return to London so that the child would be born in England. The journey was too much for Adelaide, and she miscarried in Calais. In December 1820, she gave birth to a daughter, but the baby died after four months. The miscarriage of twin boys in 1822 spelled the end of William's hopes of producing an heir – if the twins had lived, the choice of heir might have been tricky. It was now clear that even if William became king, he would be followed by the daughter of his late younger brother, the Duke of Kent.

Belatedly, William agreed to accept the increase of £6,000 a year in his allowance, and he also claimed the arrears as Adelaide improved his finances and his behaviour. Within three years, both Frederick Duke of York and George IV had died, and at the age of 64 William became the oldest person to be crowned the British monarch.[38]

---

38 If the present Queen reigns until 18 September 2013 and is succeeded by Prince Charles, he will take William's record.

In the light of George IV's behaviour, the monarchy had become very unpopular. All that was done to commemorate him was to erect a 60 foot high monument with a statue of George on the top at a crossroads in north London. Even that was demolished a few years later, although in its memory the area became known as King's Cross.

In stark contrast to his predecessor, William insisted that as little as possible was to be spent on his coronation. He took every opportunity to show himself in public, and little by little the position of the monarchy was restored.

The only people who were not satisfied with the new king were his grasping illegitimate sons, the Fitzclarences. They had very high ideas about themselves, and were constantly demanding peerages, official positions and money. Even when the oldest had been created Earl of Munster and the others had been given the precedence of the younger child of a marquess, entitling them to the prefix 'Lord', they did not stop their complaints. On the other hand, the Fitzclarence daughters were no trouble at all; indeed, one of them, Elizabeth, is the 4 x great-grandmother of Prime Minister David Cameron.[39]

One thing that did not please William was the newly-completed Buckingham Palace. He refused to move in, offering it unsuccessfully to the army for a barracks and to the Government as a replacement Houses of Parliament when the original parliament building burned down in 1834.

More serious problems came with demands for parliamentary reform. Apart from the recent emancipation of Catholics, nothing had changed for years. In particular, no changes in representation had been made to take account of the population growth of the great cities. Cornwall had 44 MPs; Manchester, Birmingham, Bradford and Leeds had none. Voting was limited, with qualification differing from place to place. Also, the absence of a secret ballot meant

---

39 He is therefore a fifth cousin twice removed (a fifth cousin separated by two generations) of the Queen; but as his descent from William IV is via illegitimacy, it gives him no place in the line to the crown.

that the rich and powerful could control voting in many constituencies.

New Prime Minister Wellington defended the system, saying it was "as near perfection as possible", and would not countenance any changes. Following an attack by protesters on Wellington's London home, he had the windows covered with metal shutters. It was for that reason, nothing to do with his military accomplishments, that he acquired the nickname 'the Iron Duke'. Parliament was not with Wellington, and he was forced to resign. William called on the leader of the Whigs, Earl Grey, to form a government. He had to act quickly – executions and transportations to Australia would not silence protest for long.

The Reform Bill of 1831 proposed greater changes than anyone expected: redistribution of seats, reduction in the property qualification for voters, disenfranchisement of many rotten boroughs with only a handful of voters and of pocket boroughs in the gift of wealthy patrons, a two-day ballot instead of 40 days of voting, and a 60% increase in the electorate. In the Commons it was close, the second reading passed by 302 votes to 301. Then the Government was defeated by eight votes, and an election was called. The result was an increase in the number of members supporting reform, as those who controlled votes did not dare to oppose reformers for fear of violence. Once more, the Reform Bill was introduced, and it was passed by the House of Commons. The real test was the House of Lords; they threw it out by 41 votes.

A Lords versus Commons battle was exactly what William had feared. The obduracy of the House of Lords, whose own position was entirely unaffected by the proposed changes, led to riots across the country. Nottingham Castle was burned to the ground, and there was huge damage and considerable numbers of casualties in Bristol, Derby and elsewhere. A new Bill had to be introduced in Parliament before the situation got out of hand; mass insurrection was a distinct possibility.

Negotiations with the Lords got nowhere, and in late 1831 a slightly modified Bill was introduced. Grey asked the King to create a sufficient number of new peers to ensure victory in the Lords. William agreed, but on condition that peerages went only to people who were already heirs to peerages, so that in time the membership of the House of Lords would be unchanged.

When the lords learned of the plan, many of them moved from support or undecided to opposition. That meant that more new lords than originally anticipated would be needed. All the Royal Family pressured the King to refuse to help Grey. The Queen, brought up in a minor despotic state, was most vociferous, only to be told by William that "English politics are not to be understood by any German".

Grey informed the King that he needed about 50 new peers. The problem was that there were not that many adult heirs to peerages available. William told Grey that he would never agree to ennoble commoners. Defeated in a Lords vote, the Government resigned.

William's quandary was that he could not find anyone willing to lead an administration that would agree to minor reform. Whigs were for full reform, Tories were against any reform. The country was on the edge, with mass demonstrations, refusals to pay tax and a run on gold. William's popularity vanished overnight; his opposition to the creation of peers was seen as the main obstacle to change.

Finally, as a matter of duty, the Duke of Wellington agreed to head a new government. Faced with a hostile House of Commons, he was forced to resign within weeks. William had no alternative; he asked Grey to assemble an administration and to present a less radical Reform Bill. Grey accepted on condition that enough peers were created to ensure success. After some delay, William reluctantly agreed.

When the lords heard this, they knew that the game was up. Rather than allow commoners to join them in the House of Lords, most of those against reform merely failed to attend the votes. The Lords passed the 'Great' Reform Bill with only 22 voting against, while the peers fumed and the King sulked. As a result, 20% of adult males had the vote. Unrest disappeared, the mood subdued as an epidemic of cholera killed 20,000 people.

It was June 1832. As in every year, the King and Queen travelled the short distance from Windsor to Ascot for the four-day festival – the Royal Meeting. After the first race, William and Adelaide were in the royal box talking to friends. About 20 yards away, an elderly man took careful aim and hurled a smooth flint stone, about the size of an egg, at William. It struck him on the forehead.

William staggered backwards and fell to the ground, shouting out: "Oh my God, I am hit!", believing that he had been shot. Then another stone was hurled, but it did not hit anyone. Fortunately, William was wearing a hat, and the stone had hit it before deflecting on to his forehead. The hat had absorbed much of the force of the stone, and for that reason William suffered nothing more than mild concussion and severe bruising.

The elderly man was seized and taken away. He was wearing a tattered sailor's uniform and had a wooden leg. Questioning revealed that he was an Irishman named Dennis Collins, who had served in the navy aboard HMS Kangaroo and HMS Atlanta. On the second ship, there had been an accident when stowing the booms, and it had been necessary to amputate Collins's left leg.

Collins's story was that on being invalided out of the navy, he had been granted a pension of £10 a year. He had later been admitted as a resident at Greenwich Hospital. Board and food being provided, his pension was naturally suspended. He had then been expelled from the hospital for making a minor complaint, and his pension had not been restored. The King had rejected a petition to restore Collins's pension, and Collins had come to Ascot to seek revenge.

Investigations revealed a different story. Collins had indeed been admitted to Greenwich Hospital for four years.

He had left voluntarily and his pension had been restored. Then he found a job as a cook in Halifax, but was dismissed for misconduct. Having returned to Greenwich Hospital, he continually caused trouble, and was expelled for disorderly and disgraceful behaviour. His pension was restored. Collins was once more employed as a cook, only to be dismissed for striking an officer. He was again admitted to Greenwich Hospital, leaving voluntarily and having his pension restored. Admitted to Greenwich for a fourth time, he was expelled after a year for disgraceful behaviour. Yet again, his pension was restored. He was admitted to Greenwich for a fifth time, and was expelled for riotous conduct. Now, his pension was forfeited.

Collins was tried at Berkshire Assizes for treason. The charge was that he had attempted to kill the King, which the prosecution said is what Collins had planned to do, and what would have happened if the King's hat had not cushioned the impact. Collins was found guilty of intending to do bodily harm, intending to wound or maim His Majesty; a capital offence. He was sentenced to be hanged until dead, his head to be severed and the body to be quartered. The sentence was commuted to transportation for life. Collins was taken to the penal colony in Van Diemen's Land (now called Tasmania), one of nearly 7,000 convicts sent to Australia that year.

On arrival at the penal colony, Collins was insubordinate and rebellious, but the terrible conditions and the brutal punishments quietened him down. Within a year of his arrival, Collins died. He starved to death, having said that he "would neither do the King's work, nor eat the King's bread".

Back at Ascot, it was decided to build a royal enclosure so that in future royalty could be kept a safe distance from commoners.

In 1833, Parliament abolished slavery in most British territories; it had never been lawful in Britain, and slave trading had been outlawed in 1807. Then the Factory Act banned the employment of children aged under nine in factories, and limited the working hours of older children and women. With those achievements, Prime Minister Grey retired. Yet he is better known for the tea that bears his name – a tea flavoured with oil from the rind of the bergamot orange, made under a formula said to have been given by Earl Grey to Jacksons of Piccadilly.

Attention now turned to the Continent, with Britain's foreign policy being directed by Lord Palmerston, the enemy of despotic monarchies. However, Palmerston was no liberal at home. Years later he would say: "I deny that every sane and not disqualified man has a moral right to vote. What every man and woman too have a right to, is to be well governed and under just laws ..." Presumably, the ruling classes would determine whether they were well governed and whether the laws were just.

As far as other countries were concerned, Palmerston was unbending. When Belgium gained independence they of course needed a king, and William favoured the Prince of Orange. The Belgians elected the son of the King of France. Palmerston would not have either of them, and he saw to it that Leopold of Saxe-Coburg, the widower of Princess Charlotte, was offered the Belgian throne.

Next it was Austria and the German states with their autocratic rulers. Palmerston disapproved of the repressive measures imposed by the reactionary Austrian Chancellor, Metternich. But William, as King of Hanover, would not support Palmerston, quite the opposite. So Metternich had his way.

Portugal had a different problem. The barbaric King Miguel had seized the throne from his niece, Maria (the only European monarch not to have been born in Europe – she was born in Rio de Janeiro). William took Miguel's side, but Palmerston provided Maria with the assistance of the navy, and Miguel was forced to abdicate. Spain was wracked with civil war. In a similar situation to Portugal, in Spain Don Carlos had seized the throne from his niece, Isabella. With the intervention of

British troops, Isabella recovered the throne.

So, in Belgium, Portugal and Spain, William had backed the repressive candidates, but in each case Palmerston ensured that monarchs offering a more liberal constitution succeeded. In Austria and the German states, Palmerston was overruled, so those states lurched further to the right.

At home, there was a problem with the Duchess of Kent, mother of the heir to the throne. Although William and Adelaide had comforted the Duchess when her husband died, as soon as William took the throne, the Duchess terminated the friendship. She now considered that as the mother of the infant heir, she was regent-in-waiting and was to be treated with high regard.

William and Adelaide had no surviving children of their own, and they treated their niece with considerable affection. When the Duchess saw this, she decided that she could use her daughter to advantage. The Duchess was supported in her plans by the scheming Sir John Conroy, her comptroller (superviser of her finances). He had his eyes on power when William died. First the Duchess stopped her daughter from visiting the King and Queen on the pretext that she might come into contact with the illegitimate Fitzclarences, whom the Duchess always snubbed. Then she stopped Alexandrina from attending William's coronation, the Duchess (as so-called regent-in-waiting) refusing to acknowledge Queen Adelaide's precedence.

When William's popularity collapsed in the reform crisis, the Duchess and her daughter embarked on a series of progresses around the country, the Duchess letting it be known that she was in favour of reform. So it went on. Having refused to attend the Queen's birthday party, the Duchess and Alexandrina did attend the King's birthday party. In his speech, William declared that his last ambition was to live for another nine months, until his niece's eighteenth birthday, so that "a person now near to me … herself incompetent to act with propriety" would not become regent.

William achieved that last ambition. On 24th May 1837, Alexandrina celebrated her eighteenth birthday. By then William was already very unwell, his heart hardened and his liver swollen, his breathing difficult because of asthma. He died on the morning of 20th June, Queen Adelaide (after whom the Australian city is named) at his side, where she had sat continuously for ten days.

A reign of only seven years, but one that had seen the abolition of slavery, the great reform of Parliament, similar reform of local government and legislation on factory employment. Those liberalising enactments helped to save Britain from the revolutions that would sweep through Europe during the nineteenth century. Of course, William had been against all the changes, but he had backed them in the end in what he saw as his duty to support his ministers. As he said, "I have my view of things, and I tell them to my ministers. If they do not adopt them I cannot help it, I have done my duty." It was an arrangement that allowed the monarchy to survive – it still does.

If Dennis Collins had been successful in his assassination attempt, the Duchess of Kent would have been the Regent, and, having been brought up in a German state, she would probably not have adopted such a relaxed attitude towards the monarch's, or the regent's, powers.

****

VICTORIA

20 June 1837 – 22 January 1901

The Duke of Kent wanted to name his daughter after her two godfathers, Tsar Alexander I of Russia and the Regent, the future King George IV. She would be called Alexandrina Georgiana. The Regent stopped him, saying that in Britain the name 'George' could not be second to any other name; so the Duke replaced Georgiana with his wife's name, Victoria.

Throughout her childhood, the Duke's daughter was called 'Drina' by her family. On the day she succeeded to the crown, numerous official documents were put before her for signature. Expected to reign as Queen Alexandrina Victoria, she signed 'Victoria'; and that was how it would remain.

Victoria's father received his military training in Germany, and he was later appointed Governor of Gibraltar. He treated his soldiers so harshly that they mutinied, and the Duke was recalled. In England, he joined the race to produce an heir to the crown, and he married Princess Marie Louise Viktoria of Saxe-Coburg-Saalfeld; she was the sister of Prince Leopold, the widower of George IV's daughter Princess Charlotte.

Years before that, on the death of her aunt, it had been arranged for the 17-year-old Princess Viktoria (she used her third name) to marry her late aunt's 40-year-old husband, and she bore him two children – to be Queen Victoria's half-brother and half-sister. Princess Viktoria of Saxe-Coburg-Saalfeld's husband/uncle died, and four years later she married the Duke of Kent. Alexandrina Victoria was born one year later.

After less than two years of marriage, the Duke of Kent died, and the Duchess was left with nothing but debts and £300 a year. Impoverished and unable to speak English, she decided against returning to Coburg; she gambled all on her daughter's succession, and remained in England. Fortunately, the Duchess' brother Leopold had an income of £50,000 a year, given to him by Parliament at a time when he was expected to become consort to Charlotte, so he was able to help. As Alexandrina came nearer to the throne, the Duchess was given an income by Parliament, but she remained bitter about the way she had been treated.

Young Alexandrina's upbringing was miserable and lonely as the Duchess and her comptroller and secretary, Sir John Conroy, prepared to take power through Alexandrina. They were encouraged by the Regency Act, which appointed the Duchess as regent should her daughter become queen before the age of eighteen.

Conroy enforced a strict set of rules regulating Alexandrina's life. She was not allowed to attend court, could not have friends other than Conroy's daughter, had to sleep in her mother's room and was never allowed to be apart from one of her mother, her tutor or her governess. Alexandrina was brought up almost as a recluse, everything possible being done to develop her into a weak woman, totally compliant with Conroy's will.

As Alexandrina grew older and William IV showed no sign of dying, the Duchess and Conroy started to get nervous; once Alexandrina reached the age of eighteen there would be no regency. Then, in 1835, Alexandrina fell ill with typhoid.

Now the two plotters (said to be lovers) saw their chance. Like vultures they sat at Alexandrina's bedside, and they tried to force her to sign a document appointing Conroy as Alexandrina's private secretary and treasurer after her accession. Somehow she found the strength to resist; she refused to sign.

There was a temporary relaxation when Alexandrina's uncle, Ernest Duke of Saxe-Coburg and Gotha (the Duchess' and Leopold's older brother), visited England with his sons, Ernest and Albert. Victoria was unimpressed with Albert, who fell asleep during a ball.

On the eve of Alexandrina's eighteenth birthday, the two schemers made one last effort. The Duchess and Conroy demanded that Alexandrina sign a document under which she agreed that her minority would be extended to the age of twenty-one. Alexandrina had held out for so long, she was not about to stumble at the last hurdle. She did not sign.

With the death of William IV, Victoria became queen. Eighteen years old, just over 5ft tall and brought up in seclusion, she began her reign. Fortunately, for much of her reign there would be a man of experience on whom she could rely. The first such adviser was the Prime Minister, Lord Melbourne (after whom the Australian city is named).

As soon as she became queen, Victoria asked to be left alone for an hour – something her mother and Conroy had never allowed. She moved into the recently completed Buckingham Palace where, to Victoria's joy, she was allowed her own bedroom. The Duchess was sent to rooms at the far end of the Palace, convention demanding that being unmarried, Victoria must live in the same building as her mother. Conroy was excluded from court life, but he was still secretary to the Duchess.

Although Victoria was now Queen of the United Kingdom as the only child of the fourth son of George III, she did not inherit the crown of Hanover. The Salic Law applied in Hanover, a woman could not become sovereign. So Victoria's uncle, Ernest Augustus Duke of Cumberland, became King of Hanover as the fifth son of George III. The 123-year link between the two countries was broken for ever.

If the Salic Law had applied in the United Kingdom, Ernest Augustus would have become king. Ernest Augustus was unpopular in England, a man rumoured to have murdered his valet, to have fathered a child by his sister Princess Sophia, and to have attempted to rape the wife of the Lord Chancellor. Victoria's mother claimed that the reason she had made Victoria share a room with her was because she was frightened that Ernest Augustus would murder Victoria so as to gain the throne.

Ernest Augustus had fallen in love with his cousin, Frederica of Mecklenburg-Strelitz, who was married to the Prince of Solms-Braunfels. The Prince conveniently died (poison was suspected), and Ernest married Frederica.

Once he was King of Hanover, Ernest revoked the liberal constitution and took absolute power. Ernest Augustus was succeeded by his son, George, who lost the sight of one eye through illness and then lost the sight of the other eye in a riding accident, so that he was blind at the age of thirteen. In the Austro-Prussian War, Prussia demanded that Hanover remain neutral. The Hanoverian Parliament agreed, but George was a supreme autocrat like his father; he overruled Parliament and supported Austria. As a result, Prussia invaded and annexed Hanover; it was the beginning of modern Germany. George lost his throne and went into exile.

He was succeeded in exile by his son, Ernest, who sided with Germany in the First World War. He was accordingly stripped of his title of Duke of Cumberland. In 1923 he was succeeded by his third son, Ernest (the first son having been killed when the car he was driving to the funeral of his uncle the King of Denmark went off the road and hit a tree, the second son having died of appendicitis). That third son married the daughter of Kaiser Wilhelm II, and was succeeded in 1953 by his son Ernest, who was succeeded by his son Ernest. Having divorced his first wife, that son is now married to Princess Caroline of Monaco.

So, if the Salic Law had applied in the United Kingdom, Ernest would now be king and Princess Caroline of Monaco would be queen, provided Ernest was not deprived of the crown under the Act of Settlement for marrying a Catholic.

Hypothetical as that may be, the reality was that for so long as Victoria had no children, Ernest Augustus was next in line in Britain. It was not a happy situation, with Ernest Augustus a reactionary autocrat and suspected murderer. Victoria hated Ernest Augustus, the ill-feeling inflamed when he demanded delivery of most of Victoria's personal jewellery (passed down from Queen Adelaide), claiming that he was entitled to inherit the jewellery as the male heir of William IV. His son continued the claim and won the eventual arbitration; the jewels were handed over. India and South Africa would compensate Victoria's loss.

There was only one way to deal with the problem of Ernest Augustus, and it would also take care of Victoria's personal problem, her desire to evict her mother from the Palace – Victoria must marry and produce an heir.

It was clear to Victoria that her uncle Leopold wanted her to marry his nephew Albert (the younger son of Leopold's and the Duchess' older brother), who was Victoria's cousin. Albert was sent to England in October 1839 to take matters further. When he was four years old, Albert's parents separated and were later divorced. Albert's mother was banished from court, and she married her lover; Albert was never allowed to see his mother again. Then Albert's father married his niece, Albert's cousin.

This time Albert's visit was successful; Victoria was attracted by his good looks, and before long her mind was made up. Of course, as queen it was for her to propose – or at least to tell Albert of her decision. She did so; they were deeply in love, both aged twenty. They married in St James's Palace in February 1840, Victoria introducing the custom of the bride wearing white. So, one of Albert's cousins was now his stepmother and another cousin was now his wife.

However, not everyone was enamoured with the young queen. In the late afternoon on most fine days, Victoria and Albert took an open carriage ride through the royal parks. An 18-year-old man from Birmingham, working at the Hog-in-the-Pound pub in Oxford Street, knew of this practice, as did many people in London.

Henry Oxford made his way to the Blackfriars Road, where he bought a pair of pistols for £2. Over the following days, Oxford went to shooting galleries in Leicester Square and the Strand, where he practised shooting at a moving target.

On the afternoon of Wednesday 10th June 1840, Oxford went to Constitution Hill (so named because Charles II used to take a 'constitutional' walk there), which runs along the side of Buckingham Palace, and he waited for the royal coach. At six o'clock, the low open carriage drawn by four horses with two outriders ahead, and carrying Victoria and Albert, set out from Buckingham Palace, turned left and proceeded along Constitution Hill. Oxford was standing on the far side of the road, by the railings dividing Constitution Hill from Green Park. When the carriage came close, he aimed his pistol and shot at the Queen. He missed. Oxford then drew the second pistol and fired. He missed again. The carriage raced away.

Out of the many watching, a man named Lowe rushed forward, grabbed Oxford and took the two firearms. Others hurried to the scene, and seeing Lowe with the pistols, they believed him to be the assassin.

"You confounded rascal! How dare you shoot at our Queen?" But Oxford stepped forward. "It was I," he said.

A search of Oxford's lodgings revealed more bullets and powder, and some documents relating to a revolutionary society called 'Young England', presumed to be Oxford's invention, as no other members were ever discovered.

At his trial for treason at the Central Criminal Court (the Old Bailey), Oxford pleaded 'not guilty'. Oxford's counsel contended that as no bullets had been found, the pistols were not proven to have been loaded. Second, he said that as she had not been hit, that was evidence that Oxford was not trying to kill the Queen; he intended to miss and was only trying to frighten her. The third defence was insanity. Counsel proposed that Oxford must be insane because no sane Englishman would try to kill the sovereign, and the proof was that all previous assassination attempts on British sovereigns had been by madmen.

More credibly, witnesses, including Oxford's mother, gave evidence of his bizarre behaviour and the mad conduct and brutality of his father. Medical evidence supported them. After a two-day trial, the jury found Oxford not guilty by reason of insanity. He was sent to Bedlam to be detained during Her Majesty's pleasure. Several years later, the doctors declared that they could find nothing wrong with Oxford, and he was released on condition that he left the country. He went to Australia, where he was imprisoned for theft and then for vagrancy. A later report suggested that he had changed his name to John Freeman and published a book; another that he became a house painter.

Oxford's assassination attempt

Now the young queen dealt with enemies at home. She moved her mother out of the Palace. Conroy accepted that his ambitions would never be fulfilled, and left for the Continent (questions were being asked about major discrepancies in the Duchess' accounts and in the accounts of Princess Sophia, Victoria's great-aunt). Victoria's joy was completed when Princess Victoria was born. It was the first time an English or British queen regnant (as opposed to the consort of a king or Anne before she acceded) had given birth.

An election brought the Tories to power in 1841. Lord Melbourne was replaced by Robert Peel, a man Victoria did not like. With that change, she began to rely on Albert, who as a foreigner had not been allowed to interfere in political matters, not even to discuss them with his wife. In fact, Albert was denied a peerage so as to keep him out of Parliament and prevent him from meddling in politics and matters of state.

On 28th May 1842, Queen Victoria and Prince Albert were travelling through St James's Park in an open carriage. Waiting for her with a pistol was 19-year-old John Francis, a man who was outraged at the cost of maintaining the Royal Family. As the Queen passed close to him, Francis took out the pistol, aimed at the Queen and pulled the trigger – but the gun did not fire. No one had noticed, and Francis ran away. He returned the next day, as the Queen and Albert took the same route. This time Francis aimed, fired and missed. He was immediately seized, and was later tried for treason. Francis was convicted and sentenced to death, but the sentence was commuted, and he was transported to Australia for life.

Then, on 3rd July 1842, the day after Francis's sentence was commuted, another young man, 18-year-old John William Bean, decided to imitate Francis. He was lying in wait for Victoria as she passed by in her carriage. Bean aimed at Victoria and fired his old flintlock pistol. However, it was loaded with paper and tobacco, so it was hardly a genuine assassination attempt. Nevertheless, it was treason. A declared anti-monarchist, Bean said that he was tired of life and wanted to die.

Albert believed that Francis and Bean had been encouraged by Oxford's acquittal. He also believed that death was far too severe a penalty for Bean. Discussions with ministers led to the speedy passing of the Treason Act of 1842. Under this Act, assault with a weapon in the monarch's presence with the intent of injuring or alarming the monarch was made punishable by up to seven years' transportation or up to three years' imprisonment, and during the imprisonment to be publicly or privately whipped not more than three times. Tried for this lesser offence, Bean was convicted and sent to prison for 18 months. No one ever received a whipping.

In time, Victoria managed to establish a working relationship with Peel, but a problem arose when he was replaced by Lord John Russell who appointed Lord Palmerston to the office of Foreign Secretary. It was a period of revolutions and uprisings threatening just about every throne in continental Europe except Russia. Palmerston opposed autocratic rulers, and he supported those who demanded constitutions in foreign countries, as well as those who sought independence. Victoria, on the other hand, was related to those autocratic rulers, and wanted Britain to assist them. She was totally against any insubordination by subjects.

However, Palmerston was backed by the British people, who admired his strong attitude towards other countries and his policy of increasing British power throughout the world. The main issue was that Victoria and Albert favoured Germany in various territorial disputes, Palmerston always took the side of their opponents.

Surprisingly, it was Greece that next felt the force of Palmerston's principles. Surprising, because he was a lover of Greece and had been instrumental in using Britain's power to obtain Greece's independence. But in 1847, David 'Don' Pacifico, the Portuguese consul in Athens, was a victim of anti-Semitic riots encouraged by the Greek Government, and soldiers looked on approvingly as Jews were attacked and their homes were ransacked and set ablaze. Don Pacifico's house was destroyed. But Don Pacifico had been born in Gibraltar, and he was therefore a British citizen. So Palmerston sent the fleet to blockade Athens' harbour, Piraeus, until the Greeks paid Don Pacifico compensation. After two weeks of blockade, the Greeks paid up. Of course, the House of Lords condemned Palmerston's support of a Jew; but the House of Commons was with him, inspired by his five-hour oration, known as 'the Civis Romanus sum speech'. In it Palmerston said, "As the Roman in days of old held himself free from indignity, when he could say 'I am a citizen of Rome', '*Civis Romanus sum*', so also a British subject in whatever land he may be shall feel confident that the watchful eye and the strong arm of England will protect him from injustice and wrong."

Memories of past attacks were revived in May 1849. On a sunny day in the late afternoon, Victoria, accompanied by three of her children, left Buckingham Palace in an open carriage on a drive through several parks. Prince Albert was riding alongside. When they left Regent's Park, Prince Albert rode on to return to the Palace. The others continued, and after crossing Hyde Park, the carriage turned into Constitution Hill. An angry unemployed 17-year-old named William Hamilton, recently arrived from Ireland, was waiting for them. Earlier that afternoon, Hamilton, who lived nearby in Ecclestone Place, had gone to his landlord and had asked to borrow a pistol, saying that he wanted to shoot some birds. With the old-fashioned pistol in his pocket, he walked to Constitution Hill and waited behind the railings on the border with Green Park.

Seeing the carriage approaching, Hamilton moved forward, took out the pistol and fired at the Queen. He missed. Inspection of the pistol suggested that it may not have been loaded. Hamilton was charged under the 1842 Treason Act. He pleaded guilty, and was sentenced to seven years' transportation to a penal colony in Australia.

A year later there was a more successful attack. Prince

Hamilton's assassination attempt

Adolphus Duke of Cambridge, Victoria's uncle, was nearing death. On the afternoon of 27th June 1850, Victoria went to her uncle's residence at Cambridge House in Piccadilly to pay her last respects. Shortly after six o'clock, she left to go home. Victoria climbed into her carriage, and the journey began. As the carriage was leaving the courtyard, a man ran forward. He was Robert Pate, a former Lieutenant in the 10th Light Dragoons. Pate was carrying a brass-topped cane. On reaching the carriage, Pate leaned in, raised his cane and struck the Queen repeatedly about the head until he was dragged away. Fortunately, like her uncle William IV at Ascot, Victoria was wearing a hat. The bonnet took some of the force of the blows. Nevertheless, Victoria was heavily bruised by the attack, also suffering a black eye.

No motive for the assault was ever discovered. Pate was charged under the 1842 Treason Act. The plea of insanity was supported by medical evidence, but the judges found him sane. Pate was convicted and sentenced to seven years' penal transportation to Van Diemen's Land. After serving his sentence, Pate stayed on in Australia, and is said to have made a considerable sum of money mining gold. Years later, on

369

hearing of the death of his father, Pate returned to England. His father had been Deputy Lord Lieutenant of Cambridgeshire; he had also been a successful corn trader, and he left a substantial estate. With his share of the inheritance, Pate settled in his home town of Wisbech, to live with his wife.

Pate's attack

Constitution Hill finally gained a victim in 1850. Former Prime Minister Robert Peel was riding past the gate to Green Park after calling at the Palace, and was thrown by his horse and then killed when the horse fell on him. Peel is credited with introducing the Police Force, policemen being popularly called 'Peelers' after his second name, and then 'Bobbies' after his first name. He had opposed Catholic emancipation, and had therefore been given the nickname 'Orange Peel', the Irish Protestants being called Orangemen after their hero, William of Orange.

Victoria's reign saw a massive increase in population and a shift to industrialisation. The positive side of progress and Britain's self-confidence was portrayed in the Great Exhibition of 1851. This was Albert's triumph; 13,000 exhibitors contained within the Crystal Palace built in London's Hyde Park, extending across 26 acres. It included the world's first public toilet, and more than 800,000 visitors 'spent a penny' – the price for its use. Parliament had refused to finance or even guarantee payment of the cost of the Exhibition, so it was left to Albert to find individuals willing to provide the necessary money. The £186,000 profit was used to buy land and build museums in South Kensington in London along and around what is now Exhibition Road, an area with buildings and memorials dedicated to Albert and therefore informally known as 'Albertopolis'.

Overseas, serious trouble was coming. By 1851, the Ottoman Turkish Empire (founded by Osman I, who was called 'Ottoman' by the Europeans) was disintegrating. Russia, always eager to increase its territory, was eyeing the Black Sea. France gave them the excuse. The Holy Land had been a Turkish territory since 1517, and the French pressured the Ottomans into confirming France and the Catholic Church as the supreme Christian authority there, so taking control of the Church of the Nativity from the Greek Orthodox Church. Naturally the Russians were outraged, and the Tsar ordered his armies into Moldavia and Wallachia, which were both under Ottoman rule.

Britain was determined to halt Russia's territorial enlargement, fearing that their next step would be to expand into the Mediterranean. The British and French fleets were sent to the Dardanelles – a long narrow straight connecting the Aegean Sea with the Sea of Marmara, and therefore dividing Europe and Asia Minor. In October 1853, the Sultan declared war on Russia. The Russians promptly destroyed a major part of the Ottoman Navy. In response, Britain and France declared war on Russia; it was the start of the Crimean War.

Before long, Russia withdrew from Moldavia and Walachia (later united as Romania); but the war had already acquired a momentum, and the British and French wanted to end the

Russian threat to the Ottomans. The focus of the war was Sebastopol (on the Crimean peninsula, located to the north of the Black Sea), the home port of the Russian Black Sea fleet. British and French armies besieged the city, which fell after a year. Fighting continued as the allies tried to move forward, but with little success. From beginning to end, the war was marked by incredible incompetence in the leadership of both sides, and casualties were high.

Then Tsar Nicholas I died, and in 1856 his successor Alexander II agreed terms of peace. Russia was forbidden from establishing military or naval bases on the Black Sea coast, and the pre-war treaty under which only Turkish warships could traverse the Dardanelles in peacetime was confirmed. It was merely a delay; the Russians attacked the Ottomans again 20 years later, leading to the independence of Bulgaria, Romania, Serbia and Montenegro.

By 1857, Victoria had given birth to nine children over a period of seventeen years: Victoria, Edward Prince of Wales, Alice, Alfred, Helena, Louise, Arthur, Leopold and Beatrice. Unusually, all survived infancy and all would be married. Alice and Leopold died in their thirties, the others all lived beyond 55, some by a long way. Albert was appointed prince consort; acceptance of the foreigner was now almost complete.

There were problems with two of the children. Leopold, the eighth child, was a poorly baby. He was found to be suffering from haemophilia, a genetic disorder that impairs blood clotting or coagulation. No scab forms, and even in the case of a minor injury or bruising the bleeding goes on for a long time, in some cases until death. Haemophilia is incurable, although nowadays it can be controlled with regular infusions of the deficient clotting factor.

It is mainly suffered by males. Females have two X-chromosomes, so if one is defective the second one compensates. Males have only one X-chromosome, so if it is defective they will suffer haemophilia. As a result, if they have the defect, men are always carriers and sufferers. A woman with the defect is generally only a carrier; but if she inherits the defect from both parents, so damaging both X-chromosomes, she will be a carrier and a sufferer – but this is very rare.

A carrier and sufferer will always pass it to a daughter; if a man, he never passes it to a son, if a woman, she has a 50% chance of passing it to a son. A woman who is merely a carrier has a 50% chance of passing it to all children.

Clearly the defect must have come from Victoria, as a man could not be a carrier without being a sufferer, which Albert was not; anyway, a man does not pass it to a son. It was a surprise, as there was no history of the disease in the Royal Family. Nor was there evidence of the disease in the family of Victoria's mother or in Victoria's half-sister and half-brother and their descendants. Studies show that about 30% of haemophilia cases are not inherited; they are spontaneous gene mutations, suddenly starting in one person – and with three of Victoria's daughters passing the disease to descendants, it must have originated in Victoria, not Leopold. Now both haemophilia and porphyria were diseases of the Royal Family.

The other problem concerned the second child, Edward Prince of Wales, heir to the crown. His parents wanted him to be studious and responsible like his father, but he turned out to be unacademic and pleasure-loving like his Hanoverian great-uncles. He was a grave disappointment to his parents.

It was time for celebration when Victoria's first child, Princess Victoria, married the son of the King of Prussia. In 1859, she gave birth to Queen Victoria's first grandchild, William – eventually to become the Kaiser. Two years later, Victoria's great happiness came to a sudden halt. In March 1861, Victoria's mother died. The Queen had become reconciled with her mother, largely through the efforts of Albert (the Duchess was after all not just his mother-in-law, but also his aunt), and Victoria was very upset when she died. Far worse was to come.

There were more of the usual problems with the behaviour of the Prince of Wales, particularly his involvement with an actress. Albert, though feeling unwell, travelled to Cambridge to lecture his son. When Albert returned to London, he immediately suffered severe rheumatic pains. On 14th December, just two weeks after returning from Cambridge, Albert died of typhoid at the age of forty-two.

Victoria was absolutely shattered; she mourned for the rest of her life. She resolved that the remainder of her reign would be spent in putting Albert's wishes into effect. For a start, their third child, Princess Alice, married Prince Louis of Hesse. Then Victoria arranged for the Prince of Wales to marry Princess Alexandra of Denmark. Of course, Victoria would not attend any of the festivities.

The fourth child, Alfred, was offered the crown of Greece after the dethronement of the German-born King Otto. Victoria turned down the offer as Albert had decided that Alfred should succeed to the title of Duke of Saxe-Coburg and Gotha on the death of Albert's childless older brother (Prince Edward having waived his prior right to the dukedom).

In 1868, Prince Alfred was sent on a world tour; it included the first royal visit to Australia. Alfred joined the Sailors' Picnic on a beach near Sydney. Henry O'Farrell, sidled up to the Prince and shot him in the back. Police seized O'Farrell in time to prevent the angry crowd from lynching him; it would only be a delay. It was claimed that O'Farrell was acting for an Irish nationalist organisation. He was certainly violently anti-British and anti-monarchist, but it seems that he was acting alone. Although he had a history of mental illness and had only recently been released from an asylum, the plea of insanity was rejected. He was sentenced to death and was hanged, despite Alfred's plea for clemency. Of course, the alternative sentence of transportation was not available – he was already in Australia. Having spent two weeks in hospital, Alfred was able to return home.

After years of mourning by Victoria, the British public felt that it had gone on for long enough. Convention set the mourning period for a husband at two years; for a wife, it was six months. However, Victoria just could not put her grief aside. For 40 years she would insist that at Windsor Castle, Albert's clothes were laid out and that hot water was brought to his room every morning, and that his linen and towels were changed daily.

Two very different men came to Victoria's rescue. Having managed working relationships with Prime Ministers Lords Derby, Aberdeen and Palmerston, a new era opened as Prime Minister Benjamin Disraeli, leader of the Conservative Party (the protectionist Tories who remained after the Peelites joined the Whigs to form the free-trade Liberal Party), slowly drew Victoria back into public life. She opened the new Albert Hall in 1871, although when it was time for Victoria to mention the name 'Albert', she was overcome with emotion and the Prince of Wales had to speak the necessary words. Nevertheless, Victoria was still unpopular with the masses. Their view was that she was not doing the job she was paid to do, and she should abdicate.

The other man was Victoria's Scottish servant, John Brown, who saw to every need in her private life. He treated Victoria like a woman, rather than as a queen. The relationship was unpopular with the Royal Family and with the public, but it helped to drag Victoria back to some semblance of normality.

Victoria lost the support of Disraeli when he was replaced as Prime Minister by Gladstone, whose rapport with the Queen was uncomfortable because of his awkward manner and his lengthy speeches to her. Unfortunately, the Prince of Wales was not able to comfort his mother. She blamed him for the death of Albert, writing in a letter: "I never can, or shall, look at him without a shudder".

Then, in 1871, Edward fell ill with typhoid, and Victoria hurried to his side. For a time Edward's life was in the balance, but he recovered. Victoria attended the Thanksgiving Service at St Paul's Cathedral, and the waiting crowds cheered her as she made her way through the city.

Two days later, as Victoria was entering the grounds of Buckingham Palace in her carriage, she was accosted by a young man who waved a pistol at her demanding the release of Irish prisoners. The man was Arthur O'Connor. John Brown seized O'Connor, who was taken away.

At his trial, O'Connor insisted on pleading guilty, despite his counsel producing several doctors who testified that he was insane. The jury found O'Connor to be "perfectly sane when he pleaded guilty to the indictment and perfectly sane now". He was sentenced to one year's imprisonment and 20 strokes of the whip. The Queen complained to Gladstone that O'Connor would be on the streets again within months, so a proposal was made and O'Connor agreed to go and live in Australia instead of the whipping. A year later he returned to England and was committed to Hanwell Asylum. Released after 18 months, he went back to Australia.

Now Victoria had been seen once more by her people, and there was sympathy because of the recent confrontation. The reconciliation with her subjects was complete. Although she continued to dress in black and to mourn for her beloved Albert, Victoria returned to public life. In 1874, it all became so much easier when Disraeli was once more appointed Prime Minister.

Then there was a bonus. The rulers of the Mughal dynasty had governed most of India, and they had used the titles 'Badshah' and 'Samrat', both of which translate to 'Emperor'. They were deposed by the East India Company (which had been authorised by Britain to administer India), and the company steadily increased its area of control – when General Napier conquered Sindh, he reported his victory in the famous one word message and pun: Pecavi, Latin for 'I have sinned'.

Although there were many grievances, the Indian Mutiny was sparked when the army introduced a new rifle cartridge that had to be bitten open. It was widely believed that the cartridges were greased with lard (pork fat) that was regarded as unclean by Muslim soldiers, or with tallow (beef fat) that was sacrilege to the Hindu soldiers – the instruction to bite the cartridges caused outrage. The East India Company put down the mutiny, but was then dissolved, and India became a British possession. Disraeli took the opportunity to revive the former rulers' designation, and he presented Victoria with the title: 'Empress of India'.

Victoria joined the Emperors of Russia, Austria and Germany, equal in rank. More importantly, it raised Victoria to the level her oldest daughter would attain when she became Empress of Germany eight years later; and it was now Germany rather than Prussia. Bismark, the Prime Minister of Prussia, had been determined to see to the unification of the German states under the leadership of Prussia, and to ensure that it would be an authoritarian regime. As a first step, Prussia invaded Schleswig, and agreed to Austria taking Holstein. Prussia then seized Holstein. Austria declared war, but was quickly defeated, and in the resultant treaty Prussia annexed Frankfurt, Hanover, Hesse-Kassel and Nassau.

The next issue for Bismark was that Crown Prince Frederick and his wife Victoria (Queen Victoria's oldest child) were admirers of Britain's constitutional monarchy and parliamentary system, so Bismark separated them from their son, the future Kaiser, to ensure that he would be brought up to believe in divine right and autocratic rule.

After victory in the Franco-Prussian war (provoked by Bismark), Prussia acquired Alsace and Lorraine. Eager to share in the victory, 25 German states, duchies and cities joined Prussia in the German Federation of which the King of Prussia was to be the Emperor. Bismark became Chancellor of the new empire, and as a strict Lutheran he introduced anti-Catholic legislation, which was followed by anti-socialist laws and severe curtailment of the freedom of the press.

Emperor William I died, but his successor Frederick's reign lasted only three months. He was succeeded by his son William II, the Kaiser. However, the strong personalities of the Kaiser and Bismark led to conflict, and in 1890 the Kaiser demanded Bismark's resignation. By then he had accomplished his aims. Before leaving office, Bismark predicted a war from Moscow to the Pyrenees and from the North Sea to Palermo. He wrongly thought it would be about Bulgaria ("a little country ... far from being an object of adequate importance") rather than Serbia, but correctly added that "At the end of the conflict we should scarcely know why we had fought."

At home, Victoria had to deal with further tragedies. Her daughter, Alice, died in 1878 on the seventeenth anniversary of Albert's death. In the following year, Waldemar, youngest son of Victoria's first child, Princess Victoria, died; a poorly boy, he suffered from haemophilia. Then a turn for the better when Queen Victoria's seventh child, Arthur, married Princess Louise of Prussia – Victoria joined the celebrations.

In 1880, Gladstone was reappointed Prime Minister when the Liberal Party took office. Two years later Disraeli died. Victoria had grown to detest Gladstone with his moralising sermons. She longed for Disraeli and his ambitions for the Empire. There was nothing she could do about it; Victoria was on her own, but now she could cope with the situation.

On 2nd March 1882, Victoria travelled by carriage to Windsor Railway Station. A large crowd was waiting to cheer the Queen as she arrived. Suddenly a man ran forward, raised a pistol and shot at Victoria. Yet again, the assassin missed. Scotsman Roderick MacLean was tried for treason. He had already spent time in various lunatic asylums. MacLean suffered from delusions of persecution combined with extreme anti-royalist views. It seems that he was angry because he had sent a poem to the Queen, and had received only a curt reply. Doctors produced by both the prosecution and the defence gave evidence that MacLean was insane. The jury took only five minutes to agree. MacLean was found 'not guilty by reason of insanity', and was sent for life to the new Broadmoor Hospital for the criminally insane.

Now Victoria had had enough. How could these people be found not guilty? "Insane he may have been, but not guilty he was most certainly not, as I saw him fire the pistol myself", she complained bitterly. She was not impressed by the proposition that not knowing right from wrong, MacLean could not have formed a criminal intent. In accordance with Victoria's demand, the law was changed so that in future the verdict

McClean's assassination attempt

would be 'guilty but insane'. The accused was still locked up in an asylum, but the verdict satisfied the Queen. The form of verdict would not be changed back to 'not guilty by reason of insanity' until 1964.

As time went by, Victoria became increasingly exasperated with Gladstone and his high moral tone and devotion to the rehabilitation of prostitutes. It was not only Gladstone's manner, Victoria believed his policies were damaging to Britain. After the massacre of the British mission in Afghanistan was avenged by the capture of Kandahar, Gladstone gave it back. In Cape Colony in southern Africa, the Boers (Dutch for 'farmers') crossed the Vaal River and proclaimed the Republic of Transvaal, later adding the Orange Free-State (north of the Orange River; named after the House of Orange). Gladstone abandoned Britain's claims to the territory, a decision that Victoria opposed not just because it diminished the Empire, but because she believed that the Boers would mistreat the native Africans.

There was a crisis when General Gordon was besieged in Khartoum. Despite Victoria's urging, Gladstone delayed sending reinforcements. When he finally did so, they arrived two days too late; Gordon had been killed, his head paraded along the streets on a pike. Victoria and the British public blamed Gladstone, and he was forced from power. He was soon back, and this time it was his programme of home rule for Ireland that enraged Victoria. She could not abide rewarding agitators, she saw it as the first step in the destruction of the Empire.

After Gladstone left office for the last time, Victoria's relationships with his successors, Lord Rosebery and Lord Salisbury, were much easier; but it would never be as it was with Melbourne and Disraeli.

There was a problem when it was time for the last child to leave home. Princess Beatrice decided to marry Prince Henry of Battenberg, and Victoria showed her displeasure by not speaking to her daughter for seven months, communicating with her by written messages. In the end, Victoria gave her consent to the marriage, but only on condition that Beatrice and her husband agreed to live with Victoria.

Queen Victoria was now an institution, cheered by her people wherever she went. Her Golden Jubilee in 1887 drew enormous crowds, with more than 50 kings and princes attending, as well as numerous queens and princesses.

The celebrations were unaffected by newspapers revealing details of the 'Jubilee Plot'. It was claimed that a plot by Irish nationalists to blow up Westminster Abbey, killing the Queen and her ministers, had been discovered. Two Irishmen, Callan and Hankins, were charged with bringing dynamite into the country. They were not charged with anything more serious because they had missed their ship in New York, and only arrived in Liverpool on the day of the Westminster Abbey celebration – too late to carry out their mission.

At their trial, it emerged that a man called Francis Millen had organised the proposed assassination. It seems that Millen was a British spy who had encouraged the plot in order to draw Irish nationalists into the conspiracy so that they could be identified and imprisoned. Also, it was hoped to discredit the Home Rule movement. Callan and Hankins were sentenced to 15 years' imprisonment; Millen was allowed to escape to America. Presumably the bombing would not have been allowed to take place.

Ten years later it was the Diamond Jubilee, and the celebrations were repeated.

Although Britain had annexed the Boer South African Republic in 1877, the Boers regained their independence after the First Boer War in 1881. The discovery by the Boers of massive gold reserves changed everything. Thousands of men rushed from Britain's Cape Colony to find work and fortune in the gold mining areas, so much so that they soon outnumbered male Boers by two to one. To preserve their control, the Boers limited the political and economic rights of the *uitlanders* (foreigners). Britain demanded that they be given full rights; the Boers refused. Really, the issue was the new wealth of the Boer territories that threatened to overwhelm Cape Colony and also challenged London's position as the world gold trade centre. War looked inevitable, and the Boers launched a pre-emptive attack in 1899, starting the Second Boer War.

It was now that Victoria became increasingly frail, and in early 1901 it was clear that the end was approaching. The Queen's surviving children and grandchildren rushed to her bedside. On 22nd January, at 12.15pm, she stretched her arms forward and called out "Bertie!". It was her last word. At 6.30pm, aged 81, she died and was taken to lie beside Albert in the mausoleum at Frogmore House near Windsor. Once more with Albert, in accordance with her instructions she was dressed in white.

It had been, and still is, the longest female reign in history, the longest reign by any British monarch. She was also the oldest British monarch, having beaten George III by four days, although she was overtaken by Queen Elizabeth II in 2007.

Victoria's family had extended across Europe. It would not stop them going to war against each other – far from it – but it was the most amazing set of royal connections in history; so many kings and queens in the same family. Nine children, forty-two grandchildren and eighty-five great-grandchildren. In fact, the first grandchild to die was Sigismund, who died in 1866; the last to die was Princess Alice, who died in 1981 – the same generation, but separated by 115 years.

There can have been few, if any, monarchs in the history of the world who had been the victim of so many assassination attempts. And they all failed.

****

QUEEN VICTORIA AND HER CHILDREN

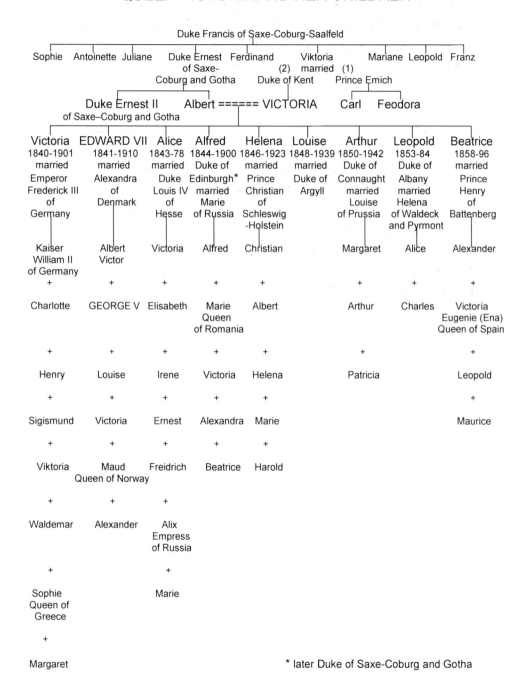

Duke Francis of Saxe-Coburg-Saalfeld

Sophie　Antoinette　Juliane　Duke Ernest　Ferdinand　　　　Viktoria　　　Mariane　Leopold　Franz
　　　　　　　　　　　　　of Saxe-　　　　　　　(2)　married　(1)
　　　　　　　　　　　Coburg and Gotha　　　　Duke of Kent　Prince Emich

Duke Ernest II　　　Albert ====== VICTORIA　　　Carl　Feodora
of Saxe–Coburg and Gotha

Victoria	EDWARD VII	Alice	Alfred	Helena	Louise	Arthur	Leopold	Beatrice
1840-1901	1841-1910	1843-78	1844-1900	1846-1923	1848-1939	1850-1942	1853-84	1858-96
married	married	married	Duke of	married	married	Duke of	Duke of	married
Emperor	Alexandra	Duke	Edinburgh*	Prince	Argyll	Connaught	Albany	Prince
Frederick III	of	Louis IV	married	Christian		married	married	Henry
of	Denmark	of	Marie	of		Louise	Helena	of
Germany		Hesse	of Russia	Schleswig		of Prussia	of Waldeck	Battenberg
				-Holstein			and Pyrmont	

Kaiser	Albert	Victoria	Alfred	Christian		Margaret	Alice	Alexander
William II	Victor							
of Germany								
+	+	+	+	+		+	+	+
Charlotte	GEORGE V	Elisabeth	Marie	Albert		Arthur	Charles	Victoria
			Queen					Eugenie (Ena)
			of Romania					Queen of Spain
+	+	+	+	+		+		+
Henry	Louise	Irene	Victoria	Helena		Patricia		Leopold
+	+	+	+	+				+
Sigismund	Victoria	Ernest	Alexandra	Marie				Maurice
+	+	+	+	+				
Viktoria	Maud	Freidrich	Beatrice	Harold				
	Queen of Norway							
+	+	+						
Waldemar	Alexander	Alix						
		Empress						
		of Russia						
+		+						
Sophie		Marie						
Queen of								
Greece								
+								
Margaret								

* later Duke of Saxe-Coburg and Gotha

383

Victoria's descendants:
Kings, Queens, haemophilia and porphyria

The first child, Victoria the Princess Royal, married Prince Frederick of Prussia. She became EMPRESS OF GERMANY and QUEEN OF PRUSSIA when her husband succeeded to the throne. Albert had hoped that his daughter and her husband would have a liberalising influence on the growing state. However, Frederick was already dying of throat cancer, and he reigned for only 99 days. He was succeeded by their son William II, EMPEROR OF GERMANY and KING OF PRUSSIA, the KAISER; anything but liberal. Although he was devoted to his grandmother, he was fiercely anti-British, leading Germany into the First World War. After defeat, he abdicated and died in exile in Holland.

The Princess Royal's seventh child, Sophie, became QUEEN OF GREECE, and two of Sophie's children became KING OF GREECE; one child became QUEEN OF ROMANIA.

Charlotte, the Princess Royal's second child, suffered from porphyria, as did Charlotte's daughter, Feodora. Two of Charlotte's sons, Waldemar and Heinrich, were haemophiliacs.

The Princess Royal did not become queen on the death of Queen Victoria because of the rule that sons take precedence over daughters regardless of age. It has recently been decided to introduce legislation to change that rule so that age, not gender, will be the only factor. If that had been the case in 1901, the Princess Royal would have become Queen, and on her death six months later, the Kaiser would have become King.

The second child, Edward Prince of Wales, became KING EDWARD VII OF THE UNITED KINGDOM and EMPEROR OF INDIA. His second son succeeded him as King George V. Two of George's sons became KINGS and EMPERORS: Edward VIII and George VI.

Edward's fifth child, Maud, married her cousin Prince Carl of Denmark who became King Haakon VII of Norway, and Maud became QUEEN OF NORWAY; her son became KING OF NORWAY.

One of Edward's great-grandsons, Prince William of Gloucester (son of George V's son, Henry), had porphyria.

The third child, Alice, married the Grand Duke of Hesse. Their first child, Victoria, married Louis of Battenberg and their daughter Louise married Crown Prince Gustave who became King Gustave VI of Sweden, and she became QUEEN OF SWEDEN; another daughter, Alice, married Prince Andrew of Greece and their son is Prince Philip, the husband of the Queen.

Alice of Hesse's second son, Friedrich, suffered from haemophilia and bled to death at the age of two after a fall. Alice of Hesse's daughter, Alix, married Grand Duke Nicholas who became Tsar Nicholas II of Russia, and she became Alexandra EMPRESS OF RUSSIA (the TSARINA); she was murdered with the rest of her family in the Bolshevik Revolution – her son Alexei, the TSAREVITCH, was a haemophiliac.

Another of Alice of Hesse's daughters, Irene, who married her cousin Prince Heinrich of Prussia, passed haemophilia to two of her sons: Waldemar who died aged 56 without issue and Henry who died aged four.

The fourth child, Alfred, had not been allowed to become King of Greece. He became Duke of Saxe-Coburg and Gotha, thought to be a greater honour by his mother. Alfred married Grand Duchess Marie of Russia (the daughter of the Tsar). Their son Alfred shot himself during his parents' 25th wedding anniversary celebrations.

Their daughter Marie married Prince Ferdinand who became King Ferdinand of Romania, and she became QUEEN OF ROMANIA. Marie's son Carol became KING OF ROMANIA. Marie's daughter, Elisabeth, married Prince George who became King George II of Greece, and she became

QUEEN OF GREECE. Marie's daughter Maria married King Alexander, and became QUEEN OF YUGOSLAVIA, their first son becoming KING OF YUGOSLAVIA.

The fifth child, Helena, married Prince Christian of Schleswig-Holstein. None of her children gave her legitimate grandchildren.

The sixth child, Louise, was the only one not to marry a foreigner. She married the Duke of Argyll. Victoria approved of the introduction of new and British blood into the family, but they had no children.

The seventh child, Arthur, married Princess Louise of Russia. Their daughter, Margaret, married Prince Gustaf of Sweden, but she died before he became king (Gustaf then married Louise, granddaughter of Victoria's third child, Alice). Margaret's grandson is Carl XVI the present KING OF SWEDEN. Her granddaughter Ingrid became QUEEN OF DENMARK, and Ingrid's daughter is the present QUEEN OF DENMARK; another daughter is the present ex-QUEEN OF GREECE.

The eighth child, Leopold, married Helena of Waldeck-Pyrmont; it was believed that he had previously wished to marry Alice Liddell – the Alice who was the inspiration for Lewis Carroll's *Alice's Adventures in Wonderland*. Leopold had haemophilia, and died at the age of 31 when he slipped on the stairs at the Yacht Club in Cannes and hurt his knee.

The disease was passed through his daughter Princess Alice (Alice Liddell called her second son 'Leopold') to her son Rupert, and it led to his death from a brain haemorrhage after a car crash.

Leopold's posthumous son Charles was not infected, and he succeeded his uncle as Duke of Saxe-Coburg and Gotha, and had a daughter, Sibylla; she married her second cousin Prince

Gustav of Sweden, and their son is Carl XVI, the present KING OF SWEDEN.

The ninth child, Beatrice, married Prince Henry of Battenberg. Their second son, Leopold, had haemophilia; he died aged 32 during a minor operation.

Beatrice's daughter Victoria married King Alfonso XIII of Spain and became QUEEN OF SPAIN; it was controversial as she had to convert to Catholicism. She was known by her last forename: Ena. Her mother had chosen the name Eua (Gaelic for Eve) and had written it down at the christening, but it was misread. At Ena's wedding, an anarchist threw a bouquet of flowers concealing a bomb at the royal couple; Ena's dress was covered in the blood of one of the guards, but she was unharmed although several bystanders were killed. Their son, Alfonso, was the heir. When he was circumcised, he bled for a long time – it was haemophilia. Ena was unpopular with the Spanish as a former Protestant; now they hated her for introducing haemophilia to their royal family. In 1931, Republicans won the election, and the royal family went into exile. The King eventually blamed Ena for introducing the disease, and the couple separated. Their first son, Alfonso, died following a car crash when he suffered very minor injuries. He had already renounced his rights to the crown on marrying a commoner – anyway he left no children. The next son, Don Jaime, renounced his rights because of infirmity; he had become deaf and mute as a result of a childhood operation. The third son, Don Juan, became the heir despite Don Jaime having sons, because Don Jaime had renounced not only his own right but also the rights of his descendants (yet Don Jaime remained Pretender to the French throne as Henry VI, being the senior legitimate male heir of the House of Capet and the head of the House of Bourbon). However, when the Spanish monarchy was reinstated, the dictator Franco bypassed Don Juan as he considered him too liberal. Instead, he chose Don Juan's son to become KING OF SPAIN, the present King Juan Carlos –

great-great-grandson of Queen Victoria (chosen despite the fact that Juan Carlos had apparently killed his younger brother when fooling around with a revolver). Ena's fourth son, Don Gonzalo, had haemophilia. He was involved in a minor car accident (he hit a wall when avoiding a cyclist); although he appeared to be unhurt, internal bleeding had started and he died two days later.

Gonzalo is the last senior royal descendant of Queen Victoria known to have had haemophilia. However, the damaged gene can remain hidden in females for generations before re-appearing. It seems that the only ones at risk are the female-line descendants of Beatrice, and that means the Spanish royal family.

After Queen Victoria died, Beatrice was given the task of editing hundreds of volumes of Victoria's daily journals, instructed by Victoria to delete confidential and offensive sections. It took Beatrice 30 years to transcribe the acceptable parts and then destroy the originals – she left out almost 70%, which was lost forever.

A lesser-known descendant of Queen Victoria, Ferdinand Soltmann (173rd in line to the throne), born in 2005, the son of Princess Xenia of Hohenlohe-Langenberg, is a haemophiliac. Princess Xenia is a 4 x great-granddaughter of Queen Victoria through her third child, Princess Alice.

Even today, Victoria's direct descendants include Queen Elizabeth II, Prince Philip (who is 489th in line to the throne), King Harald V of Norway, King Carl XVI Gustaf of Sweden, Queen Margrethe II of Denmark, King Juan Carlos of Spain, Queen Sophia of Spain, ex-King Constantine II of Greece, the ex-Queen of Greece, ex-King Michael of Romania, the pretenders to the thrones of Serbia, Russia, Prussia, Germany and France, and the claimants to the rule of Saxe-Coburg and Gotha, Hanover, Hesse and Baden.

EDWARD VII

22 January 1901 – 6 May 1910

Along with Henry III, V and VI, Edward I, III and VI and George IV, Edward is one of only eight English/British sovereigns who, provided he survived, had been certain to succeed his predecessor from the moment of his birth right up to his coronation, with no future births having a chance of priority. For Edward it was a long wait – over 59 years. No other heir apparent[40] to any throne had to wait so long.[41]

Edward was brought up by his parents with the intention that he should become a copy of his father, studious and sober. They even gave him 'Albert' as his first name. It did not help; he was a different type of person.

The strict education only helped Edward to develop into a lover of travel and good-living. With it came the gifts of charm and diplomacy.

Yet diplomacy would not help Edward with his parents. In 1861, he was sent to Ireland for military training. It was there that Edward started a brief association with an actress,

---

40 'heir apparent' meaning that he was entitled to the throne if he survived, rather than 'heir presumptive' meaning that he was first in line but would be displaced if someone was later born with a prior right.

41 Prince Charles will overtake Edward on succeeding to the crown; he passed Edward's waiting period on 20 April 2011.

Nellie Clifden. A few weeks later, Edward went to Cambridge University. Now his father was told of the actress.

Albert was horrified, and he treated the matter as a disaster that could lead to the abolition of the monarchy. Having given instructions that Edward was to be despatched on a visit to Turkey, Albert travelled to Cambridge. Although feeling unwell, Albert insisted on taking Edward for a long walk in the rain to lecture him on his responsibilities. Two weeks after returning from Cambridge, Albert was dead from typhoid. Victoria blamed Edward, and she made no secret of it. She never forgave him.

When Edward came home – the visit to Turkey took place despite Albert's death, as Victoria was committed to doing all that Albert had wanted – it was time for Edward to marry. Something else that Albert had decided.

Edward's sister, Victoria, had introduced him to Alexandra of Schleswig-Holstein-Sonderburg-Glucksburg, the oldest daughter of Prince Christian, who became King Christian IX of Denmark on the death of the previous king without issue. Christian was chosen by the great powers and the Danish Parliament out of several claimants largely because his wife was the niece of an earlier king. The Danish royals were not highly regarded, they were not wealthy and there was little diplomatic advantage. Quite the opposite, as Denmark was the enemy of Germany, which was demanding the transfer of Schleswig-Holstein. However, Edward had been quite taken with Alexandra, she was Protestant and Albert had approved. When Victoria travelled to Coburg to visit her late husband's childhood home, she met Alexandra and gave her consent. Edward, who had accompanied his mother, proposed and was accepted. The only notable event at the wedding was when Edward's nephew, the future Kaiser, was told by two of his uncles to stop throwing things at the choir, and in retaliation he got down on his knees and started to bite the legs of Prince Alfred and Prince Leopold – no joke for Leopold who was a haemophiliac.

Until his accession nearly 40 years later, Edward was given

few public duties; Victoria saw to that. She remembered only too well Albert's views of his son's inadequacies, and for Victoria the memory of what Albert had said was what counted, even when Edward reached middle age and beyond. Edward spent his time hunting, shooting, going to the races (he would eventually own three Derby winners and one Grand National winner), partying and travelling. But what else was there for him to do?

Although they cared little about his activities, Victoria, the establishment and the press objected to Edward's choice of friends, Victoria complaining that they included actresses, low nobility and Jews. Her displeasure was proved justified to a degree with regard to the low nobility. Many of them became involved in scandals: fraud, bigamy, perversion and more. Edward's reputation was tainted not just by association but in some cases by involvement. It may have been no worse than for many previous Princes of Wales, but now there was a growing and ravenous press.

Edward was said to be spending his Civil List income on gambling and to have been unable to pay his losses. Visits to Paris apparently involved evenings at the Chabanais brothel, where Edward liked to bathe in champagne with a prostitute. All night parties did not help; nor did a stag chase through the streets of London with the animal being killed at Paddington Station.

One of Edward's friends, the wealthy Henry Chaplin, was engaged to marry Lady Florence Paget, better known as 'the Pocket Venus', the daughter of the Marquess of Anglesey. It was to be the society event of the year. Florence asked Chaplin to take her to high-class department store Marshall & Snelgrove so that she could buy some items for her wedding outfit. Arriving at the store, she told Chaplin to wait for her in the coach. She went in through the front door and walked straight to the back door where Chaplin's friend, the Marquess of Hastings, was waiting – they were married within hours. Hastings died in poverty at the age of 26, having lost the present-day equivalent of £3 million betting against Chaplin's horse in the 1867 Derby. It won by a neck; the fastest horse in the first 120 races.

In 1870 it became more serious. Harriet Moncrieff had married Sir Charles Mordaunt. He came home one day to find Harriet entertaining Edward. Mordaunt told Edward to leave, and then forced his wife to watch as he shot her ponies. When her first child was born with defective eyesight, Harriet believed that it was the result of venereal disease contracted from one of her many lovers, and she confessed all to her husband, saying that she had "done wrong with Lord Cole, Sir Frederic Johnstone and the Prince of Wales often and in open day".

Sir Charles Mordaunt petitioned for divorce. Sensationally, Edward was served with a subpoena requiring him to give evidence[42]. In the witness box he denied adultery, and there was no cross-examination. The petition was dismissed on the basis that Lady Mordaunt was deranged when she made her admission. A later petition was successful, and Lady Mordaunt spent the rest of her life in an asylum.

It was an escape for Edward, but then it got worse as his name was linked at various times with, amongst others:

> Jenny Jerome, a New Yorker from a wealthy family. She married Lord Randolph Churchill, a fiery member of parliament who became Chancellor of the Exchequer and had every chance of becoming Prime Minister. However, he offered his resignation once too often, and it was accepted. His career went downhill and he died young – perhaps drugs, perhaps syphilis. As a result, Jenny threw her energies into promoting the career of their son, Winston, whom she and her husband had ignored until then. She had a large number of lovers, including Edward and Count Charles Kinsky, as well as two further husbands the age of her sons.

---

42 A subpoena ad testificandum; a court order to testify sub (under) poena (penalty), generally fine or imprisonment, for failure to obey.

When she was 67, wearing new high-heel shoes, she fell downstairs and broke her ankle. Gangrene set in, and her leg was amputated. It was too late, and she died.

Lillie Langtry, originally Emilie le Breton, who moved with her husband from Jersey to London where she became a well-known 'socialite' after her portrait was painted by Millais, Whistler and others. She became Edward's mistress in 1877, and he had a house built for them in Bournemouth. Lillie fell out of favour when she misbehaved at a dinner, putting an ice cube down Edward's shirt. She became the mistress of the Earl of Shrewsbury, and later had a child by Prince Louis of Battenberg, although by then she was the mistress of Arthur Jones. Lillie left it to her mother to bring up the child. When Lillie's husband lost all his money, on the advice of Oscar Wilde she took to the stage, and had great success in America and in England. In America she lived with millionaire Frederic Gebhard and later with millionaire George Baird. In the end, she married Hugh de Bathe and died in Monte Carlo where she and her husband lived separately.

Sarah Bernhardt, said to have been the most celebrated actress the world has ever known. She was famed in Europe and America, on stage and on film. A 'courtesan', she was for a time the mistress of the Prince de Ligne by whom she had a child. Sarah then married a Greek actor, and was later the mistress of Edward. She injured her knee jumping off a parapet on stage. It was never properly remedied, and in time gangrene set in. Her leg was amputated, but her career, as an actress at least, continued.

Daisy Greville was a descendant of Charles II's mistress, Nell Gwynne. Daisy married Lord Brooke, who became the Earl of Warwick. She had three children with him, and one with someone else. Mistress of Edward and of Lord Beresford, she was apparently the inspiration for the song: "Daisy, Daisy, give me your answer do; I'm half crazy all for the love of you".

Hortense Schneider was a French opera singer. She was the mistress of Edward and of many members of the nobility, and was therefore known as 'Le Passage [thoroughfare] des Princes'.

Cora Pearl (really Eliza Crouch) was a very expensive prostitute. She was famed for her party tricks of dancing in the nude and bathing in champagne in front of all the guests. Another speciality was being brought to the dinner table as a dessert, covered only in cream. Mistress of many, including Edward, she was for a time wealthy. Her career went downhill after one of her lovers shot himself on her doorstep and she calmly closed the door and went upstairs for a sleep. She died in poverty.

Agnes Keyser was the daughter of a successful English businessman. It is possible that her relationship with Edward was platonic. Agnes and her sister Fanny converted their home into a hospital for wounded officers returning from the Boer War. She named the hospital after Edward: 'The King Edward VII Hospital for Officers'[43], now the favoured hospital for the Royal Family.

Alice Keppel was the wife of George Keppel, son of the Earl of Albemarle. Edward's last mistress, she had

---

43 In 1960, they extended their range of care by opening a wing for 'patients of the educated middle class of moderate means but not necessarily with service connections'. In 2000, they dropped 'for Officers' from their name, and opened their doors to all military ranks.

previously been the mistress of Lord Arlington. As soon as she was married, Alice gained a reputation for adultery, having a large number of affairs, most with her husband's knowledge. Keppel always made sure that he was out of the house when Edward was 'paying a visit'. When Alice's daughter had a lesbian relationship with Vita Sackville-West, Alice objected. But when Violet had a lesbian relationship with Winaretta Singer, Alice approved – after all, Winaretta (whose mother was said to have been the model for the Statue of Liberty) was the Singer sewing machine heiress. Anyway, it ran in the family; Keppel's ancestor was Arnold van Keppel, the rumoured homosexual lover of King William III. Alice's great-granddaughter is Camilla, the wife of Prince Charles.

For all these women it was just standard conduct to have affairs with men of higher standing, so elevating their own social status, at the same time trying to move on to someone of even higher standing. The husbands nearly always knew what was going on, keeping out of the way and generally raising no objection, as they expected advancement as a result of their wives' efforts. It was said that in London members-only clubs where wives of members could come as guests, a man might bring his mistress provided he could show that she was the wife of another member.

More scandal when Lord Randolph Churchill's brother, Lord Blandford (the future Duke of Marlborough), decided to run off with Lady Aylesford, who had already given birth to his child. Lord Randolph talked his brother into changing his mind. However, Lord Aylesford learned of the relationship, and he petitioned for divorce. Trying to get him to change his mind, Lady Aylesford and Lord Randolph Churchill showed Princess Alexandra some compromising letters Edward had written to Lady Aylesford, saying that Edward would be required to give evidence in open court. As a result, Edward persuaded Lord Aylesford to abandon the petition, although he and his wife later separated. Edward and Lord Randolph did not speak to one another for eight years.

The next scandal was the Crawford divorce case in 1885, when another of Edward's friends, Sir Charles Dilke (well on his way to becoming Prime Minister), was cited as co-respondent in a divorce petition brought by a fellow MP. Twenty-two-year-old Virginia Campbell confessed that from the age of 19 she had been having an affair with Dilke, adding that he had forced her maid to join them. Having already had an affair with Virginia's mother, Dilke's career was ruined.

In 1889, the police discovered a male brothel in Cleveland Street in London, staffed by post office messenger boys. It was at a time when homosexual acts were punishable by up to two years' imprisonment with hard labour. Edward's equerry, Lord Somerset, was a customer, as were other members of the nobility. Prince Albert Victor, Edward's first son, was rumoured to have been involved, though it was never proved. The whole matter was eventually hushed up. Apart from the post office employees, the only person to be prosecuted was Lord Somerset's solicitor, Arthur Newton, who was imprisoned for six weeks for helping his client escape abroad (he was later struck off for forging a letter to help another client – the murderer Crippen).

Yet a scandal unconnected with sex caused greater damage to Edward's reputation. Sir William Gordon-Cumming had shared many of Edward's mistresses, including Lillie Langtry, Sarah Bernhardt, Lady Randolph Churchill and Daisy Brooke. Gambling would be his downfall. At a country house called Tranby Croft, Edward and others were playing baccarat, which was illegal at the time. Cumming was caught cheating. A deal was agreed under which Cumming undertook never to play cards again, and in return the five witnesses were to keep the matter secret. In 1891 the story came out; Daisy Brooke was suspected – not for nothing was she known as 'the Babbling Brooke'. Cumming sued the five witnesses for slander. Although he was not a defendant, Edward had to give evidence in open court. Cumming's case was dismissed, and he was expelled from the army and various clubs. Damagingly, Edward's own testimony showed that he had been playing an illegal game and was in breach of Queen's Regulations for failing to report a fellow officer's dishonourable conduct.

Then Edward became unnecessarily involved in yet another scandal. Lord Beresford's mistress, Lady Brooke again, wrote to Lord Beresford complaining of his return to his wife. Lady Beresford somehow got hold of the letter. At Lady Brooke's request, Edward tried to get the letter back. When Lady Beresford refused to hand it over, Edward saw to it that she was excluded from court and society. On hearing of this, Lord Beresford (who was at sea with the navy) threatened to tell the press all he knew of Edward's 'private life'. In the end, it was agreed to allow the Beresfords back to court and to exclude Lady Brooke for a short period. Edward acted the injured party, but this time he had really behaved disgracefully.

Throughout the period of these scandals, although the press, Parliament and the public expressed their disgust, most of the establishment, the Royal Family and even Queen Victoria supported Edward. However, there was one area where the upper classes and Victoria continued to be outraged, and that was in Edward's choice of friends. They felt that he should socialise exclusively with royals and high nobility, but Edward insisted on spending time with foreigners and newly-made millionaires such as:

Sir Blundell Maple, who enlarged his father's small shop, Maples, to become the world's largest furniture store.

Sir Thomas Lipton, who developed his parents' grocery store into a chain of 300 shops, buying tea cheaply direct from Ceylon, so establishing tea as the drink of the working class.

William Waldorf Astor who, having inherited his father's estate, was the richest man in America. He became a British citizen, leaving his house in New York to be turned into the Waldorf Hotel, to which his cousin later added the neighbouring Astoria Hotel. Astor's daughter-in-law would be the first woman member of parliament.

The Rothschilds, the European banking dynasty, the London branch of which had funded Wellington's army in the Napoleonic Wars. Later, when Britain was desperate for money to rebuild the economy, the Rothschilds bought the entire issue of government stock. They also helped finance the Bank of England, the building of the Suez Canal, Cecil Rhodes' creation of Rhodesia, and De Beers.

Baron Hirsch, a German banker and railway and commodity investor who became the world's most generous philanthropist. Hirsch was a Jew, so there was outrage in Vienna when Edward stayed at Hirsch's home. When Baron Hirsch visited England, Victoria refused to allow him to attend a state concert.

To his credit, Edward had no prejudices on race, religion, nationality or colour. Indeed, when Edward visited India he was appalled at the treatment of Indians, saying, "Because a man has a black face and a different religion from our own, there is no reason why he should be treated as a brute". Although Edward opposed home rule for Ireland, this did not involve any anti-Catholic feeling. In fact, at his coronation Edward clearly found the anti-Catholic statements in the declaration he was required to make under the Bill of Rights distasteful, and made a point of reading them in a very low and quiet voice. When the Kaiser addressed Edward at length on the evils of the Jews,

Edward walked away in disgust; it confirmed everything he thought of his nephew.

Edward despised the Kaiser, considering him to be an arrogant bully. It did not help that Queen Victoria treated the Kaiser as her favourite grandchild, whereas Edward was her least favourite child. Although always opposing Germany's territorial ambitions, Edward had no hatred of Germans themselves – his nephew excepted. Naturally, Edward supported Denmark (his wife's country) when the Germans invaded and annexed Schleswig-Holstein taking 40% of Denmark and 25% of its population; he also supported France (a country he loved) in the Franco-Prussian War. Queen Victoria took victorious Germany's side.

However, in one area Edward had no problems. His wife Alexandra's care for her family and her amazing tolerance were more than Edward deserved. She produced six children: Albert Victor (Queen Victoria had insisted on the names), George, Louise, Victoria, Maud and Alexander (he lived only a few hours). They were all said to have been born prematurely, but in fact Alexandra had announced late dates for each expected birth so as to ensure that Victoria did not attend and interfere. Unfortunately, some of the births were difficult, leading to Alexandra suffering from a limp, increasing deafness and deteriorating sight.

There were problems with the first child, Albert Victor, who was the heir to the throne after his father. He seemed to have a weak mind, his lifestyle became dissolute and he was heavily linked with the Cleveland Street homosexual brothel scandal. Finding a wife for him would not be easy. He rejected Princess Margaret of Germany, and was himself rejected by his cousin Princess Alix of Hesse – a mistake for her, as she later married her second cousin the son of the Tsar, and Alix (by then called Alexandra) was murdered with her husband Tsar Nicholas II and their children in the Bolshevik Revolution. It was an escape for Britain, as she was a carrier of haemophilia (which she gave to her son and probably to some of her daughters as carriers), and she would have reintroduced the disease to the British Royal Family had she married Albert Victor. Later, Albert Victor fell in love with Princess Hélène d'Orléans (daughter of the Pretender to the French throne), and the marriage was agreed. She undertook to become a Protestant, but her father and the Pope objected, so the wedding was called off.

Finally, it was arranged for Albert Victor to marry his second cousin once removed, Princess Mary of Teck. Six weeks later, Albert Victor died of pneumonia in an influenza pandemic. The following year, Edward's second son, George, married his late brother's former fiancée. Strangely, the same thing had happened to Queen Alexandra's sister, Dagmar. She was betrothed to the oldest son of Tsar Alexander II; after her fiancé died of meningitis, Dagmar instead married his brother, the future Tsar Alexander III (it was their son, Nicholas, who later married Alix of Hesse).

By 1900, Britain's reputation in the world was at its lowest level in centuries, hardly a friend in Europe. The problem was the Second Boer War. It was not just that it was the war of a major power against a weaker opponent, there was another issue. Britain adopted a scorched earth policy, burning Boer homes. To house the refugees, a series of camps was established. Under General Kitchener, a new method of denying the Boer fighters food and assistance was adopted; Boer women and children were seized and put in the camps. They were called concentration camps, earlier introduced by the Spanish in Cuba and the Americans in the Philipines to imprison families of enemy soldiers and their supporters. These were not the camps of sadism and mass murder later to be established by the Germans. However, conditions quickly deteriorated. The treatment of the prisoners was horrific. They were given little food (women and children whose husbands or fathers were still fighting got even less as punishment) and there was virtually no hygiene or medical assistance. The prisoners were left to rot. As a result of typhoid, dysentery and starvation, over 28,000 prisoners died. Camps for natives, who did not even support the Boers, saw 14,000 deaths.

Despite the anti-British sentiment, Edward and his wife decided to pay a visit to Denmark to attend the 82nd birthday celebrations of Alexandra's father, King Christian IX. The route was via Belgium, and Edward was to change trains in Brussels at the Gare du Nord on 4th April 1900. A young Belgian boy, named Jean-Baptiste Sipido, was one of many enraged at reports of British atrocities in the Second Boer War.

Sipido was a tinsmith's apprentice, and was described as a socialist and an anarchist. He made his way to the station and walked on to the platform where Edward's train was waiting. Sipido watched Edward board the train. Edward sat down in the compartment with Alexandra and one male attendant.

At 5.35pm, with flag waved and whistle blown, the train moved off. Sipido drew a revolver, ran forward, jumped on to the footboard of the carriage and fired twice at Edward through the window. Both shots missed. Sipido pulled the trigger twice more, but the cartridges misfired. As he was about to shoot again, a law student, Louis van Mol, rushed forward and snatched the revolver from Sipido's grasp. The stationmaster then knocked Sipido down from the footboard, and two railway employees wrestled him to the ground.

Hearing the shots, the engineer applied the brakes and brought the train to a halt. When Edward was found to be unhurt, the waiting crowd cheered him loudly. Edward asked if the assassin had been arrested. When this was confirmed, Edward decided to continue with his journey.

The only person to be hurt was the blameless law student Louis van Mol. Seeing him holding the revolver, some of the crowd thought that he was the assassin. He was grabbed and heavily beaten.

On being questioned, Sipido said, "When I learned from the papers that the Prince was going to pass through Brussels I immediately resolved to become the avenger of humanity and to kill this assassin... I regret that I have not accomplished it as I desired."

The facts that Sipido's pockets were stuffed with anarchist literature and that he had given what sounded like a strange speech for a poorly educated 15-year-old suggested that he had learned the words and had been put up to it by others.

Sipido's assassination attempt

Following Sipido's interrogation, the authorities arrested three men from the extreme wing of the Socialist Party: Peuchot, Meire and Meert. In court, sympathy was with Sipido and his colleagues. Sipido said that the assassination attempt was not his idea; he had been encouraged by another person. It was widely assumed that this person was Meert. Then Sipido told his story. He had gone to the Old Market on Sunday and had bought a second-hand revolver and cartridges for three francs. On the Tuesday, Sipido had put on his best clothes and borrowed some money from his father, saying that he was going out to look for a job. Instead, he went to meet the unnamed person at the Maison du Peuple (the socialist meeting-house), where they had drinks. Then they moved on to a wine shop to drink some more.

The two of them later made their way to the Gare du Nord. They went to a café in the station, and Sipido had gone to the toilet where he loaded his revolver. He then bought a platform ticket, and walked on to the platform where the Prince of Wales' train was waiting.

Sipido aged 13

Evidence of the many witnesses at the station described exactly what had happened once Sipido was on the platform. Then Meert gave evidence that Sipido was the one who had said that someone should kill the Prince of Wales because he was responsible for the Transvaal War, Meert adding that he and his colleagues had thought it was a joke. Other witnesses who had been at the Maison du Peuple testified that Sipido had announced that if Edward came to Brussels, he ought to have a bullet in his head, and that he had offered to bet anyone five francs that he would do it.

The jury retired to consider the verdicts. After one and a half hours of deliberation, they returned and announced that they found Peuchot, Meire and Meert not guilty because they had thought it was a joke. They found that Sipido had shot at the Prince of Wales, but that by reason of his age he could not be considered *doli capaux* – that is, legally responsible for a crime. He was therefore not guilty. Sipido was released to the cheers of the crowd.

But Sipido had been mistakenly released, because the Court had not yet handed down the written order. The Court later reconvened and ordered that Sipido should be confined in a reformatory until he was twenty-one. However, Sipido had three days in which to appeal the decision and according to the Belgian Government he could not be arrested during that three-day period. He immediately ran off to France.

The Belgian authorities did little or nothing to obtain Sipido's return, causing considerable anger in Britain. In the end, the Belgians reluctantly had Sipido extradited.

On his release from reformatory in December 1905, Sipido enrolled in the army ambulance corps. He later became technical and commercial director of the General Society of Belgian Socialist Cooperatives, eventually retiring to Cagnes in southern France where he died in 1959.

Finally, after waiting over half a century, Edward succeeded to the throne. He announced that the name Albert (his first name) should forever be reserved for his father, and declared that he would reign under his second name, Edward, even though he had always been called 'Bertie' by his family.

Peace came to South Africa when the Boers surrendered in May 1902, so ending the Second Boer War. Transvaal and Orange Free State were incorporated within the Empire into what later became the Union of South Africa.

Back in England there was a problem for the new king because he was an autocrat at heart. Edward struggled to adapt, and his conversion to the role of constitutional monarch was made more difficult when Prime Minister Lord Salisbury, with whom Edward had a good relationship, was succeeded by his nephew, Arthur Balfour.

On the other hand, in foreign matters Edward was useful to the Government as he had instant access to most heads of state. At some stage, his nephews included the Kaiser, the Tsar, the Grand Duke of Hesse, the Duke of Saxe-Coburg and Gotha and the Prince of Brunswick-Luneburg; his nieces included the Queen of Spain, the Crown Princesses of Sweden, Romania and Greece and the Tsarina; the King of Norway was his wife's nephew and Edward's son-in-law; the Kings of Greece and Denmark were his brothers-in-law; and second cousins included the Kings of the Belgians, Portugal and Romania.

Europe was now divided into four: first, the Dual Alliance of France and Russia; second, the Triple Alliance of Germany, Austria and Italy; third, Britain; and fourth, everyone else. For a time, Britain revelled in its 'splendid isolation', but it was soon time to find allies. The first choice was Germany. Edward went there twice and met with the Kaiser, but he just complained endlessly about Britain's dishonesty and Edward's ignorance. So Edward gave up.

Maud Gonne was born near Farnham in southern England, her father being an officer in the 17th Lancers. Maud fell in love with married French right-wing politician Lucien Millevoye, and they dedicated themselves to fighting for the recovery of Alsace-Lorraine by France and independence for Ireland (Maud had been partly brought up in Ireland when her father was stationed there). She then fell in love with the poet William Butler Yeats, but before long she returned to Millevoye, and had two children with him. Their son died after a year; their daughter was conceived in the son's mausoleum in the hope of reincarnating his spirit.

Leaving Millevoye, Maud went to Ireland where she discovered that the Irish nationalists did not welcome women members, so she founded 'The Daughters of Ireland'. Next, she converted to Catholicism. She rejected Yeats's proposal of marriage, as he refused to convert (Yeats later proposed to Maud's daughter, but was rejected again). Maud then took up with Major John MacBride, an Irishman who had fought with the Boers against the British.

They decided to assassinate Edward. The problem was that they did not dare go to England, fearing that MacBride would be arrested as a traitor. Then, in early 1903, they learned that Edward was planning a visit to Gibraltar. Maud married MacBride; she later said that it was so that they could travel to Gibraltar using their honeymoon as cover. The two of them made their way south through France and Spain. Their plan was that once they were in Gibraltar, Maud would act as a decoy while MacBride met up with his co-conspirators, who would assist him in killing Edward.

Having taken lodgings in Gibraltar, MacBride went off as Maud waited patiently in their rooms. Hour after hour passed, until finally late at night there was a knocking on the door. Maud opened the door, only to watch as MacBride staggered into the room totally drunk. Nothing had been done. It was the opposite of Sipido: criminal intent without action rather than action without criminal intent.

Maud and MacBride returned to France the next day. In time they separated, Maud having accused MacBride of molesting her daughter. He was executed by a British firing squad in 1916 after taking part in the Easter Rising. Maud lived in Ireland until she died in 1953, her son with MacBride becoming Chief of Staff of the IRA, Irish foreign minister and winner of the Nobel Peace Prize for his campaigns against other peoples and countries who had used military force.

Maud Gonne

Edward travelled on to France. He was met with cries of *"Vive les Boers!"* and, slightly ridiculously, *"Vive Jeanne d'Arc!"*.

Yet Edward never stopped complimenting France and the French in speech after speech. So much so, that by the time he left the cries were, "*Vive notre Roi!*". The new friendship allowed France and Britain to settle all territorial disputes in Africa.

It made the Germans even more hostile. Nevertheless, Edward continued his efforts to reach some sort of agreement with the Kaiser. Then the Kaiser gave an interview to an American newspaper in which he said that Edward was a corrupt monarch at the head of a corrupt court.

So Edward paved the way for a treaty with Russia, which was signed in 1907. That infuriated the Germans. Edward was convinced that there was no way to stop the Kaiser from starting a major war; he felt that it was only a matter of time. The Kaiser was more explicit; Edward was a Satan, and the world's press was controlled by British money.

There were two more clouds on the international horizon. One was Edward's decision never again to have anything to do with Emperor Franz Josef of Austria, who he considered had lied to him before Austria annexed Bosnia-Herzegovina. Also, Edward refused to speak to King Leopold II of the Belgians because of his appalling policy in the Congo. Leopold believed that the only route to wealth for him and for Belgium was by establishing colonies. The Belgian government did not agree. So Leopold acquired the Congo as a personal possession, buying the land from 500 local chieftains through the operations of Livingstone's discoverer, the American journalist H.M. Stanley (he was in fact a Welshman named John Rowlands who emigrated and changed his name). The great powers gave their approval, as each thought it was better than one of their rivals getting it.

Leopold made a fortune by extracting ivory, then he turned to the Congo's main resource: rubber. Unlike the tapping of rubber trees in many other countries, in the Congo the rubber came from vines in the jungle. The natives were forced to slash the vines, covering themselves in rubber latex, which hardened and was scraped off them at collecting points. When collection targets were not met, the punishment was death or the extermination of a village. Just as bad, Leopold's soldiers were not given replacement bullets unless they had used the previous supply efficiently – killing natives rather than animals. New bullets were supplied on the basis of one for every severed hand produced. In the end, soldiers just cut off natives' hands. This led to natives raiding neighbouring villages to cut off hands so that they could deliver them to the soldiers rather than suffering the mutilation themselves. Thousands of handless men, women and children populated the country, and hands became the currency. Up to 10 million natives died, either from disease or killed by Leopold's mercenary army. When details of the scandal became public, the great powers forced Leopold to transfer the Congo to the Belgian state.

Back in Britain, the Liberals replaced the Conservatives in power in 1905, and Campbell-Bannerman and then Asquith became Prime Minister. Edward had a good relationship with Campbell-Bannerman, but he did not like Asquith. Yet, over time, Edward learned to get on with him, instead reserving his dislike for two of Asquith's fiery younger ministers, David Lloyd George and Winston Churchill, son of Lord Randolph Churchill.

Although they had lost the election, Balfour declared that the Conservatives would control the country through the House of Lords. He was right; the Lords threw out Bills passed in the House of Commons, which was controlled by the Liberals who had been voted in by a huge majority. Of course, a Bill only became an Act of Parliament, and therefore the law, if it was passed by both Houses (the Royal Assent was now an automatic formality). It could not go on.

The Government said that they would deal with the matter once and for all by presenting a Bill to change the House of Lords' power to block legislation to a right merely to delay it. In response, the Lords continued to reject Bill after Bill; and in 1909 they voted down Chancellor Lloyd George's 'People's

Budget', which proposed increased taxation, benefits for the poor and the imposition of a land tax. That rejection was contrary to the convention that the Lords would not oppose the annual Finance Bill. Lloyd George was supported by Winston Churchill, who had already introduced the minimum wage and employment exchanges.

Parliament was dissolved. At the ensuing general election, the Liberals were returned to power, but their numbers were reduced, and they now needed the support of the Irish Nationalists in order to govern.

In April 1910, the Government introduced the Parliament Bill. It provided that the Lords could continue to veto Bills extending the life of Parliament, but Money Bills (exclusively concerning taxation and Goverment spending) could only be delayed by one month and other Public Bills could only be delayed by two years. However, Balfour and the Lords would not budge. Asquith asked Edward to appoint a sufficient number of Liberal peers to ensure a majority in the Lords so that the Parliament Bill would be passed. Edward refused, saying that the matter should be put to the people in another election.

Numerous options were available, important decisions would have to be taken by the King. There was a strong possibility that Edward would call on Balfour to form a minority government. Meanwhile, the Lords agreed to pass the Finance Bill after the land tax was dropped so that the life of the country could continue. But the Parliament Bill was out of the question.

Parliament went into recess. The atmosphere was explosive. There were secret meetings and proposals, negotiations and constitutional debates. Edward would soon have to act. What would he do? He adopted none of the proposed options; instead, he died. After a series of bronchial attacks (no doubt the result of having smoked 20 cigarettes and 12 cigars every day), Edward suffered a number of heart attacks and passed away on 6th May 1910, the only monarch both to be born in and to die in Buckingham Palace.

His final words were said to have been: "I am very glad". It was not at the prospect of death or to sum up his life; rather it was because his son, George, had just told him that Edward's horse 'Witch of the Air' had won the 4.15 race at Kempton Park.

Edward was genuinely mourned by the British people, who had grown to love a monarch with flaws. His weaknesses were mainly women, gambling, food and alcohol – all to excess. Edward was also a stickler for correct dress, frequently reprimanding others. He was open-minded enough to invite 'working class' MP Henry Broadhurst to stay at Sandringham House; but as Broadhurst had not brought correct evening dress with him, he had to eat his dinners alone in his bedroom.

Fashion items popularised by Edward include the Norfolk jacket, wearing tweed, the Tyrolean hat and the unbuttoning of the lowest button, particularly on waistcoats – but this was a necessity rather than a choice, as Edward's waist already exceeded 48 inches at the time of his coronation. Queen Alexandra popularised the 'choker'; this was also a necessity, in order to cover a scar on her neck from a childhood operation. When in India, Edward insisted on everyone dressing formally for dinner, even in the wild. After complaints, he compromised and allowed the men to cut the tails off their evening coats before coming to the table, so inventing the dinner jacket. He then introduced the fashion of wearing a black tie with a dinner jacket instead of a white tie with tails.

Another of his innovations was the custom of the Sunday Roast, particularly the combination of roast beef with horseradish sauce, roast potatoes and Yorkshire pudding.

Edward's coronation had not been attended by large numbers of foreign royals because after they had arrived in London, Edward fell ill and the coronation was postponed for an appendix operation. Most of the foreign royals went home and did not return for the postponed ceremony. However, Edward's funeral saw one of the largest gatherings of royalty and nobility in the history of the world (it included the Emperors of Germany and India, the Kings of Britain, Norway,

Greece, Spain, Bulgaria, Denmark, Portugal and the Belgians, the Dowager Empress of Russia, the Archduke of Austria and over 30 princes as well as former US President Theodore Roosevelt)[44]; and with the list of monarchs decreasing steadily from 1914 onwards, the numbers will probably never be equalled.

****

Perhaps the only photograph of four kings of the same country (George V, Edward VIII, George VI and Edward VII) – it was taken by Queen Alexandra

44 For a fuller list of attendees and what became of them, see Appendix B.

GEORGE V

6 May 1910 – 20 January 1936

George was brought up together with his older brother, Albert Victor. In 1877 they were sent to the navy; George was just two days past his twelfth birthday. Albert Victor left the navy ten years later; George remained at sea.

Then, in the winter of 1891/2 both boys fell ill, George with typhoid and Albert Victor with influenza. George recovered; Albert Victor's influenza developed into pneumonia, and he died. So George left the navy, having succeeded his brother as heir after his father, and also as the fiancé of Princess Mary of Teck. Mary was the daughter of Francis Duke of Teck and Princess Mary Adelaide of Cambridge, granddaughter of Adolphus the seventh son of George III; so she was George's second cousin once removed.

Teck was in Wurttemberg. Francis was the only son of the Duke of Wurttenberg's marriage to a Hungarian countess (she was later thrown by her horse during a troop review and trampled to death by the cavalry). However, it was a morganatic marriage, so Francis could not inherit the Wurttenberg title;

instead he was given the lower title of Teck. With no inheritance rights, Francis found it hard to find a royal bride; but Mary Adelaide was in her thirties, ugly and obese. The marriage was soon agreed. Surviving on Mary Adelaide's small income, the couple lived in England, where their daughter, Mary, was born.

George and Mary married in 1893, and they went on to have six children. The first was Edward (named after Albert Victor who had always been called 'Eddie') Christian (after his Danish great-grandfather) and then the four patron saints: George Andrew Patrick David; he would be know by his last forename – David. The second child was born on the 34th anniversary of the Prince Consort's death; he had to be called Albert. They were followed by Mary, Henry, George and John. The youngest child, John, developed epilepsy and lived apart from his family; he died at the age of thirteen.

On the death of his father, George was crowned King George V. At last the coronation ceremony went ahead without the anti-Catholic statements. George always behaved in a correct manner; so did Mary, but in a much more austere way. They were therefore known as 'George and the Dragon'.

First George had to deal with the Lords versus Commons constitutional crisis his father had managed to avoid. The solution was found during a secret meeting between George and Prime Minister Asquith. There would be another general election; if the Liberals won, George would create a sufficient number of Liberal peers to ensure that the Parliament Bill was passed in the Lords.

The second 1910 general election produced a dead-heat between the Liberals and the Conservatives, but the Liberals held on to power with the support of Labour members and the Irish Nationalists. Now George's promise to create Liberal peers became public. Just as with the Reform Bill, rather than see commoners join them in the House of Lords, many Conservative peers abstained. Even so, the Bill was passed by a majority of only 17 votes. Anyway, the crisis was over.

With all his years in the navy, George had already visited many countries. He decided to return to India. Wearing the newly-created Crown of India embedded with sapphires, rubies, emeralds and 6,170 diamonds[45], George made a magnificent progress. However, the decision for George to ride on horseback meant that the waiting Indians did not recognise him, they were used to seeing their ruler on an elephant.

When George arrived back in England, he learned that Japan had seized Korea, and Italy had seized Libya. Lower on the scale of importance, American Sam Zemurray (a refugee from Russia) financed the overthrow of the government of Honduras in return for land and tax concessions for his banana business – Honduras therefore became the first country to be known as a 'banana republic'.

At home, George found a country torn by strife. The first four years of the reign saw strikes by miners, dockers, seamen, lightermen, railway workers and others, as trade unions grew powerful with workers disappointed at the failure of their Labour members of parliament to do anything to improve living or working conditions. In fact, conditions deteriorated with the economy going downhill as Britain's domination of world trade was overtaken by the United States and Germany.

It was not just the working classes. Dissent spread throughout the population, including increased militancy by the Suffragettes seeking votes for women. Another problem had been growing for generations: it was the demand for home rule for Ireland. Dealing with it was horribly complicated by religion. Protestants were the majority in the north-east of the island, Catholics were the majority elsewhere; and the Protestants wanted to remain part of the United Kingdom.

As a first step, in 1912 a Bill was passed by the Commons giving Ireland its own Parliament. The Bill was opposed by the Lords, but now that meant a delay of two years. When

_____

45 To prevent the loss of the crown jewels to the country, the law prohibits their removal from the United Kingdom so as to stop monarchs from selling or pawning them abroad. So George had to have a new crown made for his visit to India.

1914 came along and civil war in Ireland was a real possibility, it was decided that there should be further negotiations on how to deal with Ulster where six of the eight counties were predominately Protestant. It was all put aside as attention turned to the Balkans.

In 1914, few remembered Bismark's throw-away remark that "One day the great European war will come out of some damned foolish thing in the Balkans". He was about to be proved right.

When Austrian Emperor Franz-Josef's son killed his mistress and then shot himself at the Mayerling hunting lodge, that left the Emperor's brother, Karl, as the heir. Karl died seven years later, and his son Franz Ferdinand became the heir. The new heir wished to marry Countess Sophie Chotek. She was not royalty, and the Emperor forbade the marriage; in order to marry a member of the Imperial House of Habsburg one had to be a member of a reigning or formerly reigning European dynasty. Following pressure from the Tsar, the Pope and the Emperor of Germany, Franz-Josef reluctantly consented to the marriage provided it was morganatic – a legal union, but not entitling the passage of the husband's succession, titles or property to his wife and children (also known as a left-handed marriage because at the wedding the groom holds the bride's hand with his left hand instead of the right one). It meant that after they married, Sophie did not become the Archduchess, she had no royal status and she could not even stand or sit with her husband at formal events or ride beside him in the royal carriage.

However, Franz Ferdinand was a Field Marshal and Inspector General of the Austrian Army, so on military occasions, as the wife of a senior officer, Sophie could accompany him. When General Potiorek, the Austrian governor of Bosnia, invited Franz Ferdinand to attend military manoeuvres and to open the state museum in the capital, Sarajevo, in June 1914, Franz Ferdinand jumped at the chance. He would be able to celebrate his wedding anniversary with his wife at his side.

Bosnia used to be a Turkish territory, but since 1878 it had been governed by Austria-Hungary, and they annexed it in 1908. Tension grew because the population was largely Serb. The Serbs, humiliated by the annexation, wanted to be part of Serbia, not Austria-Hungary; and Serbia was eager to rebuild its fourteenth century empire, having already conquered Macedonia and Kosovo.

A secret Serb organisation, 'Unification or Death' but better known as 'The Black Hand', angered that the Archduke should visit Sarajevo on the anniversary of the Turks' conquest of Serbia in 1389, decided to assassinate Franz Ferdinand. Three young Serbs agreed to carry out the killing, and they made their way to Sarajevo where they were joined by four others. They were given hand grenades, pistols, ammunition, money and suicide pills.

After watching the manoeuvres in the early morning of Sunday 28th June, their wedding anniversary, the Archduke and his wife arrived at Sarajevo railway station. The motorcade made its way to the Filippovic barracks. Having reviewed the troops, at 10.00am they left for the town hall. Franz Ferdinand and his wife were in a Gräf & Stift convertible with its roof folded down; it was owned by Count von Harrach, a friend of the Archduke. The route to the town hall was via Appel Quay, which ran alongside the Miljacka River. Franz Ferdinand gave instructions to drive slowly, and the cars proceeded at about 10 mph.

All seven assassins were stationed along Appel Quay. The cars passed the first assassin, Muhamed Mehmedbasic; he had a hand grenade, but he did nothing. The second assassin, Nedjelko Cabrinovic, also had a hand grenade. It was not designed to explode on impact, rather it exploded 12 seconds after the cap was snapped off. Cabrinovic knocked the cap off against a lamppost, but he could not wait the necessary few seconds before throwing the grenade because by then the Archduke's car would have gone past him. Desperate to play his part, Cabrinovic threw the grenade straight away. It hit the folded-down roof behind the Archduke, and bounced into the street, exploding as the next car drove over it. Two of the passengers and several policemen and bystanders were injured. The other cars sped away to the town hall, travelling too fast for the remaining assassins to do anything.

Cabrinovic swallowed his suicide pill, and immediately vomited it up. So he threw himself into the river. However, the water was only five inches deep, and he was pulled out by the angry crowd and beaten until he was taken away by the police. It was all over; or was it?

When the reception at the town hall ended, Franz Ferdinand announced that rather than open the museum, he wanted to go to the hospital to visit those who had been injured by the grenade. When a staff officer warned against it, Potiorek responded: "Do you think Sarajevo is full of assassins?" Off they went, General Potiorek sitting next to the driver, and Count von Harrach standing on the left running-board as extra protection. They drove back along Appel Quay, and then turned right into Franz Josef Street. But that was the way to the museum, not the hospital. The driver had not been told of the change of plan. "Stop! This is the wrong way!", General Potiorek shouted. "We are supposed to take the Appel Quay!". The driver stopped, and prepared to reverse into Appel Quay.

In the meantime, one of the assassins, Gavrilo Princip, having accepted that the venture had failed, decided to go to Schiller's Café and Delicatessen for lunch. After finishing his meal, Princip left the premises. As he stepped on to the pavement on Franz Josef Street, imagine his surprise; there, right in front of him was the Graf & Stift convertible with the Archduke and his wife on the back seat like sitting ducks. Princip pulled out his pistol, stepped on to the unguarded right running-board and shot Sophie in the abdomen and the Archduke in the neck. Both died within minutes.

Back in Austria, the Emperor could barely conceal his joy. The two bodies were taken to Vienna to lie in state for four hours, no foreign dignitaries being allowed to pay their respects. Then, in the middle of the night, the coffins were put on a railway carriage, attached to a milk train and taken away.

Princip and many of those connected with the assassination (other than Mehmedbasic) were arrested and put on trial. Some were executed, some imprisoned, a few acquitted. As Princip was under 20 years old, he could not be executed; he was sentenced to 20 years in prison. He died of tuberculosis in April 1918 (weighing only six stone, that is 84 pounds or 38 kilos, as a result of malnutrition, disease and the amputation of an arm), by which time most of the world was engulfed in the war started by his bullet.

Having checked that they would have German support, the Austro-Hungarian government delivered a 48-hour ultimatum to Serbia with demands that they knew could never be accepted. Although they made every effort to agree to the terms, Serbia could not stomach all of them, particularly the requirement that Austrian police should be entitled to go into Serbia to halt all anti-Austrian activity and propaganda. On 28th July, Austria-Hungary declared war on Serbia. It was clear that Russia would support their fellow Slavs; also, the Russians could not allow a major power to move south and threaten the entrance to the Black Sea through which most of Russia's foreign trade passed.

There was a short period of caution. The Austro-Hungarians could not attack Serbia, then they could not defend against Russia; Russia could not attack Austria-Hungary, then they could not defend against Germany; Germany could not attack Russia, then they could not defend against France, which was bound by treaty to support the Russians.

Mobilisation, making troops ready for war, was the trigger. Germany was ready to mobilise; it would take them a few days. Russia, with its vast territory, poor administration and antiquated rail system, needed weeks to mobilise. The Russians could not allow the Germans to mobilise first; if the Germans then attacked, they would be deep into Russian territory before the Russian Army was in a position to resist. So the Russians mobilised. It was seen as an act of war in itself, as it was said that no army ever mobilised without going to war.

Now the Germans could put their great plan into operation. They would attack the French and defeat them before the Russians were ready to fight. Then with France defeated, the Germans could deal with Russia. So Germany declared war on Russia and France. The French had built a defensive fortification along their border with Germany, although not along their border with Belgium – Belgium was no threat. Adopting a long-planned strategy, the Germans marched into Belgium so that they could go around the French defences and into France. Britain was bound by treaty to preserve Belgium's independence, and, unwilling to see Germany control the entire continent, gave Germany an ultimatum to withdraw. When the ultimatum was ignored, Britain declared war on Germany. The Germans could not believe that Britain would go to war over 'a scrap of paper'. Over the following days, Montenegro declared war on Austria-Hungary, Serbia declared war on Germany, Austria-Hungary declared war on Russia, Montenegro declared war on Germany, France declared war on Austria-Hungary, Japan declared war on Germany and then Britain declared war on Austria-Hungary. Others soon joined, and two groups formed: the Allies against the Central Powers.

Nothing went as planned. Austria-Hungary attacked Serbia, but they were repelled by the Serbs. Russia could have left the Serbs to look after themselves, and the whole chain reaction might not have happened. But it was all long beyond stopping now; everyone had a new reason for war.

The French took the opportunity to attack the Germans in Alsace-Lorraine, hoping to recover their lost territory. They were thrown back at a cost of 250,000 dead. The Germans were less successful in the north; they had not counted on Belgian resistance. Germany's policy of terrorising people into submission was bravely resisted. In their anger, the Germans authorised their soldiers to execute civilians and to slaughter women and children. Cities were completely destroyed, notably Louvain with five days of mass shootings and destruction including the famous university library and many churches.

In the end, the Germans did manage to move through Belgium and deep into France. However, they decided not to enter Paris until they had defeated the British and French armies. The relieved French counter-attacked, and together with the British they pushed the Germans back. Then both sides dug in, with trenches running from Switzerland to the Channel. It meant that the Germans could not dispose of France and then deal with Russia.

Certain of a German victory, Turkey joined the Central Powers, hoping to recover lands previously lost to Russia. This was later balanced when Italy (desperate to show itself as a major power on one side or the other) joined the Allies, having been promised territory and money after the Central Powers were defeated.

Seeing the Germans tied down in the west, the Russians attacked Germany. However, the Germans were wrong; they could indeed deal with France and Russia at the same time. The Russians were heavily defeated and forced to retreat.

In England, the mood changed; it would not 'be all over by Christmas'. First Sea Lord, Prince Louis of Battenberg (grandfather of Prince Philip), was removed from office. His father was Prince of Hesse, but as Louis' parents' marriage was morganatic, he had the minor title of Battenberg. He had joined the Royal Navy at the age of fourteen and later took British citizenship and married a granddaughter of Queen Victoria, but his name was German. In the East End of London, mobs ran riot, looting and destroying shops and homes of people with foreign names.

The turmoil spread to Parliament. Having put Irish home rule aside, Asquith could no longer rely on the Irish Nationalists for support. So he formed a coalition with the Conservatives.

Attention moved from the north of the continent to the

Dardanelles as Britain and France (aided by Australian, New Zealand and Indian troops) attacked Turkey, hoping to secure a sea route to Russia and force the Germans to come to Turkey's aid by transferring troops from the western front. It was a disaster; the Gallipoli Peninsula campaign cost tens of thousands of lives before it ground to a halt and then continued for no purpose until it was abandoned. First Lord of the Admiralty Winston Churchill was demoted, and later resigned, joining the Royal Scots Fusiliers and serving on the western front. Elsewhere the trench warfare was getting nowhere.

Although the Government had suspended dealing with Irish home rule until the war was over, for the Irish it was a time of opportunity. During Easter 1916 (expecting assistance from Germany – which never arrived) there was a violent uprising as nationalists seized the Dublin central post office and proclaimed the Irish Republic. After five days of fighting and several hundred deaths, the uprising was put down.

Meanwhile, Sir Douglas Haig had taken command of British forces in Belgium and France. It brought no great improvement as the four-month Battle of the Somme gained seven miles at a cost of over 600,000 Allied casualties and almost 500,000 German casualties. With all the evidence being that defence was easier than attack, the Germans took defensive positions. Then, horrifying the world, they started to use poison gas.

At home, Asquith was overthrown as leader of the coalition government, having been blamed for mismanaging the war, the criticism brought to a head in the Shell Scandal – an allegation that defeats had been caused by the failure to supply the army with sufficient quantities of high explosives. Asquith was replaced by the dynamic David Lloyd George, born in Manchester but brought up in Wales. He would lead Britain through the war and beyond.

With the anti-foreigner sentiment in England increasing, King George was made very aware of his German antecedents. It did not help that the German aircraft sent to bomb London was called the 'Gotha'. George decided to change the name of his House from 'Saxe-Coburg and Gotha' to the very English 'Windsor'. When the Kaiser (not a man known for wit) was told, he is said to have responded by saying that he would celebrate by going to the theatre to see the well-known Shakespeare play, *The Merry Wives of Saxe-Coburg and Gotha*. At the same time, all German titles held by George's family were abandoned; Battenberg became Mountbatten, and Teck became Cambridge. In addition, the peerages of those who fought with the Germans (such as the Prince of Hanover who had also been Duke of Cumberland, and Queen Victoria's grandson the Duke of Saxe-Coburg and Gotha who had also been Duke of Albany) were revoked.

Then, on 31st January 1917, in response to the British Navy's blockade, the Germans announced unrestricted submarine warfare; all shipping, including neutrals, would be sunk on sight in the eastern Atlantic. America immediately broke off diplomatic relations with Germany. Anger in America rose with the torpedoing of seven US merchant ships and the revelation (by British code-breakers) that the Germans had promised to help Mexico recover New Mexico and other territories lost to the United States.

Good news came for the Allies in June 1917: America joined the war. When British and American troops were fighting in Belgium, they became aware of the custom of the locals of accompanying their meals with small river fish, which they deep fried. In winter, when the rivers were frozen, the fish were not available, so instead the locals cut potatoes into narrow strips to resemble the fish and then deep fried the potato strips. They called them *'frieten'* or *'frites'*, Flemish and French for 'fries'. French being the official language of the Belgian Army, the British and Americans who tried the *frites*, called them 'French fries'.

Although the Russians had defeated the Austro-Hungarian Army, they could not cope with the Germans. The incompetence of the Russian leadership and the heavy casualties (after two years the Russians had already suffered two million dead, wounded or taken prisoner) led to military and civil unrest. Tsar Nicholas had been forced to abdicate in March, and a liberal government had taken over. In an effort to cause trouble, the Germans sent the exiled revolutionary Lenin from Switzerland to Russia in a sealed train. It was a success; by November the Bolsheviks had seized power. They were the faction of the Marxist Party led by Lenin, called Bolsheviks (meaning 'the majority') as they won a particular vote on membership against the other leading faction who then became known as the Mensheviks (the 'minority'). The Bolsheviks later became the Communist Party.

Immediately agreeing an armistice with the Germans, the Bolsheviks signed a treaty in March 1918 under which huge areas of territory were ceded to Germany. That allowed the Germans to withdraw troops from the east and send them to the western front. With those additional troops, the Germans launched a major offensive in the west, seeking victory before the bulk of the American troops arrived. After initially being driven back, the Allies halted the German advance 56 miles from Paris. Like the British before them, the Germans were worn down by their own offensive. They now saw the prospect of victory disappearing.

There was bad news for George when he heard that his cousin the Tsar and his immediate family had been shot. Perhaps not realising the danger the Tsar was in, George had overruled the Government's plan to offer the Tsar sanctuary, unwilling in times of unrest and republican sentiment to be associated with his despotic cousin. Also, the Tsarina was German and even more autocratic than her husband. However, after the war was over, a ship was sent to Sebastopol to rescue the late Tsar's mother (George's aunt, Dagmar) and some other aristocrats and their servants.

Finally, in the summer of 1918 the Allies started to make progress as the 'One Hundred Day Offensive' forced the German Army back towards Germany all along the line. The

Germans lost troops by the thousand to death and captivity, as fresh American troops arrived at the rate of 10,000 a day. In the Middle East, British forces drove the Turks back to Turkey. On 30th October, Turkey capitulated; on 3rd November it was Austria-Hungary; the German fleet having mutinied, on 9th November the Kaiser abdicated and the Germans declared themselves a republic; on 10th November the Kaiser escaped to exile in the Netherlands; and on the eleventh hour of the eleventh day of the eleventh month, the Armistice came into effect.

King George had been injured in the war, although it was not in battle. When visiting the troops in October 1915, in a repetition of his 4 x great-grandfather King George II's experience at Dettingen, King George V's horse took fright at the cheers of the Royal Flying Corps. This time, rather than galloping towards the enemy, the horse reared twice on the muddy ground, threw George, and then fell on top of him. George's pelvis was broken in two places. As a result, he would suffer from pain for the rest of his life.

With the war over, negotiation of the Treaty of Versailles commenced. France was eager for revenge, the USA was more interested in establishing a new ideal world, and Britain was looking for colonial scraps. As Lloyd George said, "It was like sitting between Napoleon and Jesus Christ".

At President Wilson's insistence, the Treaty included the creation of the League of Nations, an organisation that would prevent war. However, the US Senate refused to ratify the Treaty, so the US never signed it (instead signing a separate treaty two years later) and did not join the League of Nations, rendering that organisation ineffectual.

France recovered Alsace-Lorraine, Poland was recreated, German colonies were shared out, and Germany lost part of Schleswig and other European territory. In addition, the size of Germany's army and navy was limited, and they were banned from having submarines, tanks and aircraft. Other provisions included the payment of reparations totalling £6.6 billion (at today's value: £284 billion – the final instalment was paid in October 2010). Lloyd George correctly feared that France's demands for money and territory would lead to another war. Finally, Germany and its allies had to accept guilt for starting the war. Germany had not been a party to the negotiations, they were just told where to sign. The Germans were furious, they said that Austria and Russia were responsible for starting the war, and the Jews and the Communists were responsible for Germany losing it. The Germans now decided that they were the victims. French Major-General Foch declared: "This is not peace, it is a 20-year armistice."

Britain's gain was some former German colonies in Africa, but little else. The loss of 750,000 dead and 1,500,000 injured or crippled by gas brought almost full employment and an increase in wage levels. Other problems were dealt with as all men over 21 and 78% of women over 30 were given the vote. A general election in 1918 returned the coalition government led by Liberal Prime Minister Lloyd George, although two-thirds of the coalition's members were Conservatives.

Now Ireland had to be dealt with. Financed and armed from America, the Irish Republican Army began a guerrilla war for independence to include the Protestant north-east. British troops responded with violence and reprisals. In the end, Ireland became independent as a dominion within the Empire, with the parliament of Northern Ireland opting for its territory to remain part of the United Kingdom. The Irish Parliament ratified the Anglo-Irish Treaty, but many Irishmen objected to the loss of the six Ulster counties. Irish President de Valera (actually born in New York to an Irish mother and a Cuban or Mexican father (Juan de Valeros)) refused to accept the vote and resigned (as he was not a UK citizen, he had escaped execution for treason after the Easter Rising). Civil war began, and anti-treaty forces murdered the leader of the Irish government, Michael Collins. Nevertheless, the pro-treaty side prevailed.

There was a story that de Valera had organised a plot to

assassinate George. If true, it was the first attempt to kill George; but nothing came of it.

In Britain the Government was more concerned with domestic matters as union agitation and strikes broke out across the country. Conservative minister Stanley Baldwin started a revolt in 1922 against Conservative membership of a coalition led by a Liberal. Lloyd George resigned, and the Conservatives took power under Andrew Bonar Law, the only foreign-born Prime Minister – he was born in the colony of New Brunswick, soon to be part of Canada.

For George there was celebration as his second son, Albert, married Lady Elizabeth Bowes-Lyon in 1923. In politics, Bonar Law fell ill with throat cancer, and was replaced as Prime Minister by Baldwin. The Conservatives won the 1923 election; although with three large parties, they no longer had an overall majority. Baldwin refused to consider a coalition, and he resigned. Labour leader Ramsay MacDonald became Prime Minister, but he needed the support of the Liberals to govern.

A Labour government did not prevent further strikes, and unemployment grew to one million. Then MacDonald lost the support of the Liberals, and in the 1924 election Baldwin and the Conservatives took power. The Liberals were destroyed; it was once again a two-party system.

Political stability may have returned, but the economy was rocked by the General Strike[46]. It all started when German and Polish coal became cheaper than British coal on the European market. The coal companies' response was to increase working hours and lower wages. That was rejected by the unions, and the pit owners reacted with a lock-out. The transport workers, railwaymen, builders, and gas and electricity workers came out in sympathy. After nine days, the strike was called off. The miners remained out for six months, going back to increased working hours and lower wages.

---

46 The word 'strike' was first used for a withdrawal of labour in 1768, when support for anti-government demonstrations in London saw sailors strike (lower) the top-gallant sails of merchant ships, thereby preventing them from leaving port.

Following the 1929 election (women could now vote at 21, like men), Ramsay MacDonald again became Labour Prime Minister with Liberal support. It was the time of the Great Depression, and unemployment grew to three million. There was a run on sterling and panic in the City. The Government had to borrow, but banks would not lend unless the Government took steps to mend the economy. That had to include a reduction in unemployment pay. Labour ministers were unable to take such a decision. First they did nothing, then rather than act they resigned. So MacDonald was forced to form a coalition with the Conservatives.

Most Labour members left the coalition, Labour supporters treating MacDonald as a class traitor. However, with a reduction in unemployment pay, devaluation of the pound and £80 million borrowed, the economy slowly recovered.

At the 1931 election, the National Government of Conservatives, Liberals and Labour supporters won a massive majority, MacDonald leading a coalition that was composed mainly of Conservatives.

In the same year, after a gap of centuries, a challenge was made to the monarch's right to the throne. Anthony Hall, a former police inspector from Shropshire, claimed that he was the true king. He said that he was the descendant of Thomas Hall, the son of Henry VIII and Anne Boleyn, born before they were married. An illegitimate child had no right to inherit the crown, but perhaps Hall contended that Thomas Hall was legitimised by his parents' subsequent marriage.

He is unlikely to have known that as a peculiarity, it is well established that an illegitimate passed over in deciding succession to the crown does not have his or her right created on being legitimised. As far as the crown is concerned: 'once a bastard, always a bastard'. Otherwise, people could turn up years later to upset the current monarch – just as Hall was trying to do.

In the Midlands, Hall held public meetings that were attended by crowds of several hundred. They approved of his rants against the German occupants of Buckingham Palace and his promise that once he became king he would abolish the government, end taxation, build houses for working men, pay off the national debt, electrify the railways, provide free medical and dental treatment and would popularise portrait painting, wrestling and boxing.

Then Hall went too far; he said that he would have no hesitation in shooting the King as he would shoot a dog, adding that he wanted to become the first policeman to cut off the King's head. George wanted it stopped, but he did not want Hall to be sent to prison. Hall was arrested, and two doctors were appointed to examine him. To the Palace's disappointment, the doctors refused to certify Hall as insane, one of them saying that Hall had "... a case of a sort."

Instead, Hall was fined £10 for using quarrelsome and scandalous language liable to cause a breach of the peace. He was also bound over to keep the peace in future, failing which he would be fined £25 or sent to prison for two months with hard labour.

He made one more speech, ending by saying that he was going away for a while, and would be back later. "Goodnight my friends, you may be my subjects one of these days." With that he ended his campaign.

Hall's wife, [Queen] Ethel, divorced him for desertion, and he died in 1947 leaving no children to pursue the claim of 'the last Tudor'. Hall had a younger brother living in America – however, he was not interested in the nonsense.

Not really an assassination attempt, nonetheless it was a threat of murder that the Palace felt had to be stopped.

With his mental and physical health deteriorating, and worn down by the difficulty of managing a coalition where his party was in the minority, in 1933 MacDonald was once more replaced by Baldwin.

It was a dangerous time. The burden of war reparations aggravated by the effects of the Depression and perhaps their natural inclination saw Germany move to the extreme right. The National Socialists ('Nazis') were now the second largest party. Under their leader, Hitler, they were more active in the streets than in parliament, some towns becoming almost war zones as those who opposed the Nazis or were disliked by them were beaten or killed. Not for the first or the last time, anti-Semitism started in universities as Jewish students were vilified and attacked in Germany and in Austria. The next step was a boycott, introduced under the pretence that it was for political and economic reasons. Jewish lecturers were boycotted in universities, Jewish actors and musicians were boycotted with their performances interrupted by chants and abuse, and Jewish-owned businessess were boycotted and picketed, as the media and politicians either justified the boycotts or denied that it was a serious problem. The denial continued when boycotts and chants moved on to the next steps of violence and then murder.

In the first 1932 election, the Nazis with their ideology of fascism and racism gained 37% of the vote; in the November 1932 election their share of the vote fell to 33%. They had to seize power before it fell lower. With the other parties refusing to unite, President Hindenburg appointed Hitler as Chancellor.

Only one European power had the military might to cause the Germans any concern, and on 9th February 1933 an English university sent out a message: the Oxford University Union resolved that "this house refuses in any circumstances to fight for king and country".

On 27th February, the German parliament was burned down, and civil liberties were suspended. A week later, Dachau, the first concentration camp, was established. Within another week, Jews were expelled from jobs, many beaten or killed, and their shops and homes were attacked. The justification was, and still is, that the German Jews had taken jobs from Germans – there were only about 169,000 male Jews of working age in Germany (70,000 by 1939) out of a population of 70 million, and they actually thought that they were Germans.

By July, all political parties other than the Nazis were banned. In November, the Secret State Police, the _**Ge**heime **Sta**ats**po**lizei_, was established. Nazi control of Germany was now complete. Portugal and Spain became fascist dictatorships, joining

Germany and Italy (Mussolini having already seized power and banned opposition parties). Everyone watched and did nothing as Germany re-armed, established an air force, formed armoured divisions and introduced conscription, all in breach of the Treaty of Versailles.

George was horrified at the rise of fascism, with Japan having long since conquered Manchuria and with Italy in the process of seizing Ethiopia, while the Germans concentrated on attacking their own people. He was convinced that within 10 years the Germans would start another world war, and he told the German ambassador of his views. George also warned the British ambassador in Germany not to trust the Nazis.

Then, within months of celebrating his Silver Jubilee, George, who had been in poor health for several years, fell ill. On the night of 20th January 1936, at Sandringham House, George's doctor, Bertrand Dawson, determined that the King was dying of bronchitis. Would George be the first English or British monarch to die without anyone having tried to kill him? Would he avoid the curse? Now Dawson found himself faced with a problem. With the cut-off time for printing the next morning's edition of The Times fast approaching, if George did not die soon, the announcement of his death would not be in The Times, it would be, as Dawson said, "in less appropriate evening journals". That was unacceptable.

Dawson (the President of the Royal College of Physicians) told his wife to advise The Times to hold back printing for a short time. A sedative was given to Edward by a nurse, to whom he uttered his last words: "God damn you." Then, without consulting George's family, Dawson gave the King lethal injections of cocaine and morphine. The news of the King's death was given to The Times, and the print-run could start.

King George V was killed by his doctor. 'A peaceful ending at midnight' was the headline. The truth only emerged on publication of Dawson's diaries 50 years later, Dawson adding that it prevented "hours of waiting when all that is really life has departed [that] only exhausts the onlookers…" He was elevated to Viscount Dawson of Penn later in the year.

Bertrand Dawson

George was a traditionalist, but he was always in favour of moderation. In India he expressed his disgust at racial discrimination; when someone described the strikers in the General Strike as revolutionaries, George replied: "Try living on their wages before you judge them."

His father may have reversed Victoria's lack of communication, but George reversed his father's life of scandal. Also, George did not repeat his decision not to rescue the Russian royal family. After the war, he sent an officer to escort former Emperor Charles of Austria and his family to Switzerland. Then, when in 1922 the King of Greece was deposed, George agreed to a naval vessel being sent to collect the King's brother, Prince Andrew, his wife and their children, amongst whom was the one-year-old Philippos (carried in an orange box) – now Prince Philip Duke of Edinburgh.

****

431

EDWARD VIII

20 January 1936 – 11 December 1936

Edward VIII preparing to make his abdication speech

Like many of his predecessors, George V preferred a younger son to the oldest one. George could not stand Edward's flippancy and lack of propriety, telling Prime Minister Baldwin, "I pray to God that my eldest son will never marry and have children, and that nothing will come between Bertie and Lilibet and the throne".

Prince Albert's first daughter, Elizabeth, was King George's favourite. He called her 'Lilibet', and she called him 'Grandpa England'.

Edward ('David' to his family) was a disappointment academically, but he behaved well in the First World War, insisting on visiting the front on several occasions.

The three-day Battle of Loos was a British offensive in September 1915. During the battle, Edward asked his driver to take him nearer to the front line so that he could see what was happening. After a short drive they stopped, and Edward left the car to look for a vantage point. They were spotted, and a mortar barrage was fired in their direction. Edward ran back to his car. It was no longer there, a high-explosive shell had destroyed the vehicle and killed the driver. Edward was lucky, the attempt to kill him had failed. Others were not so fortunate. After initial success, the battle ended with British troops exactly where they had started. Twenty thousand men had been lost, including Princess Elizabeth's brother, Captain Fergus Bowes-Lyon (the present Queen's uncle).

Some months later, Edward had another close call. Near the front line there was a small stone building that had been partially destroyed. On an inspection trip, Edward and several officers went into the building in order to use their field glasses unobserved. They had been seen, and the Germans began firing shells at the house. When the first one burst, General Wardrop shouted to the Prince, telling him to flatten himself on the floor. Edward did not move quickly enough, so the General threw himself at the Prince, lying on top of him until the attack ceased. The house was not hit, and Edward avoided death again.

A week afterwards, while making their way to an observation post on a hill, Edward and another officer crossed a field under artillery fire. The officers in the post were watching. Suddenly a heavy shell burst on the hillside. "Great God! It's got him!" one of the officers shouted. He was wrong; when the smoke had cleared, the Prince could be seen sprinting to a recently captured German pill-box. Edward had escaped with his life once more.

With the war over, Edward carried out many public duties, and he was keen to visit the most deprived parts of the country. Yet something else in his character emerged after a visit to Australia, when he declared of the Aborigines, "They are the most revolting form of living creatures I've ever seen. They are the lowest form of human beings and are the nearest thing to monkeys."

Nevertheless, Edward was considered dashing, the most eligible bachelor in the world, setting men's fashions (but not the Windsor tie-knot, which was introduced by Edward VII), photographed and admired – one of the first 'celebrities'.

Eligible or not, Edward's interest in women was largely restricted to older women and always directed at married women. His father was disgusted, saying of Edward, "After I am dead, the boy will ruin himself in twelve months".

Bessie Wallis Warfield was born in Pennsylvania, and she would move on from her modest origins, fuelled by a fierce ambition. After a number of affairs, she divorced her alcoholic husband, US Navy pilot Earl Spencer, by which time she had already become involved with Ernest Simpson. Born in America, Simpson had become a British subject and an officer in the Guards, and was at the time a shipping executive. He divorced his wife and married Wallis.

Simpson's financial position later deteriorated, and at the same time Wallis' friend, Lady Furness (who was the current mistress of Prince Edward), held a party at which she introduced Wallis to the Prince. Some time later, Lady Furness invited Wallis to lunch at the Ritz, and told her that she would be going to New York for a short time. "Oh", said Wallis, "the little man is going to be so lonely." "Well dear, you look after him while I'm away", Lady Furness replied. Wallis did just that. When Lady Furness returned to England, Edward refused to see her or take her calls; Wallis had supplanted her friend as Edward's mistress. Although Wallis was slightly younger than Edward, her abrasive and dominating behaviour was that of an older woman, and Edward was besotted with her. He showered her with money and jewels. The King was appalled, not least when Edward produced Wallis at court, where divorced people were not allowed.

When George V died, Edward automatically succeeded to the throne. As George V's funeral procession made its way to Westminster Hall, all of a sudden the cross at the top of the Imperial State Crown resting on the coffin broke off and fell into the gutter. The watching Edward said: "Christ, what's next?" He was right, it was a bad omen. It did not take long for the royal curse to strike. On the morning of 16th July 1936, Edward took part in a ceremony in Hyde Park to present new colours to six battalions of Guards regiments. Shortly after noon, with the ceremony over, the King's procession rode down Constitution Hill on its way back to Buckingham Palace. Crowds lined the route, a military band leading, followed by Edward in uniform and bearskin.

In the watching crowd a nervous-looking man in a shabby brown suit made his way forward. The man dropped his newspaper as the parade approached, revealing a revolver in his hand. A woman standing next to the man screamed, and Special Constable Anthony Dick spun round as the man aimed the revolver at the King. Dick instinctively struck out and punched the brown-suited man on the arm. The blow knocked the loaded gun out of the man's grasp, and it flew into the road, hitting a hind leg of Edward's horse. Although the horse shied, Edward kept it under control, and he continued to ride to the Palace.

The assassin was an Irishman, Jerome Bannigan, a Nazi supporter who had distributed fascist newspapers in Paddington in west London. When questioned, Bannigan said that he had intended to shoot himself as a protest against the Home Secretary, but had suddenly changed his mind and decided to throw his gun at a leg of the King's horse. Records

Bannigan arrested

435

showed that Bannigan had been sentenced to 12 months' imprisonment on a conviction for criminal libel. After three months in prison, his conviction was overturned on appeal. However, the Home Secretary rejected Bannigan's claim for compensation, and he was incensed.

At his trial at the Old Bailey under the 1842 Treason Act, Bannigan told a new story. He claimed that he had been contacted by a foreign power (later revealed as Germany) and that a senior embassy official, a baron, wanted to promote a coup by English fascists. As part of the plot, Bannigan had been paid £150 to assassinate the King. Bannigan said that he had informed MI5 of the plot, and had proceeded with their knowledge so as to facilitate the arrest of the others involved, and without intending to kill the King.

Under cross-examination, Bannigan admitted that after his arrest he had told the police words to the effect that he wished he had done the job properly. The jury rejected Bannigan's defence and found him guilty. He then asked the judge to give him the heaviest possible sentence so as to save his life. Surprisingly, Bannigan was sentenced to only 12 months' hard labour, a light punishment in the circumstances, suggesting that either there may have been something to the defence or that the judge wanted to keep matters low-key and not create a martyr.

At the beginning of the Second World War, Bannigan was denounced as pro-Nazi. In 1940 he was again in trouble when (already having three convictions for fraud) he was found to be in possession of several important paintings, including a Gainsborough and a Romney. The police reluctantly accepted his explanation that he had been entrusted with the paintings so as to secure sales. Bannigan died in 1970.

Worse trouble awaited the new king: the consequence of his love for Mrs Simpson. On 16th November 1936, Prime Minister Baldwin was summoned to the Palace, and Edward announced that he intended to marry Mrs Simpson as soon as her divorce came through. The Prime Minister told Edward that the British people would find such a marriage unacceptable. In addition, Edward was Supreme Governor of the Church of England, which did not allow a divorced person to remarry while the former spouse was still alive – Wallis would have two of them. She was also believed to be having sexual relations with a duke and with a car salesman. Baldwin said that if the King married Mrs Simpson, the Government would resign. The Labour and Liberal leaders added that they would refuse to form a replacement government – it was after this that the 'Leader of the Opposition' became an official post carrying a state salary.

Baldwin warned the King that there would be a constitutional crisis, one that might threaten the very existence of the monarchy. Opposition also came from the dominions. The Prime Ministers of Australia, Canada and South Africa voiced their disapproval, as did the Irish leader who said Edward could not remain King of Ireland; but the New Zealand Prime Minister expressed no opinion, saying that he had never heard of Mrs Simpson. Edward's response was to say that he did not care, and there were "not many people in Australia".

For the British Government, no less objectionable was Edward's meddling in foreign affairs, particularly his friendship with Germany. During his father's reign, Edward had been in constant contact with the German ambassadors, Hoesch and then Ribbentrop, approving Germany's remilitarisation of the Rhineland in breach of the Treaty of Versailles, which Hitler used to test the reaction of other countries to his territorial ambitions. Edward had even advised the Germans to proceed, and assured them that Britain would not fight. He was right – no country took any action.

Edward refused to halt his pro-German activities, and he would not budge on the question of his marriage. Wallis encouraged him to go on the radio and appeal to the British people, but Baldwin would not permit it. In the end, Edward told Baldwin that if he could not marry Mrs Simpson and remain king, he would abdicate. And that is what he did, just six weeks short of the 12-month time limit his father had predicted. Edward's brother, Prince Albert, succeeded him as King George VI, and a law was passed excluding Edward's issue from the succession.

Edward became HRH (His Royal Highness) the Duke of Windsor, and he married Wallis in France at the home of a prominent Nazi supporter; at 39 she was by seven years the oldest bride of an English/British king (the average age is 20). The wedding was on 3rd June 1937, George V's birthday – Queen Mary believed it was a deliberate insult. Wallis became the Duchess of Windsor; but she would not be HRH, nor would any children. Edward and Wallis were furious at the denial of HRH for Wallis, and at King George who had banned members of the Royal Family from attending the wedding. The Windsors were also angered by the Government's refusal to grant the Duke an annual payment from the Civil List. Instead, King George agreed to make annual payments out of his entitlement.

The Windsors moved to exile in France. Relations between the two brothers deteriorated when George had to buy Sandringham House and Balmoral Castle from the Duke (they were private properties, not passing with the Crown, and in his will George V had left them to Edward in the belief that he would be crowned king). Even after that, the Duke continued to demand more money from his brother. Friendship came to an end, George believing that Edward had misled him on his wealth and the moneys he had received as Prince of Wales and Duke of Cornwall. In the end, George refused to take the Duke's calls, having warned him that if he ever returned to England uninvited, the annual payments would cease.

From then on, the Windsors never failed to show their dislike of Britain and the British. At the first opportunity, and against the Government's wishes, the Windsors insisted on going to Germany to visit Hitler as his personal guests. It was said that the Duke favoured appeasement towards the growing menace, as did so many. Yet it was much more than appeasement, it was clearly friendship, admiration and support.

After the outbreak of the Second World War, the Duke was appointed Major-General and was attached to the British Military Mission in France. Nevertheless, the Windsors continued to socialise with Nazi supporters. Some people accused the Duke and Wallis of supplying the Nazis with secret information, but nothing was ever proved.

When the Germans invaded France, instead of returning to England with his regiment, the Duke took a car and drove with Wallis to Biarritz, then to the safety of Spain and then to Portugal. Before he left, the Duke asked the Germans to protect his properties in France by stationing soldiers outside them – and the Germans obligingly did so.

In Spain and Portugal, the Windsors continued to consort with Nazi sympathisers. The Duke actually gave an interview in which he forecast a German victory. He also advised all countries to accept 'reorganisation of the order of society' as the Germans had done. Incredibly, he told the German ambassador that continued heavy bombing would make England sue for peace. Prime Minister Churchill was furious.

Churchill wanted the Duke back in England. The Duke was willing to return, but he insisted on several conditions, the main one being that "my wife and myself must not risk finding ourselves once more regarded by the British public as in different status to other members of my family." Churchill (who had been a leading supporter of the Duke during the abdication crisis) had no time for this sort of thing when the nation was fighting for survival. "Your Royal Highness has taken active military rank", he replied, "and refusal to obey direct orders ... would create a serious situation." It seems he was quite prepared to court martial the Duke.

In response, the Duke sent a message indicating that he would settle for a short meeting at which he and the Duchess would be received by the King and Queen, and that notice of the meeting was to be published in the Court Circular. After speaking to King George, who wished to keep his brother out of England at all costs, Churchill decided that the best way to deal with the matter was to send the Duke to the Bahamas as Governor.

Edward accepted the appointment. Then it emerged that he wished to go to the Bahamas via New York. The Foreign Office suspected mischief by the Duchess, and objected. However, the Duke was adamant; they must spend some time in New York first. The Duchess was livid, and she was also angry that they were being forbidden from taking with them as servants two young men of military age.

Churchill was advised that he must treat the Duke as a petulant child, so he allowed him to take one of the servants, but New York was out of the question. The Duke agreed, provided he did not have to sail for a week. Churchill, who was at the time trying to run the war, gave way. Before the Duke sailed, Churchill warned him that, "Many sharp and unfriendly ears will be pricked up to catch any suggestion that your Royal Highness takes a view about the war, or about the Germans, or about Hitlerism, which is different from that adopted by the British nation and Parliament. ... In particular, there will be danger of use being made of anything you say in the United States ..."

After complaints from the ship owners, the Duke did not get his week-long delay. He left, complaining bitterly to Churchill about possessions he had to leave behind.

In the Bahamas (a group of islands separated from each other by shallow water and therefore called by the Spanish after Columbus landed there: the *Baja Mar* – the Shallow Sea), the Windsors continually moaned about living in a 'third class colony'. In case there was any doubt about her feelings, the Duchess said of the British during the Blitz, "I can't say I feel sorry for them". As for the Duke, he did not hold back on his continued contempt for non-white people, saying of one official that "due to the peculiar mentality of this race, they seem unable to rise to prominence without losing their equilibrium". The Duchess was more blunt, calling them "lazy, thriving niggers".

Then the Duke gave an interview to an American journalist in which he described Hitler as a great man, adding that it would be a tragedy for the world if he were overthrown, and advising the US to mediate and not join the Allies. When the interview was published in Britain, Churchill wrote to the Duke cautioning him again and telling him that it "will certainly be interpreted as defeatist and pro-Nazi, and by implication approving of the isolationists' aim to keep America out of the war". This was at a time when Churchill believed that victory over Germany depended on America joining the war.

Many suspect that the Windsors were looking forward to the promised call from Hitler to return to London as king and queen once Britain had been conquered. As the Duke said, "After the war is over and Hitler has crushed the Americans, we'll take over. The British don't want me as king, but I'll be back as their leader." There were no doubts about the Windsors as far as the Americans were concerned. The FBI kept an eye on them, believing that the Duchess had been the mistress (which she denied) of fanatical Nazi Ribbentrop when he had been the German ambassador in London; and now that he was the German foreign minister, she was still in touch with him, passing on classified information obtained from the Duke.

It is alleged that MI5 later retrieved from Germany the correspondence between the Duke and Hitler so as to prevent its disclosure. As late as the mid-fifties, the Duke blamed the war on Anthony Eden for his treatement of Mussolini "and of course Roosevelt and the Jews". Even in the sixties, when all the horrors of the war were known, the Duke said that he did not think that "Hitler was such a bad chap".

Returning to Europe in 1945, the Windsors spent the rest of their lives in France, living tax-free in a house provided for them at nominal rent by the city of Paris and a country home next to their friends, the former British fascist leader Oswald Mosley and his wife. Queen Mary would not meet her daughter-in-law, and other members of the Royal Family refused to receive her formally. However, the Duke did on rare occasions see his family, and in later years so did the Duchess. When George VI died, the Duke came to England for his brother's funeral; the Duchess did not – she had already said on an earlier visit, "I hate this country; I shall hate it to my grave".

The Duke died in 1972, aged 77. Wallis died fourteen years later, and the sales of her jewellery produced over £40 million. Both of them were buried at Windsor. They never had any children.

Amazingly, Edward had seen his great-grandmother as Queen, his grandfather as King, his father as King, himself as King, his brother as King and his niece as Queen. Yet his life was a life of contradictions. Hugely popular, he became hated; a king, he was never crowned[47]; an admirer of the Germans, they nearly killed him; a supporter of the Nazis, but a Nazi supporter tried to assassinate him. Strangest of all, he was the man who was forced to give up the throne because he was head of a church that would not agree to the remarriage of a divorced person while the former spouse was still alive; yet that church was created as a result of Edward's predecessor, Henry VIII, demanding that he should be allowed to remarry while his former spouse was still alive.

As for Wallis, her ruthless ambition endangered the monarchy; but in the long run, unintentionally, she probably did Britain and the monarchy a great favour. Underlined when Hitler's deputy, Albert Speer, said of Edward, "His abdication was a severe loss for us."

****

---

47 One of the three uncrowned monarchs: Jane Grey, Edward V and Edward VIII – some would add Harold Harefoot and Matilda, but Harthacanute (although overseas) and Stephen (although imprisoned) respectively remained king.

GEORGE VI

11 December 1936 – 6 February 1952

George (Albert or Bertie to his family)[48] only realised that the crown might be coming his way three weeks before his brother's abdication, and it was something he did not want.

He had grown up in the shadow of his older brother. More sensitive and more often chastised by his disciplinarian father, George was a nervous child, and by the age of eight he had become burdened with a serious stammer. It did not help that as a left-hander (as was Queen Victoria and as are Prince Charles and Prince William), on his father's instructions he was forced to write with his right hand.

Yet George did not lack determination. Despite being judged the most nervous candidate the examiners had ever seen, George passed the entry examination to naval college at the age of thirteen. But it was just too much for him. In his first year-end examinations, he finished sixty-eighth out of sixty-eight. He did at least excel at sport, particularly as he was allowed to play tennis left-handed.

---

[48] Bizarrely, most recent sovereigns have not adopted as their regnal name the name by which they were known within their family. Victoria was Alexandrina, Edward VII was Bertie, his original heir Albert Victor was Eddie, Edward VIII was David, and George VI was Albert.

The following year, George's examination results improved; he moved up six places. He ploughed on, and in 1913 he became a midshipman and went to sea. George performed his lowly duties manfully, despite suffering from sea-sickness. In the First World War he saw action as a Sub-Lieutenant at the Battle of Jutland. Then, after surgery for a duodenal ulcer, in 1917 George joined the Royal Naval Air Service, which in 1918 became part of the newly-formed RAF. He was stationed in France, although he did not qualify as a pilot until 1919 and was therefore not involved in combat.

Taking up tennis again after the war, George became the RAF doubles champion in 1920, and he played in the men's doubles at Wimbledon six years later, losing in the first round to former champions.

In April 1923, accepted at the third proposal, George married Lady Elizabeth Bowes-Lyon, the ninth child of the Earl and Countess of Strathmore, whom George had met at a dance (coincidentally, her uncle was a former winner of the men's doubles at Wimbledon).

However, despite being the daughter of an earl, Elizabeth was technically a commoner and the marriage was seen as a modernising move[49]. She convinced her husband to consult an Australian speech specialist who did much to reduce George's stuttering through breathing exercises, although it would never be completely cured.

Two daughters were born; Elizabeth in 1926 and Margaret in 1930. Now George was everything his older brother was not: conventional, diligent and humble, a family man. There was a further difference – George had not been brought up to be king. With his weak constitution and his lack of self-confidence, the crown would be a great burden.

His fear showed in his remarks to his cousin, Lord

---

49 The previous marriages of a sovereign to a commoner (Edward IV to Elizabeth Woodville – although her grandfather was a count; James II to Anne Hyde – although her father was an earl; and Edward VIII to Wallis Simpson) had each been followed by the removal of a king.

Mountbatten, "… this is absolutely terrible. I never wanted this to happen, I'm quite unprepared for it. David has been trained for this all his life. I've never even seen a state paper. I'm only a naval officer, it's the only thing I know about." It might have helped if he had known that of the 44 prior English and British monarchs, arguably only fifteen had been brought up to be the sovereign.[50]

The coronation went ahead on the previously arranged date, but with a different king. Albert Frederick Arthur George, known by his first forename took his last forename as his title, unlike his brother who was known by his last forename (David) and had taken his first forename (Edward) as his title. George VI became monarch while his predecessor was still alive, just like eight earlier English sovereigns – it was the same for Edward III, Henry IV, Henry VI, Edward IV, Richard III, Mary and William & Mary.

Prime Minister Baldwin helped to ease George into his position, and he continued to help even after he was succeeded as Prime Minister by Neville Chamberlain in May 1937.

The problems with the monarchy having been resolved, more serious matters needed to be addressed. The ever-growing aggression of Germany was a menace that all could see, but few wished to admit, far less to confront. Anyway, it was thought only fair to allow Germany to rearm.

In the 1930s, it had become accepted that it was not humans but the possession of weapons that was the main cause of war, so disarmament became a policy of all three political parties. When he was Chancellor of the Exchequer, Chamberlain followed that policy, providing smaller and smaller funds for the forces as Prime Minister Baldwin constantly gave out figures understating the extent of Germany's re-armament and overstating British numbers.

Concern at Germany's growing military power was eased because many saw fascist Germany as their champion

50 Henry III, V, VI; Edward I, III, V, VI, VII, VIII; Richard II; Charles II; George II, III, IV; and Victoria.

against communist Russia where Stalin had started his purge of opponents, officers, intellectuals and peasants, with hundreds of thousands being killed and others sent to labour camps, followed by the murder or deportation of ethnic groups and the starvation of millions. On the other hand, many saw communist Russia as the only hope to stop fascists in Germany and Italy, who were supporting Franco's fascists fighting the left-wing Spanish government, then bombing Guernica so as to test the German plan of conquest by terror.

Winston Churchill had been wary of Germany's military ambitions since 1932. Every year saw his warnings get louder. In 1934 he proclaimed that "only a few hours away by air there dwells a nation of nearly 70 million ... who are being taught from childhood to think of war and conquest as a glorious exercise ... a nation which has abandoned all its liberties in order to augment its collective might." However, even in England, it was Churchill not Hitler who was denounced in Parliament and in the press.

Eventually, Chamberlain realised that things had gone too far, and he started to increase spending on the forces to vociferous opposition from the Labour and Liberal parties, who called it disgraceful.

By May 1936, Italy had completed its conquest of Ethiopia after a war in which Italian forces with 595 aircraft and 795 tanks defeated Ethiopian forces with 3 biplanes and 3 tanks, spraying the country with poison gas and murdering over 760,000 people. The conquest was accepted for fear that Italy might otherwise side with Germany. On the other side of the world, Japan launched a full-scale invasion of China.

Then, in March 1938, Germany occupied and annexed Austria, where there was huge support for the Nazis. Within days 70,000 people had been sent to concentration camps. In London, The Times said that it did not differ much from Scotland joining England 200 years earlier.

Nearer home, to Churchill's fury, Chamberlain restored to Ireland three ports over which Britain had retained sovereignty for the use of the navy in order to protect Atlantic shipping, an arrangement that Churchill had negotiated in 1921. Chamberlain accepted Irish Prime Minister de Valera's promise that in the event of war, the British Navy would have access to the ports. Even with the establishment of the Irish state, there was still massive resentment, even hatred, of the English after centuries of conflict. The parliament of Northern Ireland had opted to remain part of the United Kingdom. However, in the south, the Irish were determined that the six Ulster counties should be part of their state. On 28th July 1937, King George and Queen Elizabeth visited Belfast. While they were attending a reception party, a bomb went off in a nearby street. Presumably it had been planted by the Irish Republican Army. Fortunately, no one was hurt.

There is also a story that film star Errol Flynn (born in Australia to parents of mixed Irish/English/Scottish descent) provided most of the $200,000 finance for a joint Nazi/IRA plot to plant a bomb and assassinate the King and Queen as they crossed the Canada/US border on their way from Ontario to Detroit. Although there is no evidence of Flynn financing the plot, he was certainly on friendly terms with a senior Nazi agent to whom he had written, "I do wish we could bring Hitler over here to teach these Isaacs a thing or two." But the FBI bugged the room where the IRA and Nazi operatives were meeting. The IRA operative was arrested and for some reason was charged only with an immigration offence. However, that ended the murder plot.

Back in England, Churchill had few supporters in Parliament as he complained endlessly about Germany's mounting aggression and the inadequacy of British forces. Churchill could be ignored as a maverick, but Chamberlain would not tolerate any opposition to his policies in the Cabinet, and that led to the resignation of the Foreign Secretary, Anthony Eden. He was replaced by Lord Halifax, the man who said in 1936 that the Nazi regime was "absolutely fantastic".[51]

In 1937, Halifax was invited to go shooting in Germany by Hermann Goring. On arriving at a reception, as the super-aristocratic Halifax left the car, without diverting his gaze he held out his coat to the first person on the pavement assuming that he was a footman. A German officer whispered to him: "Der Fuhrer". Hitler was not amused. Halifax recovered the lost ground, commending Hitler for his policies and for keeping communism out of Germany – the communist and socialist leaders had been sent to concentration camps. Perhaps Halifax would have become less effusive about Germany's treatment of those it did not like if (having been born with a withered left arm with the hand missing) he had known of the event some months later when Hitler was told of a disabled baby girl called Sofia Knauer. Hitler ordered his personal physician to kill the child. In January 1939, Hitler extended the order to all disabled infants and then to all disabled adults.

Chamberlain visited Germany three times. The first time, he agreed to Germany's demand to annex the Sudeten area of Czechoslovakia, where most of the people were of German origin, on condition that the Germans negotiated the terms of the annexation with the Czechs. On the second visit, Hitler announced that what had been agreed at the first meeting would not do any more, and that the Sudetenland must be annexed immediately. Chamberlain said it was a matter for Germany and Czechoslovakia.

Next, Chamberlain and French Prime Minister Daladier went to meet Hitler and Mussolini in Munich on 29th September 1938. The Czechs, having no choice, agreed to transfer the Sudetenland, and Chamberlain presented Hitler with a three-paragraph document confirming the desire of Germany and

---

51 In an unsavoury set of connections, Halifax's mistress and confidante Alexandra (daughter of former Viceroy of India Lord Curzon) was married to Edward VIII's best friend and equerry Edward Metcalfe (a fascist supporter), and she was also the sister-in-law and mistress of British fascist leader Oswald Mosley, and for a time the mistress of Mussolini's ambassador in London.

Britain never to go to war again. Both signed. Chamberlain was delighted, announcing: "I've got it!". When Ribbentrop complained, Hitler said, "That piece of paper is of no further significance whatsoever."

The security of the rest of Czechoslovakia was guaranteed by Britain and France. Returning to England with his piece of paper, Chamberlain said that it guaranteed "peace for our time". He also reported Hitler's promise that the Sudetenland was his last territorial demand in Europe. In Parliament, Churchill told Chamberlain, "You were offered the choice between war and dishonour. You chose dishonour, and you will have war." Alfred Duff Cooper resigned as First Lord of the Admiralty. In the vote, only Churchill, Eden, Duff Cooper, Macmillan and about 20 other Conservatives abstained. It was a great success for Chamberlain, and the nation celebrated.

Despite the piece of paper, to vociferous opposition from the Labour and Liberal parties who accused Chamberlain of militarism, efforts were made to re-arm and enlarge the forces, and limited conscription was introduced.

In March 1939, Germany invaded and seized most of the rest of Czechoslovakia. Even now, there was no need to annoy Hitler; as Chancellor of the Exchequer John Simon said of Czechoslovakia, it was impossible to fulfil a guarantee to a country that had ceased to exist. However, Chamberlain and the British people could now see that Munich had been a fraud and that Hitler had been lying all the time.

Of course, Hitler had not finished; in fact, he had barely started. He demanded that Poland hand over the city of Danzig on the Baltic coast together with a coastal strip connecting it with Germany. Chamberlain considered that this was one of Germany's most justified demands; after all, the majority of the people in Danzig were ethnically German. Halifax urged the Poles to transfer the city. As if to underline the way things were going, Franco's fascists won the Spanish Civil War and Mussolini's fascists invaded Albania.

Next, Britain gave guarantees against German aggression

to Greece, Romania, the Netherlands and Denmark. Poland had been happy to seize a piece of Czechoslovakia when the opportunity arose; nevertheless, Britain guaranteed Poland as well, fearing that they might otherwise side with Germany.

Then the great blow came. News arrived that on 24th August the Russians had signed a non-aggression pact with Germany, each promising to remain neutral if the other was at war; and there was also a secret provision agreeing to split Poland between them. Now the Germans could take half of Poland and then turn west to deal with France and Britain – all without having to worry about Russia to the east. It changed the mood in Britain; right-wingers saw that Hitler was not confronting the communists, and left-wingers saw that Russia was not the answer to the fascists.

With Danzig and western Poland the next targets, Hitler wanted to create some justification for the invasion. He decided that it would be in response to Polish aggression. Hitler said of his plan, "Its credibility does not matter. The victor will not be asked whether he told the truth."

On the night of 31st August, German SS operatives in civilian clothes staged assaults in Germany, attacking a customs post at Hochlinden, a forest headquarters in Pitschen and the radio station in Gleiwitz where they broadcast a statement in Polish saying that the station had been seized and was now in Polish hands. Before running away from each of the targets, they left behind the bodies of several prisoners from Dachau concentration camp dressed in Polish uniforms, all of them having been injected with lethal drugs and then shot so that it would look as though they were Polish soldiers who had perished in the attacks.

At 00.40am on 1st September, Hitler signed the order to invade Poland; at 4.45am the invasion began. Concerns expressed by German Generals were dealt with by Hitler saying: "Our enemies are small worms. I saw them at Munich." Later in the day, Hitler broadcast to the nation, complaining of numerous Polish atrocities including three that were "quite serious". The conquest of Poland was speedy, the mass-murder of civilians began on the first day. Soon the Germans had all of western Poland; within three weeks, as agreed, Russia took eastern Poland.

In London, the Cabinet met. Chamberlain and the appeasers still wanted negotiation. Some members of the Cabinet, totally exasperated, refused to leave the room until it had been resolved to send an ultimatum to Germany. In the end Chamberlain and Halifax agreed. At 9am on 3rd September, a two-hour ultimatum to withdraw from Poland was handed over. Of course it was ignored, and at 11am Britain declared war on Germany. France, Australia and New Zealand followed, so did South Africa after some argument with the Boers, and then Canada. No other nations ever declared war on Germany, not even the great powers of the USA and Russia.

It was now impossible to ignore Churchill. Also, if he were in the Government, he could not criticise the Government. After a decade on the backbenches, he was appointed First Lord of the Admiralty. A signal was sent to all naval vessels: "Winston is back".

The British Expeditionary Force was sent to France, although at first there was no fighting. At sea, Britain suffered massive losses from mines, submarines and warships. The situation was made worse when Irish Prime Minister De Valera went back on his promise and refused Britain access to the ports handed over by Chamberlain.

Copying the Germans' staged attacks, on 26th November the Russian Army fired seven shells at the Russian village of Mainila, causing no casualties. Announcing that the Finns had attacked them, the Russians launched an invasion of Finland. They met with stiff resistance and were forced to sign a truce. Russia acquired a tenth of Finland, but in doing so they made Finland an ally of Germany.

Elsewhere on land little was happening in the period of the so-called 'phoney war'. Chamberlain even announced that "Hitler has missed the bus". Then, in April 1940, the Germans invaded Denmark and Norway. Churchill had wanted to send troops to Norway or mine Narvik harbour so as to deprive Germany of the Swedish iron ore they needed for their war machine (the iron ore being exported through Narvik in Norway when the Baltic was frozen). The Prime Minister had vetoed the plan, Halifax declaring that it would be seen as bullying neutrals. Chamberlain, Halifax, Simon and Home Secretary Samuel Hoare were still living in a different world, hoping for a negotiated truce with Germany brokered by Italy, the United States and the Pope.

Troops were hastily landed in Norway. It was too late; although Narvik was briefly captured, the surviving troops had to be withdrawn.

The Norway debate began in the House of Commons on 7th May 1940. Chamberlain's speech was weak and poorly received. Churchill had to speak in support of his colleague, but there were many who had had enough and could say so.

The crushing blow came from Conservative Leo Amery, quoting Cromwell's words to the Rump Parliament in 1653: "You have been sat too long here for any good you have been doing. Depart I say, and let us have done with you. In the name of God, go!"[52]

The vote was put. It was only a motion to adjourn, and the Government won by 81 votes. However, it was treated as a vote of confidence, and the Government's majority of MPs was over 200. A total of 39 Conservatives had voted against their party and more than 60 others had abstained. Chamberlain left the chamber to cries of 'Go!'.

Realising that he might have to resign, on 9th May Chamberlain met with his potential successors, Halifax and Churchill. Halifax had the support of most Conservatives, and

---

52 Paradoxically, Amery's elder son made pro-Nazi broadcasts from Berlin and tried to enlist British POWs to the Nazi cause. He was hanged after the war, one of only two men (the other was Summerset Fox in 1654) ever to have pleaded guilty in England to a charge of treason.

Labour and the Liberals would approve. Taking Chamberlain by surprise, Halifax said that as a lord he could not speak in the House of Commons, and that was unacceptable for a Prime Minister. It was unconvincing reasoning; there were many ways out in times of crisis: the two Houses could have sat together, he could have been an exception, or his peerage could have been suspended. Nevertheless, it was clear that he did not want the job. Very likely, he expected that Britain would soon have to surrender and he did not want to be Prime Minister at such a time; quite possibly he was hoping to become leader after the surrender, or maybe he just believed that Churchill was the right choice. Churchill said nothing. Next, Chamberlain asked the Labour leaders if their party would join a coalition. They agreed to consult their colleagues. That night, the Germans invaded Holland, Belgium and Luxembourg.

The French defensive fortification, the Maginot Line, stretched along the border with Germany, but not the border between France and Belgium. To plug the gap, Churchill had wanted to station British and French troops in Belgium. King Leopold III would only agree if he was promised the restoration of Belgium's African colonies and compensation after the war. As that was being negotiated, Leopold added that anyway, British and French troops could only arrive after Germany had attacked Belgium, as he wished to remain neutral. It was now too late, the German invasion had begun. After three weeks of resistance by the Belgian Army, without consulting his Generals or his ministers, Leopold surrendered and ordered his army to lay down their weapons[53]. The road from Germany to Paris was open; the advance was unstoppable.

With a changed situation, Chamberlain announced that he must stay on. Then, Labour's answer came. They would join a coalition, but not one Labour MP would join so long as Chamberlain was Prime Minister. The Liberals were also against

---

53 When the Allies liberated Belgium, Leopold called it an occupation. Five years after the war, he dared to return to Belgium, but was forced to abdicate.

Chamberlain. All blamed him for weakness and gullibility, when they had opposed even his limited strengthening of the forces.

Chamberlain knew it was over. He went to see the King to offer his resignation. George suggested Halifax as the next Prime Minister, but Chamberlain explained that Halifax was reluctant. So, as a last resort, the best man would have to get the job. In the evening, at the age of 65, Churchill became Prime Minister.

Churchill had been a soldier, journalist and author as well as a politician, and had seen action in India, in Sudan (taking part in the last British cavalry charge), in the Second Boer War and in the First World War. He had switched parties twice, so he was not trusted by the Conservative Party hierarchy, but he was the only man who could unite Parliament and lead the nation.

Taking complete control of the Government and the armed forces, Churchill's energy, brilliance and determination captured Parliament, the people and in time the free world. The King also became an admirer, writing that "I could not have a better Prime Minister". Churchill returned the compliment, judging his relationship with the monarch as being without precedent since the days of Queen Anne and the Duke of Marlborough. It was an appropriate comparison; George was the 6 x great-grandson of Anne's successor King George I, and Churchill was the 6 x great-grandson of Marlborough.

However, even with Churchill at the helm, British forces were thrown back. The sudden Belgian surrender enabled the German advance to accelerate, and the British Expeditionary Force and the French Army were driven on to the beaches near Dunkirk. It was here that 850 naval and merchant vessels, as well as a flotilla of fishing boats, paddle steamers and pleasure craft, crossed the Channel and rescued 224,000 British soldiers and 111,000 French soldiers; but thousands were killed, and all the army's equipment was lost.

The disaster of complete defeat in Europe was somehow turned into a triumph as Britain lived to fight another day.

Churchill was not fooled, wars were not won by evacuations. Britain had not been so vulnerable since 1066.

Certain of which side would win, the Italians joined Germany and declared war on Britain and France. Churchill was not amused: "People who go to Italy to look at ruins won't have to go so far as Naples and Pompeii again." Russia saw another opportunity, and seized Estonia, Latvia and Lithuania. Then northern France surrendered, with southern France being administered by collaborators.

Britain, the dominions and the colonies were now on their own. Nevertheless, Hitler told his Generals that there would be no invasion until the Luftwaffe had air superiority over Britain and the Channel. On 10th July, the Battle of Britain began as the Germans bombed factories, ports and installations. They encountered fierce opposition from the RAF – on 15th August alone, 76 German planes were shot down.

Bomber Command retaliated by bombing Germany. Hitler was furious. Having lost the Battle of Britain despite a numerical superiority of almost five to one over the RAF, the Luftwaffe started to bomb British cities, and the Blitz (from *Blitzkreig*, German for 'lightning war') began. London was bombed every day from 7th September to 2nd November 1940. As a consequence, the factories and airfields had some relief.

The King and Queen stayed in London for much of the time, taking their chance like everyone else, although later they spent their nights and weekends at Windsor. The Foreign Office had advised the King that the royal princesses should be sent to Canada for safety. The Queen replied, "The children will not leave unless I do, I shall not leave unless their father does, and the King will not leave the country in any circumstances."

Now the Luftwaffe sought to kill one of the most symbolic lives amongst its enemies, King George VI, making several attempts to bomb Buckingham Palace. In the first attack, at night, a bomb exploded under the King's study; fortunately he was at Windsor, and there were no casualties.

On 13th September 1940, the King and Queen were at the Palace. They were standing by a window as the Queen was trying to remove an eyelash from her husband's eye. At that moment, they heard the engine noise of a bomber. The King said to the Queen, "Ah, a German". Then there was the scream of a bomb hurtling to the ground. The bomb flew straight past them and exploded in the courtyard, blowing out several windows, with large amounts of smoke and debris being thrown into the air. The royal couple stood transfixed, no time to move. According to the Queen, her knees trembled a bit. Then another bomb crashed through a glass roof, and a third bomb destroyed the chapel, injuring three members of the palace staff. But the attempt to kill the King failed.

King George and Queen Elizabeth surveying the damage to Buckingham Palace

It was not over. Two days later, on the morning of Sunday 15th September, the Germans launched a bombing raid on London from airfields in northern France. One plane, a Dornier Do 17 twin-engine bomber, suffered an engine malfunction and a loss of power. As a result, it fell back from the main formation. However the plane was still airworthy and carrying bombs, so the pilot flew on.

As the Dornier crossed south London, it was attacked by Hurricanes of 310 (Czech) Squadron. The bomber suffered some damage, the gunner was killed and two of the crew bailed out as the pilot, Oberleutnant Robert Zehbe, continued on his own. He saw a solitary building – it was Buckingham Palace. Flying along the Mall, the route from Trafalgar Square to the Palace, Zehbe levelled out to begin his bombing run. At that very moment, the Dornier was spotted by Sergeant Ray Holmes who was piloting a Hawker Hurricane fighter flying towards the bomber.

Holmes decided to make a head-on attack. Once within range, Holmes pressed his machine-gun firing button; nothing happened – he was out of ammunition. The planes were closing at 400 mph.

Realising that the only way to stop the bombing was to ram the Dornier, Holmes climbed and then dived, aiming his plane at the bomber, and sliced off the Dornier's twin-tail with his left wing. Having somersaulted and then dived as the wing tips broke off, the Dornier smashed on to the forecourt of Victoria Station, but not before a bomb had spun out of the plane and exploded in the grounds of the Palace. The injured pilot parachuted to the ground, where he was attacked by an enraged mob, mainly women with kitchen knives. Although rescued by members of the Home Guard, Zehbe died of his injuries the next day. Badly damaged, the Hurricane also went into a dive. Holmes managed to bail out, coming down in Chelsea, but his parachute caught on the guttering of a building leaving him dangling with his feet resting on a dustbin. He was helped down and taken to the

Orange Brewery in Pimlico for a brandy, and after a check-up at Chelsea Barracks he was returned to RAF Hendon in a taxi.

The Dornier crashing

The Hurricane crashed so heavily that the crater was simply filled in and covered up. In 2004, the remains were excavated in Holmes's presence; the machine-gun button was still set to 'FIRE'.

The attacks on Buckingham Palace by Goring's Luftwaffe were somewhat ironic. In the mid-seventeenth century, the owner of the building on the site of Buckingham Palace was, in fact, Lord Goring, and the building was known as Goring House until it burned down in 1674. Probably Hermann never knew.

By coincidence, 15th September became Battle of Britain Day, as the weather over the Channel deteriorated and a turning point was reached. Hitler postponed the invasion indefinitely. Instead, progress was made elsewhere, as Italy invaded Greece, and then Hungary, Slovakia, Romania and Bulgaria joined the fascist powers. The Italian attack on Greece was repulsed, but then the Germans took over and conquered both Greece and Yugoslavia.

The relentless bombing of British cities and factories continued well into 1941. However, it became increasingly costly for the Luftwaffe, and there was little strategic benefit. So Hitler turned his attention to the East. On 22nd June 1941, the German Army began its march into Russia, eventually penetrating 1,000 miles, murdering millions of civilians as they advanced. Churchill said: "We are in the presence of a crime without a name."

Britain had won the battle for survival, yet Churchill knew that the army had to be held back from continental Europe until America joined the war. The problem was that although there were many American supporters of Britain's cause, including President Roosevelt, the vast majority of the people and of Congress opposed any involvement. It was as much as Roosevelt could do to provide ships, weapons and supplies, even in return for payment and territory.

The Germans actually hoped that their invasion of Russia might gain them support in the United States. However, the torpedoing by German submarines of British ships carrying American passengers, and even of some American ships, put paid to that hope. September saw a change in the American attitude as Roosevelt threatened German and Italian vessels entering American waters: "When you see a rattlesnake poised to strike, you do not wait until he has struck before you crush him."

Despite the fine words, America did indeed wait until the rattlesnake struck. When Japan occupied French Indo-China in mid-1941, America, Britain and colonial Holland (controlling East Indies oil) imposed economic sanctions. In response, on 7th December 1941 Japanese aircraft attacked the US fleet at Pearl Harbor in Hawaii, the Japanese hoping to cripple the American Navy so that they could seize territories and oil wherever they wished in the Far East. On the same day, Japan invaded British-ruled Malaya; Britain re-acted immediately, declaring war on Japan before the US did. In the US, a declaration of war could only be made by Congress, so it had to wait until after the Senate and House of Representatives had been addressed by the President.[54]

The British fear was that America might go to war with Japan, and remain neutral as regards Germany. Three days later, supporting their ally, Germany and Italy declared war on the United States. Now there was hope. Mercifully, at the time of the attack on Pearl Harbor the American aircraft carriers had been at sea, and devastating as the attack was, the US Navy with its carriers and submarines was still a force in the Pacific. However, the Japanese were now able to extend their conquests in the Far East, capturing Hong Kong, Singapore, Burma, Thailand, Malaya and the Philippines.

At last, in 1942 the momentum changed. The Americans went on to the attack in the Pacific, winning the critical Battle of Midway, and the Russians halted and then reversed the German advance. In North Africa, the British Eighth Army defeated the Germans and Italians at El Alamein; now the Germans would not gain access to Middle East oil fields.

In February 1943, despite suffering two million casualties, the Russians defeated the German Army at Stalingrad, taking over 100,000 prisoners including 22 Generals and a Field Marshall. May 1943 saw the Germans surrender in North Africa. Next, Sicily fell to the Allies who soon started to make their way through Italy, and before long Mussolini was deposed. The Italian fascists surrendered, and Italy changed sides; although German troops in Italy continued to resist.

The big question for the Allies was where the second front was to be established. Stalin, Roosevelt and Churchill met in Teheran. Stalin had refused to attend the earlier conference in Cairo saying it was because Chinese anti-Communist leader Chiang Kai-shek was attending. Really it was because Stalin

---

[54] Fearing a Japanese assassination attempt during the President's journey from the White House to the Capitol, efforts were made to acquire a bullet-proof car. It was impossible, because federal law limited the price of the President's car to $750. The Treasury came to the rescue, providing a car that had been confiscated after the arrest of a gangster; so President Roosevelt rode to the Capitol in Al Capone's 1928 Cadillac with its 3,000 lbs of armour, bullet-proof glass, police radio receiver, and false police siren.

was afraid of flying. Now, swaggering with Russian victories, he was eager to come to Teheran – the only time he ever flew. The Americans wanted to attack the Germans from the west, through northern France, with the Russians continuing to attack from the east. Stalin quickly agreed this with the Americans; he was content to leave France and the Low Countries to the Americans and British while the Russian Army conquered eastern Europe. Churchill was not happy. He wanted the American and British forces to attack through the Balkans, link up with the Russians and attack the Germans from the south and the east. Churchill did not want to allow Russia to seize the whole of eastern Europe.

However, Roosevelt was suspicious of Churchill's motives, believing him to be eager to protect British territories in the Middle East and India, when one of America's war ambitions was to see to the break-up of all colonial empires. So the American plan was accepted, and it was also agreed that east Poland would be transferred to Russia and that the Russians would set up governments in eastern European countries and in the Baltic states.

All available resources were now put into Operation Overlord – the Normandy landings. At great cost in lives, on 6th June 1944 the joint force of Americans, British, Canadians and allies landed in northern France, securing beachheads and then moving inland. A British memorial was erected in Bayeux reading: "We, once conquered by William, have now set free the Conqueror's native land". In August, Paris was liberated, and in the east, Romania surrendered to the Russians. The war was going to be won, but not for another year.

In early 1945, the three allied leaders met again, this time in Yalta on the north coast of the Black Sea, to debate the future of Europe. Stalin demanded that Russia must have its own 'sphere of influence'. Churchill told Roosevelt that Communist Russia was the next threat to the free world. But Roosevelt trusted Stalin. When warned by one of his advisers, Roosevelt said, "I just have a hunch that Stalin is not that kind of man …

if I give him everything ... he won't try to annex anything and will work with me for a world of democracy and peace." Not a very good hunch.

The leaders agreed that they would accept nothing but the unconditional surrender of Germany plus reparations, and that Poland would be re-created but would have a communist government. Also, ethnic Germans living in Poland and Czechoslovakia were to be transferred to Germany so as to remove the excuse for the future.

As the Russians moved west, the British and American forces in France had their advance slowed by stiff German resistance and counter-attacks, finally meeting the Russians on the River Elbe to the south of Berlin on 25th April 1945. It was much further west than anticipated, and it left the Russians with the countries they wanted plus half of Germany.

Mussolini tried to escape to Switzerland, but he was caught by Italian partisans and executed. Hitler committed suicide, and on 8th May 1945 Germany surrendered unconditionally. The war in Europe was over.

Churchill told cheering crowds in Whitehall: "This is *your* victory!" They shouted back: "No, it is *yours*." He had borne the weight of the war for years, had carried the country and driven the free world to victory. It was an incredible physical and mental effort. No other person could have done what he did.

In the East, the war against Japan continued. The Americans gave the Japanese an ultimatum to surrender or meet with utter destruction. The ultimatum was ignored. War with Japan ended after the nuclear attacks on Hiroshima and Nagasaki in August.

The Second World War had cost the United Kingdom, France and the USA half a million lives each, six million were murdered in the Holocaust (so over 97% of the victims were from outside Germany), up to twenty million Russians were killed, and so were many millions more in other countries, particularly in the Far East – in total, over 2.5% of the world's population.

In settling affairs at the end of the war, the American leadership was concerned to ensure the end of the old colonial empires; in their place came a new colonial empire. At a speech in Fulton, Missouri, Churchill declared that an Iron Curtain had descended across Europe. The Cold War had begun: a situation of tension without direct military action; the Soviet Union and its satellites and allies on one side, and the US and its western allies on the other side.

With peace came a general election. Churchill and the Conservatives were defeated, and Labour took power under Prime Minister Clement Attlee. The new government proceeded with its manifesto promises of nationalising the coal mines, road and rail transport, gas, electricity and the Bank of England, and creating the National Health Service. The Lords opposed iron and steel nationalisation, so the Lords' delaying power was reduced from two years to one.

The post-war years were a time of economic collapse. Britain found itself with crippling debts, an overvalued pound and a decline in exports. Taxes were raised, bread was rationed and there was a coal shortage. Ireland finally cut all ties, and India gained independence; the Empire became the Commonwealth – the King was no longer Emperor.

In all the gloom, there was cause for celebration in November 1947 when Princess Elizabeth married the exiled Prince Philip of Greece and Denmark, her third cousin (they were both great-great-grandchildren of Queen Victoria), who was at the time a Lieutenant in the Royal Navy.

The 1950 election saw Labour's overall majority reduced to eight. Attlee was forced to call another election in 1951, and the Conservatives under Churchill took over. Both governments had to deal with the Korean War of 1950-53, which saw the communist north invade the south, western forces and the United Nations push them back into the north, Chinese troops advance into the south, only to be driven back, and after a stalemate a truce confirming the division of the country very much as it was when the war began.

By now, King George was ill; he had already had an operation for arterio-sclerosis in 1949. In mid-1951, he became increasingly weak. He had lived all his life under strain with his education, the crown, the war and then the economic downturn. In addition to all that, George was a heavy smoker. At the back of Buckingham Palace, outside the King's bedroom, there were flagstones upon flagstones, so to reduce the noise of their marching, the guards wore bedroom slippers at night rather than boots. At Windsor Castle (now the largest and oldest occupied castle in the world) in the years after the war, they provided an additional service. The Queen had tried to limit her husband's smoking. So, the sentries at the back of the gardens were each required to have a pack of cigarettes available for the King, who (when his wife was not around) would approach one of them asking, "I don't suppose there's any chance of a gasper?"

In September cancer was diagnosed and a lung was removed, but the tumour was malignant. Weak and grey, George insisted on going to London Airport on 31st January 1952 to see off Princess Elizabeth and her husband, now the Duke of Edinburgh, who were going on a short tour of East Africa before flying on to Australia.

On 5th February, King George went shooting at Sandringham. During the night he died, aged only 56 – the youngest British monarch to die since Queen Anne in 1714. He had been a hard-working sovereign, admired by his people, and he repaired much of the damage to the monarchy caused by his predecessors, struggling throughout against personal and national problems. Churchill's wreath bore a card reading simply: 'For valour' – the inscription on the Victoria Cross.

The last Emperor of India. Cigarettes and strain succeeded where the Luftwaffe had failed.

****

EDWARD VII to ELIZABETH II

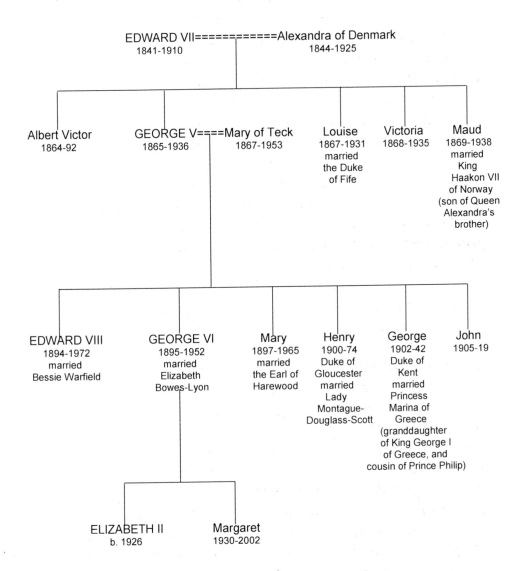

EDWARD VII=============Alexandra of Denmark
1841-1910   1844-1925

Albert Victor
1864-92

GEORGE V====Mary of Teck
1865-1936   1867-1953

Louise
1867-1931
married
the Duke
of Fife

Victoria
1868-1935

Maud
1869-1938
married
King
Haakon VII
of Norway
(son of Queen
Alexandra's
brother)

EDWARD VIII
1894-1972
married
Bessie Warfield

GEORGE VI
1895-1952
married
Elizabeth
Bowes-Lyon

Mary
1897-1965
married
the Earl of
Harewood

Henry
1900-74
Duke of
Gloucester
married
Lady
Montague-
Douglass-Scott

George
1902-42
Duke of
Kent
married
Princess
Marina of
Greece
(granddaughter
of King George I
of Greece, and
cousin of Prince Philip)

John
1905-19

ELIZABETH II
b. 1926

Margaret
1930-2002

ELIZABETH II

since 6 February 1952

Born at her maternal grandparents' home in Mayfair, London, Elizabeth was the first child of the Duke and Duchess of York. There was little expectation of the crown until her uncle Edward VIII abdicated ten years later. Even after her father became King George VI, there was a chance that Elizabeth would not be his successor – if the King and Queen had a son, he would take precedence.

Towards the end of the Second World War, having been forbidden to volunteer as a nurse in bombed areas, at the age of eighteen Elizabeth joined the Women's Auxiliary Territorial Service as Second Subaltern Elizabeth Windsor. Here she trained as a driver and mechanic, although she has apparently never obtained a driving licence.

By this time, Elizabeth had fallen in love with a young man she had met some years earlier, and in 1947 she married Prince Philip of Greece and Denmark.

After Greece won independence in 1832, Prince Otto of Bavaria was appointed king, but he was deposed and exiled in 1862. In a vote of 240,000 to decide who should be the new

THE CONNECTIONS BETWEEN QUEEN ELIZABETH II
AND PRINCE PHILIP
(with relevant issue only)

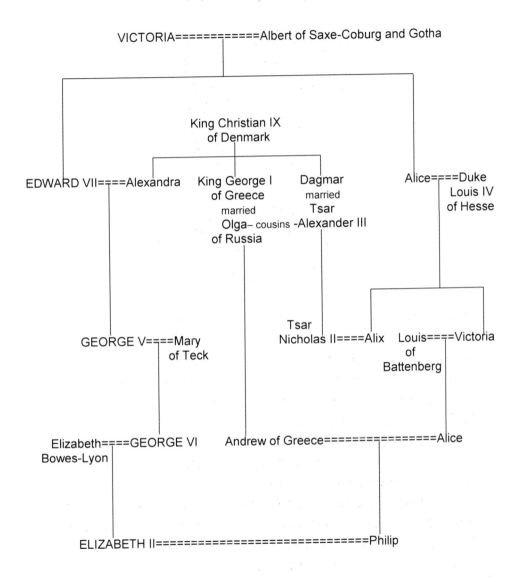

Queen Elizabeth II and Prince Philip are (through Victoria) third cousins; and are (through Christian) second cousins once removed.

king, Queen Victoria's son Alfred received 95% of the votes, only one person voted for ex-King Otto. However, Victoria would not allow Alfred to take the Greek crown, as he was destined for the rule of Saxe-Coburg and Gotha. So the Greek parliament elected as their new king the 17-year-old Prince William of Denmark, second son of future King Christian IX.

William took the Greek crown as King George. He was assassinated by an anarchist in 1913, and his son Constantine became king. In the First World War the Greek government wished to support the Triple Powers (Britain, France and Russia), whilst King Constantine was pro-German and wanted Greece to remain neutral. So Constantine was forced to abdicate in favour of his second son, Alexander (Constantine's first son, George, was pro-German and unacceptable).

After the war, when King Alexander was taking a walk, his dog was attacked by a monkey. Alexander went to the dog's assistance, and was bitten by the monkey. The monkey's mate then came to its aid, and it also bit Alexander, causing a deep wound. Both monkeys were diseased, and King Alexander died a few days later. Constantine returned as king. After an unsuccessful war against Turkey in 1922, the army revolted and Constantine was deposed again, this time succeeded by his first son who became King George II. In the fury of defeat, many political and military leaders were arrested, and some were executed. One of those put on trial was Constantine's brother, Prince Andrew, who was accused of disobeying orders. He was convicted and banished. However, there were fears for his life. Andrew was Queen Alexandra's nephew, and his wife Princess Alice of Battenberg was a great-granddaughter of Queen Victoria, so Britain sent a cruiser to rescue them and their family including Philip their one-year-old son.

Philip's older sisters all married German noblemen and went to live in Germany. He eventually went to school in England under the eye of his uncle, Earl Mountbatten. In 1933, Philip was sent to secondary school at Schule Schloss Salem in Germany, part-owned by one of his brothers-in-law. The Schule Schloss

Salem was one of the finest schools in Europe, scholastic and also teaching social skills, community duties and diversity. The other part-owner was the headmaster, Kurt Hahn, and he was Jewish. Hahn was seized by the Nazis, but on the intervention of Ramsay MacDonald he was released from prison and allowed to flee to Scotland. He then founded Gordonstoun School, which in due course acquired the reputation of Hahn's first school. A little later, Philip followed his former headmaster to Scotland to complete his education. If it were not for those circumstances, Philip might have remained in Germany like his sisters.

Philip left Gordonstoun in 1939, and he joined the Royal Navy, serving throughout the Second World War. Once engaged to Princess Elizabeth, in the post-war anti-foreigner mood, Philip was advised by Earl Mountbatten to give up his Greek and Danish titles, to renounce his allegiance to the Greek crown (his cousin, Paul, was now king), to take British citizenship and to convert from Greek Orthodox to Church of England. He did all of those things, and then discovered that he did not have a surname, the name of his House (Schleswig-Holstein-Sonderburg-Glucksburg) not being the same thing as a surname.

The solution was simple. Philip's mother was a Battenberg, so like his uncle's family Philip adopted the English version of that name: 'Mountbatten'. The wedding took place on 20th November 1947. As Philip was no longer a prince, he was given the title of Duke of Edinburgh. He was made Prince of the United Kingdom ten years later. Philip's German relations, including his sisters and brothers-in-law, were not invited to the wedding. They had all supported Germany during the war, most were Nazis, and one brother-in-law had been an officer in the SS.[55]

It was while Elizabeth was in Kenya with Philip that she learned of the death of her father. When asked what her regnal name would be, Elizabeth responded, "My own, of course – what else?" Elizabeth was crowned Elizabeth II on 2nd June 1953.

---

55 Philip's mother, however, is buried in Israel and honoured as Righteous among the Nations.

The coronation of Queen Elizabeth II

The Queen is wearing St Edward's Crown. It is named after Edward the Confessor's crown, used to crown later monarchs until it was lost by King John in the Wash. Its replacement was destroyed in the Civil War. The present crown was created for the coronation of Charles II, and used to crown all subsequent monarchs other than the small Victoria and the aged Edward VII, who found it too heavy (2.2kg). Jewels for the crown were hired for each coronation and then returned, until in 1911 permanent jewels were affixed.

On other formal occasions, the Imperial State Crown is worn (see the front cover). It was made in 1937 and contains 2,868 diamonds, 273 pearls, 17 sapphires, 11 emeralds and 5 rubies.

One of the diamonds is the Cullinan II. The Cullinan was the largest rough gem-quality diamond ever found, at 3,106.75 carats (621.35g). The other part, the Cullinan I, is in the Sceptre.

The large ruby at the front of the Imperial State Crown is the Black Prince's Ruby. It was obtained by the Black Prince in the fourteenth century as a reward for assisting Don Pedro of Castile to defeat a revolt led by his illegitimate brother. Don Pedro had stolen the ruby from the body of Abu Said, the Moorish Prince of Grenada, after murdering him.

Henry V wore the ruby in the crown on his helmet at Agincourt, as did Richard III in his desperate attack against Henry Tudor at Bosworth.

In Scotland there was anger at the name 'Elizabeth II'. The Scots complained that Elizabeth I had not been Queen of Scotland, so the current Queen is the first Scottish Elizabeth. As a compromise, it was announced that in future all monarchs will take either their English number or their Scottish number, whichever is the higher. Fortunately, going back to the union in 1707, no numbers would have been different.

Next, the question of the royal surname arose. It was a matter that had interested Queen Victoria. She had asked for an investigation, and the result was that having married Prince Albert, the Royal House was Saxe-Coburg and Gotha and the surname was Wettin. The duchies of Saxe-Coburg and Saxe-Gotha[56] were held by the Wettin dynasty, the rulers of much of Saxony for centuries, and they took their family name in about the year 1000 from the Castle of Wettin when they captured it from the Slavs.

During the First World War, George V issued a royal proclamation changing the name of the Royal House and the Royal Family to Windsor. That dealt with both House and surname.

By the time of his marriage, Philip had renounced his titles, yet he was still a member of his House, and he had taken the surname of Mountbatten. In 1952, the Queen declared that the Royal House name and the Royal Family name would continue as Windsor, despite her marriage. Philip's reaction was to say that, "I am nothing but a bloody amoeba. I am the only man in the country not allowed to give his name to his own children." There would be four children: Charles, Anne, Andrew and Edward.

In 1960 there was a slight concession, when it was proclaimed that those of the Queen's descendants who are not princes or princesses would have the surname Mountbatten-Windsor. In practice it works the other way round; the Queen's sons use the name Mountbatten-Windsor despite being princes, and the

---

56 So it is not (i) Saxe-Coburg and (ii) Gotha. Rather it is (i) Saxe-Coburg and (ii) Saxe-Gotha, contracted to Saxe (Coburg and Gotha).

grandchildren use their parents' title name as a surname, thus: Wales, York, Wessex, etc.

As to the House, the Queen's children are members of the House of Schleswig-Holstein-Sonderburg-Glucksburg and also of the House of Windsor, which is a branch of the House of Saxe-Coburg and Gotha.

The Queen is also the Queen of 15 other Commonwealth countries, and holds various other titles. Not the least are Duke of Lancaster and Duke of Normandy. Mainland Normandy is now part of France; the Duchy of Normandy comprises the Channel Islands (not part of the United Kingdom, but a crown dependency of the British monarch), where the loyal toast is "*La Reine, notre Duc*". Linking the two historic enemies, the Queen is the 27 x great-granddaughter of William the Conqueror and the 29 x great-granddaughter of Harold.

For Britain, the remainder of the Fifties saw the end of food rationing, the start of independence for British colonies, the end of the Korean War, the retirement of Prime Minister Winston Churchill in 1955 and his replacement by Anthony Eden, and the Suez Crisis when Egypt seized the Suez Canal and Britain, France and Israel invaded, but America (still in its anti-colonialist mood) took Egypt's side and despite military success, Britain and its allies had to withdraw. Prime Minister Eden was replaced by Harold Macmillan in 1957, and 1958 saw the introduction of life peerages and consequently the right of women to sit in the House of Lords.

The Sixties witnessed the end of conscription, further independences for British colonies and a resurgence of British success and influence in popular music, fashion and theatre. In 1963, Prime Minister Macmillan was replaced by Alec Douglas Home (he was Neville Chamberlain's private secretary at Munich, and followed the premierships of three of Chamberlain's Conservative opponents). In 1964, Labour won the general election and Harold Wilson became Prime Minister. The following year, Sir Winston Churchill died on 24th January, the 70th anniversary of his father's death.

In August 1969, in Londonderry in Northern Ireland, after a Protestant march celebrating the failure of James II's siege of the city in 1689, serious fighting broke out between Catholics and Protestants. British troops were sent to keep order, but the rioting spread to Belfast and led to several deaths. Within a short time, the Provisional IRA had split away from the Irish Republican Army, intent on ending British rule in Northern Ireland. Now the 'Troubles' began, leading to decades of shootings, bombings and murders in Northern Ireland and England.

Despite this new eruption of violence, after a reign of nearly 20 years, Elizabeth had apparently still not been struck by the royal curse. However, a recent revelation by an Australian former police officer suggests that the curse did indeed strike. In the spring of 1970, the Queen and Prince Philip were on a tour of Australia. On 29th April, they were travelling by train from Sydney across the Great Dividing Range of mountains. It is claimed that assassins, possibly IRA sympathisers, possibly anti-monarchists, decided to kill the royal couple. Whoever it was, they took a large log and placed it on the rail track not far from Lithgow Station, intending that the royal train would hit the log and be derailed, killing the passengers.

The royal train was heading for Orange, where the Queen and Prince Philip were to spend the night. Two hours out from Sydney, going through a winding cutting just before Lithgow, the train struck the log. Fortunately, the train was travelling very slowly, far slower than expected. So, instead of toppling off the track and into the embankment, the engine continued with the log trapped under its front wheels. It still took over 700 yards before the train came to a complete halt. The story is that the Queen was unaware of the incident, and the embarrassed authorities hushed the matter up.

In Britain, the Seventies was a time of increased political awareness, protest, terrorism and completion of the cycle of independence for nearly all colonies as the country looked towards Europe. In 1970, the Conservatives returned to power with Edward Heath as Prime Minister, 1971 saw decimalisation of the currency and measurements and the death of the Duke of Windsor (leaving no children, so even without the abdication Elizabeth would have succeeded as his niece); and in 1973, the United Kingdom joined the European Economic Community. In 1974, Labour led by Harold Wilson won the election, Wilson retiring in favour of James Callaghan in 1976; then the Conservatives took over in 1979 under Margaret Thatcher. The entire decade was marked by constant violence in Northern Ireland and IRA bombings in England, as well as the assassination of Earl Mountbatten.

The Trooping the Colour ceremony repeats the practice begun in the seventeenth century of parading in front of infantry regiments their colours or flags before battle so that the soldiers would recognise the flag, either to follow it in attack or to head for it as a rallying point. The Royal Artillery carries its colours on its guns, the rifle regiments on their drums, so they do not troop colours. For over 200 years, the ceremony has taken place in London on the monarch's official birthday (a date chosen to coincide with the probability of fine weather) when one of the five Foot Guards regiments troops its colours in the presence of the sovereign.

On 13th June 1981, the annual ceremony began. Seventeen-year-old Marcus Sarjeant joined the crowds, standing at the junction of the Mall and Horseguards Avenue. As the Queen rode by on her horse, Sarjeant drew a pistol and fired six shots. The Queen's horse was startled, but the Queen kept it under control. The shots were blanks. Sarjeant was arrested and taken away, saying that he wanted to be famous.

Sarjeant had been a military fanatic at school, and was fascinated by assassinations. He had left the Royal Marines after three months, after which he tried to enlist in the army, quitting after two days of the induction course. Following that, he failed in his attempts to join the police force and the fire service. He later became a member of an anti-royalist group. A note found in his home, where he lived with his mother, read: "I am going to stun and mystify the world. I will become the most famous teenager in the world."

Marcus Sarjeant aiming at the Queen

At his trial under the 1842 Treason Act, Sarjeant's story emerged. He had taken his father's .455 revolver, but was unable to find any ammunition for it. Then, having failed in an attempt to obtain a gun licence, he bought two starting pistols by mail order. Next, Sarjeant wrote letters to two magazines, one with a photograph of himself holding his father's revolver. He also sent an assassination warning to Buckingham Palace; it arrived three days after the incident.

The judge said that Sarjeant carried out a fantasy assassination only because he had been unable to carry out a real one, adding that nonetheless he would be sentenced for what he had done rather than what he would have preferred to have done. Sarjeant was sentenced to five years' imprisonment. After three years, spent mainly in a psychiatric ward, he was released. He changed his name and started a new life. Several

Marcus Sarjeant

years later he was admitted to a psychiatric hospital with a psychotic illness, suffering from religious delusions.

In the autumn of that year, the Queen attended the Commonwealth Prime Ministers Conference in Australia, and then she went on a short visit to New Zealand. On 14th October 1981, the Queen went on a walkabout in Dunedin. Waiting for her was 17-year-old Christopher John Lewis. Still at school, Lewis had set up a small fascist group that he called the National Imperial Guerrilla Army, made up of some of his schoolmates. He already had two convictions for theft, but neither of them had resulted in a sentence of imprisonment.

Lewis stole seven rifles, five pistols, four guns and ammunition. On 9th October, Lewis and two of his friends put on black outfits and held up a post office during their lunch break. They made off with $5,000, and cycled back to school. Five days later, Lewis wrapped up one of the stolen rifles in a pair of old jeans, and went to the steps of the Mission Building in Dunedin. Lewis judged that this would give him a clear shot at the Queen. But just as he was taking his rifle out of its wrapping, two policemen arrived and stood in front of him. Furious at having his carefully-prepared plan upset, Lewis charged off, and in his anger he raised the rifle and fired a shot along the street in the direction from which the Queen's party was approaching. It was too early, the Queen was out of range.

Christopher John Lewis

Most people thought that the noise came from a car backfiring, and Lewis escaped. Several days afterwards, one of Lewis's friends was spotted by the police wearing the black flak jacket he had worn at the post office robbery. He was arrested, and he disclosed the names of his colleagues. Once in custody, Lewis was only too happy to boast that he had tried to assassinate the Queen on her walkabout on 14th October. He was sentenced to eight and a half years in prison for robbery, unlawful possession of firearms and discharging a firearm near a public dwelling. Lewis escaped from prison, but was later recaptured. After release, he spent most of the following years committing offences and receiving short prison sentences.

However, when the Queen returned to New Zealand 14 years later for a further Commonwealth Prime Ministers Conference, Lewis was no longer in prison. As a precautionary measure, the New Zealand police (who had been advised that Lewis was a dangerous psychopath) sent him on an all expenses paid holiday to the Great Barrier Island, 62 miles out to sea.

It was a wise move. In the following year, Lewis was arrested for the murder of a young woman. The accusation was that he hit her on the head with a hammer when trying to kidnap her daughter, intending to hold her for ransom. It was alleged that having hit the woman too hard, he hit her again and again until she was dead. Whilst in prison awaiting trial, Lewis wrapped a wet cloth round his head, and then took the power supply lead from the television in his cell and attached it to his temples, electrocuting himself. He left a suicide note denying his guilt of the murder, and indeed his former cellmate (who may have informed on Lewis and whom Lewis blamed for the murder of the young woman) killed another young woman with a hammer two years later.

And since 1981, nothing.

Perhaps, hopefully, on 14th October 1981, one thousand years after the birth in 981 of Canute, the first King of all England, the 1,000 year curse finally came to an end.

The Queen in 1982 – the curse is over

****

Appendix A

The Jacobite succession

If it were not for the flight of James II and the subsequent exclusion of Catholics and those married to Catholics, his successors would have been the kings and queens of England and Scotland, then Great Britain and then the United Kingdom. Instead, they have been 'pretenders'; although Jacobite supporters have always been at pains to point out that the word 'pretender' has no connection with pretence or falsity. Rather, it is derived from the French word *pretendre* meaning 'to claim as a right', so that a 'pretender' is a 'claimant'.

James II died on 16th September 1701. He had four legitimate children: Mary, Anne, James and Louisa. On James II's death, his heir was his son James Stuart (the Old Pretender). James Stuart died in 1766, leaving two children: Charles (Bonnie Prince Charlie) and Henry. Charles therefore became the Young Pretender. He died in 1788, leaving no legitimate issue.

Charles's brother, Henry, then became the Jacobite claimant, the third Pretender. He was a cardinal, and died without issue in 1807.

To find the next pretender, it was therefore necessary to go back to James II's daughters. However, all three had already died leaving no issue: Mary (1694), Anne (1714) and Louisa (1692).

So it became necessary to go back one stage further, to James II's siblings, the six other children of Charles I. Charles II had died in 1685, leaving no legitimate issue. Mary had died in 1660, leaving a son, William of Orange (later King of England),

and he had died in 1702 leaving no issue. Elizabeth, Anne and Henry had also died leaving no issue. That left only Henrietta (Minette). Minette had died in 1670; she left legitimate issue, and it is through her that the Jacobite claim runs.

Minette was survived by two daughters: Marie and Anne. Her heir was therefore the older daughter, Marie. She married King Charles II of Spain, but she had died without issue in 1689. So, her sister Anne became the heir. Anne married King Victor Amadeus II of Sardinia. She had died in 1728, and she had four children who survived infancy: Maria Adelaide, Maria Luisa, Victor Amadeus and Charles Emmanuel. The oldest son, Victor Amadeus, had died in 1715 leaving no issue. Anne's heir was therefore her second son, King Charles Emmanuel III of Sardinia.

But King Charles Emmanuel III had died in 1773. He left as his heir his first son, King Victor Amadeus III of Sardinia, and he had died in 1796. However, he left as his heir his first son, King Charles Emmanuel IV of Sardinia. It was King Charles Emmanuel IV of Sardinia who, but for the exclusion, should have become King of Great Britain when Cardinal Henry died in 1807, being Cardinal Henry's second cousin twice removed. He became the fourth Pretender.

King Charles Emmanuel IV died in 1819 without issue. He was therefore succeeded as pretender by his brother King Victor Emmanuel I of Sardinia (the fifth Pretender). He died in 1824, and was succeeded by his oldest daughter Maria Beatrice, and she became the sixth Pretender. She married her uncle, Archduke Francis of Austria-Este, who later became Duke of Modena (a bloody tyrant, he was grandson of Empress Maria Theresa of Austria and head of the House of Habsburg).[57]

---

57 He was the 5 x great-grandson of John Frederick, the uncle of George I. See footnote on page 298.

Maria Beatrice died in 1840, and she was succeeded as pretender by her son, Duke Francis V of Modena (the seventh Pretender). He died without issue in 1875. Next in line was his brother Ferdinand, but he had died in 1849. However, Ferdinand had married Archduchess Elisabeth of Austria and he left one child, a daughter, Maria Theresa of Austria-Este. She succeeded her uncle Duke Francis V as the Jacobite claimant – she became the eighth Pretender.

Maria Theresa married Prince Ludwig of Bavaria, who became King Ludwig III in 1913. He was deposed in 1918. When ex-Queen Maria Theresa of Bavaria died in 1919, she was succeeded by her first son, Crown Prince Rupprecht of Bavaria – a German Field Marshall in the First World War. Rupprecht became the ninth Pretender.

Having fallen out with the Nazis, Rupprecht went to live in Italy. His son, Albrecht, was an anti-Nazi. Albrecht took his mother and the rest of the family to his estate in Hungary. But Hungary joined the Nazis, and before long Albrecht, his mother (Rupprecht's wife) and the rest of the family were arrested and sent to Sachsenhausen concentration camp and then to Dachau. They survived the war, although Rupprecht's wife never recovered, and she refused to return to Germany, dying several years later in Switzerland.

Rupprecht died in 1955, and was succeeded by his son, Duke Albrecht of Bavaria, who became the tenth Pretender. Duke Albrecht died in 1996, and he was succeeded by his son, Duke Franz of Bavaria, great-grandson of the last king of Bavaria and claimant to its throne.

Duke Franz (the eleventh Pretender) lives in an apartment in the Nymphenburg Palace in Munich, the former summer residence of the kings of Bavaria. But for the Catholic exclusion, Duke Franz would today be King of the United Kingdom. He is the present Jacobite Pretender, the eleventh cousin of Queen Elizabeth II.

Duke Franz of Bavaria

Duke Franz has never married. His heir is his brother, Max Duke in Bavaria. Max married the Swedish Countess Elisabeth Douglas, a descendant of Robert Douglas, a Scotsman who became a senior officer in the Swedish Army (his grandfather was one of Riccio's murderers – see Elizabeth I). They have five daughters, and Max's heir is the oldest daughter, Sophie, who married Alois the Hereditary Prince of Liechtenstein, the present regent and heir to the princedom of Liechtenstein; his father, multi-billionaire Prince Hans-Adam[58], is Europe's wealthiest monarch.

Their first son, Prince Joseph Wenzel Maximilian Maria of Liechtenstein is therefore the ultimate heir to the throne of Liechtenstein and (but for the exclusion) to the throne of the United Kingdom. Conveniently, if he succeeds to both thrones, only one national anthem would have to be played.

---

58 Prince Hans-Adam's full name is Johannes Adam Ferdinand Alois Josef Maria Marco d'Aviano Pius von und zu Liechtenstein; so he is named after the alleged inventor of the capuccino (see page 300).

Prince Joseph Wenzel was born in 1995 at the Portland Hospital in London (also the birthplace of Queen Elizabeth II's granddaughters Beatrice and Eugenie), and presently attends Malvern College in Worcestershire[59]. He will be the first pretender to be born in England since James II fled the country in 1688.

However, since the death of Cardinal Henry, no Jacobite pretenders have publicly claimed the throne.

Prince Joseph Wenzel

****

---

59 The school was formerly attended by Prince Ernest Augustus, the heir of the House of Hanover, the House that took the throne from the House of Stuart of which Prince Joseph Wenzel is the heir.

THE JACOBITE SUCCESSION
(with Jacobite claimed regnal names listed alongside the Hanoverian line)

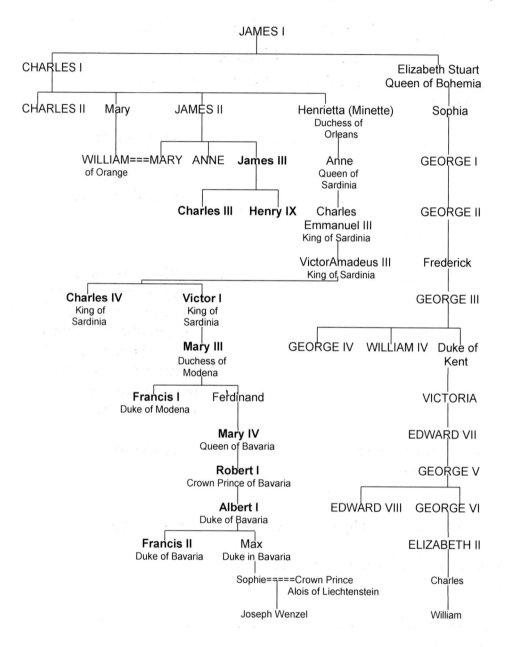

Appendix B

Principal attendees at the funeral of King Edward VII
<u>– and what became of them</u>
[relationship to Edward VII]

<u>On horseback</u>

King George V...................................…........killed by his doctor
[son]

Kaiser Wilhelm I.................................….........abdicated and exiled
[nephew]
son of Edward's sister Victoria

Prince Arthur Duke of Connaught.............entitled to become
[brother]   Duke of Saxe- Coburg
                                                                          and Gotha on the death of
                                                                          his elder brother Prince
                                                                          Alfred, he renounced his
                                                                          rights in favour of his
                                                                          nephew, Charles, son of
                                                                          Prince Leopold

King George I of Greece.........................…......assassinated
[brother-in-law]
brother of Queen Alexandra

King Alfonso XIII of Spain.......…...............…...abdicated and exiled
[nephew-in-law]
husband of the daughter of Edward's
sister Beatrice

King Haakon VII of Norway...................…........temporarily exiled
[son-in-law]
husband and cousin of Edward's
daughter Maud

King Frederick VIII of Denmark..................found dead on a park
[brother-in law]   bench in Hamburg
brother of Queen Alexandra

King Manuel II of Portugal ....exiled and monarchy
[second cousin twice removed]   abolished; died
2 x great-grandson of Queen Victoria's   suddenly in England
maternal uncle   in suspicious
                                                circumstances

Tsar Ferdinand I of Bulgaria....................abdicated and exiled
[second cousin]
grandson of Queen Victoria's maternal uncle

King Albert I of the Belgians.....................died while
[second cousin]   mountaineering on
grandson of Queen Victoria's maternal uncle   his own

Archduke Franz Ferdinand of Austria..........assassinated

Crown Prince Yusuf.............................suicide, but murder
of the Ottoman Empire   was suspected

Grand Duke Michael Alexandrovitch...........murdered
of Russia
[nephew-in-law]
son of Queen Alexandra's sister

Prince Emanuele Duke of Aosta.................lost his rights as heir
[seventh cousin once removed]   to the Spanish throne
6 x great-grandson of King George I's   when his father
uncle John Frederick   abdicated

Duke of Sparta.................................abdicated, recovered the
later King Constantine I of Greece   throne, abdicated again
[nephew-in-law]   and exiled
son of Queen Alexandra's brother

Crown Prince of Romania.......................……….succeeded by his
later King Ferdinand   grandson who abdicated
[nephew-in-law]
husband of Marie, the daughter of
Edward's brother Alfred

Crown Prince Rupprecht of Bavaria….....…….exiled
[eighth cousin once removed]
the Jacobite pretender
both he and Edward were descendants of
King James I; Rupprecht a 9 x great-grandson,
Edward an 8 x great-grandson

Duke Albrecht of Wurttemberg…………....…..heir to the throne of
[second cousin once removed]   Wurttemberg, but
great-grandson of Queen Victoria's   following his cousin the
maternal aunt   king's deposition and
                                                          abdication, the kingship
                                                          was abolished

Prince of Serbia……………..………………..…….assassinated
later King Alexander I of Yugoslavia

Prince Hendrik of the Netherlands………..…..his wife abdicated in
[fifth cousin once removed]   favour of their
consort of Queen Wilhelmina   daughter
and descendant of George I's daughter

Grand Duke Ernest of Hesse………………...…..deposed
[nephew]
son of Edward's sister Alice

Grand Duke Adolphus……………………...…….succeeded by his son,
of Mecklenburg-Strelitz   who committed
[second cousin]   suicide
he and Edward both being great-grandsons
of George III

Prince Heinrich of Prussia...............................two sons died as a result
[nephew]   of haemophilia (Heinrich
son of Edward's sister Victoria   having married his
                                                                         cousin Irene, a
                                                                         granddaughter of Queen
                                                                         Victoria), the third son
                                                                         settled in Costa Rica

Duke Charles of Saxe-Coburg.....................deprived of his English
and Gotha   titles in WW1 and
[nephew]   deprived of his German
son of Edward's brother Leopold   ducal title a year later, he
                                                                         was, before and during
                                                                         WW2, a senior Nazi

Prince George of Saxony............................died without issue
[second cousin once removed]
great-grandson of Queen Victoria's
maternal uncle

Prince Carl of Sweden...............................expected to become the
[third cousin twice removed]   king of Norway on its
3 x great-grandson of George III's sister   independence from
                                                                         Sweden, he was
                                                                         overlooked when a
                                                                         Danish prince was
                                                                         preferred

Prince Friedrich of Waldeck......................deposed
and Pyrmont
[fourth cousin once removed]
descendant of George III's sister

Prince Mohammed Ali of Egypt...................exiled

Prince Arthur of Connaught.........................succeeded by his son,
[nephew]   who whilst in Canada
son of Edward's brother Arthur   fell out of a window one
                                                                     night when drunk, and
                                                                     died of hypothermia,
                                                                     leaving no issue

Prince Christian of Schleswig-Holstein.........forced to abandon the name
[brother-in-law]   Schleswig-Holstein in
husband of Edward's sister Helena   1917, he died three
                                                                     months later without
                                                                     replacing it, and was
                                                                     succeeded by his son
                                                                     who died without issue

Prince Alexander of Battenberg..................forced to abandon the name
[nephew]   Battenberg in 1917, he
son of Edward's sister Beatrice   became Lord Carisbrooke;
                                                                     but the title became
                                                                     extinct on his death

Duke of Fife..after being shipwrecked
[son-in-law]   and later rescued, he
husband of Edward's daughter Louise;   died of pleurisy in Egypt
also a great-grandson of William IV
and Dorothea Jordan, and therefore second
cousin once removed of Edward, both being
descendants of George III

Duke Adolphus of Teck.........................forced to abandon the name
[second cousin]   Teck in 1917, he became
like Edward, a great-grandson of George III;   Marquess of Cambridge;
also a brother of Edward's daughter-in-law   succeeded by his son
Queen Mary   on whose death the
                                                                     peerage became extinct

Prince Francis of Teck............................he died without issue
[second cousin]   five months after the
like Edward, a great-grandson of George III;   funeral
also a brother of Edward's daughter–in-law
Queen Mary

Prince Alexander of Teck.......................became Earl of Athlone;
[second cousin]   died without issue
like Edward, a great-grandson of George III;
also a brother of Edward's daughter-in-law
Queen Mary; he married Alice, daughter of
Edward's brother Leopold, and was therefore
also Edward's nephew-in-law

Prince Andrew of Greece.......................father of Prince Philip;
[fifth cousin twice removed]   exiled
descendant of George II's sister

Grand Duke Michael Mikhailovich...........banished from Russia
of Russia   for life for making
[fifth cousin once removed]   an unsuitable and
descendant of George II's sister   illegal marriage
                                             (he married Countess
                                             Sophie of Merenberg
                                             the granddaughter
                                             of Pushkin, through
                                             whom she had one 3 x
                                             great-grandparent who
                                             was a former African
                                             slave given to Peter the
                                             Great and brought up
                                             by him as a son); the
                                             banishment saved him
                                             from the Bolsheviks

Prince Maximilian of Baden.....................heir to his cousin who
[fifth cousin twice removed]   abdicated, but the
descendant of George II's sister   duchy was abolished

Crown Prince Danilo of...........................abdicated and exiled
Montenegro

Prince Christopher of Greece....................declined the thrones of
[fifth cousin twice removed]   Portugal, Lithuania
descendant of George II's sister   and Albania to marry
                                                an American
                                                millionairess, his son
                                                lost all rights to the
                                                Greek throne for his
                                                descendants on making
                                                a morganatic marriage

Prince Philipp of Saxe-Coburg...................neither of his children
and Gotha   had issue, his son
[second cousin]   having died after a
grandson of Queen Victoria's uncle   prostitute threw acid
                                                in his face

Hereditary Grand Duke Adolphus..............committed suicide, his
of Mecklenburg-Strelitz   mind deranged from
[second cousin once removed]   pressure to divorce his
2 x great-grandson of George III   commoner wife,
                                                leaving no issue

Prince Wolrad of Waldeck.......................killed in WW1, leaving
and Pyrmont   no issue
[fourth cousin once removed]
descendant of George III's sister

Prince Bovaradej of Siam...................….....exiled

In carriages

Queen Alexandra...............................…....died of a heart attack,
[wife]   already partly deaf,
also fourth cousin, as both 4 x great-   partly blind and with
grandchildren of George II   her speech and
                                                memory impaired

Empress Maria (Dagmar) of Russia..............exiled
[sister-in-law]
sister of Queen Alexandra; also fourth
cousin of Edward as both 4 x
great-grandchildren of George II

The Princess Royal.............................when she and her
Louise Duchess of Fife   family were
[daughter]   shipwrecked off
                                           Egypt, while the
                                           others reached
                                           lifeboats she was
                                           swept overboard
                                           and almost drowned;
                                           she was saved, but
                                           her jewellery was lost

Princess Victoria............................never married
[daughter]

Queen Mary.................................predeceased by
[daughter-in-law]   three of her six
wife of Edward's son, George; also second children, she
cousin of Edward, both being great-   nevertheless saw
grandchildren of George III   her husband, two
                                           sons and
                                           granddaughter as
                                           sovereigns

Queen Maud of Norway.......................died of heart failure
[daughter]   after an operation

Duke of Cornwall...........................abdicated
later King Edward VIII
[grandson]
son of George V

Princess Mary...forced to marry	
[granddaughter]	Viscount Lascelles,
daughter of George V	she refused to attend
	the wedding of the
	present Queen as her
	brother the Duke of
	Windsor had not been
	invited; he was later
	invited to the
	wedding of Princess
	Margaret, but he
	refused to attend

Princess Mary...forced to marry
[granddaughter]
daughter of George V
Viscount Lascelles, she refused to attend the wedding of the present Queen as her brother the Duke of Windsor had not been invited; he was later invited to the wedding of Princess Margaret, but he refused to attend

Princess Christian of Schleswig-.....................lost the name
Holstein
[sister]
Schleswig-Holstein in 1917

Princess Louise Duchess of Argyle.................died without issue
[sister]

Beatrice Princess Henry of Battenberg..........her husband died of
[sister]
malaria contracted in the Anglo-Ashanti War; she survived him by 48 years

Duchess of Connaught......................................the first member of
Princess Louise of Prussia
[sister-in-law]
wife of Edward's brother Arthur; also
Edward's fifth cousin twice removed as
a descendant of George II's sister
the Royal Family to be cremated (at Golders Green Crematorium in NW London)

Duchess of Albany Princess Helena...............her husband died of
of Waldeck and Pyrmont
[sister-in-law]
wife of Edward's brother Leopold; also
Edward's third cousin twice removed as
a descendant of George III's sister
haemophilia after two years of marriage

Princess Patricia of Connaught..................relinquished the title
[niece]   on marrying a
daughter of Edward's brother Arthur   commoner

Princess Alexandra of Fife.......................left no issue
[granddaughter]
daughter of Edward's daughter Louise;
but when her husband died of pleurisy,
she married her mother's cousin (Edward's
nephew Arthur)

Princess Maud of Fife............................title of princess
[granddaughter]   abandoned as
daughter of Edward's daughter Louise   demanded by George V
                                                who disapproved of
                                                his father having
                                                elevated George's nieces
                                                to the rank of princess
                                                when their father was
                                                merely a duke

Princess Helena Victoria of Schleswig-..........lost the name
Holstein   Schleswig-Holstein in
[niece]   1917; never married
daughter of Edward's sister Helena

Princess Marie of Schleswig-Holstein...........lost the name
[niece]   Schleswig-Holstein
daughter of Edward's sister Helena   in 1917, her marriage
                                                was annulled by her
                                                father-in-law the
                                                Duke of Anhalt who
                                                was said to have
                                                discovered his son in
                                                bed with a male
                                                servant; left no issue

Prince Albert later King George VI
[grandson]
son of George V

Prince Henry, later Duke of Gloucester.......his first son (diagnosed
[grandson]
son of George V

with porphyria) died in a plane crash, as did Henry's brother George Duke of Kent. Henry's wife (Princess Alice) lived to the age of 102, the oldest ever member of the Royal Family

Prince George of Hanover.....................…....killed in a car crash; left
and Cumberland
[second cousin once removed]
2 x great-grandson of George III;
also Queen Alexandra's nephew

no issue

Prince Tsai-tao of China.........................…........uncle of the Emperor of
China; dynasty
collapsed in 1912

(Former) President Theodore Roosevelt.......survived assassination
[17th cousin twice removed]
Roosevelt being a 16 x great-
grandson of Edward III, and
Edward VII being an 18 x great-
grandson of Edward III

in 1912 as the bullet, before entering his chest, passed through the steel eyeglass-case and 50-page speech in his jacket inside-pocket (the bullet was never removed)

****